Shogam Publications
Carlton North, Victoria 3054
www.shogam.com

National Library of Australia Cataloguing-in-Publication entry

Creator: Bkra-sis-rnam-rgyal, Dwags-po Pan-chen, (1512 or 1513–1587), author.
Title: Moonbeams of Mahamudra / Dakpo Tashi Namgyal; oral translation by Traleg Kyabgon.
ISBN: 978-0-9805022-3-7 (paperback)
978-0-9805022-4-4 (ebook)
Notes: Includes bibliographical references and index.
Subjects: Mahamudra (Tantric rite)
Mahamudra (Tantric rite)--Early works to 1800.
Meditation--Buddhism
Spiritual life--Buddhism.
Buddhism.
Other Creators/Contributors:
Kyabgon, Traleg, (1955–2012), translator.
Dewey Number: 294.34435

Moonbeams of Mahamudra

Dakpo Tashi Namgyal

Oral translation

Traleg Kyabgon

Moonbeams of Mahamudra

Phyag rgya zla ba'i 'od zer

Moonbeams: Eloquence that Illuminates the Definitive Meaning of the Graduated Path of Mahamudra

Nges don phyag rgya chen po'i sgom rim gsal bar byed pa'i legs bshad zla ba'i 'od zer

SHOGAM
PUBLICATIONS

Books by Traleg Kyabgon

The Essence of Buddhism: An Introduction to its Philosophy and Practice, Shambhala Publications, 2002 & 2014

Benevolent Mind: A Manual in Mind Training, Zhisil Chokyi Ghatsal, 2003

Mind at Ease: Self-liberation Through Mahamudra Meditation, Shambhala Publications, 2004

Nyima Tashi: The Songs and Instructions of the First Traleg Kyabgon Rinpoche, KTD Publications, 2006

The Practice of Lojong: Cultivating Compassion Through Training the Mind, Shambhala Publications, 2007

Influence of Yogacara on Mahamudra, KTD Publications, 2010

Ninth Karmapa Wangchuk Dorje's Ocean of Certainty, KTD Publication, 2011

Four Dharmas of Gampopa, KTD Publications, 2013

Asanga's Abhidharmasamuccaya, KTD Publications, 2013

Karma: What It Is, What It Isn't, Why It Matters, Shambhala Publications, 2015

Moonbeams of Mahamudra, Shogam Publications, 2015

Luminous Bliss: Self-realisation Through Meditation, Shogam Publications, 2015

DEDICATION

Dedicated to the 10th tulku of the unsurpassed Traleg lineage. May he swiftly guide beings on the pure path again and may his vision for Buddhadharma in the West continue to flourish for the benefit of all sentient beings.

Contents

Biography

TRALEG KYABGON RINPOCHE IX

Traleg Kyabgon Rinpoche IX (1955–2012) was born in Nangchen in Kham, eastern Tibet. He was recognised by His Holiness XVI Gyalwang Karmapa as the ninth Traleg tulku and enthroned at the age of two as supreme abbot of Thrangu Monastery. Rinpoche was taken to Rumtek Monastery in Sikkim at the age of four where he was educated with other young tulkus in exile by His Holiness Karmapa for the next five years.

Rinpoche began his studies under the auspices of His Eminence Kyabje Thuksey Rinpoche at Sangngak Choling in Darjeeling. He also studied with a number of other eminent Tibetan teachers during that time and mastered the *Hevajra Tantra*, *Guhyasamaja Tantra*, and the third Karmapa's *Zabmo Nangdon* (*The Profound Inner Meaning*) under Khenpo Noryang (abbot of Sangngak Choling). Rinpoche studied the *Abhidharmakosha*, *Pramanavarttika*, *Bodhisattvacharyavatara*, *Abhidharmasamuccaya*, *Six Treaties of Nagarjuna*, the *Madhyantavibhaga*, and the *Mahayanuttaratantra* with Khenpo Sogyal. He also studied with Khenpo Sodar and was trained in tantric ritual practices by Lama Ganga, who had been specifically sent by His Holiness Karmapa for that purpose.

In 1967 Rinpoche moved to the Institute of Higher Tibetan Studies in Sarnath, and studied extensively for the next five years. He studied Buddhist history, Sanskrit, Hindi, and English as well as Longchenpa's *Finding Comfort and Ease* (*Ngalso Korsum*), *Seven Treasuries* (*Longchen Dzod Dun*), *Three Cycles of Liberation* (*Rangdrol Korsum*), and *Longchen Nyingthig* with Khenchen Palden Sherab Rinpoche and Khenpo Tsondru.

When Rinpoche had completed these studies at the age of sixteen, he was sent by His Holiness Karmapa to study under the auspices of the Venerable Khenpo Yeshe Chodar at Sanskrit University in Varanasi for three years. Rinpoche was also tutored by khenpos and geshes from all four traditions of Tibetan Buddhism during this time.

Rinpoche was subsequently put in charge of Zangdog Palri Monastery (the glorious copper coloured mountain) in eastern Bhutan and placed under the private tutelage of Dregung Khenpo Ngedon by His Holiness Karmapa to continue his studies of Sutra and Tantra. He ran this monastery for the next three years and began learning to speak English during this time.

From 1977 to 1980, Rinpoche returned to Rumtek to fill the honoured position of His Holiness Karmapa's translator at Rumtek in Sikkim, where he dealt with many English-speaking Western visitors.

Rinpoche moved to Melbourne, Australia in 1980 and commenced his studies in comparative religion and philosophy at La Trobe University. Rinpoche established E-Vam Institute in Melbourne in 1982, and for the next twenty-five years gave weekly teachings on classic Kagyu and Nyingma texts. After a break of a few years, Rinpoche established a Buddhist college called Shogam Vidhalaya at E-Vam Institute in 2010 and again instructed students on a weekly basis.

Traleg Kyabgon Rinpoche founded two more Dharma centres in Australia and one each in New Zealand and the United States. He first established Maitripa Centre in Healesville, Australia in 1997 where he conducted two public retreats every year until 2012. He oversaw restricted annual retreats based on the traditional Tibetan three-year and three month retreat format at Maitripa Centre. Rinpoche founded Nyima Tashi Kagyu Buddhist Centre in Auckland, New Zealand in 2004 and Yeshe Nyima Centre in Sydney, Australia in 2009, where programs that teach yoga and pranayama are regularly held. Rinpoche opened E-Vam Institute, New York in 2000 and established practice and study groups in Milwaukee and West Virginia. He also accepted responsibility for the spiritual direction of Kamalashila Institute in Germany for five years during the 1980s.

Rinpoche was also active in publishing during the last two decades of his life, beginning with his quarterly magazine Ordinary Mind which ran from 1997 to 2003, and culminating with his own publishing imprint when he founded Shogam Publications in 2008. Rinpoche released a number of Buddhist books on history, philosophy, and psychology and left instructions for the continuation of this vision with future publications.

Rinpoche's ecumenical approach can be seen in his other activities aimed at bringing buddhadharma to the West. He established the biannual Buddhism and Psychotherapy Conference (1994 to 2003), the Tibet Here and Now Conference (2005), and the annual Buddhist Summer School (1984 to the present).

Traleg Kyabgon Rinpoche passed into parinirvana on 24 July 2012, on

Chokhor Duchen, the auspicious day of the Buddha's first teaching. Rinpoche stayed in meditation (*thugdam*) for a week after his passing. A traditional cremation ceremony was conducted at Maitripa Centre and a stupa has been erected on the centre's grounds in Rinpoche's honour.

Foreword

Mahamudra is the highest teaching in the Vajrayana. It is the most profound and sacred realisation of the enlightened ones. The late Traleg Kyabgon Rinpoche was an authentic master of this enlightened lineage. What he expresses in this comprehensive book, *Moonbeams of Mahamudra*, comes from his vast readings and knowledge, but especially from his own realisation. This carries tremendous blessings for the reader.

What Rinpoche has kindly shared here with us is not ordinary. It comes from his deep love and care for beings in general, and particularly for western students. He gives these teachings so that we may make a genuine connection to the enlightened nature and its practice. I have always been moved and in awe of Rinpoche's tireless work and achievements. He has set a great example for us all to follow, and has served as an immense inspiration to me personally.

Dzigar Kongtrul Rinpoche
April 2015

Preface

Moonbeams of Mahamudra is one of the three most important meditation manuals of the Kagyu tradition. Together with the ninth Karmapa, Wangchuk Dorje's *Ocean of Certainty* and *Illuminating the Darkness of Ignorance*, it tells us everything we need to know about Mahamudra practice. This is a specific type of practice inherited from our forefathers, the mahasiddhas of India. The mahasiddhas were not monks and nuns but lay practitioners and very serious ones at that.

This text discusses the common meditations of tranquillity and insight in Book One and then provides a comprehensive overview of the Mahamudra approach to tranquillity and insight in Book Two. Mahamudra meditation is an extension of basic tranquillity and insight practices so Tashi Namgyal has been careful to put these common practices into perspective. If we are mistaken about the common techniques our Mahamudra practice will also be distorted.

Moonbeams of Mahamudra is meant to be used as a manual. As beginners we should practise Mahamudra in a step by step manner but the essence of this practice is to realise that the person doing the meditation and the actual practice of meditation are not separate. We normally think of the spiritual path as a vehicle or process through which we systematically eliminate all the undesirable aspects of ourselves and gradually acquire all the positive aspects that will lead us to our desired destination. Mahamudra does not regard these qualities as separate things. The practice, the path, and the person travelling that path are the same. That is the essence of this teaching.

When approaching this manual it would be best to focus on one exercise at a time and practise that for a long time. It is pointless to try to go through these meditative exercises quickly. It would be much better to approach the text in a slow and systematic manner without engaging in too much examination. If you want to sharpen your intellect you can learn Buddhist logic or study its philosophical texts. The type of analysis that we are practising here is not intellectual. It may be best to start at the beginning of the book and work through the exercises but that will vary from person to person. You should just see how you go with the whole process. Continue with each vipashyana exercise until you experience some kind of insight from your analysis. There is no hurry. As many Tibetan lamas say, 'If you apply yourself to whatever you are doing properly you will become good at it.' There is nothing in the world that does not become easier through practice.

It is important to understand that this Mahamudra system goes beyond Tantra. The text contains a discussion on the relationship between Tantra and Mahamudra but Mahamudra is not confined to conventional tantric practices. The goal of all higher tantric practices is to realise mahamudra, but Mahamudra meditation is a distinct meditative system. Conventional tantric practices include visualisations of deities, mantra recitation, ritual practices, chanting, and so on. Not so in Mahamudra meditation. Mahamudra does not rely on any of these things or even regard them as important. We can practise Mahamudra without practising Tantra or we can practise it in conjunction with Tantra, but the Mahamudra system as presented in this manual is a complete and distinct practice in its own right.

We need to remember this fact. Many people make the mistake of thinking that Mahamudra is just an extension of Tantra. Mahamudra is a practice that allows the individual to access his or her spiritual condition directly. It is often called 'signless meditation' for this reason.

Enlightenment may be the most important thing within Buddhism but there are many different ways to attain it. We can do tantric practices, we can practise analytical meditations that break the phenomenal world down into minute constituents, or meditations that recognise those constituents as having no intrinsic reality. In Mahamudra, we don't spend too much time analysing the phenomenal world at all. We simply concentrate on exploring our mind and the various aspects of our consciousness. According to the Mahamudra teachings we will never attain enlightenment for as long as we remain ignorant of our own consciousness no matter how well we are able to apprehend ultimate reality.

This mind has the capacity to confuse us, to delude us, to lead us astray, and to corrupt us; it can even send us over the edge into madness. Mind also has the capacity to take us to enlightenment and to reveal aspects of our consciousness that have remained totally foreign to us. We can become confused, depraved, lost beings (a state normally referred to as a 'samsaric existence' in Buddhism) or we can become a buddha, an enlightened being, an 'awakened one.' Enlightenment is not given to us as a gift. We attain enlightenment by realising the different aspects of ourselves until nothing remains hidden.

We often talk about the fact that we do not understand other people and we think that other people do not understand us, but the truth is that we do not even understand ourselves. Our levels of delusion and confusion may remain hidden from ourselves but they continue to influence the way we think about the world and the way that we interact with other people. We cannot become enlightened while we remain ignorant of the workings of our own minds.

Where does all this confusion and delusion come from? We assume that our senses are neutral media that we use only to apprehend the world so that everything we see, hear, smell, taste, and touch is unadulterated. We do not have this kind of direct perception of the world. The truth is that we are constantly constructing the world that we inhabit. Our sensory perceptions are connected to our consciousness—we have five senses and five sense consciousnesses—and these consciousnesses have to be selective. If there were no consciousnesses attending to each of our senses we would be completely overwhelmed by our sensory impressions. We cannot process everything we hear, see, smell, touch, and taste.

We have a central organising consciousness that manages these five sense consciousnesses and all six of these are connected to the 'ego-consciousness.' We do not just see things or have certain experiences, we constantly think in terms of I, me, and mine. We automatically think, 'I saw this,' 'I heard that,' 'I experienced this,' 'I hated that,' 'I enjoyed this,' and so on. All of our experiences are assimilated by ego-consciousness in this way.

In addition, nothing that we experience goes to waste. Every experience leaves an impression on the mind and those impressions are stored within an underlying level of mind called the 'storehouse consciousness.' Those stored impressions give rise to certain proclivities and tendencies until we become so habituated to the ways we react to things that we are completely unaware of what is going on. Certain emotional experiences become so much a part of our psychological makeup that we do not even realise they are there. That is how karmic cause and effect comes into being. That is how the mind becomes deluded according to Mahamudra teachings.

As practitioners, we need to be more attentive to the ways that our minds function on the sensory level, to the ways that we organise and interpret our sensory impressions, to the kinds of reactions we have, and to how we relate all this to a sense of 'self.' Our ego is so fragile it sees everything we experience as either friendly or threatening. We must learn to be more aware of the ways our ego functions in terms of how it reacts to the world and how it sees itself within that process. We learn to become familiar with these psychological tendencies through meditation practice. Mahamudra meditation gives us the ability to recognise our mental habits and the kinds of thoughts that persist within our minds. We do not all think alike. Every individual has different thoughts and emotions. We all have our themes and tendencies and fixate on certain thoughts and emotions that we either favour or revile.

We will gradually learn to become more awake through this process of meditation. Instead of trying to understand ultimate reality or ultimate truth—we have a lot of obsessions like that—we simply learn to become more familiar with ourselves. As a result many of our anxieties, fears, angers, and frustrations will subside. When we know our own minds, we will begin to understand ultimate reality, but without that self-understanding, ultimate reality will just be a version of whatever we believe it to be. We cannot have the experience of ultimate reality without self-understanding.

As you proceed with Mahamudra meditation you will start to gain insight into a more positive aspect of your mind; an aspect that is spiritual, pure, uncorrupted, and incorruptible. You may be confused and bewildered, you may be the victim of your own conflicting emotions, but when you understand more about your mind you will begin to see that your mind is intrinsically pure. This is called our 'true nature.' Our ignorance, jealousy, pride, greed, lust, anger, and so on have no power to corrupt our spiritual nature. When you begin to understand that you will develop a real sense of confidence. This confidence is not based on the manufactured sense of self that comes from your ego identity. It is a real form of confidence; a transcendental confidence that does not have its basis in any one thing.

This confidence is being-itself because to dwell in our own spiritual being is the same thing as confidence. In other words, we do not have confidence, we do not acquire confidence, we *are* confidence. Confidence is simply being in our spiritual state. We have become alienated from this state as a result of all kinds of misunderstandings and delusions. Nonetheless, even though we have become alienated from our spiritual state, we have never lost it. We can never lose it. The state of enlightenment is attainable for that reason.

If we had no enlightened nature within ourselves, it would require really drastic measures to change us from an ignorant, confused, and bewildered person into a liberated, awake, and enlightened being. As the Mahamudra teachings say, 'You cannot extract oil from coal.' If we did not have an inherently spiritual nature, our aspirations to enlightenment would be just another fantasy or dream. We would not have what it takes to secure enlightenment. Ignorance cannot lead to enlightenment but enlightenment can overcome ignorance. If our authentic and intrinsic nature is spiritual and uncorrupted, and it is there to be discovered, then enlightenment is not a fantasy. It is a tangible and reachable reality.

Mahamudra meditation puts us in touch with our spiritual being. You will stop thinking, 'I am just someone who gets angry, jealous, resentful, bitter, despondent, passionate, and worked up about things.' You will begin to feel ease, mental clarity, sharpness, and pure presence because you are becoming totally alert and aware. Normally even when we think we are conscious, we are not aware at all. The teachings say that we are not even conscious. For example, when you react with anger to someone or something, you may be able to catch yourself after the fact and recognise your reaction, but during the actual experience you were completely carried away by the current of emotion. We cannot say we are fully present within our experiences or fully conscious of them.

Mahamudra meditation teaches us to dwell within our own spiritual well-being so that all of the problems that we create in life have less of an impact. According to the teachings, the real source of our mental disturbances is not having confidence. We usually feel so vulnerable, we are always on the defensive; our behaviour is always so protective, and filled with so much fear and anxiety. We generate all kinds of emotional responses to protect ourselves. If we can learn to be at ease with ourselves, if we can find comfort and ease in the spiritual well-spring within ourselves, nothing will overwhelm or threaten us. We will deal with whatever life situations present themselves. We gain access to this spiritual energy when we feel enriched and can overcome the poverty mentality that is associated with the samsaric mind, which makes us feel confined and constricted and unable to express ourselves, unable to even *be* ourselves.

Technique takes pride of place in traditional meditation approaches, but that is of much less importance in Mahamudra. Mahamudra does use some meditative techniques but very little. Even when techniques are applied, they are only meant to be used when needed, they are not to be relied upon. We are trying to transcend our ordinary states of consciousness by approaching our meditation practice in a natural way, without trying too hard and without exerting ourselves too much.

We exert ourselves in meditative techniques and practices when we are somehow uncomfortable with ourselves. When we want to overcome some basic level of corruption or dis-ease. Mahamudra meditation is about releasing our confusions, delusions, mental obscurations, and conflicting emotions because when disturbing thoughts and emotions are allowed to arise and dissipate without interference or fixation, they are naturally self-liberated. Self-liberation occurs when you stop deliberately trying to create a particular state of mind and can just be with whatever arises. Everything can be self-liberated if you are able to maintain your awareness. You can enter into your own natural authentic state where suffering is unknown and where delusions have no hold, and you can enter into that state even while you are in the state of delusion. By going past that state of delusion and remaining in your natural state you can overcome delusions and suffering. You don't have to abandon your negative thoughts and emotions and cultivate positive ones, you don't have to purify your disturbing thoughts and emotions, and you don't have to transform a negative thought into a positive one. By just letting our thoughts and emotions be, they will dissipate of their own accord.

This is how we come in touch with our authentic condition. Our true condition is not about dividing ourselves up and saying, 'That is my false self, this is my true self.' We have to see all of our experiences, thoughts, and emotions as ourselves and not to feel so bad because we have these negative things inside us. We will become less self-divided in that way. We cannot even think of wisdom if we are trying to reject conflicting emotions. Wisdom comes from being able to deal with, accept, and incorporate those emotions, not from making a huge effort to reject them or deny their existence. Our conflicting emotions will then be self-liberated into wisdom. Wisdom and conflicting emotions are in a mutual dialogue. Mahamudra meditation is a way to remain in our own natural state so that our thoughts and emotions are naturally self-liberated into wisdom.

Introduction

Introduction

THE RESOLUTION TO COMPOSE THIS TEXT

Buddha's teachings include many important instructions, the most essential of which is the practice of meditation. These days people pay great attention to hearing, contemplating, and analysing the teachings but very few actually translate that into direct experience by meditating on what they have heard. There are also people who do meditate but who go about it in the wrong way because they lack experience. I composed this text for the sake of those people and for students who rely on me. When approaching this text I had a choice between two perspectives: the strictly logical method of conceptual analysis and the more lyrical method of poetic expression and metaphor. I chose the latter because of its directness and because its meaning is more readily available to untutored or philosophically unsophisticated readers.

WHY WE MEDITATE ON THE NATURE OF MIND

This has three sections:

- Everything is determined by mind
- The harm of not doing meditation
- The benefits of doing meditation

§ Everything Is Determined By Mind

Everything that we experience arises from the mind itself, whether it comes from our samsaric nature or from our higher aspirations for nirvana.[1] The *Dasabhumika Sutra* says:

> Oh sons and daughters of the Victorious One,
> All three modes of existence are nothing but mind itself.

The *Vajrapanjara Tantra* says:

> There is nothing outside of mind.
> Without mind, there would be no mention
> Of ordinary beings or buddhas.

The *Samputa Tantra* says:

> External phenomena and mental experiences
> Are all fabrications of mind.
> Nothing exists independently of mind.

Sakya Pandita says:

> The various material things
> That exist in the world
> Are all determined by mind itself.

We may wonder how we have come to be laden with this mistaken yet implicit belief in an external world that exists independently of our minds. This belief arises from ignorance. We create duality between the self and external things and view those things as independently existing objects.[2] This mistaken belief is consolidated by our karmic traces and dispositions.[3] The *Lankavatara Sutra* says:

> Due to turbulence created by
> Our karmic traces and dispositions,
> We perceive an independent and external world.
> But no such external world exists independent of mind.

The *Samputa Tantra* says:

> Our various impressions of the world
> Are nothing but the creations of mind.
> Distorted perception leads to its appearance.

Saraha says:

> When freezing winds blow across a lake,
> They turn water to ice.
> Just so the turbulent activities of mind
> When stirred by karmic traces and dispositions
> Make our impressions appear solid.
> This gives rise to the mistaken belief
> In a self-existing and substantial world.

This very mind is responsible for our state of bondage in samsara and has the capacity to free us from that bondage. We are bound when our mind is filled with defilements and delusions and we are liberated when our mind is cleansed of those defilements and delusions. The *Hevajra Tantra* says:

> We wander in samsara when delusions are present;
> We attain nirvana when delusions are removed.

The *Samputa Tantra* says:

> As long as we proliferate conceptual confusions
> We are mad men, constantly yielding
> To the unwholesome tendencies
> Of desire, lust, anger, and resentment.
> When this same mind is understood
> We realise the nature of mind,
> And free ourselves from bondage
> By seeing the ineffectiveness
> Of desire, lust, anger, and resentment.
> A mind free of adventitious defilements
> Is the state of nirvana.

Master Nagarjuna says:

> By purifying the causes of samsara
> We automatically obtain nirvana.
> Mind is the maker of everything;
> It binds us to samsara and it frees us in nirvana.

The *Lankavatara Sutra* says:

> Just as a mirror reflects many objects,
> Mind experiences many things.
> Just as we cannot find
> Objects within a mirror,
> The perceptions of mind
> Are insubstantial and hard to find.
> This is how it should be understood.

The *Ratnamegha Sutra* says:

> Ordinary beings are constantly led by mind,
> Because their minds do not realise their own nature
> And cause wholesome and unwholesome deeds.

Just as a burning stick makes luminous circles
When waved through the air;
Mind revolves in perpetual motion.
It rolls like a turbulent ocean.
It rages like a forest fire.
It floods like a valley when swamped with desire.

The *Vajrapanjara Tantra* says:

Due to our mistaken conceptions,
We perceive the external world
As solid and substantial
Existing independently of mind.

It also says:

Mind does not realise
That it determines its perceptions thus.
This harm that comes from
Failing to meditate on the nature of mind.

§ The Harm Of Not Doing Meditation

We will not gain any real benefit from the teachings if we don't engage in meditation. Hearing and contemplating certain teachings or spiritual ideals will do us little good. Only meditation can provide us with spiritual experiences. The *Gandavyuha Sutra* says:

We too will be like that unfortunate fellow.
Like a man extremely generous with food and drink
Who dies of thirst and malnutrition;
If we do not meditate
We too will be like that unfortunate fellow.
Like a physician who devoted his entire life to others
Only to die of a terrible disease;
If we do not meditate
We too will be like that unfortunate fellow.

Like the caretaker of a wonderful treasure
Who counts the gems but does not own any;
If we do not meditate

We too will be like that unfortunate fellow.
Like the servant of a king
Who lives in the midst of luxury without owning anything;
If we do not meditate
We too will be like that unfortunate fellow.
Like a blind man commissioned to paint a street scene
Without being able to see anything;
If we do not meditate
We will not get a true picture of anything.

Like a ferryman devoted to helping others cross a great river
Only to drown when his boat capsizes;
If we do not meditate
We will put an end to our spiritual life.

Like a man at a crossroads praising others
Without achieving anything himself;
If we do not meditate
We will deprive ourselves of all spiritual qualities.

As the following verses demonstrate, another outcome of failing to practise meditation is that we easily succumb to defilements. The *Manjushrivikridita Sutra* says:

Without meditation, mind is completely without power;
And automatically yields to desires and distractions.
Afflicted more and more by mental torments,
It is increasingly mired in the samsaric state.

Shantideva's *Bodhicharyavatara* says:

Beings who are constantly subject to distraction
Live in the midst of emotional turmoil.

It also says:

Realising the nature of mind is most important of all;
Our whole effort will be futile if we do not know this secret.
Even if we want to attain happiness and avoid suffering,
We are just not approaching it in the right way.

Nagarjuna's *Suhrllekha* says:

> Insight will not manifest if we do not meditate.
> If insight does not manifest,
> The idea of obtaining enlightenment is remote.

Even if we are trying our level best to lead a commendable life by practising proper ethics and engaging in contemplation and analysis, we will not gain the full benefit from our efforts if they are not backed up by meditation.

§ The Benefits Of Doing Meditation

Meditation will endow us with extraordinary spiritual capacities and enable us to tap into all our spiritual resources with ease. The *Tattvaprakasa Sutra* says:

> Oh Shariputra, it is far better to meditate for a split second than to contemplate and analyse for aeons. Shariputra, for that reason it is important to lead others to the state of meditation.

The *Mahosnisa Sutra* says:

> Meditating for one day is far better than studying and analysing the teachings for two aeons. Why is this so? Only meditation will help us to overcome the anxieties related to life and death.

The *rTogs pa rgyas pa'i mdo* says:

> It is far more beneficial to practise meditation for one moment than to practise charity for the benefit of all sentient beings for an indefinite period.

Only the practice of meditation will allow you to be less obsessive in your attachment to possessions. It will also enable you to cut through your doubts and uncertainties. Meditation helps you gain insight, develop the spiritual quality of compassion, and cultivate the spiritual power to benefit others and lead them on the spiritual path. The *Prajnaparamita-samcayagatha* says:

> Meditation gives you the capacity to discard your bad habits and replace them with higher ideals. It is also how you gain spiritual insights and attain meditative states.

The *Dasacakra-ksitigarbha Sutra* says:

> Only meditation enables us to cut through doubts. That isn't

> possible without meditation. That's why the wise ones rely on it.

The *Dharmasamgiti Sutra* says:

> When the mind is put to rest, we realise the way things exist. Realising the nature of things is how we attain enlightenment.

The *Sutralamkara* says:

> Everyone can be transported to the three states of enlightenment through the practice of meditation.[4]

BOOK ONE

A Brief Description of the Common System of Meditation

1

Common Meditation

TRANQUILLITY AND INSIGHT MEDITATION

We will begin by discussing the common system of meditation and then turn to the extraordinary meditation practices of Mahamudra. The common system of meditation has two aspects: tranquillity meditation and insight meditation. Tranquillity meditation is found in Buddhist texts such as the *Samdhinirmocana Sutra*, the *Abhidharmasamuccaya* and *Yogacarabhumi* of Asanga, the *Prajnaparamitopadesa* of Santipa, the three *Bhavanakrama* of Kamalashila, and others. If you want to understand the general practice of meditation you should study these texts as they are readily available. All of the meditation techniques that can be found within Buddhist practice can be subsumed under these two categories. As the *Samdhinirmocana Sutra* says:

> Many of the aspects shown by me of the meditative equipoise demonstrated by the shravakas, bodhisattvas, and buddhas came about through tranquillity and insight meditation.

The second *Bhavanakrama* says:

> Yogins should constantly dwell within tranquillity and insight meditation. All forms of meditative equipoise come together within these two.

A tree has only one trunk but it can have many branches. In much the same way, there may be various meditative methods, but they all lead to tranquillity and insight.

The Hinayana and Mahayana teachings distinguish between meditation with an intentional object and meditation without intentional object. The tantric teachings also distinguish between meditation with symbol and meditation without symbol. Mahamudra meditation distinguishes between experiences of bliss, luminosity, and non-conceptuality. Whatever method we adopt, it is always an extension of the techniques of tranquillity and insight.

No meditative technique could be regarded as a substitute for, or as an addition to, these two methods. Whenever we employ an intentional object or symbol we are practising tranquillity meditation and whenever we meditate without an intentional object or symbol we are practising insight meditation. Tranquillity meditation is associated with form because through it we try to develop mental concentration. Insight meditation is linked with formlessness because through it we try to give rise to insight. As the *Mahayanapradadsa-prabhavana Sutra* says:

> Understand, oh sons and daughters of the Buddha, the faith and attainment of all bodhisattvas originates in an undistracted mind and in insight into the nature of reality.

Mahamudra meditation begins with training in an undistracted mind, which is the practice of tranquillity meditation. It expands as we learn to let the mind be in its natural state with translucency, which is the practice of insight meditation. Tranquillity meditation generates a state of one-pointed concentration and insight meditation generates discriminating awareness. The third *Bhavanakrama* says:

> Even though Buddha taught an infinite number of meditation practices, they can all be subsumed under the major practices of tranquillity and insight meditation. No meditation practice should be regarded as a substitute or addition to these two.

2

Common Tranquillity and Insight

THE CAUSES OF TRANQUILLITY AND INSIGHT

The *Samadhinirmocana Sutra* says:

> Maitreya: 'Buddha, what is the cause of tranquillity and insight?'
> Buddha: 'Maitreya, the causes of tranquillity and insight are pure morality, contemplation, and analysis.'

Gampopa says:

> Tranquillity arises when we meet with an authentic teacher under favourable circumstances for then we are in a situation where removing defilement is easy. This also applies to insight.

The second *Bhavanakrama* of Kamalashila says:

> Being in a favourable environment, being free from excessive desire, being content, refraining from excessive activities, having pure morality, and having no conceptual proliferations are the six necessary causes for attaining tranquillity.
> Consulting with an authentic teacher, becoming acquainted with the written material, and engaging in correct contemplation are the three causes for attaining insight.

Being in a favourable environment is a situation where food, drink, and shelter are immediately obtainable; where your life is not endangered by wild animals, human beings, or infectious diseases; where you are able to mix with people of a similar disposition and ideals; where there is little commotion during the day, and it is peaceful at night. As the *Sutralamkara* says:

> The environment where the wise seek realisation

Is one where proper food and drink are obtained,
Where shelter is found, safety assured
And companions are of good disposition.

Being free from excessive desire means you can let go of attachment to food and clothing and exercise moderation about the quality and quantity of food and drink you consume. Being content means being satisfied with the requisite sustenance and attire and not desiring more than you already possess. Refraining from excessive activities means not engaging in business transactions, associating with laity or monastics, or practising medicine and astrology.[1] Having pure morality as a layperson means immediately rectifying any behaviours that are discordant with that goal. You eliminate conceptual proliferation by gradually freeing yourself from the fixation on worldly possessions by contemplating the harm of obsessive attachment to things and becoming familiar with the idea of separation by contemplating impermanence.

Consulting with an authentic teacher means associating with someone with the knowledge to teach the three trainings: hearing, contemplating and meditating. Such a person must be capable of explaining the subtle nuances of tranquillity and insight meditation. Becoming acquainted with the written material means familiarising yourself with teachings that have a direct meaning without getting embroiled in teachings with a conventional meaning.[2]

Engaging in correct contemplation means developing the right view, which is free from extremes, once you hear teachings with a direct meaning.

ERADICATING OBSTACLES TO TRANQUILLITY AND INSIGHT

This has two sections:

- How to recognise obstacles
- The antidotes to apply when obstacles arise

§ How To Recognise Obstacles

The *Samadhinirmocana Sutra* says:

> Maitreya: 'How many of the five obstacles relate to tranquillity meditation and how many relate to insight?'
> Buddha: 'Mental agitation and resentment relate to tranquillity meditation. Dullness, stupor, and doubt relate to insight meditation. Excessive desire and harmful thoughts relate to both.'

The *Abhidharmasamuccaya* states:

> What is mental agitation? Mental agitation comes about when the mind focuses on a pleasant object and becomes obsessed with it so that mental peace is disturbed.

It also says:

> Resentment comes about when the mind does not remain at rest after going out of its way to entertain a particular thought. You then engage in a variety of conscious and unconscious acts, which are either wholesome, unwholesome, or neutral in nature. These are performed in a timely or untimely, worthy, or unworthy manner.

These actions are a product of ignorance and disturb our peace of mind. The *Abhidharmasamuccaya* says:

> When your mind is agitated in this way, you behave in an obsessive manner, and think repeatedly of the rightness or wrongness of certain objects. As a result, your mind is never at peace.

The *Abhidharmakosa* says:

> What is dullness? Dullness is defined as a heaviness of mind and body whereby both become unserviceable.

We lose our clarity, sharpness, or translucency of mind when we succumb to such mental dullness. The *Bhavanakrama* says:

> Dullness is similar to stepping into darkness, suddenly closing your eyes, or becoming blind. The mind becomes completely foggy and loses its perceptiveness.

It also says:

> What is stupor? Stupor comes about when the mind becomes preoccupied with what is wholesome, unwholesome, or neutral, timely or untimely, worthy or unworthy. This results in a total state of ineffectiveness, which causes our attention to waver. When we become mentally ineffective, we are beset by a lack of resilience.[3]

Again, it says:

> What is doubt? Doubt is to become two-minded about something.

In this context it is a mind beset by doubts about the relationship between ultimate and relative truths and the Four Noble Truths.[4] Excessive desire means wanting to acquire more and more of the same thing and so never being at rest. Harmful thoughts mean harbouring the intention to injure someone physically or mentally. The *Samadhinirmocana Sutra* says:

> Buddha lists five types of distraction: distraction in relation to mental activity, distraction in relation to the external world, internal distraction, distraction with sign, and emotional distractions that lead to lower states of existence.

It also says:

> 'Distraction in relation to mental activity' refers to bodhisattvas who take the vows but suddenly waver in their intention and fall to the state of an arhat or shravaka.[5]
>
> 'Distraction in relation to the external world' refers to those bodhisattvas who become fixated on sensory objects and give rise to various mental afflictions.
>
> 'Internal distraction' refers to bodhisattvas who become prone to dullness and vulnerable to mental afflictions. 'Distraction with sign' refers to bodhisattvas who are distracted by external things and thus lose their concentration.
>
> 'Emotional distractions that lead to lower states of existence' refers to bodhisattvas who think in terms of an 'I' or 'self' and thus open themselves up to various mental afflictions.

The *Madhyantavibhanga* says:

> Laziness, forgetfulness, dullness, agitation, non-exertion, and over-exertion are the six obstacles to tranquillity meditation.

The five obstacles become six if we count dullness and agitation separately. If we look at it simply in terms of obstacles, we can subsume them all under dullness, agitation, lack of effort, and entertaining thoughts. These obstacles disturb our serenity and make it very difficult to realise tranquillity.

§ The Antidotes To Apply When Obstacles Arise

1. The general explanation of obstacles and antidotes

The obstacles we are concerned with here are mental agitation and dullness.[6] These obstacles can manifest in a variety of ways. When mental agitation arises we should contemplate impermanence. When resentment manifests, avoid entertaining the thoughts that gave rise to it. When dullness comes about, think of something pleasant and uplifting.[7] We can overcome drowsiness by visualising light to illuminate the mind. If you experience doubt, examine the origin of that doubt. If sensual craving arises, contemplate its harmfulness. If spite arises, generate compassion. The *Madhyantavibhanga* says:

> We match the five obstacles to their corresponding antidotes.

To counteract laziness, we should cultivate confidence, interest, effort, and pliancy. To counteract forgetfulness of the necessary meditation practices, we heighten our practice of mindfulness. To counteract dullness and mental agitation, we generate vigilance. To counteract falling into non-exertion, we cultivate mental effort. When we find ourselves applying too many antidotes, we try to remain in a state of equanimity. The *Abhidharmasamuccaya* says:

> What is the state of perfect ease? We cultivate pliancy of body and mind to make them serviceable so that they no longer yield to the obstacles that arise. This is how we become free from dullness, drowsiness, and so on.

If we do not cultivate this pliancy of body and mind they will remain unworkable in the sense that they remain resistant to obtaining higher goals and achieving wholesome aims. When pliancy is cultivated, the body will become light, serviceable, and full of joy because the mind is free from mental anguish. Master Sthirmati says:

> When the body becomes pliant it is light, resilient, and free from dullness. When the mind becomes pliant it will be responsive to a higher mental orientation and find it easier to be contemplative. Physical and mental pliancy does not automatically arise; we only develop it after repeated effort in meditation.

The *Sravakabhumi* says:

> It is very important to practise breathing exercises, to lighten the mind, and to diffuse the vital air within the body. A significant mental component is attached to that.

The *Abhidharmasamuccaya* says:

> What is mindfulness? Mindfulness is the antidote that allows the mind to fixate on a meditation object without the problem of distraction.

Mindfulness means not forgetting to pay attention so that we remember the object of our focus. If we have to remember something in our daily lives, we think about it constantly. Forcing ourselves to fixate on a meditation object enhances memory in just the same way. The *Madhyantavibhanga* says:

> It is important to have a sense of non-forgetfulness when we meditate. Once we achieve some mindfulness, we can then maintain our awareness and detect the arousal of obstacles, such as dullness or agitation, as they manifest.

The *Bodhicharyavatara* says:

> Intention is the mental event that propels us to take action in either a wholesome, unwholesome, or neutral manner. It is the propelling factor behind all of our actions.

The *Abhidharmasamuccaya* says:

> Intention propels us to make effort to practise meditation so that we can remove the obstacles of dullness and agitation.

Equanimity means the mind is not disturbed by the obstacles of dullness or agitation. We can therefore hold our attention on the practice of tranquillity or insight meditation. The *Sravakabhumi* says:

> The experience of equanimity is associated with the experience of joy, mental pliancy, peace, and so on.

We become free of the obstacles of dullness and agitation by cultivating equanimity. This enables us to develop a balance between tranquillity and insight meditation. It also says:

> Once we develop equanimity, we no longer need to force ourselves to fixate on a meditation object. We experience equanimity when our minds are no longer distracted by the obstacles of dullness and agitation.

2. Specific methods for removing dullness and agitation

(i) Refraining from the causes of dullness and agitation

All other obstacles can be subsumed under these two main categories of dullness and agitation. These arise from a number of factors. The *Sa'ingosha* says:[8]

> Mental dullness arises from the following factors: having no

> control over our sense impressions; not knowing when to stop eating; not meditating regularly at dawn and dusk; not leading a life of awareness; not training our mind to be resilient so that it becomes prone to dullness, drowsiness, and sleep; not developing the skills to better our situation; being plain lazy; not generating interest; not making an effort; not engaging in analysis; not training in or failing to master tranquillity meditation properly; getting obsessed with certain aspects of the practice and forgetting others; allowing the mind to become completely dark and dull; and failing to take joy in the object of meditation.

Mental agitation arises from the first four: not having control over our sense impressions, eating too much, avoiding meditation, and a lack of awareness. It also arises from not controlling our desire, not paying attention to our aggressiveness, and not generating despair towards certain negative conditions. It also results from not having the skill to improve our situation. We make no effort to control our desires and allow ourselves to get overly involved in domestic matters.

(ii) Eliminating dullness and agitation

To counter mental dullness, think of the qualities and attributes of the Buddha or try to analyse or expand your mind. To uplift your spirits, contemplate something joyful that gives rise to pleasant feelings. The first *Bhavanakrama* says:

> When the mind is affected by dullness so that the object of meditation is taken away, try to visualise the Buddha and his qualities. If you become discouraged, try to lift your spirits.

The *Prajnaparamita-samcayagatha* says:

> If you are overcome by depression, lift your spirits
> by persevering in the development of insight.

The *Madhyamakahrdaya* says:

> You can equalise a depressed state of mind
> By meditating on an object of great size.

The *Sravakabhumi* says:

> Visualise the light of a lamp, a fire or the sun; then imagine that your whole being is illuminated by it.

Depression is eliminated by concentrating on bright objects that illuminate the mind. If dullness becomes overwhelming, discontinue your meditation session, wash your face and go for a stroll. If it is night, gaze at the stars to clear your head. When mental agitation arises, contemplate impermanence and the insubstantiality of everything. It also helps to lift your mood if you settle your mind in tranquillity. As the first *Bhavanakrama* says:

> If your recollections give rise to mental agitation during your meditation, contemplate impermanence as the antidote.

The *Madhyamakahrdaya* says:

> When it comes to distractions and their causes,
> View them as harmful and eliminate them.

The *Prajnaparamita-samcayagatha* says:

> When the mind is distracted by mental agitation,
> Eliminate it through tranquillity meditation.

Try to control your sense impressions, refrain from engaging in rigorous physical exertion during post-meditation, and avoid thinking about things that give rise to mental agitation. It is also very beneficial to do numerous prostrations. If a subtle form of dullness arises, tighten your concentration and if mental agitation arises, loosen or relax your attention.

THE TRUE NATURE OF TRANQUILLITY AND INSIGHT

The *Samadhinirmocana Sutra* says:

> Sit in solitude, pay attention to your chosen meditation object, and attain a state of inner purity where you develop physical and mental pliancy; that is tranquillity meditation.

It also says:

> When you engage in analysis in a state of calmness and apply this analysis to everything knowable; that is insight meditation.

The *Ratnamegha Sutra* says:

> Tranquillity meditation is one-pointed concentration.
> Insight meditation is the full comprehension of reality that is found through analysis.

The *Sutralamkara* says:

> Know this. When the mind is at rest,
> That is tranquillity meditation.
> When you analyse things,
> That is insight meditation.

It also says:

> A mind settled in its own purity is tranquillity.
> When you can analyse that state, that is insight.

Vasubandhu says:

> When you can direct your mind to the meditation object, the mind is fully gathered and when you cannot, it is scattered. When the mind can continuously fixate on a particular object, that is tranquillity meditation. When you engage in the analysis of things to determine reality and give rise to insight, that is insight meditation.

Tranquillity meditation is about remaining in a non-conceptual state where the mind is completely settled without generating any concepts. Insight meditation relies on that tranquillity to wilfully use concepts to determine reality. That is the difference. In tranquillity meditation, you simply pay attention to the meditation object without analysing it, while in insight meditation you use analysis. The *Samadhinirmocana Sutra* says:

> Maitreya: 'Victorious One, how many objects are used in tranquillity meditation?'
> Buddha: 'Only one, the object of non-conceptuality.'
> Maitreya: 'Victorious One, how many objects in insight?'
> Buddha: 'Only one, the object of conceptuality.'

The *Prajnaparamitopadesa* says:

> Tranquillity meditation grasps the extent of things and the nature of things in a non-conceptual way, whereas insight meditation grasps the extent of things and the nature of things in a conceptual way.

The second *Bhavanakrama* says:

> Tranquillity meditation is the ability to maintain the pliancy of body and mind by being able to focus on an inner object of

> meditation joyfully, naturally, and without interruptions once distractions have been pacified. Insight meditation is analysing the nature of that pliancy.[9]

Unless you have a well developed pliancy of body and mind, you will not have fully attained tranquillity and insight. You have attained a proximate experience of tranquillity and insight. The *Samadhinirmocana Sutra* says:

> Buddha: 'Until we attain that physical and mental pliancy we have not fully attained tranquillity and insight, it will only be a proximate experience of those two. We attain tranquillity when we overcome dullness and drowsiness. We attain insight when we overcome mental agitation and resentment.'

The *Prajnaparamitopadesa* says:

> When you stay in solitude, abandon all conceptual proliferation and focus continuously on your mental perceptions, you have mastered a simulated tranquillity. However, real tranquillity is the attainment of mental and physical pliancy.

How do we attain pliancy of body and mind? By overcoming dullness and agitation, by attaining insight, and by eliminating resentment. As the *Samadhinirmocana Sutra* says:

> Maitreya: 'Victorious One, when do we attain pliancy of body and mind?'
> Buddha: 'When we eliminate dullness and agitation.'
> Maitreya: 'Victorious One, when do we attain insight?'
> Buddha: 'When we completely eliminate resentment.'

DISTINGUISHING TRANQUILLITY FROM INSIGHT

Tranquillity meditation is divided into three types. These are: 1) transcendental tranquillity, 2) blissful tranquillity, and 3) the nine stages of tranquillity. The *Sutralamkara* says:

> When concentrating on an object of meditation,
> Do not allow your mind to become distracted.

Vasubandhu says:

> The nine stages of tranquillity are 1) resting the mind, 2) continuous resting, 3) patch-like resting, 4) close placement, 5) pacification, 6) subjugation, 7) thorough subjugation, 8) one-pointedness, and 9) meditative absorption.

The *Abhidharmasamuccaya* says:

> What is tranquillity meditation? When we regularly settle the mind in a peaceful state with full attention and pacify it completely, we are in one-pointed concentration and develop meditative equipoise.

The nine stages of tranquillity are discussed in the following chapter. Now when it comes to insight the *Samadhinirmocana Sutra* says:

> Maitreya: 'Victorious One, how many ways are there to practise insight?'
> Buddha: 'Three: conceptual enquiry, logic, and analysis.'

It also says:

> Maitreya: 'Victorious One, what will arise from conceptual enquiry?'
> Buddha: 'Insight from examining an object of meditation.'
> Maitreya: 'Victorious One, what arises from logic?'
> Buddha: 'Insight from logically investigating unknown aspects of mind.'
> Maitreya: 'Victorious One, what arises from analysis?'
> Buddha: 'Insight from analysing the mental aspects of reality.'

The *Abhidharmasamuccaya* says:

> What is insight? Insight comes from systematically analysing the apparent and true nature of all things. It also comes from analysing duality and non-duality and from analysing the obstacles and conceptual proliferations of mind to determine what must be abandoned and what must be cultivated.

Insight meditation has four stages: 1) the insight that determines all aspects of reality, 2) the insight that determines ultimate reality, 3) the insight that analyses the concept of duality and 4) the insight that understands duality. The *Sravakabhumi* says:

> Buddha: 'What are the four kinds of insight?'

> Monk: 'Determining the nature of all phenomena, determining the nature of ultimate reality, analysing dualistic concepts, and understanding non-duality.'

The mind must remain in tranquillity meditation while practising these four stages of insight. The *Sravakabhumi* also says:

> Buddha: 'How do we determine the nature of phenomena?'
> Monk: 'By 1) clear analysis, sharp intellect, purifying the mental object of meditation, 2) seeing the nature of reality for what it is, 3) complete analysis of dualistic thoughts, and 4) analysing the mind that directly perceives ultimate reality.'

Again, it says:

> There are three gateways and six methods for establishing insight. All types of insight are subsumed within these three. Insight may also be established by analysing the nature of mind in six ways: 1) analysing its reality, 2) analysing its substance, 3) analysing its characteristics, 4) analysing it in terms of space, 5) analysing it in terms of the three times, and 6) analysing it through logical reasoning.

THE DIFFERENT STAGES OF TRANQUILLITY AND INSIGHT

The Sutric or exoteric teachings emphasise tranquillity. They urge us to practise tranquillity meditation first and then to follow that with insight meditation. The *Sutralamkara* says:

> By depending on the former, we do the latter.
> What is superior must depend on what is inferior,
> What is subtle must depend upon what is gross.
> This order has to be maintained.

The same thing is said about the transcendental actions.[10] We must first engage in the practice of generosity, then patience, then morality, effort and so forth because the preceding transcendental action is always cruder than the succeeding one. The *Suhrllekha* says:

> We will not give rise to insight
> Without depending on tranquillity meditation.

The *Bodhicharyavatara* says:

> It is only through tranquillity meditation
> That we can develop insight meditation
> And eradicate our emotional conflicts.
> We should practise tranquillity meditation first.

Other texts, such as the *Sravakabhumi* of Asanga and the *Bhavanakrama* of Kamalashila, also make this point. Some people become mistaken about the relationship between tranquillity and insight meditation through these statements and then insist that insight meditation must follow tranquillity meditation under all circumstances. They say that unless we develop pliancy of body and mind it will be impossible to attain the state of tranquillity, and this will in turn make it impossible to attain insight.

That is also incorrect. It is possible to experience both types of meditation without attaining this pliancy of body and mind. As the *Bodhisattvabhumi*, *Abhidharmasamuccaya*, and *Prajnaparamitopadesa* point out, it is not true that only the ninth stage of tranquillity meditation is proper meditation and the earlier stages are only to be regarded as a prelude to that. All nine stages of tranquillity meditation are legitimate forms of meditation. The same is true for the four stages of insight meditation.

Why is this so? While it may be impossible for beginners to develop this pliancy of body and mind initially, it is possible for them to experience both tranquillity and insight meditation. If the view that insists on differentiating between tranquillity and insight and formalising their relationship in this way were true, there could be no relationship between the two at all. But we can't make this kind of absolute distinction between them. As the *Abhidharmasamuccaya* says:

> It is possible to attain insight without relying on tranquillity
> And it is possible to develop tranquillity by practising insight.

The *Sa'ingosha* says:

> People who gain insight into the Four Noble Truths can put their minds into a state where they attain insight without having first accomplished tranquillity meditation.

When we visualise deities in Tantric meditation, we engage in 'meditation with sign' and 'meditation without sign' in the same session. It is not always true that insight must follow tranquillity. There are examples of people who achieved insight without doing tranquillity meditation in the life stories of the siddhas. Moreover, within the Kagyu tradition it is sometimes possible to attain insight just by establishing the view. At other times, we can establish insight by practising tranquillity meditation. It depends upon the individual. There is no strict order that everybody must follow.

PRACTISING TRANQUILLITY AND INSIGHT TOGETHER

This has two sections:

- Why we need both tranquillity and insight
- How to combine the two

§ Why We Need Both Tranquillity And Insight

Tranquillity and insight meditation should be practised together, because our mind will be like turbulent water without any rest if we do not engage in tranquillity meditation and we cannot recognise our authentic state if the mind is not at rest. To practise insight meditation without first engaging in tranquillity would be like placing a lamp in the wind; we will only ever have a flickering experience of insight. The first *Bhavanakrama* says:

> The mind of an ordinary sentient being is always in a state of turbulence. Unless we train it to rest in tranquillity meditation, it will be impossible to uproot our mental conflicts. However, if we only practise shamatha and neglect vipashyana, we will also have trouble. Shamatha may suppress our emotional conflicts and give us some control over them, but it will not uproot those conflicts. There will still be underlying unconscious processes that have not been dealt with, that will prevent our liberating ourselves from the anguish of birth, old age, and death.

The second *Bhavanakrama* says:

> We may gain some control over our mental instabilities through practising tranquillity alone, but we will never uproot them. Many of our underlying mental processes will remain undealt with and we will never liberate ourselves from the anguish of birth, old age, sickness, and death.

No matter how much we practise tranquillity meditation, it can only temporarily subdue our mental defilements and obscurations; it can never eliminate them. Tranquillity meditation does not uproot hidden mental defilements and cannot liberate us from the karmic traces and dispositions that we have accumulated in samsaric existence over incalculable lifetimes. The second *Bhavanakrama* says:

> If we practise tranquillity meditation alone, we will only put our mental processes into temporary suspension; they will never be eradicated completely. This is so, because insight has not been born in us. We still have various latent defilements that need to be removed.

The *Samadhinirmocana Sutra* says:

> It is through the process of tranquillity meditation that we learn to control our emotional conflicts. It is through the development of insight that we learn to eradicate them at their unconscious origin.

We must learn to develop an unwavering, concentrated mind if we are to learn to combine tranquillity and insight meditation. Having developed concentration, we need to develop the analytical capacity to dismantle all our wrong views. The *Candrapradipa Sutra* says:

> Tranquillity meditation makes the mind unshakeable.
> Insight meditation makes it as unmovable as a mountain.

§ How To Combine The Two

When you attain the ninth stage of tranquillity meditation and can remain in a state of meditative equipoise, you engage in the analytical process of insight meditation. The state of tranquillity is free from dullness and agitation; the kind of clear mind we need to engage in the analysis of insight. If we practise tranquillity, the ability to engage in insight will arise automatically, without having to make a great deal of effort. The two are interrelated. The *Sravakabhumi* says:

> When do tranquillity and insight meditation merge and why is this described as a unifying path? Tranquillity and insight meditation merge when we attain the ninth stage of meditative equipoise.[11] We can then strive to attain the discriminating wisdom that can perceive ultimate reality, so that we are naturally drawn onto the path of insight meditation. At this level, insight meditation requires no effort. This is where tranquillity and insight meditation are combined.

The third *Bhavanakrama* says:

> When mind settles naturally in meditative equipoise, free from dullness and mental agitation, it will vividly perceive its own nature. Relax your efforts and maintain that even state. This is the attainment of the union of tranquillity and insight meditation.

The *Prajnaparamitopadesa* says that the resultant ability to focus on discriminating awareness is described as 'the integration of tranquillity and insight meditation.' This is called *'zung 'brel*, where *'zung* means 'integration' and *'brel* means 'their interrelationship.'

Generally speaking, tranquillity and insight meditation are distinguished by their differences because the former emphasises non-conceptuality and the latter emphasises conceptuality. However, we have to remember that this distinction is not absolute. If it were, how could we visualise deities when practising a meditation that relies on images and symbols? If we were to say that tranquillity meditation is non-conceptual, we would have to say we do not use concepts when we visualise deities, but that is false.

If tranquillity and insight meditation were completely different, there would be an enormous gap between them. They would have two totally different natures; one non-conceptual and the other conceptual. We cannot say tranquillity meditation is non-conceptual.

Some people might argue visualising a deity is not a conceptual process; it is simply the appearance of an image. We can only ask in response, 'How can there be the appearance of an image without the use of concepts?' It is also incorrect to say that all types of insight meditation are conceptual, because there are forms of insight meditation that involve a contemplative or non-conceptual state. For instance, the non-discriminatory wisdom of a buddha is non-conceptual, because it is an absolute experience of insight. It is also incorrect to say tranquillity meditation is completely devoid of any mental ideation, because it is common practice for people to develop mindfulness through conceptual methods in this meditation.

Why is it said that the object of tranquillity meditation is non-conceptual? It is only generally true that the object of tranquillity is non-conceptual and the object of insight meditation is conceptual. We cannot make an absolute distinction between the two. For example, when we visualise a deity, to construct the manifestation of that deity is tranquillity meditation and to determine the nature of that manifestation is insight meditation. To realise lack of essence of the image is the experience of insight. For this reason, the experience of both types of meditation should be regarded as one experience with two different aspects rather than two different types of meditation. Your meditative experience will have both the aspect of tranquillity and the aspect of insight.

Tranquillity meditation involves concentrating on a visualised mental object without thinking about anything else. Insight meditation involves the analysis of the nature of that concentration, while remaining aware that both the object of meditation and the thoughts that examine it have no essence. As a result, tranquillity and insight meditation blend inseparably into one reality with two aspects. That is the integration of tranquillity and insight.

THE FRUITION OF TRANQUILLITY AND INSIGHT

The fruition of tranquillity and insight meditation is connected with the purification of mind on the one hand, and giving birth to wisdom on the other. The *Samadhinirmocana Sutra* says:

> We purify our minds through tranquillity meditation.
> We give rise to wisdom through insight meditation.

Purifying the mind of various conceptual distortions and giving rise to wisdom means that our consciousness becomes illuminated through the eradication of karmic traces and dispositions. Through this we can see that the two types of meditation counter two different corrupting veils. As the *Samadhinirmocana* also says:

> Maitreya: 'Victorious One, what are the roles of tranquillity and insight meditation?'
> Buddha: 'They are meant to liberate sentient beings from the two types of veils that lead to lower states of existence: the veil of conceptual confusion and the veil of emotional conflicts.'

The practice of tranquillity also helps us resist the temptations of sensory objects and to develop super knowledge. Through it, we overcome problems that arise from excessive desire, excessive concern with pleasure and our various experiences of mental anguish.[12] By overcoming these afflictions we are able to go through the four stages of absorption that correspond to the states of the gods. The *Prajnaparamita-samcayagatha* says:

> A yogin who has properly developed tranquillity meditation will develop sublime inner qualities, pliancy of body and mind, and supernatural powers.

The *Suhrllekha* says:

> By practising the four contemplations
> We eliminate excessive desire, joy, pleasure, and misery
> And achieve a bliss equal to that of the gods
> Who dwell in the realm of form.

Atisha's *Bodhipathapradipa* says:

> A yogin who achieves tranquillity meditation
> Will also develop supernatural powers.

The practice of insight enables the generation of happiness and harmony as a temporal goal and the transcendence of 3 modes of existence as an ultimate goal. This comes about when an understanding of the nature of things dawns in us.[13] The final accomplishment of these two types of meditation embodies the realisation of enlightenment. The *Prajnaparamita-samcayagatha* says:

> All the happiness of the buddhas,
> Bodhisattvas, shravakas, and pratyekabuddhas,
> As well as gods, and other sentient beings;
> Originate from supreme discriminating wisdom.

The ultimate result of the integration of tranquillity and insight meditation is complete enlightenment. The *Bodhisattvabhumi* says:

> Bodhisattvas who engage in meditation and can perfect the paramitas will be transported to the state of buddhahood.

The *Saptasatika-prajnaparamita Sutra* says:

> Oh Manjushri, great bodhisattvas, who practise discriminating wisdom will soon attain complete, great enlightenment.

Gampopa says:

> Tranquillity and insight meditation are the gateway to reality.

There are five factors attached to the practice of tranquillity and insight meditation: 1) cause, 2) function, 3) obstacle, 4) defilement, and 5) path. The cause of tranquillity meditation is proper conduct and the cause of insight is contemplation and analysis. The function of tranquillity meditation is to liberate us from the entanglements of conceptual constructions, and the function of insight meditation is to uproot the ignorance that gives rise to mental affliction. The obstacle to the attainment of tranquillity is obsessive concern for body and possessions and the obstacle to the realisation of insight is a lack of opportunity to reflect on the sublime words of the teachings. Obstacles for both types of meditation are frittering away our time in trivial pursuits and a lack of contentment.

Defilement in relation to tranquillity is agitation and resentment and defilement in relation to insight is stupor and dullness. Excessive desire and harmful intent are defilements in relation to both types of meditations. Overcoming dullness and stupor is having success on the path of tranquillity and overcoming resentment and agitation is having success on the path of insight. This completes the general elucidation of tranquillity and insight meditation.

3

Common Tranquillity Meditation

PREPARING TO ATTAIN TRANQUILLITY

You should rigorously try to avoid everything that might disturb your efforts to attain tranquillity meditation. Some causes of disturbance are failing to control your senses and indulging in gluttony. Learn to sit comfortably on a cushion by maintaining the posture of Vairochana. Your breath should be natural and even, without making noises or breathing hard. You should meditate without fear of suffering and hardship. You must try to remember these things or you will not gain the full benefit from your meditation practice. As the *Bodhipathapradipa* says:

> If your tranquillity meditation is defective,
> You will not attain tranquillity
> Even if you meditate for a thousand years.

The first *Bhavanakrama* says:

> If you don't look for praise or gains
> But abide in proper conduct
> Willingly undergoing hardships and applying effort,
> You will attain tranquillity quite quickly.

SETTING FORTH THE OBJECTS OF MEDITATION

This has four sections:

- The general explanation of meditation objects
- Relevant objects for different types of meditators
- Meditation objects to attempt at the beginning
- Retaining the visualised image during meditation

§ The General Explanation Of Meditation Objects

1. Pervasive objects

There are four aspects to this visualisation:

1. Meditation objects with concepts: 'meditation object' here does not refer to objects in the external world but to a mental image of an object.
2. Meditation objects without concepts: here the objects in the phenomenal world are used as the focus of meditation. We learn to focus on the nature of everything that exists as the object of our meditation, and try to realise the reality of things.
3. The extremities of the phenomenal world: this involves contemplating everything that exists in the entire world.
4. The object of meditation that fulfils our desire: we take whatever object of meditation is available and contemplate it repeatedly until we become so familiar with it that we will be free of defilements.

2. Antidote objects

This involves counter-attacking our desires or emotional conflicts. If a sudden emotional conflict arises, we have to do something to eradicate it. If it has not yet arisen, we need to make sure it does not arise in the future. Analytical meditation[1] has five aspects:

1. Contemplating the ugliness of the body to counter desire: we focus on aspects of the body that are undesirable, such as a hairy bum, and become automatically revolted. [2]
2. Giving rise to compassion to counter harmful thoughts: focus on our enemies, friends, and people to whom we are indifferent.
3. Analysing the twelve interdependent links to overcome ignorance: focus on understanding how certain causes and conditions result in particular effects.
4. The six spheres as an object of meditation: meditate on the psychophysical elements the spheres of earth, water, fire, air, space and consciousness.
5. The breath as an object of meditation: learning to stop our minds from wandering by focusing our attention on our breath.

3. Objects of the wise

This entails special methods that can help us realise the insubstantiality of the self. These meditations are not incorporated in the analysis of the psychophysical elements. This has five aspects:

1. Understanding the nature of the psychophysical constituents: we realise the self is not something that exists over and above the psychophysical constituents themselves.[3]
2. Understanding the spheres: we grow familiar with the eighteen spheres; which include six sense organs, six sense consciousnesses, and six sense objects.[4]
3. Understanding the sensory impressions: we come to understand that the six sense organs are the condition for the six sense consciousnesses, the six sense objects are the condition for perception, and the consciousness that follows immediately upon contact with a sense object is the instantaneous condition for the next thought to arise.
4. Sitting still with the interdependent links: here we come to understand that the twelve interdependent links are imbued with suffering and insubstantiality.[5]
5. Skilful recognition of what is appropriate and what is not: we gradually come to realise what kind of mental intentions lead to what kind of actions, and what kind of actions bring about what kind of results, thereby realising negative intentions bring about negative actions, which in turn produce negative results.

4. Objects that eradicate emotional defilement

This has two stages, one subtle and one gross:

1. The four stages of absorption: these relate to the gods, because the first stage is the realm of desire, the second is the realm of form, the third is the formless realm, and the fourth is the realm of non-mentation. We begin with the gross form of absorption and progress through the subtle forms that are the realm of the gods until we attain non-meditation.
2. The Four Noble Truths: we realise sixteen aspects of impermanence by contemplating suffering, its origin, its cessation, and the path that leads to that cessation. These contemplations are not

confined to tranquillity meditation; they are also very much a part of insight meditation. We use them as objects of concentration in tranquillity meditation and we use them as objects of analysis in insight meditation.

§ Relevant Objects For Different Types Of Meditators

The *Sravakabhumi* quotes the *Nam grus zhus pa'i mdo*:

> A monk who is overwhelmed by desire should contemplate the revolting features of the body, meditate on loving-kindness to counter hatred, contemplate the twelve interdependent links to eradicate ignorance, and analyse the six spheres to overcome pride.

It also says:

> A monk who is overcome by conceptual proliferation should practise contemplating the breath.

The *Namgrus zhuspa'i mdo* says:

> A monk who is ignorant about the characteristics of mental events, the self, and life in general should engage in analysis of the psychophysical constituents. If he is confused about their causes, he should analyse the six spheres. If he is confused about their conditions, he should analyse the sense processes. If he lacks understanding about impermanence, suffering, and selflessness, he should analyse the workings of dependent origination and learn to recognise the appropriateness and the inappropriateness of his own behaviour and intentions.

It also says:

> If a monk wishes to be free from desire, he should contemplate the form realm and practise the subtle contemplations of the formless realm. If he wants to be free from all conditioned things, he should become acquainted with the Four Noble Truths and contemplate those. If he wants to eradicate defilements, he should investigate the reality of dissatisfaction and suffering. If he leans too much toward any of these options, he should choose whichever contemplation suits him best.

Anyone who succumbs to the emotions equally or does not have a very emotional nature can choose any of the above meditations. The *Sravakabhumi* says:

> People who are equally affected by different emotions should stabilise their minds through the tranquillity method of their choosing rather than through insight meditation. The same applies to people who do not have very emotional natures.

§ Meditation Objects To Attempt At The Beginning

We can see that there are many types of meditative techniques for settling the mind in tranquillity meditation. It is important for people who are given to discursive thinking to begin by meditating on the breath. When such people introduce an object of visualisation, they should rely on a single object so as not to further disturb their minds. The *Bodhipathapradipa* says:

> Settle the mind peacefully
> On a chosen object.

Noble Aryasura says:

> You will achieve mental stability by concentrating on your chosen mental image exclusively. Do not try to focus on multiple mental images, or they will disturb your mind.

The initial meditation on tranquillity has two aspects. Master Bodhibhadra says:

> There is introspective contemplation and outward contemplation. Introspection refers to visualising your body as a deity, a skeleton, or a sacred trident. It can also include contemplating the breath, an imaginary seed syllable, a mental sphere, light, or even joy and happiness.

Some people say we should not use sticks and pebbles as objects of meditation, but that is of no real concern. Using an object of meditation such as a buddha statue seems to have many benefits. In any of these options, we use mindfulness to make sure the mind does not wander so that we can learn to hold that concentration and we use awareness to detect whether we have become distracted and lost our mindfulness.[6] The *Samadhiraja Sutra* says:

> The Buddha had a perfect form
> Which was golden in colour.

> Anyone who meditates on this image
> Will achieve samadhi.

The third *Bhavanakrama* says:

> Anyone who is trying to attain tranquillity meditation should imagine a statue of the Buddha and picture it exactly the way they have seen it or heard about it.

If you successfully concentrate on a mental image in this way, you can attempt any of the visualisations described above. The first *Bhavanakrama* says:

> When you achieve mental stability in meditation, you can focus on the psychophysical constituents, the elements, and so on.

§ Retaining The Visualised Image During Meditation

Retaining the visualised mental image during our meditation is very important if we hope to attain mental concentration. Through mindfulness, we make sure the mind does not wander. We use awareness to detect whether the mind has become distracted or whether it has lost its mindfulness. The commentary on the *Sutralamkara* says:

> Mindfulness helps to maintain the object of concentration, while awareness helps to recognise when we have become distracted and lost mindfulness.

A traditional analogy says:

> The mind is like a mad elephant, the object of concentration is like a stable pole. Mindfulness is like a rope, and awareness is like a hook. We must use mindfulness and awareness to tie the elephant of mind to the pole of the object of concentration.

The *Madhyamakahrdaya* says:

> When the elephant of mind wanders,
> It should be bound with the rope of mindfulness
> To the stable pole of the meditation object
> By consistently applying the hook of awareness.

If we make too much effort to concentrate, we will only agitate our minds and if we try too hard to relax into the meditative state, we will only fall into drowsiness and stupor. We therefore have to maintain a balance between being too uptight and too loose. Master Chandragomin says:

> If we apply ourselves too much, agitation will arise.
> If we do not apply ourselves enough, depression will set in;
> It is so hard to maintain a balance.
> What is the point in stirring up the mind?

His *Desanasatava* also says:

> Over-exertion will arouse mental agitation,
> While non-exertion will bring about depression;
> But the middle ground is hard to achieve.
> What is the point in getting agitated?

METHODS FOR REALISING TRANQUILLITY

This has four sections:

- The eight antidotes
- The nine stages of tranquillity
- The six powers
- The four mental attitudes

§ The Eight Antidotes

This covers the same subject matter as the section on obstacles and antidotes. The obstacles are laziness, forgetfulness, dullness, agitation, not making enough effort, and making too much effort. The antidotes are mindfulness and awareness because they help us recognise dullness and agitation arising. When they do arise, we remove them through the methods explained above. When we begin meditation, we take no delight in it and find pleasure in things that are distracting. We delight in three types of laziness: plain laziness, idleness, and indifference.

The first stage of tranquillity meditation is known as the 'stage of application' because we have to inject enormous effort into our meditation practice and we must continually train ourselves to dwell on the benefits of meditation. As a result, we develop three types of confidence: undiluted confidence, the confidence of certainty and inconvertible confidence.

We must also reorientate our way of thinking so that meditation becomes an important part of our lives. We have to continuously dwell on the defects and shortcomings of frittering away our time through laziness, idleness, and indifference. Recognising the harm in wasting time has to become a spur for our practice. Everyone experiences physical and mental hardships when they meditate so we should have courage in the face of difficulties. We should take them on ourselves, instead of regarding them as insurmountable obstacles that overwhelm us.

The second stage of tranquillity meditation is known as the 'stage of concentration' because we become aware of distraction when we forget to be mindful and can redirect our attention to the object of meditation. We may also encounter dullness, agitation, and doubts without being aware of them so we should learn to become aware of those obstacles as well. When we do get distracted by them, we should practise relaxing and tightening our concentration until we eventually learn to eradicate those obstacles. When dullness or agitation arises, meditate in such a way that you are not concentrating on anything; simply remain in a state of equanimity. These techniques for achieving tranquillity are a common practice and can be found in most meditation treatises.

§ The Nine Stages Of Tranquillity

The first stage of tranquillity is known as 'resting the mind' and is about trying to control our impressions in an introspective mood, because that will give us less chance of being distracted. To explain the first stage of tranquillity, the *Sutralamkara* says:

> Rest your mind on the object of meditation
> And concentrate on it,
> Without letting yourself get distracted.

We should rest comfortably in the first stage of tranquillity and maintain the continuity of that mindfulness until we can settle into the second stage. This second stage is known as 'continuous resting.' The *Sutralamkara* says:

> We should try to remain in a state of concentration without becoming distracted.

The third stage of tranquillity meditation is known as 'patch-like resting.' Here the *Sutralamkara* says:

> If we suffer from forgetfulness, we recognise it
> And then go back to the object of concentration.

In the fourth stage, we should try to gather our agitated thoughts, emotions, and concepts, instead of allowing our mind to becoming scattered. We will then gradually realise we no longer need to control the grosser mental activity. However, there are subtle forms of activity that we should continue to gather in, which is why this fourth stage is called 'close placement.' The *Sutralamkara* says:

> Skilful meditators always gather the mind
> More and more inward to increase their concentration.

The fifth stage is called 'pacification' because we completely pacify our disturbances through seeing the benefits of attaining meditative concentration.[7] The *Sutralamkara* says:

> Realising the virtues of samadhi, we train the mind in tranquillity.

The sixth stage is the state of 'subjugation,' because we have now successfully settled all mental activity that gives rise to disturbances in meditation, having realised the defects of distractions and mental disturbances. The *Sutralamkara* says:

> Realising the harmful effects of a distracted mind,
> The meditator eliminates all mental activity.

The seventh stage is where we experience 'thorough subjugation,' which means that from this point onwards no mental disturbances arise from desire, dullness, worry, and stupor. Even if such disturbances begin, we immediately become conscious of them and disperse them on the spot. The *Sutralamkara* says:

> As soon as we recognise desire, worry, and lust
> They dissipate naturally.

The eighth stage is called 'one-pointedness,' because we are in a state of one-pointed concentration without any mental disturbances and don't need to make any effort to remain in that state of contemplation. *Sutralamkara* says:

> When we really stabilise our effort to concentrate,
> We achieve perfect natural concentration.

The ninth stage is the state of complete concentration which arises from furthering the experience of one-pointed concentration. [8] The *Sutralamkara* says:

> At this level, we no longer need to make effort to meditate at all.

§ The Six Powers

We need to develop the following six powers to accomplish these nine stages of tranquillity: 1) power of hearing, 2) power of contemplation, 3) power of mindfulness, 4) power of awareness, 5) power of effort, and 6) power of familiarity.

It is through hearing about meditation and concentration that we are able to enter into the idea of practising meditation. The power of contemplation means that what we have heard is not sufficient in itself to give rise to an understanding of meditation; we have to think about that and contemplate it again and again. If we do this, it will gradually become easier to meditate.

The power of mindfulness means that it is only through the practice of mindfulness that we are able to develop concentration and overcome distraction. The power of awareness means that it is only through awareness that we can become conscious of the emotional conflicts that arise in meditation so it is awareness that enables us to overcome them. It is also through awareness that we realise the harmful effects of the obscurations and our mind ceases to han-ker after our deluded mental processes.

The power of effort empowers us to withstand the obstacles of dullness and agitation and overcome our conceptual proliferation. The power of familiarity means we only become familiar with meditation by practising it repeatedly. Only then can it start to become a natural process for us.

§ The Four Mental Attitudes

There are also the four different mental applications to employ in relation to the nine stages of meditation. These are: 1) concentrated mental application, 2) interrupted mental application, 3) uninterrupted mental application, and 4) spontaneous mental application.

We need to apply concentrated mental application during the first two stages of meditative concentration or samadhi and must invest enormous energy into developing our powers of concentration. We can then apply interrupted mental effort to our concentration in measured stages. For example, many obstacles may arise during the fifth stage of meditative concentration, such as dullness and agitation, and interrupt the length of our concentration span. We need to learn to interrupt it and reapply it. By the eighth stage of meditative concentration, we will no longer have interruptions because we will have learned how to cultivate a continuous state of concentrated mind, which is why this is called uninterrupted mental application. On the ninth level of concentration, we no longer need effort or antidotes because we are spontaneously in a state of concentration. The *Sravakabhumi* says:

> We need to use the four mental attitudes to realise the nine stages of tranquillity meditation or no results will be attained. Concentrated mental application has an effect on the first and second stages of tranquillity. Interrupted mental application affects the third to seventh stage of tranquillity, and uninterrupted mental application is how we realise the eighth stage of tranquillity. Spontaneous mental application leads to the attainment of complete meditative concentration on the ninth stage of tranquillity.

We apply concentrated mental application to the first and second stages of meditation. Interrupted mental application applies to the next five stages. Why is there a difference here? The term 'concentrated mental application' means the mind does not stay in meditative concentration during these first stages, while 'intermittent mental application' implies that it is still necessary to make an effort when mind is able to rest in meditative concentration. Tranquillity meditation needs to be conducted in the way it has been outlined here so that it doesn't become defective. A defective meditation practice will not yield results even if we were to meditate for a thousand years. The *Bodhipathapradipa* says:

> If our meditation is defective,
> No amount of effort will reward
> Our attempts to meditate.
> Even if we try for a thousand years,
> No samadhi will arise from that.

The *Prajnaparamita-samcayagatha* says:

> Exert yourself in attaining tranquillity
> Through uninterrupted meditation
> On the innate purity of mind.
> Just as striking flints together sporadically
> Will not cause sparks,
> Intermittent meditation practice
> Will not lead to tranquillity.
> Do not give up until you have attained samadhi!

This completes the explanation for tranquillity meditation.

4

Common Insight Meditation

THE GENERAL MEDITATION ON INSIGHT

There are three types of insight: 1) the mundane level, 2) the supramundane level, and 3) the insight of the Mahayana tradition. The mundane level of insight employs subtle and gross objects of meditation. The supramundane level consists in contemplating the Four Noble Truths and realising the selflessness of ego. The insight of the Mahayana tradition is the approach we will examine here. The *Samadhinirmocana Sutra* says:

> 1) Insight using concepts, 2) insight establishing the right view of reality, and 3) insight born from discriminating awareness.[1]

The *Samadhinirmocana Sutra* and *Abhidharmasamuccaya* mention four types of insight:

> (1) Insight arising from analysis because of employing concepts to understand the existence of individual things, (2) insight arising from determination because of understanding the extent of individual things, (3) insight arising from full comprehension because of using concepts to understand individual things as well as the nature of those things, and (4) insight arising from realisation because of recognising the true nature of things after applying the previous methods.

The *Sravakabhumi* says:

> There are six techniques in the practice of insight meditation: These are 1) the identification of existing things, 2) the identification of meaning, 3) the identification of characteristics, 4) the identification of a special occasion, 5) the identification of time, and 6) the identification of reason.

We gain comprehension of the nature of things through insight meditation in these ways. The *Sutralamkara* says:

> We start by using concepts
> To develop an understanding of discrimination,
> Then we allow the mind to relax,
> So that we can realise that concepts have one flavour;
> The flavour of insubstantiality.

Master Vasubandhu comments:

> We employ eleven types of investigation in insight meditation: 1) using both investigation and examination, 2) using examination without investigation, 3) using neither investigation nor examination, 4) cultivating tranquillity alone, 5) cultivating insight alone, 6) cultivating both, 7) investigating the characteristics of contemplation, 8) investigating tranquillity, 9) investigating the characteristics of equanimity, 10) investigating our own mental cultivation, and 11) investigating with reverence.

These are the eleven different types of investigation in insight meditation and they should be applied in that order. The first three establish the proper view, the following four enhance our meditation, and the last four ascertain the view. In brief, they demonstrate that concepts can be used to understand the nature of reality. As the sutras and treatises on meditation state, when we vigorously rub two sticks together, they will produce flames and be consumed by them. Similarly, if we correctly use analysis to apply concepts to the apprehension of reality, those concepts will produce insight and be consumed by it.[2] This is why it is important to establish a proper view through insight meditation. The insight that dawns will be of a non-conceptual kind.

ESTABLISHING THE VIEW OF INSIGHT

This has two sections:

- Enumerating the methods of different schools
- The relevant methods of our system

§ Enumerating The Methods Of Different Schools

The Yogacara school of Asanga and Vasubandhu places great emphasis on the mental aspect of reality by employing the reasoning of non-duality. Whatever the object of analysis, we come to realise its lack of inherent existence by understanding that everything is constructed and fashioned by the mind. We employ the same reasoning to see that even consciousness is empty of inherent existence and that it is as insubstantial as the material world.

The Madhyamaka school of Nagarjuna and Aryadeva puts the emphasis on emptiness. The svatantrika-Madhyamaka propounds the view that both subject and object are devoid of substantiality. They employ the 'reasoning of the one and the many' to get to the root of the existential condition.

The prasangika-Madhyamaka uses analysis to establish that ideas of me and mine (subject and object, perceiver and perceived) and the ignorance that gives rise to these divisions is illusory. We will thereby realise everything is insubstantial by nature because it lacks inherent existence. According to this school, the proper view is not to entertain notions of existence or nonexistence (emptiness or non-emptiness) because these ideas are just conceptual proliferations. Both schools say we realise a wisdom consciousness devoid of the differentiation of perceiver and perceived through meditation practice.

The prasangika-Madhyamaka school is also divided into two further sub-schools. The first advocates 'self-emptiness' because we realise that everything is insubstantial and empty of inherent existence. The second advocates 'other-emptiness' because we realise a wisdom consciousness that is independent of any external factors and as a consequence is self-existent.

Many Indian and Tibetan masters have said we should first try to realise the emptiness of external phenomena and then to understand that external phenomenon is determined by mind. We can then turn our attention to the mind itself and we will realise that the nature of mind is also empty of any inherent existence and thus devoid of substantiality.[3]

§ The Relevant Methods Of Our System

1. The general meditation on selflessness

(i) Why we meditate on selflessness

It is very important to understand what we mean by the notion of ego, what we mean by 'me and mine,' and so on. Our primordial ignorance and our failure to examine and analyse things properly means that we automatically conceptualise something called 'self' and 'selflessness,' subject and object, me and mine. We thus fail to realise the insubstantiality of the self and of external objects.[4] Chandrakirti's commentary to the *Catusataka* says:

> The self is conceived as existing by itself, without being dependent

on anything else. To realise selflessness is therefore to realise the non-existence of the mental implication called 'self.' Selflessness has two aspects: the selflessness of persons and the selflessness of material things.

Dharmakirti says:

> The notion of self comes from believing there is something called 'me' that is immutable, unchanging and permanent. This mistaken notion of a permanent physical body and of a permanent material world give rise to the defilements and obscurations.

The *mdo Sil bu* says:

> All phenomenal elements that have characteristics are called *dharmas*. Consciousness is called 'the person.'

The self of persons consists of an innate consciousness that regards itself as an enduring, self-existing substantial entity. It clings to the notion of 'I, me, and mine,' and mistakes the psychophysical consitituents or *skandhas* as a permanent entity. The self of phenomena is created by the mind grasping at external objects as self-sufficient, substantial realities and clinging to them as unchanging and reliable.[5] These two forms of self engender karma, mental obscurations, emotional defilement, and suffering. Sri Dharmakirti says:

> As long as there is the notion self,
> The notion of others will arise.
> If we hang onto these two notions,
> We experience attachment and aversion.
> Once we become entangled in attachment and aversion,
> Various mental afflictions start to manifest.

The *Ratnavali* says:

> As long as we fixate on the skandhas,
> We will project the notion of 'self.'
> We continually create fresh karma
> When this notion of self abides.
> If this karmic process is perpetuated,
> We will never put an end to rebirth.

It is important to contemplate the idea of selflessness because we will find it impossible to achieve liberation without it. Dharmakirti says:

If we do not purge ourselves of this mistaken notion,
There will be no way we can discard the idea of a self.

The *Catusataka* says:

If you realise selflessness in the insubstantiality of an object,
All the seeds of your samsaric disposition will cease.

The *Madhyamakavatara* says:

All our confusions and defilements
Come from having a wrong notion of the self.
When a yogi realises the notion of the self to be illusory,
He is able to eradicate that misconception.

By meditating on selflessness we can reverse the mental processes that fixate on the psychophysical constituents, the locus of the idea of self and other, me and mine. When that reversal takes place, the samsaric dispositions set up by craving, clinging, and grasping become nullified and exhausted. We then achieve liberation from samsara. The *Mulamadhyamikakarika* says:

When the idea of 'me' and 'mine' becomes pacified,
The idea of self and selflessness automatically disappear.

It also says:

When we realise no self within and no substantiality without,
We overcome the duality of 'me' and 'mine.'
All conditions that perpetuate samsaric existence cease.
Karmic dispositions, emotional conflicts,
And mental defilements also come to cease.

(ii) Ways of meditating on two kinds of selflessness

- Negating the self of the person

There can be no notion of a self. If such a self were to really exist, it must have come into existence either from itself, from something outside itself, from both, or from neither. According to the Madhyamaka view of the *Ratnavali*:

To advocate the notion of a pure self is to be deluded about the reality of things.

Since none of these options is possible, the notion of the self cannot be real.

The *Ratnavali* also says:

> The notion of the self has not arisen
> Of its own accord, from something outside, or from both
> Nor has it arisen in the three times.
> We should put an end to this mistaken concept.

For this self truly to exist, it must be either identical to the psychophysical constituents or completely separate from them. The *Madhyamakakarika* says:

> If the psychophysical constituents are the self,
> Then it too will have to experience birth and death.

If there were nothing apart from the psychophysical constituents, the notion of an eternal, immutable, and permanent self would be nullified. If the self were identical to the psychophysical constituents, it would come into being and go out of existence in the same way as the other constituents. If the self were completely identical with the psychophysical constituents, without an enduring nature of its own, it would be difficult to establish memory and responsibility because there would be no continuity.

You would not be responsible for your past negative actions because you would now be somebody different, and there could be no notion of your experiencing the consequences of those actions. Many difficulties arise from this premise. The idea of a self that is completely separate from the psychophysical constituent is refuted in the following excerpt. The *Madhyamakakarika*:

> If the self were disassociated from the skandhas,
> It would have no determining characteristics
> And would therefore be nothing.

It also says:

> If the self were a separate entity from the skandhas,
> It would be divested of all significance.
> It would have no integral determination
> Because cognition would be impossible.

The *Madhyamakavatara* says:

> We should automatically realise that what we consider 'mine'
> Is just as insubstantial as what we call 'me.'

The *Madhyamakakarika* says:

> When there is no substantial self

> How can there be a substantial other?

The *Madhyamakavatara* says:

> When we comes to realise there is no substantial self
> We realise that our actions also lack inherent existence.
> It is by understanding this nature of selflessness
> That a yogi becomes liberated.

The *Bhavanakrama* says:

> The notion of the self is dependent upon the five skandhas, the eighteen spheres and twelve sense faculties. Without these, we cannot make any sense of a self. The notion of a self, as presented by certain non-Buddhist thinkers, has no basis because it is said to be unchanging and immutable. The skandhas are composite phenomena and all are subject to change. We have to realise the idea of 'me' and 'mine' is based on a misconception.[6]

- Negating the self of phenomena

The bases for the creation of a self are the following dharmas: the psychophysical constituents, the elements, and the sense faculties. We negate this notion of the self in the following way. As the *Madhyamakakarika* says:

> Nothing whatsoever arises from itself
> Nor from others, neither from both,
> Nor without a cause;
> Nothing whatsoever comes into existence.

We employ this method of 'fourfold reasoning' to negate the notion of self. This reasoning states that if something were to arise of its own accord and from itself, cause and the effect would be identical.[7] It also says:

> If what gives rise to the effect and that effect are the same,
> The cause and the effect would be one entity.
> If that which exists comes from something other than itself,
> There could be no homogeneity between cause and effect.

Again, it says:

> Insofar as something is other than its cause,
> There can be no difference between that
> cause and anything else that exists.

If we say something arises from itself and from something else, the problems we have already encountered would again apply. As the *Madhyamakavatara* says:

> If something comes into existence without a cause
> Or in dependence upon something else,
> It cannot be substantiated.
> If we examine things properly,
> We will see that everything is devoid of self.

Both subject and object are found to be without any substance or essence when we examine them thoroughly. If they truly had substance, it would have to consist of either one or many entities. However, neither of these options can be found. Dharmakirti says:

> By examining the things of this world,
> We find that they have no substance.
> They are completely devoid
> Of any unitary or multiple nature.

The *Bodhichittavivarana* says:

> If something called 'atoms' existed,
> They could not be regarded as indivisible.
> Even they lack any inherent existence
> Being reducible to ever finer particles.
> In brief, nothing exists as a complete unity
> Or in a complete state of diversity.
> Mistaken notions about self and external world arise
> Because our karmic traces and dispositions
> Have created deluded ways of thinking.

It also says:

> Due to the turbulent activities
> Of our karmic traces and dispositions,
> We perceive substantial things.
> These notions are determined by mind itself.
> No external world exists independently
> Of these determinations of mind.

Even if phenomena arise as if they had a kind of inherent existence, that in itself is not proof that any such substantiality is actually there. A magician can conjure up images that have no reality. We perceive the world as if things had substance to them in much the same way. The *Lankavatara* says:

> Stirred up by hidden defilements,
> The mind creates the appearance of an external world,
> However, that reality does not exist.
> To perceive external phenomena as real
> Is a complete distortion.

The *Samadhiraja Sutra* says:

> A magician is able to produce the illusion
> Of horses, elephants, chariots, and so on.
> Similarly, our perceptions of a world
> Created validity, substantiality and duration.

To contemplate the insubstantiality of the phenomenal world, we need to think about it in a way that is currently foreign. The *Bhavanakrama* says:

> The phenomenal world consists of the five psychophysical constituents, the twelve sensory formations, the eighteen spheres, and so on. Without mind, these things have no existence; they are dependent on consciousness. We should realise that even if something looks as if it has validity, immutability and duration, it reveals its lack of substantiality when we look into its finer particles. Our innate and inveterate tendency to cling to things that in reality are insubstantial, makes us mistake them for substantial entities. In the same way that we take dreams to be actual events when sleeping, we take what is ephemeral and intangible to be abiding and substantial when awake. All these things are manifestations of mind. They have no independent existence.

(iii) How we gain insight through this meditation

The above negation of the two forms of self, the self of persons, and the self of the phenomenal world should be used to eradicate our attachment to things. However, we should not take this to mean nothing exists at all from the ultimate point of view. The *Madhyamakakarika* says:

> The Victorious Ones expounded the teachings on emptiness
> To eradicate absolute views.
> That things are empty of substance
> Should not be seen as an absolute view.

The *Maharatnakuta Sutra* says:

> Buddha: 'Kashyapa, holding onto a notion of ego as great like Mount Sumeru is easier to understand than hanging onto notions of emptiness as a concept. Why is this so? Because, Kashyapa, to understand emptiness, you need to dismantle all absolute views. To establish emptiness as another absolute view defeats its whole purpose.'

The *Bodhichittavivarana* says:

> To conceptualise things as unoriginated,
> Non-existent, and completely lacking in self
> Is an inferior form of meditation.
> That is not the way to meditate on emptiness!

Atisha says:

> Only through developing skilful means
> And sharpening our discriminating awareness,
> Can we attain enlightenment;
> Not from meditating on lack of self alone.

How then should we understand emptiness? Emptiness is understood by not falling into the extremes of eternalism and nihilism. We should realise that everything exists in an interrelated or interdependent manner. Things do not exist substantially, but this does not mean things do not exist at all. The phenomenal world does have independent existence. To say that something is empty is to say that something has no inherent existence. It is not a way of saying it has no existence at all. The *Madhyamakakarika* says:

> Nothing exists
> That is not a product of dependent phenomena
> And all dependent phenomena
> Are empty of substantiality.

It also says:

> To say that something exists substantially
> Is to fall into the view of eternalism.
> To say that nothing exists
> Is to fall into the view of nihilism.
> The wise ones do not fall into the extremes
> Of existence or non-existence.

The commentary to the *Satyadvaya-vibhanga* says:

> For that reason, it is not empty or non-empty.
> It is not affirmed or negated.
> It neither arises nor does not arise.
> This is the teaching of Buddha.

The human mind has the inveterate tendencies to grasp after or hang onto certain concepts because it is filled with terror and anxiety when it has no concepts to cling to. It makes us feel better when we can cling to concepts such as existence and non-existence. That is the cause of our downfall. [8] The *Ratnavali* says:

> The teachings on emptiness
> Do not give us anything on which to cling.
> Ordinary beings want concepts they can concretise
> Especially in relation to existence and non-existence
> And thus, they become distracted from reality.

We should also apply this reasoning to the mind and not presume it has any more substantiality than the things of the world just because it determines our perceptions of that world. The mind is also empty of inherent existence. We can see the mind has no inherent existence, because it is not something that can be grasped, shown or perceived in any form or shape. If we try to analyse the mind, we will see that it cannot be discovered as any kind of entity. The way to realise emptiness is to understand that the phenomenal world is determined by mind, while that same mind is devoid of substantiality. The *Lankavatara* says:

> External reality is neither existent nor non-existent.
> Even mind has no substantiality.
> The elimination of all views
> Is how we realise emptiness.

The *Bodhicharyavatara* says:

> Mind cannot be perceived
> By the senses or by itself.
> To look for the mind
> As self-existing or not
> Is like looking for a barren woman's son.
> It is an exercise in futility.

It also says:

> When mind no longer perceives
> Either composite or non-composite entities,
> There is no other reality.
> Clinging to imaginary essences
> Resolves into the non-conceptual state.

The first *Bhavanakrama* says:

> View all three planes of existence as being of mental origin, because everything is created by mind. If you analyse the mind, you are analysing the essence of everything.

When we analyse the nature of mind, we need to understand that even the mind is insubstantial. How can the mind be unreal when it is said to create the external world? Just as phenomenal things and the senses have no essence, so too is the mind without substantiality. The objects of the world have many manifestations yet they are neither one nor many in their nature. The mind is also neither one entity nor multiple entities. The mind and the external world are ephemeral.

If we examine the nature of mind with discriminating awareness, we will see that it has no external or internal reality. The mind cannot be found in the three times (past, present, or future). The thoughts and emotions that arise in the mind come from nowhere and abide nowhere. You may wonder what the nature of mind is, if it cannot be grasped or established in any way. The *Ratnavali* says:

> Buddha: 'Kashyapa, mind can't be discovered through analysis. The nature of mind can't be known. That which can't be grasped has no past, present, or future.'

This meditative method is superior to meditations that employ analysis and concepts. The *Sutralamkara* says:

> Apart from mind, nothing exists,
> Even the mind does not exist.
> Meditators who understand the unreality of both
> Can settle in emptiness without duality.

Master Vasubandhu's says:

> When we understand that we only perceive mental images, we realise the insubstantial nature of mind, because there can be no

internal reality without external reality. The realisation of this is non-duality. This is the direct perception of ultimate reality.

2. Specific methods for meditating on reality

(i) Identifying the proper view of ultimate reality

If we analyse the phenomenal world in the way described above, we will begin to think in terms of existence, non-existence, substantiality, insubstantiality, emptiness and non-emptiness, and so on. However, this is a conceptual exercise and cannot reveal the reality of emptiness. To realise emptiness properly, we first have to employ analytical reasoning and rely on the instructions, then we have to come to a non-conceptual understanding of reality. Reality-as-such cannot be comprehended through concepts alone because reality is free from concepts.

We can develop the proper view by using concepts. Reality transcends concepts because reality-as-such is not an entity; not something that exists, has come into being, or has a limit. Therefore, it is beyond our conceptual grasp.

To understand the real nature of things is to understand the nature of mind itself, because the nature of mind is unvitiated and unpolluted by concepts and ideas. The nature of mind does not exist within or without. It is not an entity of any kind. Therefore, it has been pure right from the beginning. In that sense, we cannot even speak about liberation as a process. We can only speak about liberation in relation to the nature of mind because it has always been free. The *Dharmatasvabhava-sunyatacala-pratisarvaloka Sutra* says:

> All things are innately non-arising,
> Do not dwell anywhere,
> Have no ultimate function or activity,
> And transcend existence and non-existence.

The *Prajnaparamita-samcayagatha* says:

> When we understand that all phenomena lack inherent existence,
> We realise the transcendental wisdom of the Mahayana path.

It also says:

> Not to perceive phenomena as existent, non-existent, both or neither is to realise the transcendental wisdom of the Mahayana path.

The *Dharmatasvabhava-sunyatacala-pratisarvaloka Sutra* says:

> The mind is not an entity; it has no shape or form, cannot be

> touched or seen, and does not dwell within or without. It is completely pure from the beginning, having no essence. The mind cannot be liberated because the nature of mind has never been separated from the nature of ultimate reality.

The *Yum la bstod pa* says:

> That which cannot be expressed, perceived, or defined
> Is the transcendental wisdom.

The *Madhyamakakarika* says:

> The reality that is inseparable from the nature of mind,
> Is not something we can acquire or lose.
> Nor is it something that can cease to exist.
> It is the state of nirvana itself.

Atisha says:

> The nature of mind is profound,
> Free from concepts, and luminous.
> It doesn't come into being or cease to exist.
> It is the state of nirvana itself.
> The nature of mind is never disturbed
> By obscurations, defilements, dullness, or agitation.

He also says:

> If we understand that the five skandhas,
> Eighteen spheres, and sensory impressions
> All lack substantiality;
> We have developed discriminating awareness.

(ii) Description of the Proper Meditation

Once we have established the proper view, we can engage in contemplative meditation and will remain in a state of meditative concentration as explained in the previous chapter. We need to keep our minds undistracted by using mindfulness and awareness, without entertaining any thoughts apart from mindfulness and awareness, without modulating or conditioning the mind, without decreasing or increasing the mind, without analysing the mind, and without examining the mind. We simply let the mind rest in its own natural state.[9] The *Ting 'dzin dam pa'i mdo* says:

The nature of mind
Should not be conceived as space.
We should rest in that expansiveness
For that is the state of samadhi.

It also says:

When we settle the mind in ultimate reality
Which is inseparable from it;
We will have authentic meditation experiences
That cannot be conceptually formulated.
This is the state of samadhi.

The *Saptasatika-prajnaparamita* says:

If we allow whatever arises in the mind to be
And can rest in that experience,
That is the meditation of discriminating wisdom,
The meditation of non-conceptuality, and non-elaboration.

The *Astasahasrika-prajnaparamita* says:

When we stop grasping after certain things
Trying to acquire or discard them,
We develop discriminating wisdom.

It also says:

We develop discriminating wisdom
When the mind is allowed to rest in space-like expansiveness.

The *Nam mkha' rin po che mdo* says:

The nature of mind cannot be clarified
Nor established as this or that.
When it simply rests in its own authentic condition,
We recognise its true reality and attain liberation.

The *Avatamsaka* says:

Meditate on the nature of mind
Which is just like space.
Simply remain in the state of spaciousness
Without entertaining thoughts or concepts.

The *Sutralamkara* says:

> If we settle the mind in ultimate reality
> And rest in pure awareness,
> We will soon attain buddhahood.

The *Bodhichittavivarana* says:

> The nature of mind
> Has the characteristic of space.
> So this space-like meditation
> Is the meditation on emptiness.

Atisha says:

> In the sphere of ultimate reality,
> Detached from conceptual proliferations;
> We settle the mind without discrimination.

Many more statements by past masters could be cited, but they are elaborated further in the Mahamudra section of this text.

(iii) The attitude to maintain in post-meditation

We should try to carry the power of mindfulness and awareness from our meditation into everyday life. It is important to view everything as illusion-like, because everything must be seen as lacking in inherent existence.[10] This is the perception of post-meditation. The *Prajnaparamita-samcayagatha* says:

> We should realise that the insubstantiality of the skandhas
> Is identical with those skandhas.
> It is not that insubstantiality is a separate thing
> From the skandhas themselves.
> They are identical in nature.

The *Samadhiraja* says:

> Like a mirage, an illusion,
> A magical display, or a dream,
> Meditation on sensory phenomena
> Is lacking in any substantiality.
> Know all phenomena to be this way.

The term 'magical display' is used here because we should regard everything as like an illusion during post-meditation. While we may sometimes perceive our everyday lives as illusory, this is not the meaning of 'magical display.' How should we perceive everyday life in post-meditation? Everyday phenomena should be dealt with in the same way a magician deals with his tricks; as unreal and therefore we should have no clinging to them. Even though the audience might be fooled by these tricks, the magician knows they have no reality.

In the same way, while ordinary people become attached and fixated to phenomenal experiences, the yogin is aware that nothing has any substantiality. Simply understanding that is not sufficient however, because that is only a conceptual view of the phenomenal world.[11] We need to translate that view into a direct experience of the insubstantial nature of phenomena. The *Samadhiraja Sutra* says:

> Magicians conjure up images of horses, elephants, and so on,
> But they have no attachment to these images
> Knowing they lack reality.
> Understand all phenomena this way.

Someone who realises the insubstantial nature of the phenomenal world will no longer be overwhelmed by the various presentations of that phenomenal world because he or she will have realised the unreality of things. That is why we must start by viewing phenomena as illusory. The *Prajnaparamita-samcayagatha* says:

> Just as a magician knows the unreality of his creations
> A yogi recognises the insubstantiality of the phenomenal world.
> This is direct experience, not a conceptual attitude.

If you gradually train yourself in this way, there will be a conflation of the meditative and post-meditative states, and you will no longer need to make a distinction between formal meditation and post-meditation. Whatever you perceive in the world will be perceived through the meditative mind state, for you will now be free of the conflict of perceiver and perceived. We meditate on insight to cultivate the proper view. Having established the view, we use awareness to witness the arising of dullness and agitation and to recognise the clarity of our mental state when the mind is devoid of dullness and agitation. We can also develop equanimity by not entertaining thoughts. Many techniques such as these are described in detail in Asanga's *Sravakabhumi*. You should consult that text and study those techniques. However, you should be able to understand something of the nature of insight meditation from the discussions contained in this chapter. This completes the explanation for insight meditation.

5

Misconceptions About Common Meditation

ANALYTIC AND CONTEMPLATIVE MEDITATION

Some people hold the view that only scholars should engage in analytical meditation while meditators are better served by confining themselves to the meditation of tranquillity. Other people say only scholars should study texts and then analyse what they have read during contemplation, while meditators need only concern themselves with contemplation and rely solely on meditation instructions. These are both mistaken views.

Scholars who engage in analysis also need to engage in meditative contemplation, and meditators need to complement their practice with analysis if they want to determine how their concepts work. If you engage in analysis but do not meditate, your understanding will remain on a conceptual level. If you meditate without engaging in analysis, your meditative experiences will remain subjective. You will not receive the full benefits of meditation practice if you do not combine analysis and contemplation.[1]

You might ask, 'Why then is this distinction made between tranquillity and analytical meditation?' This is more a question of emphasis than any lack of relationship. Analytic meditation uses inference and relies on textual sources and reasoning. It is called 'analytic' for this reason. Tranquillity meditation relies largely on direct, immediate experience and this is obtained through resting the mind in its own natural state without the use of analysis.[2] Analytical meditation is particularly emphasised by the followers of Nagarjuna, Chandrakirti, and so on, and tranquillity meditation is emphasised by the siddhas, such as Shavaripa, Saraha, and others. Both approaches are correct because their final understanding is the nature of reality itself. As Je Gotsangpa says:

> The analytical meditation of a scholar and the contemplative

> meditation of a yogi lead to the same goal, but contemplative meditation is a more spontaneous approach.

It is possible to realise emptiness by relying solely on textual authority and analytical reasoning, but in most cases this approach only leads to a conceptual understanding of reality. A direct experience of reality is usually only possible through contemplative meditation. For instance, great Buddhist philosophers, such as Nagarjuna and Aryadeva, became enlightened by practising the Sutric tradition, which emphasises contemplative meditation. The Buddhist masters that figure highly in the Kagyu lineage, such as Naropa and Maitripa, were great scholars who did not attain final realisation through their studies. They only became realised through the direct instructions of their meditation masters. Many of the great Indian and Tibetan masters were liberated through this central practice of contemplation.

Some people argue that if we don't establish the proper view by consulting texts and using reasoning, particularly the views of Nagarjuna and his spiritual son, we cannot gain an understanding of reality. This view is completely wrong. It is a biased assertion, which may suit the purposes of its proponents, but it can't be consistently upheld. Were it valid, no Buddhist practitioners prior to Nagarjuna would have gained any spiritual insight at all.

Strictly speaking, 'analysis' refers to the practice of analytic meditation and 'contemplation' refers to the practice of tranquillity meditation. However, this definition is not entirely correct. Contemplating the difficulty of attaining a precious human rebirth, impermanence, and the insubstantiality of the subject-object duality would have to be included in the category of analytical meditation, and employing analytical examination before letting your mind rest would have to be included under the category of tranquillity meditation.

Other people argue that we cannot engage in analysis while in a state of contemplation and we cannot engage in contemplation while using analysis. This is also incorrect. As the *Bhavanakrama* says:

> Employ analysis during the state of contemplation because this is how to cultivate discriminating awareness.

In his summary of the *Sutralamkara*, Vasubandhu explains that we can meditate by using analysis and investigation and we can also meditate using examination without investigation. We should remain in a state of contemplation while engaged in analytical meditation. When the mind detects certain obstacles arising during tranquillity meditation, that is an extension of insight meditation.

THE ROLE OF ANALYSIS AND CONTEMPLATION

Some people claim that we should not do analysis during tranquillity meditation or practise contemplation during analytical meditation because both approaches would lead to loss of insight. This is also incorrect. If it were true, we should not do any analysis during tranquillity meditation at all. It is possible to employ analysis in a contemplative state. If we were to subscribe to the negative view, it would be impossible to develop insight during contemplation or to remain in contemplation during analytical meditation.

Other texts say that insight meditation is concerned with resting the mind, not just with analysis. The people who claim that there is absolutely no room for analysis during contemplation and no room for contemplation during analysis set the two types of meditation against each other. They conclude that contemplative and analytical meditations are incompatible. But that is completely untrue.

What view should we hold about the two types of meditation then? We should begin by engaging in tranquillity meditation and practising the nine stages of tranquillity meditation and then we should engage in analysis while remaining in that contemplative state. The first *Bhavanakrama* says:

> While remaining in tranquillity meditation, you analyse the five psychophysical constituents, the eighteen spheres, and so on.

Furthermore, if overwhelming obstacles manifest during our tranquillity meditation, we need to apply the appropriate antidotes. For instance, if desire arises, we contemplate the ugliness of the body. If hatred arises, we contemplate compassion. If ignorance arises, we contemplate dependent origination. All these antidotes are an extension of analytical meditation. While we employ methods of analysis during the practice of analytical meditation, we should also allow the mind to rest and remain in a contemplative state during this meditation. This is not a deviation from the main thrust of analytical meditation, as some people assume. On the contrary, our ability to recognise the essence of analytical meditation will be enhanced if we know how to remain in a state of contemplation during this practice. The *Kasyapaparivarta Sutra* says:

> Fire is produced when two sticks
> Are vigorously rubbed together.
> It then consumes those sticks.
> Likewise, analysis consumes concepts
> So that we can remain in a state of concentration.

The *Madhyamakavatara* says:

> Human beings are bound by dualistic perceptions.
> Yogis who overcome this dualism attain liberation.
> The fruit of analysis is non-discrimination.
> So proclaim the wise.

When we have attained mastery in combining analytical and tranquillity meditation, it may still be necessary to practise analytical meditation alone. We should focus more on contemplative meditation in the beginning.[3] I will explain how to do this in detail in later chapters. For a beginner, too much analysis can lead to an agitated mind while prolonged engagement in tranquillity meditation can lead to dullness and sluggishness. This is why we have to balance the two types of meditation and cultivate a state of equanimity. The first *Bhavanakrama* says:

> We lose clarity when our mind is overwhelmed by dullness and can't attain insight. We are like blind people if the sluggish mind is not clarified. Engaging in vipashyana too rigorously results in mental agitation. The mind becomes unstable and flickers like a lamp in the wind. This will never lead to a proper understanding of reality. When our mind is agitated and unstable, we should engage in shamatha. When our mind is sluggish and dull, we should supplement that with meditative analysis.

We combine the two meditative methods in this way and try to meditate for as long as our body and mind can endure it. When we have completely synthesised these meditations, we can remain in a state of one-pointedness without need of further elaboration. The *Samadhinirmocana Sutra* says:

> Maitreya: 'When do analytical and contemplative meditation become well-integrated?'
> Buddha: 'When the mind attains one-pointedness.'
> Maitreya: 'What is one-pointedness?'
> Buddha: 'When you can recognise the essence of the meditation object and remain in that state, that is one-pointedness.'

Jnanagarbha's commentary on the *Samadhinirmocana* says:

> There is no divergence between the path of contemplation and the path of analysis. We are intentionally aware of the object of meditation through the practice of analysis and we continually dwell on the object of analysis through the practice of contemplation.

> We realise the inseparability of the object of mental concentration and mind itself through this.

ESTABLISHING THE PROPER VIEW

Some people say we must first rely on textual authority and reasoning, recognise how we apprehend the truth of emptiness, and then remain in a state of contemplation if we wish to establish the proper view. In addition, we should not dwell in the contemplative state for too long because that might dissipate our analytical ability. We should therefore return to analytical meditation after very short periods of contemplation. This view is also mistaken.

No amount of analysis that relies on textual authority and reasoning will lead to a direct experience of reality, because anything we understand through this type of analysis will remain conceptual. According to the Yogacara view, it is impossible to recognise the nature of what occurs in this way because there is a discrepancy between the state of contemplation and the practice of analysis. It also says we should not dwell in a state of contemplation after conducting analysis because that will lead to our losing the clarity we gained through meditative analysis. Another view claims that we must repeatedly engage in analysis, even if we have synthesised the two types of meditation, or we will lapse into a state of contemplation. These are all mistaken views.

If we have managed to integrate the two types of meditation and can remain in a state of one-pointedness, there is no discrepancy between the two meditative experiences. This is the state of integration. It is not one or the other meditative approach.

How then should we engage in the two types of meditation? We begin by trying to establish the proper view through reading and contemplation. We will establish discriminating awareness and gain greater confidence in our understanding through this. We will come to understand the inherently non-existent nature of things through inference. Even our apprehension of the insubstantial nature of things lacks any substantiality of its own. This type of analysis should only be undertaken in a state of contemplation, not otherwise. The first *Bhavanakrama* says:

> Having stabilised your mind in tranquillity meditation, employ analysis and develop discriminating wisdom. This discriminating wisdom will illuminate your mind in the same way light makes it possible for the eye to perceive the external world.
> You carry out this analysis in the state of contemplation because

> that enables you to recognise the insubstantiality of things. This is called 'recognition of the image and the imageless.' 'Imageless' refers to the lack of substantiality in the external world. To understand the insubstantial nature of things is to attain discriminating awareness.

Once we realise nothing can be seen through insight meditation we realise anything we can understand, see, or perceive lacks substantiality. It also says:

> When it is said 'there is nothing to be seen,' this is not the same as closing your eyes, being deprived of light, or blindness. The substantiality of things has never been present, so there is really nothing there to see.

When we realise that there is nothing to see because everything is lacking substantiality, we have understood the full meaning of the reality of things. It is so important to practise the two types of meditation conjointly—employing analysis while in a state of contemplation, and developing contemplation while employing analysis—because this is the way to develop the proper view. Even when we have the proper view, we may occasionally cling to certain concepts and ideas. It is important to return to insight meditation when this happens. When we establish the proper view, all our doubts and uncertainties will be dispelled and full confidence in the practice will develop.

ELIMINATING DOUBTS ABOUT THE PROPER VIEW

This has two sections:

- Review of other Buddhist schools
- Establishing the meditative system of our school

§ Review Of Other Buddhist Schools

Certain early Buddhist masters held the view that it is necessary to disassociate ourselves from any kind of contemplation if we are to attain a proper state of meditation. They said we should not even think positive thoughts but try to attain a thoughtless state. This view has been criticised as very similar to that of the Chinese master Hwashang Mahayana. This view is incorrect because it leads to a state of non-discrimination and ignorance rather than discriminating awareness. This was one extreme view held by some early masters.

Another extreme view held by some early Tibetan scholars was that we must rely on the proper rules of logic to understand the true nature of things. Only reasoning and logic can reveal that nothing has any endurable or immutable essence. This view is also wrong. According to Gampopa, the understanding we gain from logic and reasoning is based on inference rather than immediate experience and can therefore only ever be provisional.[4] The *Pramanasamuccaya* says:

> If you are led to the truth
> Along the path of ideas,
> It debases Buddha's teachings.

Atisha says:

> Those who claim to have understood
> The nature of emptiness,
> By employing reasoning
> And relying on direct perception and inference,
> Are making a mistaken assertion.

Other early Tibetan masters made the assertion that we need to rely on the type of reasoning found in Madhyamaka philosophy if we hope to realise that everything is devoid of essence or any kind of enduring nature. This approach to emptiness is negative in import. It is understood as a lack, the lack of substantiality or essence. According to the *Kalachakra Tantra*, the understanding that we generate from the philosophical reasoning of Madhyamaka does not lead to a full understanding of emptiness because emptiness also has some positive import.[5] It is called 'ever-perfect emptiness' in the *Kalachakra Tantra*. Emptiness should not be understood purely in a negative sense therefore, because it also has a positive aspect.

Other masters believe we must first use analysis and rely on reasoning to understand reality and then at a certain point we suspend all judgements and remain in a state of contemplation. We will then be able to give rise to discriminating wisdom from that state of contemplation. However, this view is not completely correct because we have to distinguish between experience and realisation. Our experiences are conditioned, but our realisation is not, it is unconditioned.[6] Others believed that first we have to engage in reasoning and refute the views of others without proposing any view of our own. This is also incorrect. It is a clever device, but does not lead to a proper understanding of emptiness or to a genuine view of Madhyamaka.

Yet others believed that recognising that both physical and mental entities have no substantiality and then remaining in a state of non-cogitation without dwelling on anything is the realisation of emptiness. However, this comes very close to the view of Hwashang Mahayana, which is said to be nihilistic insofar as it advocates contemplating a state of nullity.[7]

It can sometimes happen that although our understanding is correct, we cannot articulate that understanding properly because we lack proficiency in reasoning or training in logic. However, falling into an extreme state of contemplation without any element of discrimination will only lead to our becoming depressed within a state of total absorption. We should avoid this pitfall.

Some people also maintain that we must first rely on textual authority and reasoning to gain an intellectual grasp of the reality of things and then cease to engage in such analytical activity and remain in a state of non-thought. These views are also refuted. If a state of non-thought is positive in itself and worthy of cultivation, we should be able to realise emptiness simply by falling asleep, fainting or falling into unconsciousness, but that is not so. When we speak about a non-conceptual state of contemplation, we need to establish whether mindfulness and awareness are present or not. If they are not, we could easily fall into a state of absorption that is completely devoid of discrimination and not worth cultivating.

Some exponents of meditation don't go along with these three approaches, but assert that a proper meditation practice entails gaining an understanding of emptiness, establishing certainty in that understanding and then relaxing the mind in a meditative state. In this approach, we remain in the meditative state while still holding onto a proper view. We have analysed, established a proper view, and then been able to remain in a meditative state without wavering from it. This approach also avoids the defects involved in the above three techniques. We avoid the defect of not being orientated to a proper understanding of emptiness, which is inherent in the first approach. We avoid the defect of falling into a thoughtless state, which is inherent in the second approach, and we avoid the defect of not holding the proper view, which is inherent in the third.

This approach also has its critics, who say that if you establish a proper view of emptiness and then relax your mind in a meditative state, you will automatically be in a state of tranquillity rather than insight.[8] They argue that this approach is not as holistic as it should be because it emphasises tranquillity meditation at the expense of insight and does not integrate the two meditations properly. That criticism is unfair however, because you have to engage in analysis to establish the proper view. Once you have established the proper view, you need to remain in a state of rest, which is associated with tranquillity meditation. It is unnecessary to engage in analysis repeatedly once you establish the proper view so the criticism levelled against this approach is unjustified and inappropriate. This is therefore the best of the approaches reviewed so far.

Nonetheless, there is an aspect to this technique that readers should be cautioned about. It may generate a certain attachment to views established through the practice of analysis. Some learned scholars say that to formulate the right view, we must first uproot our ignorance because ignorance is the source of all our misconceptions and wrong views. Once that ignorance is exposed, we will understand that the nature of things lacks inherent existence and certainty will be consolidated. If we engage in tranquillity meditation in conjunction with analysis, we will develop confidence in our understanding of the reality of things, without being lured by our experiences of meditative absorption, as in the case of Hwashang Mahayana. Furthermore, these same scholars maintain that when we use the analysis of Madhyamaka logic to conclude that nothing has any enduring essence, there will be a reversal in the structure of our consciousness and we will no longer react to things in an impulsive manner. We will come to realise that the nature of everything is empty. Engaging in tranquillity meditation in conjunction with this sort of analysis will synthesise the two practices and establish the proper view.

This understanding is again incomplete because a view that brings certainty about emptiness and develops conviction in the empty nature of things can also give rise to a fixating on emptiness. We were previously attached to the idea that everything has enduring essence and now we are attached to the view that nothing has enduring essence. That is simply another obstacle to overcome. Realising that the self is a product of causes and conditions, subject to change, and lacks essence, and then becoming fixated on that realisation, only creates another obstacle to the attainment of discriminating awareness. The *Bhavanakrama* says:

> First contemplate the idea that nothing has enduring essence. Then try to overcome your fixation on that understanding of emptiness by applying discriminating awareness.

The *Madhyamakakarika* says:

> Anyone who views emptiness
> As something valid or real,
> Has fallen into the wrong view
> According to the teachings of Buddha.

It also says:

> We should not assert that things have inherent existence,
> Nor should we assert that they lack inherent existence.

The *Bodhicittavivarana* says:

> Making assertions about ourselves and the external world
> Saying that they have no inherent existence
> Or that they do have inherent existence,
> Is to misunderstand the teachings of Buddha.

The *Madhyamakakarika* says:

> To say things have inherent existence
> Is to fall into the eternalist view.
> To say things have no inherent existence
> Is to fall into the nihilist view.

Atisha's *Mulamadhyamaka-vrttih Prasannapada* says:

> Focusing on originlessness, emptiness, and selflessness
> Is the wrong approach to meditation.

The *Madhyamakakarika* says:

> People that affirm the view of emptiness are dull-witted
> And will suffer the consequences.
> But it is erroneous conceptions of emptiness
> That really bring the less intelligent to grief.

It also says:

> If our conviction in emptiness becomes solidified,
> We have actually developed a wrong view of emptiness.

In brief, becoming fixated on the view of emptiness is to have the wrong view. It is far better to confirm the reality of things than to fall into nihilism and say things do not exist at all.[9] Nagarjuna's *Madhyamakakarika* says:

> If we assert that things have inherent existence,
> We will still be able to attain higher levels of existence.
> If we deny the existence of things completely,
> We will be dragged down to lower forms of existence.

It is incorrect to claim practising tranquillity meditation after establishing the proper view will automatically put us in a state of absorption because it is impossible to establish the proper view if we do not combine tranquillity and insight meditation in the first place. People who believe 'analytical meditation always means insight meditation' and 'contemplative meditation always means tranquillity meditation' do not understand the importance of marrying the two. Unanagarba's commentary to the *Samadhinirmocana Sutra* says:

> What is tranquillity meditation? It is the ability to focus on the object of analysis in insight meditation. The object of analysis and the analyser of that object are one, because the same mind is operating in both cases.

If tranquillity and insight meditation were completely separable, as some people assume, such quotations would conflict with their views. However, no other exponents in Tibet or India have accepted this as a valid point of view because it assumes tranquillity and insight meditation run parallel, instead of converging. From our point of view, it is essential to view them as conjoined. The *Dharmadhatusattva* says:

> We should contemplate the nature of things
> Without engaging in the overt practice of analysis.

The great Brahmin Saraha says:

> The nature of things is unblemished
> And should not be sullied by overt analysis.
> Excessive analysis pollutes the immaculate nature of reality.
> It is like angering a poisonous snake.

Nagarjuna says:

> The nature of ultimate truth
> Cannot be grasped through purely mental cogitations.
> Only in relative truth does analysis have its home.

If we become attached to the idea of emptiness, selflessness, or essencelessness, it will only generate further confusion in our minds and prevent our ever gaining a proper understanding of emptiness. The *Prajnaparamita-samcayagatha* says:

> If we say the psychophysical constituents
> Are devoid of essence,
> We have already mistakenly fixated on the concept of emptiness.

The *Prajnaparamita Sutra* makes the statement, 'From form to buddhahood,' which is meant to imply all knowable things. 'Form' is often used in Buddhist texts to imply everything. If we say 'all knowable things are permanent, impermanent, empty, not empty, self, and lacking in self,' we are saying that all these conceptual categories have only provisional value and will not lead to a proper understanding of emptiness.[10] Saraha says:

> To find this idea appealing and hold onto it,
> Even if this attachment is very subtle,
> Will only generate constant suffering.
> We will never transcend our afflictions.

He also says:

> We must learn to let go of attachments
> Whatever they may be.

It must also be said not all states of non-conceptuality lead to the meditative state proposed by Hwashang and others. Excessive conceptuality is also a barrier to a proper realisation of emptiness. The *Bodhichittavivarana* says:

> We come to realise emptiness
> By overcoming conceptual activities.
> As long as our conceptual activities persist,
> We will be deprived of that understanding.

The *Madhyamakavatara* says:

> Conceptual activities lead to wrong understanding.

The *Mulamadhyamaka-vrttih Prasannapada* says:

> We should remain in the state of non-discrimination
> Without entertaining concepts or ideas.

If the previous critiques were correct, Atisha's position would only be an extension of Hwashang Mahayana's view but that conclusion is obviously far-fetched and incorrect. Any view that insists that tranquillity and insight meditation are separable is totally wrong. Sometimes Hwashang tried to bring the two together, but it was like trying to put an incompetent rider on a spirited horse; the partnership did not work out.

Other interpretations of tranquillity and insight meditation might also be elaborated upon, such as the prolonged practice of analysis followed by tranquillity, which gradually leads to the state of meditative absorption. This is also to be found in Hwashang Mahayana's system. But I will stop at this point because I don't want to make this text too bulky. As Unanagarbha's commentary on the *Samadhinirmocana Sutra* says:

> If tranquillity and insight meditation were separate and independent methods, quotations of this nature would be in direct conflict with the critic's view. The path of tranquillity focuses primarily on the mind, which is the actual object of insight, so tranquillity and insight must operate together; even overlap.

§ Establishing The Meditative System Of Our School

Some of the views of our own school have already been communicated in the previous discussion on insight meditation. You can also learn more about these views by relying on reasoning and logic. The views of our school will be presented in summary fashion here, but first we need to understand that to have the proper view, we need to have already attained a certain level of spiritual realisation. I will present the view with lay people in mind. The establishment of the proper view is important, no matter what kind of meditation you are doing, be it any of the tranquillity or insight techniques described in the previous sections. The establishment of the right view comes from understanding the nature of emptiness. As long as you fail to have that understanding, you will fail to cut the root of your samsaric condition, no matter how much you try to crystallise the view or persevere in the practice. The *Bodhichittavivarana* says:

> People who don't understand emptiness
> Will never attain liberation.
> They remain in the prison of fixed modes of existence
> Without disentangling themselves from the web of ignorance.

When we do make the effort to establish the proper view, we must make certain our view is correct. Naropa's *Drstisamksepta* says:

> If your view is correct and proper,
> Meditation and action will flow naturally and smoothly.
> You will attain the goal of enlightenment;
> Like a trained horse negotiating a difficult course.
> If your view is mistaken,
> Meditation and action will be erroneous and deviant,
> You will not attain the desired result;
> Like a blind person groping around in the dark.

The proper view is established through three kinds of training in insight: hearing the teachings, contemplating the teachings, and meditation. The importance of the last training in insight meditation cannot be over-stressed. Even if we have great learning and dwell extensively on various topics, we will never establish the proper view if we do not internalise our learning into experience through meditation. The trainings of hearing and contemplation must therefore lead to the practice of meditation. All the teachings of the Buddha's sutras and tantras agree on the importance of meditation. The *Guhyasamaja Tantra* says:

> We examine the nature of mind
> To realise that our perception of the external world
> Is determined by the structure of our own consciousness.
> Then we come to understand non-duality
> Of the nature of things as they are.

The *Vajrapanjara Tantra* says:

> If we meditate on the nature of mind via the promptings of jewel-like mind, we will surely attain buddhahood.

The *Lankavatara Sutra* says:

> First, we realise that our experiences of external phenomena are conditioned and constructed by mind. Once we have understood the role of mind, we have to realise that this very mind is devoid of inherent existence. We will be truly established on the Mahayana path when we realise this two-fold essencelessness.[11]

The *Sutralamkara* says:

> First realise that the creative nature of mind conditions and determines our perceptions of the external world. Then realise that this very mind, which is so prolific in the construction of things, is devoid of essence.

Saraha says:

> As long as the mind is bound, we will never find freedom.
> When the mind is free, we will also be completely free.

These quotations have been taken from various texts in both the Sutric and Tantric teachings. The Sutric teachings include both Madhyamaka and Yogacara texts. What we glean from these quotations is the importance of understanding the nature of things. However, even if we appreciate the importance of emptiness, we will not be able to understand it if we are not in possession of discriminating awareness. These quotations all point out the importance of using discriminating awareness and analysis to determine the reality of things. We should not become too obsessive in the use of analysis however. We need to become proficient in it to a certain point and then we learn to remain in the state of contemplation. The third *Bhavanakrama* says:

> All realities are devoid of essence. This cannot be understood without analysis.

The *Kasyapaparivarta* says:

> Just as two sticks that are rubbed together by a howling wind produce sparks, which then fan into flames and consume the sticks, non-dual wisdom, which arises from analysis and discriminating awareness, consumes the concepts that gave rise to it. Non-dual wisdom emerges from the ashes of dead concepts that have been burnt by the fires of discriminating awareness.

The second *Bhavanakrama* says:

> If we make use of discriminating awareness and analysis, the fire of wisdom will emerge and gradually consume the gross material of our conceptual categories.

It must be pointed out that this analysis should be done in a contemplative manner rather than in an excessively intellectual way. Another sutra says:

> If we allow our minds to rest, wisdom will emerge.

The *Bhavanakrama* says:

> First, we learn to rest our mind, then we engage in analysis, and then we give rise to discriminating wisdom through analysis.

The proper view is associated with the realisation that analytical insight is also devoid of essence. Not only is the object of analysis insubstantial, the very act of analysis itself and the insight obtained through analysis are also devoid of any essence. Another sutra says:

> When we come to realise there is nothing to be seen in relation to all existing things, we have attained wisdom.

The *Bhavanakrama* says:

> From the ultimate view, realise that there is nothing to be seen in respect to individual existent things.

We should let our mind rest in its natural condition while remaining aware of whether it is sliding into dullness or mental agitation. Letting the mind be in its natural condition means stripping it of all extraneous conceptual proliferations. Another sutra says:

> When we let our mind focus on the reality of things, we will have an experience that cannot be articulated. This is the attainment of meditative concentration.

Atisha says:

> Resting naked mind on naked reality is proper meditation.

He also says:

> The reality of things, which is emptiness, has no beginning or end, no centre or circumference. It is not subject to thought or concepts. If we allow our mind to rest in the encompassingness of reality, without being disturbed by either dullness or mental agitation, we have achieved meditative concentration.

Atisha's *Madhyamakopadesa* says:

> When we use analysis, we first analyse our mental continuum by trying to examine past mental events or states that no longer exist, and then trying to examine future mental events or states that have not yet come to be. The only thing we can properly analyse is our present mental state. When we analyse that, we discover the present state of consciousness has no shape or colour and lacks substantiality. We can also employ processes of reasoning, such as the one and the many, or cause and effect, to discover that mind has no substance and is not a static thing.

Neither the mind engaged in analysis nor the act of analysis is substantial. Just as rubbing two sticks together produces a fire that consumes them, discriminating awareness eliminates concepts by revealing them to be lacking in substantiality.[12] With this understanding, we should let the mind be, without allowing it to yield to obstacles such as dullness or mental agitation. We should not entertain any ideas or concepts and suspend our judgement.

While Atisha's explanation of this aspect of meditation is quite easy to understand, I will elaborate upon it a little further. We begin to practise meditation with the analysis of the external world and realising that subject and object, perceiver and perceived, are conceptual constructions rather than something that has any abiding reality of their own. This realisation comes from understanding that our perception of the external world is largely determined by our conceptual categories and is therefore mind-dependent. Then, the mind itself should be analysed in relation to the three times, the one and the many, origin and cessation, and so forth. This type of analytical reasoning will help us realise that even the mind has no enduring essence, after which we come to realise the non-dual awareness that perceives that this lack of essence in mind has no enduring essence either. Discriminating awareness is not an entity.

We must abandon all such misconceptions to attain discriminating awareness. Then we should let the mind rest and not allow it to be disturbed by thoughts or concepts, such as any notion of a subject and object, perceiver and perceived, and so on. We remain in that state of contemplation for as long as we can until mental disturbances resurface. The *Bhavanakrama* says:

> We should first realise that all individual existing things are devoid of substantiality. We then need to realise the very concept that things have no enduring essence is insubstantial and must therefore be discarded through insight.

We need to go beyond entertaining the idea that things lack or do not lack an enduring essence. Through the gradual development of insight, we gain certainty in our understanding that things lack inherent existence and build confidence in this understanding of reality. This confidence is obviously associated with the establishment of the proper view. The *Samadhiraja Sutra* says:

> By analysing conditioned and unconditioned things, existent and non-existent entities, the wise ones realise emptiness is not an entity.

The *Bhavanakrama* quotes the *Ratnamegha*:

> The mind that has this understanding should also be seen as lacking in enduring essence. Realising this, the meditator should rest in a state of non-duality.

The second *Bhavanakrama* says:

> When a yogi examines the mind with discriminating awareness, without clinging to its essence as the ultimate nature, he has attained the state of non-conceptuality.

Kamalashila's commentary on *Avikalpapravesa-dharani* says:

> Having engaged in analysis, we must rest in the state of contemplation.

The *Bodhipathapradipa* says:

> By first establishing that phenomena
> Lack any inherent existence
> Through the use of ideas in analytical meditation,
> We come to understand non-discriminating wisdom.

This completes the explanation of the traditional way to dispel doubts about the view and meditation. It has been accomplished mainly by relying on standard meditation materials that are available in the Sutric and Tantric teachings. We will now embark on an extensive explanation of the special technique of Mahamudra meditation.

BOOK TWO

An Extensive Description of the Uncommon System of Mahamudra Meditation

Part I: The Preliminaries

1

An Explanation to Arouse Confidence

THE DEFINITION OF MAHAMUDRA

This has three sections:

- The meaning of Mahamudra
- Identifying the nature of Mahamudra
- The benefit of knowing it and the harm of not knowing it

§ The Meaning Of Mahamudra

Mahamudra is called *phyag rgya chen po* in Tibetan. *Phyag rgya* has many synonyms, such as symbol, gesture, sign, seal, and characteristic. It can also mean a 'stamp' because just as we make an impression on something by stamping it, the phenomenal world is impressed with the stamp of the reality of things. It can also mean 'identification,' in the sense of a soldier's rank being identified by certain marks on his or her clothing; in the same way that the mark of *phyag rgya chen po* reveals the nature of both samsara and nirvana. *Phyag rgya chen po* also has the connotation of 'not going beyond.' For example, the authority of a sovereign is binding on all his or her subjects, in the same way that reality is all-encompassing and inclusive of both samsara and nirvana. Mahamudra is that reality. The *Gaganaganjapariprccha Sutra* says:

> The 'mudra' in *mahamudra* refers to the 'seal of inseparability,' which does not generate attachment, which cannot be moved and which cannot be comprehended by gods, demi-gods, and so on. This 'mudra' or *phyag rgya* is also called *chen po* or 'great' because of the all-encompassing nature of reality.

The *Guhyasiddhi* says:

> Mahamudra originates from the fourth empowerment
> Of the Anuttarayoga tantras,
> And brings about perfect enlightenment.
> Mahamudra meditation is unsurpassed by anything.

The *Mahamudra-tilaka* says:

> The particle *phyag* refers to the 'inseparability of emptiness and wisdom,' the particle *rgya* refers to the 'transcendence of the concept of emptiness' and *chen po* refers to the 'inseparability of these two.'

The *Pancakrama* says:

> *Phyag* refers to the inseparability of emptiness and wisdom.

It also says:

> *rGya* means 'not being bound by the samsaric condition' or 'transcending that condition.'

Emptiness is not encompassed by any particular thing, such as the psychophysical constituents, the senses, the feelings, the notion of subject and object, and so on. The *Guhyasamaja Tantra* says:

> Emptiness is all-pervasive
> It is not encompassed by any individual thing.
> Therefore, *rgya* stresses the aspect of transcendence,
> And *chen po* signifies the coming together of wisdom and emptiness
> In the transcendent nature of Mahamudra.

Chen po can also signify 'the inseparability of method and wisdom.' Maitripa's *Dasatattva* says:

> Practising method and wisdom is the best of all practices,
> Because it leads to the realisation of Mahamudra.

The *Padmini*, a *Kalachakra Tantra commentary*, interprets it differently:

> *Phyag rgya* refers to the great goddess Prajnaparamita, who is the mother of all buddhas, and the personification of emptiness. She is 'the mother of all buddhas' because the past, present, and future buddhas all arise from emptiness. Everyone attains buddhahood through insight into emptiness. At the same time, Mahamudra is

the experience of bliss, which comes from the realisation of nirvana. This coming together of great bliss and emptiness is *phyag rgya*. *Chen po* means that it is superior to karmamudra, jnanamudra, and so on, because it is free from the embellishments of the samsaric condition, whereas the other mudras are not.

Gampopa says:

> *Phyag rgya* means 'samsara and nirvana both participate in the same reality of emptiness.' That is represented by *rgya*, which means 'anything that arises in relation to samsara or nirvana cannot arise outside of emptiness.' The realisation of this is *chen po* or 'great.'

Serlingpa's *Thektron* says:

> The meaning of *phyag rgya chen po* or Mahamudra:
> *Phyag* is 'the ability to recognise the obscurations of karma and emotional conflicts and self-liberate them by realising the nature of mind.'
> *rGya* is 'the impossibility of a purely conceptual apprehension of emptiness.'
> *Chen po* means 'this approach transcends the techniques of all the sutras and lower tantras.'

Synonyms for *phyag rgya chen po* are reality, supreme wisdom, Samantabhadra, the great seal, and dharmakaya. Indrabodhi's *Jnanasiddhi-sadhana* says:

> Mahamudra is the absolute,
> It is the supreme wisdom;
> It is Samantabhadra himself.
> This great seal is also known as dharmakaya.[1]

The *Yogasapta* says:

> Lack of essence, nature, reality, dharmadhatu, the equality of all phenomena, ultimate truth; these are the same as mahamudra.

§ Identifying The Nature Of Mahamudra

The nature of Mahamudra is such; it does not dwell in space, cannot be found in a specific location and does not have any definable characteristics for the simple reason that it is all-pervasive.[2] Indrabodhi says:

> Just as space is not found in a specific place, Mahamudra is all-pervasive and devoid of characteristics. This is the ultimate truth.

Maitripa says:

> Mahamudra is the state of unity that transcends conceptual categories, while also being translucent and luminous. It is all-pervasive, so even though it is apparent, it does not have any essence. It is just like the reflection of the moon in water, free from embellishments of any kind. Like the dream of a mute, the experience of this reality cannot be communicated.

We need to view Mahamudra practice in three stages: ground, path, and fruition.[3] Ground Mahamudra is synonymous with buddha nature. It is the true reality that has never been corrupted, primordially speaking. It is free from the division of subject and object, primordially pure, unsullied and all pervasive. Therefore, we cannot comprehend it through conceptualisation.

Path Mahamudra involves hearing the teachings on Mahamudra, pondering those teachings, and finally practising Mahamudra meditation. Through these three activities we realise that all existing things in both samsara and nirvana participate in the same reality. That reality does not come into being, does not persist, and does not dissipate in the way that things do. The reality-of-being that is Mahamudra is not an entity of any kind. We can experience this reality if we cultivate the proper view and practise meditation. Path Mahamudra is how we become familiar with ground Mahamudra; it is the way we overcome all of the subtle defilements and attain the state of two-fold purity. Two-fold purity refers to two aspects of the mind: 1) the original state of purity, which is Mahamudra, and 2) the temporal state of purity, which is attained through the eradication of our mental defilements.[4] When we become established in this two-fold purity, we attain fruition Mahamudra. The *Uttaratantra* names three kinds of beings who correspond to different levels of understanding of ground Mahamudra. The *Uttaratantra* says:

> There are impure, pure, and extremely pure beings.
> Impure beings are ordinary human beings
> Who have not purified their defilement.
> Pure beings are enlightened beings
> Who have overcome defilement.
> Extremely pure beings are buddhas

> Who have no obscurations whatsoever.

Mahamudra must be understood in relation to four other mudras: karmamudra, samayamudra, jnanamudra, and dharmamudra.[5] The *Samvarodaya Tantra* says:

> When we differentiate emptiness, it becomes samadhi and wisdom.

Indrabodhi says:

> The path of Mahamudra is divided into these four stages: karmamudra, samayamudra, jnanamudra, and dharmamudra.

He also says:

> Just as different objects are reflected in a mirror, the nature of mind is reflected in the dharmakaya. That is the realisation of proper wisdom.

Everything that occurs in the mind is like the reflections in a mirror. When we realise this, we will eventually realise five wisdoms[6] and the three aspects of a buddha's being.[7]

§ The Benefit Of Knowing It And The Harm Of Not Knowing It

If we do not understand the practice of Mahamudra, we will not achieve final liberation, no matter how proficient we become in various spiritual practices. However, if we come to understand Mahamudra, it will help us understand everything. The *Mahamudra-tilaka* says:

> People who don't understand Mahamudra
> May gain enlightenment but will not become yogis.
> To become a proper yogi
> You have to understand Mahamudra fully.
> You may engage in mahayoga
> And practise 100,000 sadhanas,
> But you will not gain spiritual realisation.
> If you realise the nature of phenomena to be emptiness,
> You will realise Mahamudra and become a buddha.
> This is the same as becoming Vajrasattva.
> The wisdom that understands emptiness is Mahamudra itself.

The *Bodhichittavivarana* says:

People who do not understand emptiness
Will never attain liberation.
They are caught in cyclic existence
Because of their ignorance.

Maitripa says:

If you realise Mahamudra
You will know both samsara and nirvana.
Everything that exists within them
Participates in the same reality.
This is the realisation of dharmakaya.

He also says:

If you do not realise Mahamudra,
You may achieve a temporal state of release
But you will never attain proper liberation.
If you realise Mahamudra,
Nothing can bind you to the samsaric condition.

MAHAMUDRA ACCORDING TO THE SUTRAS

In the Sutric teachings, the word mudra has a broad usage. It is found in many different contexts and is used to signify many different things.[8] The *Sagaramatipariprccha Sutra* says:

> All existent things are marked by the mudra of reality. Since everything that exists participates in this reality, they are marked by the mudra of equanimity; synonymous with reality itself. The realisation of selflessness is marked by the purity of emptiness.

The same sutra lists twenty different mudras that have been enumerated in various other sutras. It says:

The nature of the phenomenal world
Is uncorrupted, unembellished, and pure like space.
Reality has never come into being.
What has not come into being cannot cease to exist.
The phenomenal world is therefore marked
By the mudra of purity.

The *Maitreyapradasthana Sutra* says:

> All dharmas are marked by the same mudra;
> The mudra of emptiness.

This text enumerates fifteen different mudras. Another well-known text lists ten. The *Bu mo rin chen gyis zhus pa* refers to the following mudra:

> All dharmas are marked by the mudra of equanimity
> Which is similar to the characteristics of space.
> Whatever is marked by this mudra is incorruptible.
> That is the mudra of emptiness.

We can see the word mudra is used in many different ways and contexts. You will also find it used in relation to wisdom, the nature of things, and so on. In the Tantric teachings, the word mudra is used in a different context again. For example, the lower tantras refer to the hand gestures that accompany rituals as mudras while other tantras refer to the implements held by deities as mudras. The higher tantras, such as the Anuttarayoga tantras, also speak of four different mudras in relation to hand gestures. These examples are stated to illustrate how the word mudra is used in various contexts in both the sutras and tantras.

In brief, Mahamudra has to be understood as synonymous with the concept of buddha nature, which is to be found in both the Sutric and Tantric teachings. Whenever the idea of buddha nature is presented, we should recognise it to be the same as the idea of Mahamudra.[9] This buddha nature is understood to be the nature of mind, which is luminous and free of defilements and obscurations. As such, it is also equivalent to the concept of ground Mahamudra, which describes the nature of the mind for what it is.

Path Mahamudra consists of understanding that the nature of mind is empty, free from conceptual proliferations, free from defilements, and free from all notions of a substantial self and then becoming familiar with this reality through the practice of meditation. Fruition Mahamudra is the final realisation of the four aspects of Buddha's being and the five wisdoms, which are actualised at the time of enlightenment.[10]

MAHAMUDRA IN THE MAHA-ANUTTARAYOGA TANTRAS

This has three sections:

- Determining whether there are three or four mudras
- Explaining the unique nature of Mahamudra
- Clearing away the confusion of other schools

§ Determining Whether There Are Three Or Four Mudras

The *Kalachakra Tantra* says:

> Abandon karmamudra and jnanamudra;
> They do not lead to ultimate spiritual realisation.
> Practise Mahamudra by experiencing union.

It also says:

> When the practice of union within karmamudra
> And the union experienced within jnanamudra
> Are unified in the experience of mahamudra,
> It will increasingly lead to an experience of immutable bliss.

Padmavajra's *Guhyasiddhi* says:

> The practice of karmamudra is unstable and deceptive.
> So is the practice of jnanamudra.
> Abandon proliferating concepts and practise Mahamudra.

Manjushri says:

> When karmamudra practice is unstable and deceptive,
> Jnanamudra is the same.
> Abandon these proliferating concepts
> And practise mahamudra.

Three different kinds of mudras are mentioned in these quotations: karmamudra, jnanamudra, and mahamudra. The *Pradipoddyotana* also mentions three mudras, but these are presented in a slightly different form:

> The three seals are the mudra of phenomena, the mudra of sign, and the great mudra.

The *Vajramala* mentions four mudras:

> There is the dharmamudra, karmamudra, samayamudra, and mahamudra.

The *Candraguhya-tilaka* also says:

> First is dharmamudra,
> Second is samayamudra,
> Third is mahamudra,
> And fourth is karmamudra.

The *Jnanagarbha Tantra* also refers to four mudra divisions: karmamudra, samayamudra, jnanamudra, and dharmamudra. The *Buddhasamayoga* of Garab Dorje lists four also: mahamudra, samayamudra, dharmamudra, and karmamudra. Master Abhayakara expounds on the creative-imagination and fulfilment stages of Tantra in his *Buddhakapala*, in which he enumerates a hundred different practices, each with its own karmamudra, dharmamudra, mahamudra, and samayamudra attached to them. In his commentary on the *Hevajra Tantra*, Naropa lists the karmamudra, jnanamudra, mahamudra, and samayamudra. In his *Caturmudraniscaya*, Maitripa lists the four mudras as karmamudra, dharmamudra, samayamudra, and mahamudra.[11]

In brief, there is no uniformity, because different siddhas gave different lists of mudras and often listed them in different orders. I mention this to give some indication of the variety of practices included in the listing and ordering of the mudras. Many more examples could be quoted, but I will finish here for fear of expanding the text too much. According to one teacher:[12]

> Naropa and Maitripa accepted the four orders of mudra:
> As karmamudra, dharmamudra, samayamudra, and mahamudra.
> This listing was accepted by all the Indian masters.

This author is mistaken. There is no consistency in the ordering of mudras even within texts authored by Naropa and Maitripa. This teacher must have failed to consult other Tantric texts, where it is quite clear there is no accepted standard in the ordering of mudras. His list of mudras is also in conflict with the lists given by Naropa and Maitripa. He also implies that Naropa and Maitripa relied on the four mudras rather than excelling in the practice of mahamudra. That is an unacceptable understanding of these great masters.

Even though Naropa mastered the sutras and tantras, he was not satisfied with them and sought out a master who could teach him more. He eventually met Tilopa and spent the next twelve years engaging in arduous and often perilous practices with him. He went to these great lengths because he was not completely satisfied with the Tantric practices. Naropa attained enlightenment through the practice of Mahamudra, under the guidance of Tilopa. His enlightenment did not come about through the purely Tantric practices that are associated with the other mudras.

These siddhas also wrote texts devoted purely to the exposition of Mahamudra teachings that do not mention the other mudras at all. For example, Tilopa sang many dohas that mainly consisted of his experiences in Mahamudra practice.[13] Naropa also expounded on the Mahamudra teachings in his texts. If the above critic's position were correct, all these texts would not exist.

The same can be said of Maitripa, the other great Indian master mentioned by this critic.

Maitripa was dissatisfied with the great learning and experience he gained through the practices of Sutra and Tantra and eventually sought out the mahasiddha Svarisvara. He eventually attained enlightenment by following him and practising Mahamudra. Maitripa also wrote many dohas about the Mahamudra teachings. These teachings could not be attributed to Maitripa if he was only involved with the mudra practices of Tantra, as the above-mentioned critic maintains.

§ Explaining The Unique Nature Of Mahamudra

Some of the texts quoted in the previous section on the three or four mudras also refer to the supreme incomparable Mahamudra. This is certainly the case with statements found in the *Kalachakra Tantra* where it says, 'Mahamudra is where wisdom and ever-perfect emptiness coincide and where we realise that wisdom and emptiness have one-flavour.' The *Kalachakra Tantra* also says, 'Immutable bliss is found in Mahamudra.' The key word here is 'immutable bliss' because we may experience bliss through the practices of karmamudra and jnanamudra, but that experience is contrived. The awareness of wisdom that arises from it is therefore refutable.

The bliss that arises from the practice of Mahamudra is known as 'spontaneous bliss' or 'coemergent bliss' and is incontrovertible. 'Incontrovertible bliss' always refers to the experience of mahamudra, not the various experiences we may endure during the practice of other mudras.[14] The forty-sixth chapter of the *Vajramala* says:

> Mahamudra is experienced
> As peace and supreme wisdom.
> It embodies all meaning;
> It is supreme bliss.
> Imbued with the extraordinary taste of oneness,
> It is the great illusion, subtle in its play
> Expansive as space itself.
> It is the great wisdom of the Tathagatas
> Only arrived at by overcoming conceptual proliferation.
> It is the place of the unmoving vajra,
> The indestructible, indivisible, unmoving mind.
> It is blissful, lacking the anxieties of conceptual activity.
> Vast as space, it is free from all embellishments.

These characteristics describe ground Mahamudra. On path Mahamudra, the *Vajramala* says:

> Mahamudra is free from duality,
> The selfless, inexpressible self-awareness of yogis.
> It is realised by not concerning ourselves
> With the skandhas, elements, or sense fields,
> Conceptual constructions,
> Or the two stages of Tantric practice.
> By abandoning these and concerning ourselves
> With relinquishing confused mind,
> Without hoping to attain wisdom,
> Without reciting mantras,
> Visualising deities, or practising sadhanas;
> We engage in path Mahamudra.[15]

Again, on fruition Mahamudra, the *Vajramala* says:

> Mahamudra transcends all existing things
> But can only be understood
> Through the attainment of wisdom.
> That is the attainment of supreme mahamudra.

If you wish to look more deeply into these verses, you should go to Pandita Alamkakalasa's commentary on the *Vajramala*, where you will find a detailed explanation of ground, path and fruition Mahamudra. This description of ground Mahamudra is in the *Mahamudra-tilaka*:

> The goddess Devi made this request:
> 'Victorious One,
> You expounded a great deal on the secret methods
> That dispel the darkness of ignorance,
> But you never revealed anything on the teachings of Mahamudra.
> What is Mahamudra?
> Please expound on this topic, Your Lordship.'
>
> The Victorious One replied:
> 'Listen to me goddess, Mahamudra is supreme bliss.
> Bliss is the secret of Mahamudra.
> It cannot be communicated verbally.
> Mahamudra has not come into being,
> So we cannot say it has form or is formless.

It has a form yet is formless,
It is gross yet subtle.
In brief, it cannot be measured by the intellect.
The unvitiated light that illuminates all;
It is non-abiding,
Cannot be found anywhere,
Yet is everywhere.
Mahamudra does not arise or dissipate,
Yet is ever-present.
Nor can we speak of it in relation to time and space
Because the ideas of origin and extinction
Do not apply to it.'

Buddha goes on to expound on ground Mahamudra in great detail, then describes the method to employ, the benefits of practising Mahamudra, the defects of not practising it, what sort of result we should expect from it, and so on. If you are interested in knowing more about this particular tantra, you should consult the commentary on it by Gambhiravajra, where you will find a very clear explanation of these ideas. The *Jnana-tilaka* says:

The Mahamudra is the most sublime of all things.
It is one hundred million times more sublime than the Brahma-loka.[16]

The *Guhyasattva*, a commentary on the *Jnana-tilaka*, says:

Mahamudra is attained
Through the practice of mystic heat
Which is the gradual cultivation of bliss.
First, you cultivate a bliss that is embellished
Then you come to realise unconditioned bliss.

It also says:

Mahamudra is present as the natural condition of all sentient beings.
It is regarded as the mother of all the buddhas.
All Buddhas began as sentient beings at one time
So there is complete continuity
Between cause and effect.

Mahamudra is free from the embellishments of conceptual proliferation and is simultaneously the nature of bliss. The Mahamudra is described in this way because it leaves its seal on everything. Saraha's commentary on the

Buddhakapala says:

> The intrinsic nature of the sphere of reality has left its stamp on all the buddhas. Therefore, it is the great seal.

The *Padmini*, a commentary on the *Kalachakra Tantra*, says:

> Mahamudra is atemporal. We cannot speak of it in relation to past or future. It is the mark of all the enlightened beings because all buddhas emerge from the same source, known as emptiness, prajnaparamita, or mahamudra.

Ramapala's commentary on the *Sekamirdesa* says:

> The mahamudra is called 'maha,' because it has imprinted its indelible mark on the other three mudras. Mahamudra is non-abiding, the source of all wisdom, unceasing, immaterial, and completely transparent; all obscurations are absent from it. Mahamudra is the source of everything that arises and it is the ground upon which everything depends. From the perspective of Mahamudra, both samsara and nirvana are equal, because both participate in the horizon of Mahamudra. At the same time, Mahamudra is the source of great compassion. Even after enlightenment has occurred, it is great compassion that prompts enlightened beings to work for the benefit of others.

We can apply these descriptions to Mahamudra and form some idea of how we should identify it and of how to understand ground, path, and fruition Mahamudra. If you want to explore this area further, there are many texts you can consult, such as the *Buddhasamayoga*, the *Samvarodaya*, the *Vajrapani*, the second half of the *Hevajra Tantra*, the *Samputa,* and others. You should go to these texts for further clarification from time to time. We will leave the discussion here for fear of making this text too long.

In summary, Mahamudra is presented as the natural condition of all things within the Tantric texts and the dohas of the great mahasiddhas. Mahamudra is represented as emptiness, the great equanimity, and great bliss. It is originless, unceasing, and free from all conceptual proliferations. Even so, some critics have said, 'this sort of Mahamudra is not present in the tantras so we don't accept these teachings as genuine.'[17] To this we can only reply that these critics have not properly applied themselves to understanding the Tantric texts and their statements simply demonstrate a limited understanding of the existing Tantric material and what it represents.

§ Clearing Away The Confusion Of Other Schools

The same critic goes on to say:

> The Tibetan system of Mahamudra and the Chinese system of Mahasandhi or Dzogchen are the same. The only change is that they use different language. For example, instead of referring to two systems of meditation, namely the Chinese and Indian systems, they change their terminology to either the 'swooping down' and 'climbing up' paths or the instantaneous and gradual approaches. The words may have changed, but the meaning and the practices are the same.

This statement is completely mistaken. *Mahasandhi*, also known as Dzogchen or Ati-yoga, has to be viewed as the culmination of Tantric practice. The Chinese system of meditation, known as Ch'an, was introduced into Tibet by Hwashang Mahayana. It relies on eighty different sutras. Not only are their approaches to meditation different, their sources are also different because mahasandhi relies on the Tantric teachings while Ch'an relies on the Sutric teachings. It has never been proven that Dzogchen was introduced from China. To say that Dzogchen is the same as the system of Hwashang is therefore a gross misrepresentation. This is equivalent to reducing something sublime to the level of something completely profane and impure.

This critic is clearly demonstrating his ignorance and has obviously not looked into the standard Mahamudra sources, such as Saraha's *Do ha skor gsum*, the *Do chung mdzod brgyad*, the *Grub snying*, the *A-ma-na-si,* and so on. He goes on to give an historical exposition of these schools, but does not seem to have consulted the relevant historical material, such as the foreword to Kamalashila's *Bhavanakrama.* This contradicts our critic's own survey of historical events and criticises Hwashang's view of Ch'an Buddhism. Furthermore, the critic says:

> The proponents of Mahamudra have hidden their sources but are simply relying on Chinese Buddhist texts, giving them new names, and calling it Mahamudra. What goes by the name of 'Mahamudra' is nothing other than Chinese Ch'an.

This statement merely demonstrates the author's own wishful thinking, which he is trying to pass off as the truth. It does not correspond with actual events. He has not shown how the proponents of Mahamudra have achieved this trickery nor been able to give any evidence of a link between Chinese

Ch'an and that of the Mahamudra that is practised in Tibet.

There is ample evidence to suggest that Mahamudra was known for a long period in India before it ever became popular in Tibet and prior to the spread of Ch'an Buddhism. This shows the historical priority of the Mahamudra teachings and proves it is not dependent upon nor copied from Chinese Ch'an. The critic therefore demonstrates his total ignorance of materials that have any bearing on this controversy. While hiding his own ignorance, he casts aspersions on the integrity of other authors and practitioners. Such wild criticisms are not a worthy object of impartial scholarly scrutiny.

Other critics of Mahamudra have said followers of Hwashang Mahayana do not believe in the veracity of karmic cause and effect. They also claim that their Sutric sources say we should have no thoughts when practising meditation. They argue, 'the sutras advocate emptying the mind of its contents' and 'refusing to entertain either positive or negative thoughts will bring all mental activities to a stop.' Their sutras also say, 'the realisation buddhahood is imminent within our own minds.' Their critics maintain that the so-called Tibetan practitioners of Mahamudra are advocating the same approach as Hwashang.

It is easy to see that these critics have not looked into the relevant Mahamudra material. They are casting wild aspersions that have no basis in fact, as they obviously have no knowledge of the real views and practices of the proponents of mahamudra. Without really attempting to understanding it, they engage in verbal abuse, which is fitting only for a person of unsound mind. Kamalashila's third *Bhavanakrama* is the source of this controversy and criticises Hwashang's position:

> According to Hwashang Mahayana, as long as we entertain thoughts of good and bad or produce positive and negative karma we will continue to be subject to the ceaseless cycle of samsara. The temporary states of happiness and suffering both prevent liberation. The only way to achieve liberation is to empty the mind of all concepts of good and evil. It is important therefore not to engage in mental cogitations. Nor should we practise wholesome deeds, such as generosity, and so on. These are only commendable for people of limited capacity. People of higher capacity should shun wholesome actions because they will ultimately only imprison us in the samsaric condition in the same way that unwholesome deeds do.
>
> Anyone who advocates this view is completely mistaken. They have abandoned the Mahayana precept of developing an altruistic

> attitude and working for the benefit of others and therefore lost the essential ingredient in the pursuit of enlightenment. Anyone who claims that we should aspire to a mind devoid of all mental activities will fail to develop discriminating awareness. Without discriminating awareness, we cannot develop discriminating wisdom and without discriminating wisdom, we cannot gain insight into the reality of things. We will therefore have no opportunity to attain enlightenment. The refusal to engage in wholesome deeds only divests us of the opportunity to accumulate merit, which is another essential ingredient in the pursuit of enlightenment.

This passage shows that Kamalashila is criticising Hwashang Mahayana's claim that we do not need to develop discriminating awareness or engage in wholesome activities to practise Buddhism. However, there is no textual evidence to suggest that Hwashang Mahayana ever actually dismissed the workings of karmic cause and effect. If Hwashang and his followers relied on certain sutras, they must implicitly have accepted the veracity of karmic cause and effect. The critic's view of Hwashang is therefore both incomplete and biased. Kamalashila never referred to the fact that Hwashang rejected the workings of karma.

While this critic intended to write a detailed description of the controversy that arose between the Indian camp led by Kamalashila and the Chinese camp led by Hwashang Mahayana, he has only composed something that is full of contradictions, inconsistencies, and wild allegations. This demonstrates his complete ignorance of the writings of Kamalashila on the so-called Samyas debate and is therefore a gross misrepresentation of that debate.

Furthermore, to allege that Mahamudra meditation is the same as the Ch'an approach is to distort the Mahamudra tradition. I don't wish to go into this subject in detail. It is unnecessary to expand on it at length. I will simply make a brief comment on the characteristics that distinguish Mahamudra from Ch'an. There is a difference in how the two traditions emphasise action. According to Hwashang, there is no need to engage in wholesome deeds because the teachings on virtuous action are for people of limited capacity. It is more important to go beyond both good and evil, from the ultimate point of view. According to Mahamudra, we need to realise emptiness and see how to mediate good and evil, but that does not imply we no longer need to engage in wholesome activities. Everything functions from the principle of interdependent origination, so the relative aspect of reality can never be negated.

There is also doubt as to whether Hwashang promoted the one-flavour of individually existing things. There is also some uncertainty about what constitutes a full understanding of relative truth in his system. Hwashang's position on the possibility of realising the Buddha's physical body is also unclear, since he says it is unnecessary to engage in wholesome activities. In the Mahamudra system, the realisation of the nirmanakaya depends upon the development of wholesome activities.

Hwashang does seem to have asserted that not entertaining any thoughts or ideas during meditation, whether positive or negative, is the supreme meditative state. The Mahamudra view is that it is very important to maintain mindfulness and awareness, even from the very initial stages of meditation, so that we can detect whether the mind is tending toward mental agitation or dullness. Hwashang not only fails to see a thoughtless, introverted, and absorbed state of mind as defective; he actually encourages it.

The Mahamudra view constantly presents this thoughtless, unconscious state of mind as something to resist rather than something to cultivate. Hwashang's meditation system didn't emphasise the importance of analytical meditation at all while Mahamudra clearly emphasises the need to engage in both analytical and contemplative meditation. Hwashang did emphasise remaining in a neutral state, while Mahamudra is clear that the emphasis should be on practising awareness so that we are present in the moment. Hwashang did not see any problems with entering into a mindless state whereas Mahamudra says that state should be avoided at all costs.

Hwashang never placed any emphasis on the importance of cultivating the right view through study, contemplation, and meditation. Mahamudra says we must engage in those activities to establish the right view. Hwashang did not seem to concern himself with establishing a view of reality at all whereas the Mahamudra system deems it essential to recognise that the root of duality lies in the perceiver and perceived and to establish a proper view about the reality of things. In terms of the fruition, Hwashang believed we could become enlightened simply by training and pacifying the mind, while Mahamudra says that enlightenment is achieved through the practices of mindfulness and awareness and by overcoming any traces of dualistic thought.

This brief comparison clearly demonstrates that this critic is completely mistaken in his views. He has wildly distorted the Mahamudra system when he says things that do not correspond to fact. This kind of abuse is not fitting for a person of his position, as many innocent people take his words seriously. He is simply passing on his misconceptions to others. The same critic says:

> According to the system of Mahamudra, a person must first receive empowerment so that wisdom can arise in association with

> the two-fold stages of Tantra. They will realise the spontaneous wisdom that occurs at the time of enlightenment.

This statement may be correct, insofar as engaging in the two-fold stages of Tantric practice is concerned, where it is based on the four mudras mentioned earlier. However, it would be a gross misunderstanding to think that the third empowerment will bestow the great bliss of Mahamudra.[18] Indrabodhi says:

> Practitioners who say that they attained great bliss
> Through the practice of sexual yoga
> Are mistaken, because that kind of bliss is conditional.
> It comes from the causes and conditions
> Of performing a particular action.
> The bliss of Mahamudra is unconditional
> Because it arises with the unfolding
> Of proper wisdom accompanied by full self-knowledge.
> For this reason, it is called the great bliss.
> This great bliss is permanent and incontrovertible.

Such statements confirm my assertion that the bliss of Mahamudra is not associated with the bliss produced by various Tantric methods. If that were not so, the *Kalachakra Tantra's* statement, 'incontrovertible bliss is Mahamudra,' would be untrue. Those experiences of bliss that are transient and impermanent are called 'experiences of worldly bliss.' Even if we experience worldly bliss as empty in nature, this is no guarantee we will experience the incontrovertible bliss of Mahamudra. The *Kalachakra Tantra* says:

> Understanding emptiness by analysing the skandhas
> Does not lead to a final understanding of emptiness.
> This final understanding is Mahamudra:
> Ever-perfect emptiness.

It also says:

> Analysing the constituents of the sensible world—the elements, particles, and psychophysical constituents—will never lead to a complete understanding of emptiness.[19]

The critic is also mistaken when he suggests we experience relative wisdom (a combination of bliss and wisdom) when we receive the third empowerment and practise sexual sublimation and are introduced to transcendental wisdom when we receive the fourth empowerment.[20]

These two wisdoms are interrelated; the first wisdom is regarded as the cause and the second wisdom is regarded as the effect. However, the critic presents the two wisdoms as unrelated and even contradictory. Another comment worth making here addresses the critic's suggestion that we must have received Tantric empowerment to practise Mahamudra.[21]

Ground Mahamudra refers to the natural condition of mind and all things. How could that natural condition be brought into being through receiving an initiation? If that were so, we wouldn't be able to practise path Mahamudra or experience fruition Mahamudra, because they are contingent on the existence of ground Mahamudra. All the treatises and songs of great Mahamudra masters like Saraha, Tilopa, Naropa, and Maitripa would then have to be regarded as distortions that lack authority. That is certainly not the case.

MAHAMUDRA AS THE EMBODIMENT OF SUTRA AND TANTRA

This has two sections:

- Identifying the essence of the path
- Condensing the deep meaning of the sutras and tantras

§ Identifying The Essence Of The Path

According to some of the doha songs and Mahamudra cycles, the Mahamudra system belongs to Vajrayana Buddhism. The Vajrayana is divided into three paths: 1) the path of blessings, 2) the path of inner solace, and 3) the path of determining reality. It is important to receive the appropriate empowerments and to understand that the other paths are stepping-stones leading to the culminating point of Mahamudra.

According to the *rGya gar gsang spyod*, we have to understand all these different paths in relation to different types of people. This typology consists of people with dull intelligence, people with modest intelligence and people with supreme intelligence. These people correspond to the Sutric teachings on emptiness in the *Prajnaparamita sutras*, the Vajrayana teachings in the tantras, and the supreme yana, which contains the Mahamudra teachings.

Mahamudra is not the same as the teachings in the *Prajnaparamita sutras*. Mahamudra is in accordance with the Tantric teachings, but it is superior to both Prajnaparamita and Tantra. Despite this, some teachings say we should receive the appropriate empowerments and permissions before embarking on the practice of Mahamudra. In other words, we still engage in visualisation of deities and so on when it is appropriate.

These texts also suggest that Mahamudra must be seen as the culmination point of Tantric practices. Nonetheless, if we look at the teachings of Saraha, a great Mahamudra master, we will see that Mahamudra is quite distinct and independent from the Tantric teachings. As Saraha says in one of his dohas:

> Mahamudra is that which is supreme,
> It is the essence of all paths.
> This Mahamudra is the fruition state
> Which has always been inherent in everything that exists.

He also says:

> Mahamudra does not involve
> Mandala visualisation, ritual offerings,
> Mantra recitation, or hand mudras.
> Mahamudra is not conditioned
> By the sutras and tantras.
> Mahamudra is the realisation
> Of self-existing, immutable wisdom.

Again, he says:

> Mahamudra is not Tantra
> It is devoid of mantras
> And practices to increase concentration.
> All of these are just devices;
> Mahamudra is free of them.

Furthermore, he says:

> What is the point of burning candles and butter lamps
> Or visualising deities?
> What use are these Tantric practices
> When you can rest in the nature of your own mind?
> That is Mahamudra.

Saraha makes it clear the Mahamudra path is independent of Tantra but that it is not in conflict with it. Mahamudra is also free from practices that transmute the three poisons of desire, anger, and ignorance. It is free from the four joys cultivated in the Tantric yogas. It is also superior to the experience of luminosity in practices of Tantric yoga. Saraha's *Queen Doha* points out that Mahamudra is not in conflict with the practices of Tantra, insofar as the karmamudra empowerment, and certain yogic exercises can serve as triggers for Mahamudra realisation. Nonetheless, Mahamudra and Tantra practices must be perceived as quite distinct. Gampopa outlines three different paths:

1. The Sutric approach employs reasoning and logic, such as the negation of one and many, and meditations that analyse the lack of intrinsic existence in all phenomena.
2. The Tantric path of blessings involves visualising deities and yogic exercises that balance energy and work with the energy pathways.
3. The direct path determines reality by directly realising the natural state of things.

Mahamudra is called the 'direct path' or the 'path that determines reality' because it involves directly entering into the natural state of being.[22] Gampopa mentions another way to understand these three approaches:

1. The path of renunciation uses analysis to cultivate what is beneficial and to abandon what is harmful. This is the path of the sutras. Sutra distinguishes between the antidotes and that which is to be abandoned and thereby eliminates them.
2. The path of transformation transmutes conflicting emotions instead of abandoning them. This is the path of the tantras. Tantra takes defilements, obscurations, and emotional conflicts on the path and transforms them into a visualised deity, into a vajra, a sceptre, or a lotus, thus using what is gross to realise what is unsullied and pure. It involves using concepts to realise nonconceptual wisdom.
3. The approach of Mahamudra does not use the techniques of renunciation or transformation, because the idea that there is something to renounce or something to transform does not arise. Instead, we realise the one-flavouredness of what we need to abandon and the techniques we use to abandon them. We discard the very concepts of abandonment and techniques and realise everything that occurs is a creation of mind. There is no need to introduce techniques to achieve a certain state of mind or bring about certain realisations. The only method is to let the mind be and rest in being-itself. The realisation of Mahamudra will then occur quite spontaneously.

Another way to understand this is that people of limited capacity and intelligence are given teachings on emptiness in the

> *Prajnaparamita sutra*s, people of modest capacity are given the Tantric teachings and people of superior capacity are given the Mahamudra teachings. Mahamudra is a distinct approach that can be practised on its own, quite independently of Sutric and Tantric teachings.

Sometimes the path of Mahamudra is called 'the path of blessings' because it can happen, as it has happened in the past, that a lama may introduce his or her student to ordinary mind.[23] In this case, a direct introduction of ordinary mind has taken place, which is quite independent from the student's training in the sutras and tantras. This is how Mahamudra was practised in ancient times. However, the later Tibetan tradition came to practise Mahamudra more and more in conjunction with the sutras and tantras. It therefore became quite essential for people to practise the tantras so that they could become spiritually ripe for the effects of Mahamudra. This involves receiving the appropriate empowerment and engaging in the four preliminary practices. There is no contradiction here, for now people with varying degrees of intelligence can all gain enormous benefit from practising Mahamudra in conjunction with Tantra.

§ Condensing The Deep Meaning Of The Sutras And Tantras

The teachings of Buddha, as contained in the sutras and tantras, have one purpose, to enable a realisation of the true nature of things. We may use many different techniques and approaches—some subtle, some general, some quite complex and some quite simple—but they are all skilful devices to help us understand reality. As one sutra says:

> All the teachings of Buddha orient us to an apprehension of reality. They all bring that reality into our consciousness.

The second *Bhavanakrama* says:

> The teachings of the Buddha are all oriented toward revealing reality through either direct or indirect means.

Atisha says:

> The eighty-four thousand teachings in the sutras and tantras
> Are designed to help us perceive reality.
> Apart from teachings on the reality of emptiness;
> Nothing else was taught.

The *Pancakrama* says:

> There are a multitude of teachings and methods
> But not one of them is not designed to reveal emptiness.

The *Nirvanaviskambhi* says:

> The teachings of Buddha
> Enable us to perceive that which is unoriginated
> And that which is in a state of peace.

Two cycles of teachings were given to make it easier to realise emptiness, those of Sutra and those of Tantra. The Sutric cycle teaches meditation, as well as hearing the teachings, contemplating the teachings, and practising the six transcendental actions. We realise emptiness when we have gained a full comprehension of all this. The *Vajrasamadhi Sutra* says:

> We will perfect the six paramitas if we do not waver from an understanding of emptiness.

The *Khyad par sems kyi zhus pa'i mdo* says:

> To not engage in conceptual proliferation is giving.
> To not get involved in discursive thought is morality.
> To not get caught up in differentiation is patience.
> To not think of abandonment or cultivation is effort.
> Non-attachment is meditation.
> Non-cogitation is wisdom.
> All six paramitas are included in understanding emptiness.[24]

Saraha says:

> Understanding the nature of the mind to be emptiness accomplishes everything at once. So read texts, ponder them, meditate on them, and master their subtle meaning.

The *Rap tu mi gnas pa'i rgyud* says:

> If you taste the food of the unconditioned nature of mind,
> All the various schools of thought become satisfied.
> However, people uneducated in spiritual matters
> Become caught in the semantics of words.
> They are unable to realise
> That everything is constructed by mind.

Furthermore, there are two different meditative stages according to Tantra: the creative-imagination and fulfilment stages.[25] These are also known as the 'stage with concepts' and the 'stage without concepts.' We must realise the stage without concepts. The *Vajradakini Tantra* says:

> To realise the unconditioned nature of phenomena, we must engage in things naturally, without contrivances. We engage in the recitation of mantras quite naturally, without deliberation and without excessive effort because if we can become free of contrivances, we will understand that which is unconditioned or that which is naturally present. Certain methods and techniques may be necessary, but only up to a point. After that, we must be free of them and learn to be natural, just as we would stop carrying a boat after we have used it to cross a river.

The *Hevajra-pindartha* (commentary on the *Vajrahrdaya*) says:

> Concepts are bound together by karmic traces and dispositions. Therefore we first need to have a conceptual understanding of this process, then once we understand it conceptually, we must slowly loosen ourselves from that conceptual bond.

In this way, we have to realise that the real essence of Tantra lies in the uncontrived, spontaneous, and unconditioned. The *Hevajra Tantra* says:

> The deities we visualise in Tantric practice
> Must certainly lie in the sphere of reality.
> From the ultimate point of view,
> Understanding the nature of mind
> Accomplishes everything at once.

It also says:

> Non-conceptual awareness embodies everything
> That we accomplish through mantras,
> Yogic exercises, rituals, fire offerings, and mandalas.
> Realise that an understanding of the nature of mind
> Is the most important thing of all.

The *Amrtaguhyatantraraja* says:

> Engaging in prayers, offering cakes, and ritual performances
> Must eventually assist us in realising the nature of mind.
> Everything is accomplished if we realise that.

It is important to have this Mahamudra perspective in our practices, no matter what practices we are engaged in. Our Sutric and Tantric practices must all be permeated by this open and expansive view. We will find it very difficult to realise the nature of mind if we rely solely on the Sutric and Tantric methods. It is the recognition of the nature of mind that enables us to accomplish realisation. As the great Mahamudra adept, Saraha, says:

> Some people become monks or nuns, leading a celibate life,
> Some teach the sutras,
> Some pursue realisation of mind,
> Some excel in study,
> Some do mandala practices,
> Some propound the significance
> Of the fourth empowerment,
> Some use space as the object of meditation,
> Some try to establish a proper view of emptiness;
> A great number of people
> End up having wrong views.
> No matter what practices you do,
> If you remain distant
> From the nature of your own mind
> You will not achieve enlightenment.

Tilopa says:

> Even if we become expert in the tantras or sutras
> And know everything about the vinaya,
> If we haven't applied ourselves to understanding
> the nature of mind,
> None of these things will be of much benefit.

These statements show that Mahamudra places greater emphasis on the ultimate aspect of the practices rather than on the relative ones. The *Abhidhana Tantra* says:

> If we engage in the practice of Mahamudra
> And our meditation becomes actualised
> We will attain buddhahood in this very lifetime.

The *Surayacandra-sadhana* says:

> Those yogis who consistently
> Engage in Mahamudra

And develop unwavering attention;
Will attain Mahamudra realisation,
In three years and three months' time.

THE GREAT QUALITIES OF MAHAMUDRA PRACTITIONERS

This has two sections:

- The lineage of realised ones in India
- The meditative lineage of Tibet

§ The Lineage Of Realised Ones In India

Vajradhara taught the Maha-Anuttarayoga tantras—especially the *Mahamudra-tilaka*, the *Sri-anavila Tantra*, the *Rap tu min gnas pa'i rgyud,* and other teachings—to Guhyapati who in turn transmitted them to the dakinis in Uddiyana. The dakinis taught the key instructions to king Visukalpa, who travelled to Uddiyana, then took those instructions back to India. After carefully examining potential disciples, he found Saraha to be of superior mind and predestined to attain instantaneous enlightenment. Saraha achieved liberation through receiving these instructions from king Visukalpa and in turn passed them on in his dohas, thus helping to liberate many fortunate people. This is how the lineage of instantaneous realisation came into being.

According to the dohas, the *Brda tsa*, *rGya gar gsang spyod,* and so forth, Buddha transmitted the quintessential teachings of Dharma around the time he began to contemplate his own paranirvana. At the request of Manjughosa and Avalokiteshvara, Buddha travelled to the south of India to transmit the quintessential instructions to an assembly of innumerable bodhisattvas like Saraha, Nagarjuna, and Savari in the city of Vidarbha. There the Buddha prophesied the emergence of exponents of this quintessential Dharma some time in the future.

The Buddha Vajradhara transmitted his teaching to the bodhisattvas, who gave it to Saraha. Saraha was the forefather of all the greatly realised ones in India. Saraha transmitted this teaching to Nagarjuna, who is renowned as the second Buddha. Nagarjuna especially guided Sri Savarisvara to liberation. Sri Savari came from the caste of dancers. He was predestined to attain instantaneous liberation. According to some traditions, Savari also received these instructions from Saraha. They attained enlightenment through the rainbow body and it is said that these masters appeared to fortunate meditators at the mountain retreat of Sriparvata until recent times.

These instructions were transmitted through a succession of authentic teachers and became known in India in the *Druppa Dendun* of Mahamudra, the *sNying po skor drug*, the twenty-four sections of the *A-ma-na-si,* and extensive dohas. These texts so impressed the wise scholars and siddhas of India in subsequent periods, they sought out the gurus of this instruction lineage.

Maitripa was one such learned yogi who had heard of the greatness of this quintessential Dharma. He travelled to Sriparvata, enduring immeasurable hardships, but his initial attempt to find Savari was in vain. Finally, when Maitripa attempted to take his own life, Savari suddenly appeared before him. Maitripa eventually received the quintessential instructions from Savari. He was later recognised as the great lord Maitripa at Bodh Gaya and made available his own numerous commentaries on the quintessential instructions in the dohas, *Brda rtsa*, *Gsang spyod,* and so on. These texts became very well known, especially after they were passed on to Vajrapani.

According to some sources within the Kagyu tradition, the great mahasiddha Tilopa was a reincarnation of Cakrasamvara. According to others, he was the reincarnation of the bodhisattva Cittavajra. It is said he visited Akanishtha in his illusory manifestation and heard Vajradhara expound on the buddhadharma in all its depth and profundity. He thus became the pre-eminent master of Tantra, just like its custodian Vajrapani. Tilopa compiled the creative visualisations into four or six classes, the fulfilment stage meditations of the father tantras into five levels, and the fulfilment stage meditations of the mother tantras into four or six mudras.

One account says that Tilopa then visited the great country of Zahor in Bengal and taught the Dharma to hundreds of thousands of people, all of whom entered the realm of dakinis by attaining a rainbow body, leaving the entire city deserted. This same account mentions Tilopa's miraculous subjugation of eight saints, who in turn liberated innumerable sentient beings. It also maintains that Tilopa still lives and will continue to perform acts in his illusory form as long as the Dharma survives. Many people were sceptical of Tilopa's assertion that he had no human teachers, so Tilopa created the impression that he had associated with teachers before attaining liberation. He received the four mystic transmissions—Mahamudra, inner heat yoga, dream yoga, and illusory body yoga—from Nagarjuna, Krsnacarya, Lavapa, and the dakini Subhagini. He attended other great male and female gurus, including Tengipa and Darika (disciples of Luyipa), and associated with Dharma brothers such as Vajraghanta and Indrabodhi before he manifested the way to enlightenment.

Then there was the great master Naropa, who achieved mastery of the sutras, tantras, sciences, and arts and realised the instructions of mysticism before he received the prophecies of Cakrasamvara and a dakini. He travelled to Zahor in search of Tilopa and after innumerable hardships and disappointments, found and pleased Tilopa with personal service. He endured twelve personal ordeals until he eventually received all the key instructions, which was like pouring the entire contents of one vase into another. Naropa brought countless disciples to realisation on his return to Magadha. Amongst his most eminent disciples were seven comparable to himself, such as Maitripa, one hundred and eight saints, fifty-four male yogis, and one thousand female mystics. In addition, there was Phamthingpa of Nepal and Marpa of Tibet. Naropa also attained enlightenment in a rainbow body.

§ The Meditative Lineage Of Tibet

Marpa the translator made the journey to India three times, studying with great realised masters, such as Naropa and Maitripa. He cleared away his doubts and assumptions by practising these profound instructions, and was renowned as a most outstanding bilingual scholar and realised master. He excelled in the vital instructions that are vast and profound. Marpa had many realised disciples, such as Mila Shepa Dorje of Kungthang, the great three (Mey, Ngok and Ram), Tsurton, Golek, and so on.

Milarepa pleased Marpa by undergoing great hardships and many arduous physical ordeals. He was then given the general teachings on the quintessential instructions on Mahamudra along with the special secret, oral instructions. He raised the victory banner of meditation by undergoing such hardship and asceticisms that everyone who hears about it is awestruck and deeply moved. Milarepa thus became the most renowned mystic of Tibet. Among his numerous great disciples were the four repas, the eight minor yogis, and the six masters.

Until the time of Milarepa, the yogis of this instruction lineage meditated mainly on the key instructions of Tantric mysticism and only sometimes incorporated the vital instructions on Mahamudra from the discourses on the yogas of inner heat and luminosity. However, the great master Gampopa was moved by immeasurable compassion to expound on the quintessential instructions of Mahamudra separately. It is due to these efforts of Gampopa that the Mahamudra became the single path for all predestined practitioners. Gampopa appears to have developed a special causal link for this innovation in the past, which I will now briefly mention.

Gampopa was the former bodhisattva Candraprabha, who was a disciple of the Buddha. At one time, the supreme Buddha expounded the *Samadhiraja Sutra* and then asked his assembled audience of bodhisattvas, 'Who among you wishes to propagate this sutra in the future and make it widely known at a time when the Dharma is declining?' Candraprabha stood up and pledged to do so. The Buddha placed his hand on Candraprabha's head, called upon the great disciples such as Maitreya and the celestial beings, and prophesied, 'When the Dharma begins to decline at a future time, Candraprabha will always maintain celibacy and make this sacred meditation widely known, thus opening the Dharma treasure of the Sugata. He will instruct more than five hundred disciples, attain enlightenment and become known as the victorious Buddha Vimalaprabha.' The Buddha then blessed Candraprabha to remove any remaining obstacles, at which point the eight hundred teachers of the Dharma stood up and pledged their assistance in preserving the same sutra. Then eight hundred million devas, nagas, and semi-celestial beings pledged to protect these holy sages. This was stated in the *Samadhiraja Sutra*.

In the *Mahakarunapundarika Sutra*, the Buddha comforted Ananda by prophesying that after his paranirvana, a monk by the name of Jivaka would appear in the north and spread the Dharma widely. Immediately upon death, Jivaka would attain enlightenment and become the tathagata Vimalaprabha, in the buddha-realm known as Gunalamkara, located within the pure land of Amitabha. He further prophesied that in the snowy land north of Bodh Gaya, close to the river Brahmaputra, a monk-physician named Jivaka would attain enlightenment along with an assembly of over five hundred disciples. More such prophecies of this nature exist, but for fear of overstating the case, I will not mention them here. You can find these references in the relevant sutras.

In accordance with these prophesies, Gampopa and at least five hundred disciples appeared in the rocky mountains of Dakpo Gampo, practised the quintessential instructions of Mahamudra, and made them known far and wide among disciples. The eight hundred bodhisattvas, in keeping with their own pledges, were reborn in Tibet and became personal disciples of Gampopa or disciples of his disciples and became renowned masters who spread the teachings widely. The snowy mountains of Tibet resounded with such echoes of their fame that it could have shaken the whole world. The glorious Dakpo Kagyu School became widely known in India, Nepal, China, and Mongolia. We can see that despite these degenerate times, there are still human beings who can completely renounce their attachment to material things and raise the victory banner of meditation. They wander through terrifying cemeteries, mountain passages, lonely caves and deserts.

This completes the explanation on how to establish confidence in practice.

Part II: Mahamudra Meditation

2

The Kagyu Tradition of Meditation

TWO APPROACHES TO MAHAMUDRA

Buddhist meditation is meant to cater for two types of practitioners and can therefore be divided into two kinds of paths. Some practices belong to the teachings of the instantaneous path. This path caters to individuals of excellent capacity and spiritual insight who have the ability to dispel doubts and uncertainties immediately and then engage in contemplation. Other practices belong to the teachings of the graduated path. This path caters to individuals of limited capacity who have not yet developed sufficient spiritual insight. These practitioners are encouraged first to engage in tranquillity meditation and then to cultivate insight meditation so they can eradicate doubts and uncertainties and establish the proper view once their minds have become settled.

The teachings of the great Mahamudra masters, such as Saraha, Savaripa, Indrabodhi, Tilopa, Maitripa, and others emphasised the instantaneous path and catered mainly for individuals of excellent capacity. The teachings of Maitreyanatha, Asanga, and Vasubandhu, the *Bhavanakrama* of Kamalashila and the *Prajnaparamitopadesa* of Santipa break the path into stages of spiritual development, thereby bringing out its systematic nature. Many streams of teachings were transported from India to Tibet, some of which contained both gradual and instantaneous approaches. A form of Mahamudra practice was passed on in the transmission of some ancient Kadampa masters in the lineage that originated with Indrabodhi and passed from Dombipa to Atisha. Most of Atisha's teachings were passed down from teacher to student before they were eventually systematised by Dromtonpa and his associates. The underlying theme in this line of transmission is the graduated path.

Gampopa brought the sudden stream of the mahasiddhas of India and the gradual stream of Atisha to spiritual realisation. He was familiar with both

Tantric and Mahamudra teachings but he chose to put the emphasis on the instantaneous path where practitioners first establish the proper view and then engage in meditation. Indian mahasiddhas like Maitripa and the authors of doha songs and pith instructions of Tantra agree with Gampopa. However, there were other teachers in Tibet who argued that it is not possible to engage in insight meditation or embark on the instantaneous path, without first becoming familiar with tranquillity meditation and the teachings associated with it. This claim is incorrect.

If that were true, much of what the great Indian and Tibetan masters have said about the instantaneous path would have to be discredited. Many authoritative texts by great masters with experience in both teachings and practices confirm the view of the instantaneous path. The following excerpt from the *Ahapramanasamyak* will help to illustrate this point:

> Teachings that are medicine for practitioners
> On the graduated path
> Become poison for practitioners on the instantaneous path.
> Teachings that are medicine for practitioners
> On the instantaneous path
> Become poison for practitioners on the graduated path.

We would have to say the people who claim, 'We must always approach the teachings from the perspective of the graduated path,' are unfamiliar with the teachings that expound the instantaneous path. Furthermore, excessive attachment to the Sutric teachings makes some people cling to the idea that it is impossible to attain tranquillity without first pacifying body and mind, impossible to practise insight without first attaining tranquillity, and impossible to gain insight into the nature of reality without first mastering these two aspects of meditation. They therefore insist on approaching spiritual realisation in a systematic and graduated manner. Some people even say that as so few individuals actually master these two types of meditation, it is no longer possible to gain insight into the nature of reality. They argue that the current climate is so unfavourable for meditation practice, it would be better to turn away from the whole idea of meditation altogether.

The only possible response to that line of reasoning is that Buddha, in his infinite wisdom, did not teach one thing. Buddha taught different things to different people in response to varying degrees of intelligence, and their different capacities, dispositions, and predilections. We should not imagine that Buddha taught only the graduated path or only the instantaneous path. Buddha gave a variety of teachings to benefit the greatest number of human beings. Some teachings are so profound and powerful; we can gain extraordinary realisations from them, even without putting enormous time and effort into their practice. We only need to look at the life stories of the mahasiddhas of India to see the truth of this.

Having made these general remarks on the two Buddhist approaches to spirituality, we now turn to the perspective of the Kagyu lineage. The Kagyu teachings embody both the instantaneous and the gradualist approaches, without disparaging one or exaggerating the importance of the other. The Kagyu tradition contains teachings that are beneficial for people who have embarked on the instantaneous path, having the ability to dispel confusions and uncertainties at the very beginning, and engage in contemplative meditation in accordance with that insight. The Kagyu tradition also has teachings that are beneficial for people who have embarked on the graduated path, needing to settle their minds through tranquillity meditation before they can gradually proceed to the practice of insight meditation. They gain proper insight by eliminating their confusions once their minds have become more settled and focused.

There are some people that say the present age is particularly suited to the instantaneous path because people are sharper, more intelligent, and have more agitated minds. Nevertheless, I will not be presenting the instantaneous approach in this text. I will stick to the more traditional graduated approach, which first deals with tranquillity meditation and then deals with insight meditation in relation to that tranquillity.

THE STAGES OF MAHAMUDRA MEDITATION

The chapters on Mahamudra meditation are divided into the following four topics:

Guiding meditators on the path
The stages of virtuous practice
Consolidating our meditative experiences
The resultant dawning of realisation

3

Tranquillity Meditation

MASTERING TRANQUILLITY MEDITATION

This has two sections:

- Creating the appropriate conditions
- Physical conduct and posture

§ Creating The Appropriate Conditions

We have to create the appropriate conditions for the practice of tranquillity meditation. We also need to be aware of the obstacles that may arise during the course of meditation. The two primary obstacles are dullness and mental agitation. The specific methods for overcoming these two obstacles were discussed in Book One. It is important for beginners to practise in a suitable environment with no human traffic and without noise at night.

Tranquil surroundings, such as staying within a forest or by a river, are extremely helpful for the development of tranquillity because we need to abandon all distractions when we train in settling the mind. We need to remain vigilant and alert between meditation sessions and during breaks. We should constantly behave in a careful and subdued manner as if we were recovering from an illness. Book One also highlighted the need to control our senses and consume a modest amount of food. It will be much more difficult to attain tranquillity if we fail to pay close attention to these details. Atisha had this to say about maintaining the appropriate conditions:

> Failing to pay attention to the auxiliary points of meditation
> Will make sure meditative concentration does not arise,
> Even if we meditate with diligence for a thousand years!

§ Physical Conduct And Posture

Naropa highlighted the importance of maintaining a perfect posture during meditation when he says the real essence of meditation lies in the physical posture. Other masters of the Practice Lineage have made similar comments. They all propose an interdependent relationship between body and mind. When we place the body in the perfect posture, the mind will automatically be put at ease. We should not underestimate the importance of maintaining the perfect physical posture because the meditative state does not arise from mind alone.

The most famous and widely used posture is the 'seven-point posture of Vairochana,' where you 1) sit cross-legged in the vajra posture if you can manage, or if not you sit in the 'posture of the bodhisattvas,' 2) place the right hand on top of the left with the thumbs lightly touching and the palms joined together about four inches below the navel, 3) straighten you spinal column so that your whole body is erect, 4) stretch out your arms so your elbows do not bend too much, 5) tilt your head forward so that your Adam's apple is slightly depressed, 6) touch your upper palate with the tip of your tongue, relax your mouth so that your teeth are barely touching, and 7) keep your eyes completely still without blinking and gaze into space with the tip of your nose in view. This is known as the posture of Vairochana purely because Vairochana is typically depicted in this posture in statues and paintings.

Some people say it is not necessary to be too careful about the mouth and teeth but it is better to keep them in the position recommended above. Kamalashila's Bhavanakrama recommends an eighth point by adding the need to pay attention to the breath. He says we should avoid breathing noisily or with force, but instead make our breathing so subtle that we may not even feel it going in and out. The *Vajramala* says:

> The shoulders should be even
> The tip of the tongue touching the palate
> Teeth and mouth left in a comfortable position
> And eyes gazing into space across the tip of the nose.

Master Pagme Dorje says:

> Sit cross-legged on a comfortable cushion,
> Hands resting on each other with thumbs touching.
> The spinal column should be straight,
> The head tilted slightly forward.

Naropa says:

> The vital aspects of the posture are these:
> The spinal column should be straight
> Like beads strung on a reed.
> Neck slightly bent and body erect
> Like a wild fully grown lily.
> Extend your arms out straight
> As if to form a square knot.
> The hands should rest together
> Pressing just below the navel.
> And the legs should cross
> Like lines on a checker board.

The line about the legs being 'like lines on a checker board' is irrelevant in this context. All the other points, such as having the spinal column straight, head slightly forward, arms straight, and hands resting upon each other, are important.

Enormous physical and mental benefit is gained from maintaining a perfect physical posture. Sitting cross-legged controls the downward psychophysical energy. Having the two hands resting upon each other just below the navel equalises the energy of mystic heat. Having the spinal column straight and body erect prevents any dissipation of psychophysical energy. Keeping the shoulders even will control the life-essence. Having the head tilted slightly forward with the tip of the tongue touching the palate will control the upward psychophysical energy. All the other psychophysical energies naturally start to flow when we adopt the perfect physical posture, particularly when we gaze into space, without blinking too much and without allowing the eyeballs to move around. If we can do this, the auxiliary psychophysical energies will be controlled because energy pathways are connected to the eyes.

Adopting the right physical posture will help you deal with the energy pathways, the psychophysical energy, and the life-essence. Harmonising these three principles ensures the five elements within the body become even and no single element can predominate and upset the balance of the others. Good health will come when all these elements are balanced and harmonised. For example, our complexion will improve and our mind will be more focused, resilient, and susceptible to meditative concentration, because of our greater physical health. An increased physical stability will ensure the mind is sharper, more settled, more resilient, and clear. It will also be naturally free of mental agitation, dullness, and drowsiness.

Failure to maintain a perfect physical posture will result in many obstacles. For example, if the body inclines to the right, there may be a certain amount of mental clarity initially, but it will be followed by proliferating thoughts. If the body inclines to the left, there may be a feeling of well-being and ease initially, but it will be followed by increasing mental agitation. When the body inclines to the right, the thoughts that disturb the mind come mainly from sensory objects, when it inclines to the left, mental agitation arises from within the mind. If the body leans forward, there may be a certain amount of mental clarity initially, but that will soon be polluted by mental agitation. If the body leans slightly backward, there may be a sense of spaciousness and ease initially but the mind will quickly become susceptible to distractions. Not maintaining the proper gaze can also result in different mental disturbances during meditation. Asanga's *Sravakabhumi* says:

> The proper physical posture makes the mind resilient.
> We can spend long periods in meditation without disturbance and without mental and physical exhaustion.
> This posture is completely different from the Hindu tradition. This perfect physical posture is a transmission,
> In itself passed down through the generations
> By the previous buddhas and shravakas.
> Its effectiveness can be gleaned from the success of the tradition.

HOW TO CONCENTRATE ON A MEDITATION OBJECT

We must also have the inspiration to practise, because without inspiration, we simply will not persevere with the practise of tranquillity meditation. Inspiration arises from contemplating the benefits of meditation. A certain sutra says:

> If the teachings are not meditated upon,
> We will not perceive the true nature of ultimate reality.
> Just as seeing and hearing about water
> Will not slake our thirst.

Such sutras highlight the importance of meditating on the Buddhist teachings. The following quotation emphasises the general benefits of meditation practice. The *Prajnaparamita-samcayagatha* says:

> Meditation will naturally teach us
> To let go of clinging and grasping to sensory stimulants.
> It also brings forth insight and psychic abilities.

The particular benefits of engaging in tranquillity meditation are that we enjoy a sense of physical and mental well-being, we can effortlessly apply concentration, we have no mental dispersion and distraction, and we develop a focus that gives us the wisdom to avoid mistakes and erroneous judgements. We may also develop psychic powers. Successful tranquillity meditation will give rise to insight meditation. In summary, we gain all kinds of benefits from tranquillity meditation. These benefits can be short-term, long-term, purely mundane, and purely spiritual. We will develop the inspiration to practise by constantly thinking about these benefits. Vasubhandu's *Madhyantavibhanga* says:

> Settle the mind in a state of dwelling
> For that is the cause and effect of meditation.

'Dwelling' means to make a constant effort to remain in meditation. To 'settle the mind in a state of dwelling' means to make a concerted effort to stay in continuous concentration. The cause of meditative concentration is the inspiration we gain from appreciating the benefits inherent in meditation practice, and the effect of meditation is pliancy of body and mind. Engage in meditation with those things in mind.

ATTAINING EQUIPOISE USING AN EXTERNAL OBJECT

This has two sections:

- The actual meditation
- Identifying with a tranquil state of mind

§ The Actual Meditation

A meditator of lesser capacity can use different methods to settle the mind at the beginning. Tilopa says:

> Using different methods and focusing on different objects
> Is how we train the mind to attain tranquillity.

Certain sutras and the *Bhavanakramas* of Kamalashila say that beginners should use a mental image of the Buddha to enhance their ability to concentrate, but the Practice Lineage considers it difficult for a beginner of limited capacity to visualise an image of the Buddha. They advise beginners to use familiar objects to anchor their minds instead. For this reason, the Practice Lineage counsels using a pebble, a piece of wood or anything familiar and ordinary as the object of meditation. We may also want to use a statue of the Buddha. To make it even easier, it is sometimes helpful to place a small object at the edge of a shadow and concentrate on that. At night, we can visualise a small dot in the form of light between the eyebrows or a similar dot of light underneath our body. The basic point of these methods is to learn how to concentrate the mind so that it does not become distracted. We should not be concerned with the colour or shape of an object while meditating. We simply focus on the object without entertaining any thoughts.

Another useful method for beginners is to break from meditation and rest for a while once the mind has become settled for a short time, even if our minds have not yet been aroused by mental disturbances. It is advisable to practise meditation in short but frequent sessions. If we break off the session while the mind is still relatively calm, it will have the added advantage of making us want to meditate again. Conversely, forcing ourselves to meditate and bear discomfort without any sense of joy will have an adverse effect on our desire to practise.

Some people are critical of using familiar objects such as pebbles or sticks as an object of meditation because these ordinary everyday objets are not mentioned in the authoritative texts. Such criticism is erroneous however. It is easier for beginners to concentrate on something that they are already familiar with rather than trying to visualise something that is quite unfamiliar to them in their everyday life. The use of ordinary objects has the advantage of making concentration easier and the attainment of meditative concentration becomes a practical reality. Nor is it true that familiar everyday objects are not mentioned in the texts. Acharya Bodhibhadra says:

> There are two kinds of meditation:
> Meditation that focuses inward on mental objects
> And meditation that focuses outward on external objects.

He also says:

> The objects of meditation can be of two kinds: extraordinary and ordinary. 'Extraordinary' means visualisations of Buddha and so on and 'ordinary' means pebbles, sticks, and other such items.

The body can also be used as an object of meditation by employing five different methods: 1) meditating on the breath, 2) meditating on a physical mark, 3) meditating on a ball of light, 4) meditating on the rays of the sun, and 5) meditating on the emotional modulations of happiness and joy.

At this point, some people may raise an objection to using pebbles and sticks as objects of meditation by arguing that meditative concentration should be achieved on the mental level through mental training. They say developing concentration with ordinary objects such as sticks and pebbles causes an over-reliance on sensory impressions and trying to attain meditative concentration through sensory impressions is inappropriate. To pacify such doubts, it is worth pointing out that the most important sense organs are the eyes. It is due to the senses, particularly the visual sense, that the mind becomes agitated. When the eyes are controlled by focusing on an external object and the visual organs and visual perception cease to waver, the mind is also stabilised. When the visual organs focus on an object, all the other senses follow suit, and when the senses become settled, the mind settles.

Sticks and pebbles are only a convenient device for the attainment of meditative concentration. They are comparable to points jotted down in a notebook. When you look at the notebook, you are reminded of the things you need to do because your notes are there to jolt your memory. Pebbles and sticks can similarly facilitate our ability to concentrate by jogging our memory whenever we see them lying around. We should understand that there is no finite number of objects that can be employed in the service of our meditative goal. Almost anything and everything can be used to develop meditative concentration. For example, to overcome excessive attachment, we meditate on ugliness, but even this technique varies greatly. We can also meditate on written words, physical forms, sound, light, or names. Nothing is definite or absolute about the objects of meditation in the context of tranquillity meditation. However, by consensus, an image of the Buddha is considered the best, because it embodies the spiritual qualities that we are trying to attain and actualise. The *Bhadrapalapariprccha Sutra* says:

> Just as a teacher is present before students when giving a discourse, bodhisattvas should visualise the Buddha sitting cross-legged before them in his perfect form, displaying his various spiritual qualities, and his immense physical beauty.

The *Samadhinirmocana Sutra* says:

> Buddha's perfect physical form is the colour of radiant gold.

The third *Bhavanakrama* says:

> While many guidelines have been given for the various stages of visualisation, Aryasura and Atisha say it is best to concentrate on one suitable visualisation to attain tranquillity.

The first *Bhavanakrama* says:

> When you have attained tranquillity,
> You can visualise any object.

In brief, there are different ways to focus the mind and different objects of meditation. Beginners should start with something familiar and ordinary and proceed from there. The essential thing is to learn to concentrate, so whatever helps you with that goal should be incorporated into your practice. Once your mind is able to concentrate on a particular object, you can apply that ability to any other object of meditation. The sutras teach us that the practice of insight meditation enables us to dispel doubts, and the attainment of mental stability enables us to eradicate emotional conflicts. Because we make use of pebbles and sticks in this type of meditation, the masters of the Practice Lineage call it 'meditation with object.'

§ Identifying With A Tranquil State Of Mind

There are many different ways and means to settle the mind. In the present context, we are employing techniques that help achieve a state of mental concentration. Tilopa says:

> Free yourself from all physical activity,
> Restrain your speech, which is like an echo,
> And allow your mind to be lucid, settled, and free from distractions,
> Like a reflection of the moon on a pool of water.

Dignaga says:

> The mind should not entertain any thoughts
> Of perceiver and perceived, duality or non-duality
> Self and others, samsara or nirvana;
> But be left in its natural state without discrimination.

It is not so very difficult to attain the state of tranquillity. If we reorientate our minds to stop being predisposed to proliferating thoughts and then learn to remain undistracted in the present moment with a sense of mindfulness, we will have attained some success with tranquillity meditation.

When beginners learn to stay in the state of mental quietude, they should break it off and rest for a short time, then continue with the practice once again. Always be alert and vigilant to your current state of mind. The mind may occasionally appear to be devoid of all activity, but this may not be mental concentration, it could also be an unconscious state without any real mindfulness or awareness. If you notice that your mind has entered an unconscious state, make every effort to correct that because it is anathema to tranquillity. However, if you can maintain a semblance of mindfulness free from gross mental activities during meditation, even when your mind is foggy and dull, do not view that as harmful. Simply continue in this state for a time, and then take a short break, before resuming the practice once again.

Another point to bear in mind is that as you gradually increase your mindfulness, you may feel you have more thoughts than ever before and that your meditative state is upset by this mental proliferation. You do not need to worry about this. Your thoughts may appear to have multiplied, but this is only because you have begun to establish mindfulness and to notice what is going on in your mind. Instead of being an indication of increasing mental distraction, it is a sign of increasing mental stability, so you should not view it as defective. Try to free your mind of all concerns and preoccupations and rid your thoughts of attachment and clinging. You should also rid your mind of the tendency to encourage certain thoughts and reject others. Observe your thoughts with mindfulness, but without following them.

You may still be unable to detect the different states of mind that transpire during the course of meditation, such as mental concentration or mental movement, even after you have been practising for a while. If that is the case, you should pay more attention to sounds, particularly sounds that are loud or unexpected. When those sounds occur, look at your mind and try to see the gap between your thoughts, where one thought has passed and another thought has not yet arisen. This gap should be identified as the state of non-discrimination. This is the state of mental rest. This method can be reinforced by using the breath as a mental object, as described in the following section.

ATTAINING EQUIPOISE WITH AND WITHOUT A MENTAL OBJECT

This has two sections:

- Using the breath
- Not using the breath

§ Using The Breath

1. Counting each breath

Breathing techniques are described in a variety of texts in both Sutric and Tantric teachings. Tilopa says:

> A person of inferior capacity
> Will have difficulty concentrating
> And should resort to using the breath.

According to the sutras, breathing practice can be done in a variety of ways. The *Abhidharmakosha* says:

> There are six breathing techniques:
> Counting the breath, retracing the breath, resting,
> Comprehension, transmutation, and purification.

According to the Sutric teachings, 'counting the breath' means counting the breathing cycle twenty-one times, then starting over with the first breath, repeating the count over and over, for half an hour to an hour, without forgetting the order of the numbers. This counting trains us to concentrate the mind. The technique of 'retracing the breath' means following the inhalation of breath from where it enters the body to where it spreads throughout the body. The technique of 'resting' is cultivating a state of non-discrimination while we feel our breath expand our body. The technique of 'comprehension' means understanding that the nature of the breath is subtle energy. The technique of 'transmutation' means we can transform our mind by following the breath. The technique of 'purification' means the mind is gradually purified of its defilements as its excessive activities are eliminated through breathing techniques and we thus attain the realisation of non-discrimination.

The Tantric teachings also have many kinds of breathing techniques that are used in conjunction with the Tantric yogas, but it is unnecessary to go into those here. I will confine myself to describing the transmission on breathing technique as passed down by the masters of the Practice Lineage. These techniques have two aspects: counting the breath and the inward retention of the breath. The *Sa'i snying po 'khor lo chos pa'i mdo* says:

> We pay attention to the outgoing and incoming breath with mindfulness and a sense of naturalness, and count an exhalation and inhalation as one. If we can pay attention to the breath as it comes in and goes out, we will develop a natural ability to realise ultimate reality.

The *Samvarodaya* says:

> A yogi should count the ingoing and outgoing breaths
> Up to one hundred thousand times.
> This counting should be done silently.

It also says:

> If we can count the breath and practise this properly
> It can even prolong our life.

We sit in the posture described above and watch our breath passing through our nostrils, without making any noise and without forcing it. It is advisable to breathe with a sense of gentleness and mindfulness, without thinking about anything other than paying attention to the breath. We start by counting up to three cycles of breath, then five, then seven, and so on. We should also take breaks between these cycles and rest. Eventually, we should be able to count up to one hundred breath cycles without a break while maintaining our mindfulness the whole time. This practice is extremely useful in conjunction with tranquillity meditation with an external object. Even if we have not achieved much success with meditating on an external object, this breathing practice can be extremely beneficial on its own.

2. The inward retention of breath

The practice of retaining the breath can be done in two ways: during normal breathing and in the technique known as vase breathing. The latter involves holding the breath in the abdomen, making the shape of a vase. The *Vajradakini Tantra* says:

> Retention of the breath will rid our body of stale air
> And purify it of all pollutants.
> It can also reduce fever.
> If we hold the breath in the shape of a vase,
> The body will be fully controlled
> And the sensory impressions
> Will cease to be a distraction to us.

The *Samvarodaya* says:

> Vase breathing can prolong our life
> And allow us to conquer death.
> We retain the breath
> So that it spreads all over our body
> Down to the tip of the toes
> And then hold it in the abdomen in the shape of a vase.

It also says:

> Vase breathing harmonises
> The upward moving psychophysical energy
> And the downward moving psychophysical energy
> At the navel centre.

> The yogi who can accomplish this
> Will achieve total physical and mental stability.

The *Kalachakra Tantra* says:

> The practitioner should breathe in through the nostrils.
> When this activates the energies within the body,
> The male or lunar energy element
> And the female or solar energy element
> Will become harmonised.
> The body will become stronger
> And feel less hunger or thirst,
> While our increased health levels
> Will prolong our life and even conquer our mortality.

Naropa says:

> There are four kinds of breathing exercises:
> Drawing in, saturating, diffusing,
> And darting like an arrow.
> A meditator should try to master all of these.

These last four exercises are not important in the context of this manual; they are only practised in conjunction with Tantric yoga. The meditation manuals of the Practice Lineage only mention the types of breathing exercises that will help us to stabilise the mind. Simply hold the breath within the body and then quieten the mind by not entertaining any thoughts. To begin this exercise of the retention of the breath, inhale a lot of air and then breathe it out forcefully so that any stale breath is expelled. Do this several times.

Then we begin the practice of retention by inhaling slowly through the nostrils in one long stream, without any noise or any kind of force and then hold that breath. We then try to feel a sense of lightness in the upper portion of our body, while pushing the breath into the lower part of our body to give it a feeling of stability and firmness. When it becomes uncomfortable to hold that breath any longer, we simply exhale it in one slow elongated breath, without any sense of panic and without any noise or force. We need to be mindful of the three stages involved in this breathing exercise: the inhalation, the retention and the exhalation. We should try to remain in a state of rest while we retain the breath, without thinking about anything but maintaining a sense of mental clarity.

You should gradually try to expand the duration of your breath retention over time. For example, begin by retaining the breath for the count of three, then five, then seven, and so on. If mental agitation arises during the practice, relax the mind while maintaining a sense of mindfulness. If dullness or mental stupor sets in, you should clear it by straightening your posture and increasing your concentration.

A mind that is constantly wandering and becoming distracted is caused by a disturbance in your prana and this can be fixed by eating nutritious food and receiving regular massages. If dullness or stupor sets in while you are holding the breath, you should open your eyes more, spread your shoulders out wide, and straighten your spinal column. If certain thoughts enter your mind during the retention of breath and you notice them while maintaining a sense of mindfulness, this should not be regarded as an obstacle to meditative concentration. Simply apply mindfulness to these thoughts.

All the techniques described so far—including the use of external objects, counting the breath, and retaining the breath within the body—have the same goal: the attainment of meditative concentration. We should try to attain a certain level of tranquillity with the aid of these techniques.

§ Not Using The Breath

As you progress with tranquillity meditation, you will reach a stage where you can abandon the breath as an object of meditation. The mental stability achieved with the help of these techniques reaches a point of stability where you no longer require external aids. Adopt the same physical posture as before, but without relying on external sticks, pebbles, or breath. The mind should now be independent of anything other than itself. Simply allow the mind to rest in its natural state.

Do not think about the past and assume you can predict your experiences from what you have done previously. Do not think about the future and anticipate anything you might achieve through your efforts thinking, 'If I do this, that may happen; if I do that, this may happen.' Do not concern yourself with what is happening in the present moment, worrying about the thoughts and emotions in your mind. Simply let the mind be. The *Guhyasamaja Tantra* says:

> The mind should be allowed to rest
> Without thinking.

The *Doha kosa* says:

> Do not be concerned with thinking
> Or the object of thought,
> Whatever arises in the mind should be left to itself.

Allow the mind to rest without cogitation. Just like a summer sky, the mind should be free from the clouds of conceptual activity. The *Doha kosa* also says:

> If we let the mind rest like space itself,
> We realise that all existent things
> Are equal in the realm of ultimate reality.

When such understanding dawns, you will no longer be disturbed or perturbed by the transient nature of things. That is why we let our mind rest in a non-wavering state free from cogitations. Certain signs associated with the mastery of the psychophysical energy will also appear and we will uproot the very cause of the ever-recurring wheel of the samsaric condition. The *Kalachakra Tantra* states:

> If you spend a single day in meditation
> Without being overwhelmed by thoughts and emotions
> There will be some sign at the end of the day
> Of having gone beyond the ordinary state of mind.
> If this is not true,
> Everything I have said is nothing but lies!

The *Doha kosa* confirms:

> When the mind is left alone in an unwavering state,
> We are naturally liberated from samsara
> Without consciously abandoning it.

You should just allow your mind to rest in its own natural state, without employing any kind of external means to achieve that natural state. You should begin by doing numerous short meditation sessions. When an obstacle arises, you should then apply the antidote. Apply exertion if the obstacle is mental dullness and apply relaxation if the obstacle is mental agitation. If mental dullness is an endemic and persistent problem despite your use of the antidotes, you are advised to purify your karmic defilements by practising confession and prostrations.

Whatever level of mental stability you were able to establish during your practice of the previous exercises, which involved the use of external objects and the breath, apply this stability to this technique of resting the mind. If you do not become completely familiar with this last technique, you will never properly establish yourself in tranquillity meditation. This particular method is sometimes called 'signless meditation,' while the methods involving external objects and the breath are called 'meditation with sign.'

ATTAINING EQUIPOISE WITHOUT AN OBJECT

This has two sections:

- How to attain formless tranquillity
- Recognising the state of formless tranquillity

§ How to Attain Formless Tranquillity

1. The vital point of balance

The Mahamudra meditation instructions place the emphasis on the techniques of exertion and relaxation. These techniques are similar to the Sutric teachings on tranquillity meditation that deal with the obstacles of dullness and mental agitation. However, unlike the Sutric approach, which employs a number of specific antidotes to deal with those obstacles, the Mahamudra approach is just to let the mind rest, applying mindfulness to observe the activities of mind so that we immediately detect the arising of dullness or mental agitation. We then apply exertion to the appearance of dullness, and relaxation to the appearance of mental agitation.

Many obstacles to a tranquil state of mind need to be overcome. Obstacles such as mental agitation, regret, drowsiness, uncertainty, attachment, resentment, and so on are listed in the sutras. From the Mahamudra perspective, all these obstacles can be subsumed under the categories of dullness and mental agitation. If we really want to be specific about these obstacles, we can see that there are subtle differences between drowsiness, stupor, and dullness, but these are regarded as one obstacle in the Sutric literature. The Sutric teachings prescribe different antidotes for each of the obstacles as they arise. Our meditation instructions say we need only use simple methods to overcome dullness and agitation because all the other obstacles are automatically eradicated when these two are overcome.

We determine what gives rise to dullness and agitation and then examine their characteristics so that we can easily identify them. Then we apply the recommended methods for overcoming them. These methods were described in general terms in Book One. In brief, the meditative state that we need to realise must consist of two things: an element of mental clarity when the mind is at rest and a sense of stability.

The obstacles of dullness and agitation must be overcome because dullness robs the mind of clarity and agitation makes it difficult to cultivate stability. The sutras recommend many different methods for overcoming these two obstacles. If dullness arises, we are advised to lift our mood by contemplating beautiful and pleasant things. If agitation arises, we are advised to use these agitated thoughts to our advantage by contemplating the harmfulness of a distracted mind or the transience of everything to give ourselves a sense of urgency.

The Mahamudra approach to these obstacles is to apply the techniques of exertion and relaxation. Meditative concentration will arise automatically if we master these techniques. Once we become proficient in these methods, we will have enough experience to gauge the degree of exertion or relaxation we need to apply in any given situation.

2. Employing exertion

The technique of exertion is primarily used for the obstacle of mental dullness but that does not mean it cannot occasionally be applied to mental agitation. In the context of Mahamudra, dullness means the diminished power of mindfulness when resting the mind in its natural state. The mind can become completely foggy and lose its concentration so that we forget to focus on the meditation object. Even if we do not lose track of the meditation object, our sense of mental clarity might still give way to a sense of vagueness. That is also the effect of mental dullness. The first kind of dullness can easily be seen for what it is but we need to pay particular attention to the second one because it is easy to mistake that state of dullness for the tranquillity of shamatha. We need to be constantly vigilant and alert to the obstacle of mental dullness. The mind will gradually grow duller if we cannot maintain an element of mental clarity during meditation. Our ability to think or remember will also start to lose its edge and the mind will be corrupted. To eradicate this obstacle, accentuate your gaze and look straight ahead with eyes wide open. The obstacle of dullness is also accompanied by a subtle form of depression. When you notice it, correct it by expanding your mind and generating a sense of confidence and cheerfulness. The short *Prajnaparamita Sutra* says:

> If depression sets in, dispel it with a feeling of expansion.

The *Madhyamakahrdaya* says:

> When depression arises, meditate on a sense of lightness.

You may gradually be overcome by the grosser forms of mental dullness but you must remain vigilant toward its more subtle expressions. Your mind should be forever vigilant during meditation, with no desires, other than the outcome of your meditation practice. You should just allow your mind to rest one-pointedly in its own natural state. As with the previous exercises, begin by practising mental exertion for a short time. Take quick breaks and then return to the meditation, practising this format repeatedly. Your sense of mental fogginess can be transformed if you apply the right amount of mental exertion. Your mind will become more resilient, lucid, and naked when it is no longer shrouded in mental confusion and conceptual proliferations. This is what we are aiming for in overcoming mental dullness, for this produces one aspect of the tranquil state; the aspect of mental clarity. In brief, even if we are not consciously thinking about overcoming these obstacles, we should be able to detect them whenever they arise in meditation by applying mindfulness and mental clarity. The *Madhyantavibhanga* says:

> Meditators should always be aware
> Of dullness and agitation.

The *Bhavanakrama* says:

> Meditators should have the ability to detect dullness and be aware of agitation when it arises in the mind.

There are people who have a natural disposition toward thinking a great deal. In such cases, mental clarity may be present, but the ability to remain in a state of non-cogitation may be brief. Do not regard this as a defect; continue to work toward maintaining that mental clarity. Even if thoughts arise, you can still realise the meditative concentration of tranquillity if you retain a sense of mental clarity. Meditators who are unable to rest the mind, but able to retain mental clarity, should simply work on maintaining that clarity. They should also try to retain an element of relaxation so that their practice does not become too forced.

3. Employing relaxation

We apply the technique of relaxation to the obstacle of mental agitation. There are again, many different ways to apply this technique, but we are only using it to dispel mental agitation in Mahamudra meditation. Sutric literature defines mental agitation as 'the attachment that arises when we think about a beautiful object.' However, we are not specifically using mental relaxation to counteract sensual excitement within the Mahamudra approach. We include a wider range of human thoughts and emotions in the definition of mental agitation, including regret, doubt, uncertainty, harmful intentions, hostility, and anger. Mental agitation refers to any kind of restlessness experienced during meditation.

We use the technique of relaxation to settle the mind and achieve mental tranquillity. The Sutric method advocates specific antidotes for overcoming specific obstacles. For example, we are advised to contemplate the harmfulness of our mental states when we yield to distraction, craving, and so on. As the *Sutralamkara* says:

> All kinds of obstacles to meditation,
> Such as distraction, ill-will, craving, and restlessness
> Should be pacified by contemplating
> The harm of such mental states.

The *Madhyamakahrdaya* says:

> When the mind becomes distracted,
> We pacify it by contemplating
> The harmful effects of those distractions.

However, in the Mahamudra context, relaxing the mind means ceasing to think about the object that gave rise to the mental agitation. We should neither encourage nor discourage those thoughts, but simply try to relax our minds. The short *Prajnaparamita Sutra* says:

> When the mind becomes agitated,
> We should try to relax
> So we can enter the state of tranquillity.

The adjustment we make to our eye gaze in this technique is the opposite to the adjustment we made to counteract the obstacle of dullness. Here, we cast our gaze downward instead of straight ahead. Do not concern yourself with thoughts about what you should be doing in meditation, do not feel any upsurges of confidence when your mind becomes stable, or feel alarm when your mind is agitated. You should not anticipate any benefits from your meditation at all. Just allow the mind to loosen and experience a sense of lightness, without thinking about any of these things.

The essence of Mahamudra relaxation is to not accept or reject any of your experience and to not condition the mind in any way. Whatever arises in the mind should be left alone to settle naturally, instead of using techniques that force the mind to settle. Apply relaxation while maintaining your mindfulness so that you remain constantly aware of the thoughts and emotions that arise during meditation.

Certain thoughts may forcefully enter the mind when you are trying to cultivate such a state, but if you do not try to suppress or follow those thoughts, they will not lead to distraction. Do not try to prevent these violent or forceful thoughts from arising, but employ mindfulness and try to remain undistracted. If subtle thoughts enter the mind, do not regard them as either good or bad and do not try to encourage or discourage them. Try to relax and just allow yourself to ease into a state of mind that can accommodate these thoughts without being disturbed by them. Persist with the practice of mindfulness as well, because mindfulness is comparable to a security guard that is always on the lookout for disturbances.

When you manage to settle the mind and start to experience a sense of mental lightness, openness and spaciousness, break from your meditation instead of indulging in that experience. It is preferable to break from your meditation session before agitation sets in and then continue the practice again in further short sessions.

When you apply exertion to counteract dullness by tightening the mind, you increase the force of your concentration because you are virtually blocking out your thought processes and creating a concentrated state devoid of cogitations. Nonetheless, this tightening technique is not as efficient as the loosening one, because loosening only requires us to be aware of whatever is arising in the mind without being swayed by it. Just allow the mind to rest in a relaxed state in a comfortable way, without forcing anything on it. If you can maintain the attitude of not accepting or rejecting anything that arises in the mind and can simply observe and be aware of those mental activities, you will no longer be overwhelmed by your gross and subtle thoughts and will be able to use whatever arises in the mind to attain tranquillity.

This method does not require you to think about anything more than remaining mindful of your mental activities. By the simple act of not concerning yourself with anything else, you will create a sense of spaciousness and relief in your mind. When you let go of thoughts about employing antidotes to the meditative obstacles, your mind will naturally loosen up. This is the essence of the relaxation technique according to the Mahamudra tradition. Saraha says:

> When a mind that has been completely
> tightened in concentration is loosened
> It will naturally remain in a meditative state.

He also says:

> A mind that is tied wants to run in the ten directions.
> When let loose, it realises it has nowhere to go,
> And will remain in a relaxed state;
> Like a dog on a leash.

Maitripa says:

> If a disturbing thought arises in a yogi's mind,

He simply lets it be, like cotton wool,
Without trying to condition the mind.

Certain people have criticised this Mahamudra relaxation technique. They argue that if you allow the mind to relax in this way, it will quickly lose mindfulness and be vulnerable to the harmful effects of dullness and agitation and they dismiss the approach as ineffective. This is an unfair criticism and reflects their ignorance of the primary sources. Tilopa says:

The mind should be left in its natural state.
That which is bound will relax
If it is let loose.

Saraha's *Doha kosa* says:

Anything we hang onto, including meditative antidotes, must be released.

All of these masters clearly advise relinquishing all attachment and clinging to anything during meditation, including meditative techniques and antidotes. Master Zhang says:

When the mind is left in a relaxed state,
It arises clear and devoid of disturbing thoughts.
That is the meditative experience.
When mind is like the sky without clouds;
This is what is meant by dharmakaya.

To answer the above criticism, using the relaxation method to overcome mental agitation does not weaken mindfulness. Any loss of mindfulness can in fact be attributed to a failure to practise the relaxation method properly. Diminished mindfulness is also regarded as faulty meditation by Mahamudra practitioners. Who would regard such a misguided use of relaxation as the supreme meditation? That would be pure craziness. Mahamudra teachings do not encourage methods that lead to mindlessness.

You must remain constantly aware of what occurs in the mind and determine whether you are mindful or not of the transitions that take place there. You should also be mindful of how much relaxation you need to apply in any given situation. If you apply too much relaxation, your meditation will be incomplete. If you apply too little relaxation, that will also cause problems. In brief, when applying mindfulness as a beginner, don't think, 'I should be mindful, I should be mindful' and reinforce that all the time. Simply relax into the state of mindfulness. You only need to generate a sense of mindfulness when you have become distracted by one of the obstacles. Maintain mindfulness and awareness in the meditative state, with a sense of clarity and stability, remaining open and aware of all your sense impressions. If you can do that, you have achieved tranquillity meditation.

§ Recognising The State Of Formless Tranquillity

The above methods are the way to give rise to the meditative concentration of tranquillity. That meditative concentration must have the qualities of clarity and stability. The clarity aspect comes from maintaining mindfulness and awareness. The stability aspect comes from being able to settle your conceptual proliferations. A mind with proliferating thoughts will have its stability disrupted. Even if your mind is not running rampant, as such, your mindfulness will be so weak, your mind will be mainly unconscious, and you will have difficulty developing the clarity aspect of meditative concentration.

Mental dullness arises when mindfulness and awareness are absent from our minds. Mental agitation arises when we have no control over our conceptual proliferations. The obstacles of mental dullness and agitation were discussed in Book One and we will return to them again in later chapters. To restate them briefly here, we overcome dullness by practising mindfulness and awareness to develop mental clarity and we overcome mental agitation by focusing on the object of meditation to loosen the mind through relaxation. We need to maintain the fine balance between relaxation and exertion and then try to maintain that mental state for as long as we can. Nagarjuna's *Tushi Nyamjor* says:

> Lift your spirits when dullness arises,
> Relax into mental agitation when it arises.

What is the difference between mindfulness and awareness? Mindfulness is the mental component that prevents the mind from being distracted from the object of meditation. Awareness detects whether we are distracted and identifies the obstacles of dullness and agitation. At the beginning, we learn to apply mindfulness so that we can stay with the object of meditation without distraction. As we persist with mindfulness, we can start to use awareness to detect distractions as they occur and to identify the presence of dullness and agitation. Awareness is not applied in the same way as mindfulness. We need to have a sense of bare awareness, where we are simply aware rather than trying deliberately to be aware of something.

This would be an appropriate place to describe the Practice Lineage's understanding of the relationship between mindfulness and awareness. Mahamudra meditation is one of the most important methods for developing these mental faculties. The sutras emphasise the difference between mindfulness and awareness and many scriptures have elaborated upon those differences. However, the teachings of the Practice Lineage blur this distinction somewhat. They either discuss mindfulness and awareness together or they discuss mindfulness at length and only intimate the presence of awareness. These different understandings of the relationship between mindfulness and awareness should not alarm the reader. As the *Bodhicharyavatara* says:

> Guard the mind with mindfulness
> This effort will ensure that awareness arises naturally.

This quotation demonstrates that mindfulness and awareness are not two different mental faculties; they are part of the same mental faculty. The difference is simply a matter of refinement because a very refined form of mindfulness is no different to awareness. Awareness is already present in that mindfulness. The *Madhyantavibhanga* says:

> Wherever there is mindfulness,
> Awareness will also become present.

At this point, the prudent among you may raise an important and relevant question, 'We still need to employ a subtle form of thought while trying to concentrate on the object of meditation. We have to determine whether the mind is stable or whether it has fallen victim to the obstacles of dullness and mental agitation. Without these subtle thoughts, we will have no way of dealing with these obstacles when they arise. How then is it possible to attain a state of non-cogitation?'

To ease your minds and dispel your perplexity, it should be said that we do not need to regard these subtle thoughts as bad. We need them to attain insight. Such thoughts are not the same as our ordinary discursive thoughts; they are in tune with the insight of vipashyana. In fact, these subtle thoughts are no different from awareness itself and are therefore something we need to cultivate. Kamalashila's second *Bhavanakrama* says:

> Having let the mind rest on the object of meditation, we persist with this point of focus by examining whether the mind is properly focused on that object. Has the mind yielded to the distractions of dullness or mental agitation? Has the mind been overwhelmed by sensory impressions and become scattered? It is important for the meditator to examine what is going on in the mind in this way.

This quotation clearly demonstrates that using subtle thoughts to maintain a sense of mindfulness and awareness is not anathema to the development of meditative concentration. We do not use these subtle thoughts in conjunction with any deliberate, conscious mental processes. Subtle thoughts are merely used as a watcher during the meditative state. We don't go over these things again and again in a forceful or deliberate manner, we maintain a sense of awareness and observe what occurs in the mind in a gentle way, where the preceding mental event of awareness is followed by a succeeding mental event of mindfulness. The mere watcher is maintained in this way.

We need to have a fine balance between exertion and relaxation in this use of mindfulness and awareness. That is the essence of this method for developing meditative concentration. Meditative concentration is the state of mind that can maintain mindfulness without becoming corrupted by dullness or mental agitation and where a sense of joy and well-being are present. These qualities constitute meditative concentration. Asanga's *Sravakabhumi* says:

> What then is one-pointed mind or meditative concentration? Meditative concentration is a state where mindfulness is continuously maintained in a proper manner so that the mind is not corrupted by obstacles and there is a sense of joy and well-being within our stream of consciousness. That is samadhi.

When Asanga says we should continuously maintain mindfulness, he means we should apply whatever we have read or heard of the teachings. The *Sravakabhumi* also says:

> We need to meditate on all the teachings and instructions that we have been given by our teachers. We should then try to translate that into direct experience by practising meditation.

MAINTAINING THE TRANQUIL STATE

We need to adopt the right attitudes if we want the inspiration to sustain our meditation practice. We have to preserve four mental attitudes: 1) a conviction in the efficacy of meditation practice, 2) the inclination to continue with the practice, 3) perseverance in the face of difficulties encountered in the practice, and 4) the mental pliancy to resist becoming mired in opinionatedness and other constricting mental biases. If you lack these four mental attitudes, you will find it practically impossible to develop the inspiration to practise and will gradually give in to laziness and complacency. You must constantly sustain these four attitudes so that your interest does not wane over time.

Focus without distraction on the object of meditation with these attitudes foremost in your minds. If your mindfulness starts to slip, the object of meditation will be lost, so never forget to concentrate on that object. Then, give rise to awareness from within that state of mindfulness, because it is awareness that notices whether dullness or mental agitation is present. Without awareness, you have no way of knowing whether your mind is free from obstacles in a proper meditative state or whether your meditation has become diluted or corrupted by obstacles.

Mindfulness helps us stay with the object of meditation so that distractions do not arise. Awareness helps us perceive when obstacles have arisen in the mind and whether our meditative state has been corrupted by them. If obstacles do arise during meditation, apply relaxation and exertion or loosening and tightening of the mind. When the obstacles of dullness and mental agitation arise, your mind will be naturally overwhelmed by them if you do not apply sufficient exertion. When these obstacles have been pacified, do not persist with exertion and relaxation. Let the mind be and remain in a state of neutrality. The mind is decentralised when it is placed in a state of neutrality. You then remain in a state of equanimity, which is the essence of meditative concentration. The *Madhyantavibhanga* says:

> If we allow the mind to rest when we settle the mind,
> The second will be the cause of the first.
> Abandoning the obstacles of dullness and agitation
> And focusing on the meditation object
> Is how we attain meditative concentration.

Due to insufficient information, some meditators are misled into thinking that it is not essential to cultivate the four attitudes described above. They therefore start to meditate without much preparation. It is difficult for such people to apply mindfulness properly because they are totally open to the influences of distractions. Their feeble awareness has no ability to detect the obstacles of dullness and agitation in the mind. Even if they do recognise these obstacles, they see them as something to be abandoned and fail to appreciate the full potential of awareness. Such meditators have no idea what qualities meditative concentration should possess and naively assume that any comforting or uplifting meditative experiences are meditative concentration. They therefore mistake certain positive or pleasant meditative experiences for real meditation. They may even accidentally stumble on the real experience of meditative concentration, but they have no ability to appreciate or understand that state, and resort to various methods of controlling the mind, thus stirring it up so that mental agitation and other disturbing states arise. All these unwholesome experiences come about from a lack of skill and knowledge. It is important for beginners to avoid falling into these traps. They can be avoided by applying mindfulness properly, for at least then the mind will stay focused on the object of meditation for a certain period.

Some people are naturally predisposed to think too much. They need to use awareness to counter this tendency, because awareness gradually helps us to first detect gross forms of mental agitation and then to detect the more subtle forms of it. If mental agitation is your predominant concern, you should deal with it without any force. It is important to relax and loosen up, because even subtle forms of mental agitation begin to subside if you do. If dullness is your predominant problem, try to make your mind clearer and more lucid by tightening it through exertion.

We gradually overcome the obstacles of dullness and agitation by applying these two methods. An unsullied and authentic meditative concentration will then arise. When this authentic and uncontrived meditative concentration is present you don't need to apply methods to sustain it. Simply remain there and be aware of that state without doing anything. As soon as you do something to extend that meditative concentration it will be disrupted. When a proper meditative concentration arises, just remain in that state of neutrality.

You need to generate mindfulness with great intensity at the beginning. When that mindfulness is firmly established and there is no further possibility of your becoming distracted, you will not lose the object of meditation. If you become partially distracted, the power of your mindfulness has diminished. If you become totally distracted, you have lost your mindfulness completely. The secret of mindfulness practice is to keep regenerating its power so that you sustain a continuity of mindfulness. Before one episode of mindfulness has lost its power, you need to regenerate it, so that continuity is maintained. In other words, we maintain our mindfulness by refuelling its power so that the mindfulness of past mental states is transferred to subsequent mental states.

Awareness does not arise independently of mindfulness; it comes from mindfulness that is firmly established and continuously maintained. Awareness is the witness that differentiates various states of mind and notices the obstacles that arise. Nonetheless, from the Mahamudra perspective, we do not use awareness as the tool of analysis, as if it were just another meditation technique. Too much analysis is an obstacle to the attainment of one-pointed concentration. You need to apply some form of exertion to overcome the obstacles of dullness and agitation, but once those obstacles have been overcome, do not persist with these techniques. The second *Bhavanakrama* says:

> Once the mind has become settled, we only create distractions by continuing to exert ourselves in mind control methods.

The aim of tranquillity meditation is to give rise to equanimity. Once the methods of tightening or loosening have been applied, with the right amount of exertion, we should ease ourselves into the state of equanimity with a neutral attitude and completely let go of any form of exertion. The ability to remain in that state is meditative concentration. The second *Bhavanakrama* also says:

> When the mind is free of dullness and agitation and can remain focused on the meditation object, let go of any form of exertion toward those obstacles, and remain in a state of neutrality for as long as you can.

Beginners at the practice of mindfulness and awareness should not remain in a meditative state for too long, because it will be too much of a strain. Your mind will soon be overwhelmed by obstacles and you lose all ability to detect them. For that reason, even the practice of mindfulness and awareness should be conducted in short sessions with numerous breaks.

As you become familiar with the practice and have confidence in the application of mindfulness and awareness, you can gradually extend these periods of contemplation. There is no real time limit for your meditation sessions; just meditate for as long as your mind is not too upset by obstacles. When obstacles do arise, apply the methods of relaxation and exertion and take frequent short breaks in your practice sessions.

I have described the essence of tranquillity meditation practice from the point of view of Mahamudra in this chapter. The way to deal with obstacles to this meditation has already been described in detail in Book One so there is no need to comment further here.

STAGES IN REALISING THE SETTLED MIND

As you gain proficiency in tranquillity meditation, you will gradually experience various stages of meditative concentration. Tilopa says:

> The beginner's mind
> Is comparable to a waterfall.
> A more settled mind
> Is comparable to the flow of the Ganges.
> A mind that has attained meditative concentration
> Is like the merging of a river with the ocean.

While these three meditative stages are not necessarily confined to the practice of tranquillity meditation, we can understand the development of meditative concentration from this description. At the beginning, your mind is like a waterfall because any attempt to rest it is made extremely difficult by mind's instability. After you grow accustomed to the practice, your gross mental disturbances subside and your increased skill in exertion and relaxation enable you to relinquish those mental disturbances so that they no longer disrupt your meditation. This is comparable to the flow of the Ganges River, because even though there is movement, it does not cause any turbulence. At this stage, you may have the ability to rest in the natural state of mind, but every now and then your mind will wander in response to sensory impressions and you will be subject to mental agitation again. When you finally attain meditative concentration, all mental agitations subside. Even if subtle forms of agitation still arise, they will not disrupt your meditative state and will begin to subside naturally. This is comparable to the merging of a river with the ocean because thoughts, feelings, and emotions can no longer rob you of mindfulness and awareness, just as the oceans' waves cannot disturb the stillness of its depths. Everything that occurs in the mind will be self-liberated.

That is the general Mahamudra view of the stages in tranquillity meditation. Don't imagine this is in conflict with the nine stages of tranquillity found in the Sutric teachings. Nine stages are also attained through this Mahamudra method. They correspond to progress in Mahamudra meditation in the following manner: 1) 'resting the mind' is attained when the practitioner tries to concentrate on a particular meditation object, 2) 'continuous resting' is attained when our meditation practice no longer wavers from the object of meditation, 3) 'patch-like resting' is attained when we can regenerate mindfulness and go back to meditation object, 4) 'close placement' is attained when we can continuously regenerate mindfulness so that its power does not diminish, 5) 'pacification' is attained when we realise the benefits of meditative concentration, 6) 'subjugation' is attained when we realise the harmful effects of dullness and agitation and learn to pacify the mind through relaxation and exertion, 7) 'thorough subjugation' is attained when the more subtle mental agitations, such as craving and clinging, become pacified, 8) 'one-pointedness' is attained by dwelling in meditative concentration with sustained mindfulness and awareness by using the methods of relaxation and exertion, and 9) 'meditative absorption' is attained when we no longer need to apply any effort to remaining in the meditative state. We can therefore see that the Mahamudra and Sutric approaches to meditation are not in conflict, even though they are presented somewhat differently. The *Mahayanasutralamkara* says:

> When the mind is able to focus on the meditation object
> We should remain in that continuity without distraction.

The Sutric Mahayana teachings also describe six powers that come from meditation practice. These concepts can be used to illuminate Mahamudra teachings. We should not think that these six powers have no relevance to our practice and understanding. From the Mahamudra perspective, 1) the power of hearing means hearing the pith instructions on how to develop meditative concentration, 2) the power of contemplation is accomplished by cultivating what we learn from the pith instructions, 3) the power of mindfulness is accomplished through sustaining mindfulness during meditation, 4) the power of awareness is applied when we detect dullness and agitation, 5) the power of exertion sustains our interest in meditation and gives us the perseverance to accomplish it and 6) the power of familiarity is realised when we are skilled in the techniques and practices of Mahamudra meditation.

The sutras describe four methods for generating meditative concentration. These correlate to the Mahamudra approach to tranquillity meditation. According to Mahamudra: 1) the 'method of entering meditative concentration with exertion' applies to beginners who must invest great energy and effort into developing meditative concentration, 2) the 'method of entering into meditative concentration discontinuously' applies to meditators who are constantly overwhelmed by dullness and agitation through not having developed sufficient mindfulness and awareness to maintain the continuity of their meditation, 3) the 'method of entering meditative concentration without interruption' applies to meditators who have become more skilled in their practice so that it is no longer disrupted by obstacles when they arise, and 4) the 'method of entering meditative concentration in a spontaneous manner' applies to meditators who have mastered meditative stability and no longer need to apply effort to overcome the obstacles. We progress through the stages this way, according to the Sutric and Mahamudra traditions.

The first to sixth stages of tranquillity meditation have to be sustained by continuously generating the right mental attitudes, such as conviction, inclination, mindfulness, and so on. Once we have attained the seventh and eighth stages of tranquillity meditation, we become so accomplished at meditation that it is no longer necessary to generate those things. This stage quickly leads to the realisation of the ninth stage of meditative concentration. Becoming accomplished in the seventh and eighth stages of tranquillity means we only have to think about meditation practice for it to follow automatically. As soon as we sit down to meditate, our minds will automatically incline toward meditative experience without becoming distracted by obstacles of any kind. This is not so different to learning how to read. At the beginning, we have to really concentrate and apply effort to the reading process, just as our ability to sustain meditative concentration requires enormous energy. After we learn the basics of reading, we still need to maintain the intention to read until reading becomes an effortless process.

After you have persisted with tranquillity meditation for some time, the meditative experiences of bliss, luminosity, and non-conceptuality may arise during your meditation. They may even spill over into your post-meditation experiences. Meditators without sufficient learning may mistake this for the ultimate experience of meditative concentration. However, such experiences are not generally regarded as portents of concentration by the masters of the Practice Lineage.

How then should we view our meditative experiences? According to Sutric teachings, tranquillity is attained when the mind has become pliant. Until that is done, our meditative concentration will not go beyond the experience of one-pointedness in the sensual realm. The sutras list three realms of concentration that can be experienced in the course of meditation. These are the sensual realm, the form realm, and the formless realm. One-pointedness is attained when the mind has been made pliant and serviceable in the sensual realm, but that does not come anywhere near the meditative absorptions of the form or formless realms. The sutras therefore call this level of one-pointedness an approximate tranquillity. The *Sravakabhumi* says:

> When we attain the one-pointedness of the sensual realm, our mind and body are made more pliant, flexible, and serviceable, and the meditative experiences of bliss, luminosity, and non-conceptuality are established to the point that we take delight in the practice of meditation. On the physical level, the body is made more pliable and serviceable through breathing techniques that make the breath permeate through the body.

Once meditative experiences start to arise, we employ six techniques for stabilising our absorption. These are discrimination, inclination, privacy, joy, analysis, and application. We gradually attain the meditative absorption of the desire realm through these techniques and then we progress on to the experiences of the form and formless realms. The *Bhavanakrama* says:

> When the mind is in a neutral state, with an element of conceptual understanding and analysis remaining, it is in the state of non-interference, which is equated with the attainment of the first level of samadhi. At this level, the mind is free of excessive desires and cravings and we begin to abandon other defiling mental factors. On this first level of samadhi, we embody the mental factors of understanding, analysis, joy, and happiness. However, the factor of understanding begins to disappear from the mind on this first samadhi.

We attain the second stage of meditative absorption when understanding and analysis completely disappear and leave only joy and happiness in our minds. We attain the third stage of meditative absorption when the mind becomes free of the defilements that were still present on the second level and when the mental factor of happiness remains with equanimity, mindfulness, and awareness. We attain the fourth level of meditative absorption when we abandon the subtle attachments that lingered on the third level, leaving the mind in a state of complete neutrality without even the experiences of pleasure or pain, happiness or unhappiness.

That is how we apply the successive stages of meditative absorption. However, there is no need to go through all four stages. When the mind and body have been made pliable and serviceable, it is easy to remain in a state of meditative concentration, because both body and mind are free of all kinds of constricting factors, and we experience a sense of physical well-being. We can therefore remain in this meditative state for a long time. For example, our own master Gampopa remained in meditative absorption for thirteen days with a butter lamp on his head.

That was a brief description of the Sutric view of the stages of tranquillity meditation. However, from the perspective of Mahamudra and the Practice Lineage, we do not need to be overly concerned about these stages of meditative absorption. According to the Practice Lineage, the ability to stabilise the mind somewhat is regarded as merely the foot of meditation. Even if we have not fully mastered the technique of making the body and mind pliant, the ability to rest the mind with some ease, even if we still need to exert ourselves to do so, is considered a sufficient level of tranquillity. We can now proceed to the practice of insight meditation.

According to the Mahamudra tradition, we should not be exclusively devoted to tranquillity meditation but instead combine the practices of tranquillity and insight. There is no real conflict between the Mahamudra and Sutric approaches here. There may be differences in how meditative concentration is cultivated, but there is no difference in the meditation itself. The practices of mindfulness, awareness, and exertion are equally important in both approaches and they both agree that we will eventually develop the ability to enter into meditative concentration with ease. From the Mahamudra point of view, it is important to establish ourselves in tranquillity and then to move on to the practice of insight meditation. The *Bodhicharyavatara* says:

> Insight comes from establishing ourselves in tranquillity.

The masters of the Practice Lineage say, 'When the mind is not tranquil, insight will not arise.' They also say, 'If insight is cultivated first, mental stability will not arise, so it is important to have some grasp on tranquillity practice.'

THE PURPOSE OF REALISING TRANQUILLITY

Tranquillity meditation must be practised because both mundane and supramundane spiritual paths rely on it. On the mundane spiritual path, we pacify the defilements of the three realms of existence through tranquillity meditation and then give rise to insight. In the sensual realm, our thoughts and emotions are very rough and rugged, so we need certain antidotes to overcome them. In the form realm, we have overcome our more subtle defilements but we still need insight to eradicate them. If we are to attain the various stages of meditative concentration that correspond to the three realms of existence—such as the eight approximate meditative concentrations, the eight actual meditative concentrations, and so on—we must attain insight by traversing one level of absorption to the next. Tranquillity is necessary for this reason.

On the supramundane spiritual path, tranquillity is necessary for the development of the insight that understands the Four Noble Truths and selflessness. According to the Hinayana, we are only able to make use of insight once we have established ourselves in tranquillity meditation. According to the Mahayana, we are only able to apply insight into two-fold selflessness and non-duality once we have established ourselves in tranquillity meditation.

All kinds of mental capacities are developed from the practice of tranquillity meditation, such as the four feet of miraculous transformation, the eight levels of absorption in the form and formless realms, the eight methods of settling the mind, the eight methods of overpowering, and the ten expansions. We cultivate tranquillity meditation to develop these mental capacities. The first *Bhavanakrama* says:

> When the meditator has abandoned all the obstacles, meditative concentration will be realised and all kinds of psychic powers will be accomplished.

It also says:

> Meditators who can apply the methods of settling the mind will develop various abilities in miraculous transformation.

We gain these mental capacities by developing one-pointedness, by attaining meditative concentration, and the absorptions of the form and formless realms. Furthermore, it is only through the practice of tranquillity that we can overcome the gross forms of emotional conflict and the dualism of subject and object.

However, from the Mahamudra perspective, the real reason to do the practise of tranquillity meditation is to make it easier to practice insight meditation. We arrive at the peak of human excellence through the mental exercises of tranquillity meditation, but it is only through insight meditation that we can go beyond that.

If we wish to practise insight meditation, it is necessary to first practise tranquillity meditation. Most people find it extremely difficult to go straight into the practice of insight meditation. Without the foundation of tranquillity, insight meditation is comparable to a waterfall or a lamp in the wind because it is virtually impossible to rest the mind without a basis in tranquillity. A mind that cannot be still will also find it difficult to focus and it will be impossible to gain insight into ultimate reality without mental focus. The first *Bhavanakrama* says:

> The untamed mind is like a fast flowing river. A mind that can't stay still will find it impossible to gain insight into ultimate reality.

The second *Bhavanakrama* reiterates:

> Insight divorced from tranquillity makes a yogi's mind more distracted. Like a lamp flickering in the wind, it eventually goes out and will never sustain the illumination of wisdom.

You may ask, 'How long should we persevere with tranquillity meditation?' You should try to attain the first level of meditative absorption in the form realm, as previously stated. If that is not possible, it is sufficient to attain the one-pointed concentration of the sensual realm. Pawo says:

> People who persevere with meditation
> Without following the spiritual path
> May progress to the attainment
> Of the final stage of absorption in the formless realm.
> However, they have not embarked on a proper spiritual path
> So conflicting emotions and delusions will again arise
> To throw them back into the samsaric condition.
> People who have embarked on the spiritual path
> May not actually attain real stages of meditative concentration
> But can use the attainment of one-pointedness
> Combined with insight
> To transcend the samsaric condition altogether.

4

Insight Meditation

WHY INSIGHT MEDITATION IS NECESSARY

You should not be content to practise only tranquillity meditation because that will never result in liberation or enlightenment. You may be able to pacify and control your mental defilements and conflicting emotions through tranquillity meditation but you will never cut them off at the root and they will continue to exert an influence over you even when hidden from consciousness. Only insight meditation leads to genuine insight into the absence of an enduring and permanent self. This recognition of selflessness is the only thing that can permanently eradicate your delusions and conflicting emotions and liberate your mind from samsaric existence. The middle *Bhavanakrama* says:

> Yogis pacify their conflicting emotions through the practice of tranquillity meditation but these emotions will not be eradicated through tranquillity alone. Without insight, yogis will remain unaware of their delusions, which continue to operate at an unconscious level.

The *Samadhinirmocana Sutra* says:

> When we establish stability of mind through tranquillity,
> Conflicting emotions subside.
> When we practise insight meditation,
> Conflicting emotions and delusions are completely uprooted.

We should engage in the practice of insight meditation with the intention of eradicating all of our mental defilements and obscurations. Only insight has the power to cut these defilements at the root and thereby remove them completely. The *Samadhiraja Sutra* says:

> Worldly people cultivate themselves in tranquillity meditation;

> This may temporarily pacify their obscurations,
> But it will not give rise to insight.
> They will fail to perceive their own true nature,
> And their obscurations will rise again in due course.
> If tranquillity is coupled with insight meditation,
> You will come to understand that the nature of self
> And the nature of reality are devoid of essence.
> Only insight will deliver nirvana.

You might experience all the stages of meditative equipoise in tranquillity meditation, but these states will not give rise to insight into self. You will never abandon your misconceptions about the self through this type of meditation. As long as you retain that fundamental misconception, all the primary and secondary conflicting emotions will continue to arise and you will wander endlessly in the samsaric condition, propelled this way and that by unresolved delusions. On the other hand, if through insight meditation you can realise the nature of self has no enduring essence, you will be able to free yourselves from your samsaric delusions and as a result you will attain nirvana. There is no other cause for the attainment of nirvana. When we have gained this insight into the inherent selflessness of the self, all the root conflicting emotions are also eradicated.

THE PRELIMINARIES FOR INSIGHT MEDITATION

Before you begin the practice of insight meditation, you need to know what things you need to cultivate, to ensure the success and efficacy of your practice. The *Samadhinirmocana Sutra* says:

> Hearing, contemplating, and establishing the proper view are the causes for attaining insight.

The middle *Bhavanakrama* says:

> Apart from meditation, relying on someone with the necessary qualities, receiving instructions from them, and contemplating those instructions are the major causes of attaining insight.

'Someone with the necessary qualities' refers to somebody who is experienced in the practices of tranquillity and insight meditation and who has the ability to impart that knowledge to others. Someone who only knows what to do from reading texts about meditation may be quite learned, but he or she will not have the capacity to give meditation instructions to others. It is therefore important to seek out someone who not only knows about meditation but also practises it.

Much can be learnt from the teachings; there are an infinite number of them. Nonetheless, we should only concern ourselves with the teachings that contain the ultimate meaning. There is a danger in becoming lost in teachings with provisional meaning and then missing the essential points. We must also contemplate the definitive teachings. Simply hearing the instructions on the ultimate meaning is not enough for us to assimilate that meaning. We have to contemplate the teachings and then to translate that contemplation into inner experience because ultimate truth is not something we can understand through logic and analysis alone. The interpretive teachings mainly emphasise relative truth and convey that truth through words, sentences, and logical analysis. Definitive teachings emphasise the true meaning and concentrate on having a direct experience of emptiness. Emptiness is difficult to comprehend through conceptual processes. The *Aksayamatinirdesa Sutra* says:

> All the sutras that expound relative truth are interpretive in intent and all sutras that expound ultimate truth are definitive. The sutras that make use of a great deal of words, letters, and sentences belong to the interpretive category, while sutras that intimate the incontrovertible meaning of ultimate truth—which is profound and stretches language to its limits—belong to the definitive category.

What is meant by relative and ultimate truth? Sutras that expound relative concepts, such as self, sentience, consciousness, life essence, and so forth, contain the relative truth. Sutras that expound on selflessness, unoriginatedness, emptiness, and so forth reveal the true intent and contain the ultimate truth. The same sutra says:

> Many sutras subscribe to a superficial impression of the notion of self, sentience, agency, or enduring personhood. These teachings are called interpretive because they contain relative truth. From a higher perspective, self, sentience, agency, and personhood do not exist. Sutras that expound the concept of emptiness, signlessness, inexpressibility, unconditionedness, unoriginatedness, lack of enduring essence, lack of agency, and lack of enduring personhood contain ultimate truth. They reveal the true intent of the Buddhist teachings and are thus called definitive.

The *Samadhiraja Sutra* says:

> We can distinguish sutras belonging to one category
> From sutras belonging to the other,
> By knowing that all the sutras that discuss emptiness
> Belong to the definitive category,
> And all the sutras that discuss sentience and agency
> Belong to the interpretive category.

You should only concern yourself with teachings that contain the ultimate meaning because by hearing and contemplating such teachings we establish the proper view. The proper view is essential for the development of insight. Your understanding should be accurate and clear. This view is established on the basis of the authentic teachings and is the cause of attaining insight.

We must spend time listening to and contemplating these teachings. That is how we will learn to deal with the obstacles of dullness and agitation, control our sensory impressions, cultivate and sustain awareness, gain the benefits of a temperate appetite, and so on. All of these things come from assimilating the proper instructions. To rely upon the personal instructions of the guru is of utmost importance in the Practice Lineage because the view is established through transmissions we receive from our teachers. The *Hevajra Tantra* says:

> Coemergent wisdom is discovered
> Through the coming together
> Of our own application
> And the blessings of the teacher.

It also says:

> This self-cognising wisdom
> Goes beyond any verbal exchange between teacher and student.
> It is conveyed only when there is a meeting
> Of the student's attitude and the teacher's blessings.

THE DIFFERENT APPROACHES TO INSIGHT MEDITATION

There are many kinds of insight meditation, including the contemplation of impermanence, understanding the Four Noble Truths, and so on. In our Mahamudra tradition, we gain insight through understanding the lack of enduring essence of all things. We understand the nature of everything—both subject and object—through this insight. Cultivating insight into the non-substantiality of existence has many methods and the texts vary slightly in their descriptions. The *Abhidharmasamuccaya* talks about four types of insight, while the *Samadhinirmocana Sutra* mentions only three. But whether there are three or four types, they all have the same aim, to understand the insubstantiality of the self and the phenomenal world.

Many Indian panditas relied on the works of Nagarjuna and Asanga and on Madhyamaka forms of reasoning—the analysis of the one and the many or identity and difference—to understand things have no enduring essence. Madhyamaka logic analyses the phenomenal world to realise the emptiness of all existent things. However, this approach is based upon negation and runs the risk of procuring only a conceptual understanding of reality. It reduces reality to a universal concept and thereby fails to convey emptiness as an experiential reality that is beyond form and expression.

The Mahamudra tradition uses the mind to gain a direct experience of emptiness because it is practically impossible to realise emptiness through reasoning alone. Meditators may gain an overview of emptiness through analysis but that is only a proximate view; based on inference and purely conceptual. The Mahamudra view follows the methods of such great Indian siddhas as Saraha, Shavaripa, and Tilopa.

This method has more in common with the Yogacara than the Madhyamaka tradition, because the Yogacarans used insight into mind to understand ultimate reality. According to the Indian siddhas, we do not gain insight into emptiness through analysis or reasoning, we gain it through contemplating and assimilating the pith instructions on meditation and then having a direct experience of emptiness. Instead of analysing external objects, we contemplate the nature of mind directly. Insight into ultimate reality comes from recognising our own mind because emptiness is present in both subject and object. This method is the same as the one in Santipa's *Prajnaparamitopadesa*, Kamalashila's three *Bhavanakramas*, and Atisha's *Madhyamakopadesa*. I will now explain Mahamudra insight meditation.

THE RELEVANCE OF INSIGHT MEDITATION

This has two sections:

- The intrinsic nature of diverse mental perceptions
- Attaining certainty about the root of samsara and nirvana

§ The Intrinsic Nature Of Diverse Mental Perceptions

1. Why we gain insight into mind

The best way to perceive ultimate reality is to gain insight into mind, because the mind determines whether we remain in the bondage of samsara or find the freedom of nirvana. Everything we experience is dependent on mind because mind is the creator of all experience, including deluded and enlightened states. It is therefore essential to meditate on mind. The *Dharmasamgiti Sutra* says:

> Thus, the bodhisattva Vikrantamati said, 'The essence of all the teachings lies in understanding individual existent things are all dependent on mind. We need to depend on mind to pacify mind. Understand the nature of mind and you will attain knowledge of everything. It is of the utmost importance to cultivate insight into the nature of mind with gentleness and ease.'

If we gain an understanding of the nature of mind, we will understand everything because if mind is freed, everything is freed. The *Aryaratnamegha Sutra* says:

> Mind is the precondition for all phenomena. Only through understanding the nature of mind can we understand the nature of everything.

The *Atyayajnana Sutra* says:

> Understanding the nature of mind is the attainment of wisdom. Attaining wisdom is to become enlightened. Enlightenment can only be found in the nature of mind.

Saraha says:

> When the mind is bound
> We remain in a state of bondage.
> When the mind is free
> We are liberated from samsara.

He also says:

> If mind comes to understand its own nature
> It will automatically become free from distorted views
> And attain great bliss.
> This is the supreme siddhi.

Tilopa says:

> Understanding the nature of mind
> Is like cutting down a tree at its root.
> Trying to gain spiritual insight through any other means
> Is like cutting off the tree's branches.

We must endeavour to gain insight into the nature of mind, for this is the root of both bondage and freedom. According to Shantideva, only suffering will result from failing to understand the nature of mind. There is no better spiritual practice than understanding mind. The *Bodhicharyavatara* says:

> If we do not understand the nature of mind,
> Suffering will be the only result.
> Even if we have strong desires to attain happiness,
> There is no better practice than understanding the mind.

It also says:

> I make the commitment to train my mind
> And guard my mind with vigilance;
> That is the real practice of asceticism.
> What use are ascetic practices that torture the body?

Certain logicians and intellectuals object to this emphasis on mind and argue that if it were truly possible to attain enlightenment by becoming intimate with our minds in meditation, without using analysis or reasoning, all sentient beings should attain enlightenment without difficulty, especially when the innate nature of an ordinary being's mind is said to be no different to the mind of an enlightened being. This criticism of the Practice Lineage is quite unjustified. It reflects a lack of knowledge about our practices. These logicians and intellectuals mistakenly believe a conceptual understanding of emptiness is something laudable and that the deluded mind is something to be abandoned.

If these logicians and intellectuals had a broader knowledge of Mahamudra literature, they would understand that the nature of the mind is no different to the nature of emptiness. In fact, the nature of mind *is* emptiness. Consequently, when we contemplate the nature of mind, we automatically contemplate emptiness, because they are not separate. Likewise, when we gain insight into the nature of mind, we gain insight into ultimate reality. This point will be elaborated on further in the ensuing chapters so I will say no more here.

When meditators assert that the nature of an ordinary being's mind is no different from that of an enlightened being, they are not making an arbitrary statement. If the logicians and intellectuals would only examine the relevant texts, they would quickly find doctrinal support for these claims. The *Lankavatara Sutra* says:

> Buddha is nothing other than a mind reversed
> By abandoning conceptual proliferation.
> That mind of enlightenment
> Enables us to perceive ultimate reality.

The *Kalachakra-mulatantra* says:

> The mind of ordinary sentient beings is uncorrupted and luminous;
> Has not come into being from the beginning,
> Has never arisen, does not persist, and cannot cease.
> It is the same as the mind of the buddhas;
> Having not been brought about by causes and conditions.

The *Tantrasamgraha* says:

> All sentient beings are enlightened insofar as buddhahood is discovered within the minds of ordinary beings.

The *Vajradakini Tantra* says:

> When mind comes to recognise its own nature
> We realise that we have been awakened from the beginning.

The *Hevajra Tantra* says:

> Buddha is not found outside ourselves.
> Buddha is found within the depth of our own consciousness.

The *Dvikramatattvabhavana-nana mukhagama* says:

> Individually existing things are all conditioned by mind itself,
> To realise this is the same as buddhahood!

These quotations from authoritative texts support our claim that the nature of mind in ordinary beings is no different to the enlightened ones. According to Mahamudra, insight meditation is the method by which we gain insight into the nature of mind because that is how we realise that the nature of mind has been pure from the beginning. It has never been corrupted by the defilements and obscurations of mind. The *Rastrapalapariprccha Sutra* says:

When we meditate on the nature of mind,
Everything is revealed as empty of essence.

The *Vajrapanjara* says:

Motivated by bodhichitta,
We meditate on the nature of mind
And attain enlightenment.
This is the sacred truth of buddhahood!

It also says:

When we meditate on the inseparability
Of emptiness, awareness, and compassion;
We embody the Buddha, Dharma, and Sangha.

We can find many statements in the tantras and commentaries that propose contemplation on mind as the best method for achieving enlightenment. These methods are not totally foreign to the Sutric approach. Two kinds of bodhichitta are discussed in the Mahayana teachings: relative bodhichitta (the cultivation of compassion toward all beings) and absolute bodhichitta (synonymous with buddha nature, nature of mind, emptiness, and ultimate reality).

2. The nature of mind is the basis for everything

(i) Scriptures that deal with this subject

Some people might wonder whether there is any textual basis for the Mahamudra view. What texts say that everything in the phenomenal world is dependent on mind so it is therefore possible to cultivate insight by contemplating the nature of mind and recognising it to be devoid of enduring essence? To ease this concern, we will quote from some of the authoritative texts that endorse the practice of cultivating insight by contemplating the nature of mind. The *Sutralamkara* says:

We must first realise nothing exists independently of mind.
We must then realise that even mind is devoid of enduring essence.
This is how we transcend the duality of subject and object
And dwell in the sphere of ultimate reality.

The *Bodhichittavivarana* says:

Seekers of the truth should first realise
That everything is contingent on mind

And then develop the insight
That reveals mind to be devoid of essence
And experience to be conditioned by mind.
Ordinary people without sufficient knowledge
Fear mind is the source of all evil, and want to abandon it.
But the nature of mind is the same as ultimate reality.
The Yogacara school sees diverse appearances
As the manifestation of mind.
Even the three aspects of reality
Are differentiated according to the structures of mind.
Mahayana practitioners should understand
That realising mind to be devoid of enduring essence
Is the same as realising the non-duality of subject and object.
The nature of mind is unconditioned and uncaused.
This very mind is therefore the mind of enlightenment.

The first *Bhavanakrama* says:

> Meditators should realise that the triple world is dependent on the mind. Mind is the key that unlocks the mystery of ultimate reality; the essential nature of physical and mental phenomena. Developing deep insight into the nature of mind will automatically enable you to penetrate into the nature of all things. You shouldn't imagine that the nature of mind is some kind of substantial entity. Just as the external world appears to have independent existence, when in reality it is devoid of substance, the mind gives the appearance of having an independent existence until properly investigated, and then it is found to have no enduring essence at all. By understanding the mind in that way, we come to understand the nature of the material world.

Many comments of this kind can be found in meditation texts. This demonstrates that the Mahamudra method, which uses the mind to gain insight into ultimate reality, has ample textual support in the conventional Buddhist schools. Mahamudra is not an unconventional approach and cannot be said to contradict established tradition.

(ii) The actual stages of insight meditation

The aim of tranquillity meditation is to focus the mind without distraction on a chosen meditation object and it emphasises overcoming conceptuality. When you are ready to embark on insight meditation practice, you should maintain the mental quietude you established through tranquillity meditation so that your mind is more resilient and perspicuous, and then employ discriminating wisdom to examine your mind. While tranquillity meditation is known as 'the meditation of rest,' insight meditation is known as 'analytical meditation' because it uses discriminating wisdom to gain insight into the nature of mind. According to the Sutric tradition, the object of analysis is normally the notion of self. In the Mahamudra context, the object of analysis is mind. The way we carry out this analysis is similar in both traditions. The physical posture is also the same as it is during tranquillity meditation. Keep your eyes open and hold your gaze without excessive blinking. Saraha says:

> The best form of yogic practice
> Is to keep our eyes open
> Without blinking in rapid succession.

He also says:

> Hindus roll their eyeballs upward and look into the sky,
> Shravakas cast their gaze downwards and focus on the ground,
> Tantric practitioners hold their gaze straight ahead.

These comments clarify the importance of a proper gaze during meditation. Remain in the state of rest with your gaze fixed straight ahead, focus your mind on itself and then examine the mind by asking the following questions: What is mind? Is mind an entity of any kind? Does mind have colour or shape? Is mind located somewhere? Is mind dependent upon anything? Does mind have some kind of independent existence? How can mind be pinpointed exactly? How can mind be identified? What qualities and attributes does mind have?

We should carry this analysis further and examine whether the mind has any shape, colour, or locality. Does mind depend on the external world for its existence? Does mind depend on our body? If you think mind resides in your body, ask yourself: Does mind reside in a certain part of the body? Does mind pervade the extremities of the body? If the mind appears to pervade the entire body, try to determine how it does so. Does mind intermingle with the physical body? Does mind stay completely separate from the physical body? Does mind stop at the skin? Does mind expand beyond our physical boundaries into the external world?

Try also to identify the nature of mind as emptiness and ask yourself: How can I identify the luminosity of mind? Examine the teaching that says the nature of mind has the qualities of being empty yet luminous. What does it mean to say that the nature of mind is emptiness? Does it mean the nature of mind is vacuous like space that is unoccupied by anything? What does this concept of emptiness mean? The same sort of analysis should be conducted into the aspect of luminosity. What does it mean to say that the nature of mind has the aspect of luminosity? Does mind illuminate in the same way as the sun and the moon? Does mind illuminate in the manner of a lamp?

Analyse the mind in this way to the point of exhaustion. It is not sufficient to be told about emptiness or to read about it in books, you need to practise this kind of analysis and discover it through your own experience. You have to analyse mind until you come to a point of incontrovertible certainty. The more you examine the mind in terms of emptiness and luminosity, the more your understanding of mind will increase because all kinds of misconceptions will start to fall away through this method. You will gradually gain a proper insight into the nature of mind and a genuine understanding of emptiness and luminosity. Maintain your mindfulness while doing these analyses and make use of discriminating wisdom.

This type of analysis is not like ordinary thinking; it is a specific type of meditative thinking. You may come to a point where you can't fully articulate your experience, because it is unlike any of your preconceived notions. Emptiness cannot be identified as this or that. When you reach a point in your practice where you recognise this; it portends advancement in your meditation. It is essential to focus on that awareness at this point. Saraha says:

> Analyse your own mind
> With total mindfulness.
> Nothing will be revealed to you
> If your mind is distracted.

The *Bhavanakrama* says:

> Analysis carried out from within the stability of tranquillity meditation will give birth to insight and produce incontrovertible, authentic, indubitable wisdom.

(iii) How this compares with the original exposition

Certain people have criticised the practice of identifying the nature of mind. They argue that we cannot probe into the nature of mind when the mind is immaterial. They say that looking for the nature of mind is not like looking for material things, which can be identified and discovered, so this exercise is pointless. Again, this criticism reveals a lack of understanding about insight meditation. These critics have not understood the nature of mind in the ultimate sense. The importance of this practice is supported by various textual citations. The *Ratnakuta* says:

> Identify the nature of mind if you wish to attain insight.

The *Ratnacudapariprccha Sutra* says:

> Meditators must identify the nature of mind.

The *Trayastrimsat-parivarta* says:

> Wise ones should seek out the path of self-discovery
> Which consists of looking for the nature of mind.
> Realise mind and the nature of mind are devoid of essence,
> For both the mind that is sought and the mind that is seeking
> Lack any enduring essence.

These quotations from authoritative texts help us appreciate the importance of this type of practice. The understanding that mind is not a material entity and therefore imperceptible to the senses, will not give rise to insight into the nature of mind. The mind has to be looked into and analysed. We have to probe deeper and deeper, further and further, until we come to realise the nature of mind is emptiness. The *Bhavanakrama* quotes the *Ratnamegha Sutra*:

> When we engage in contemplation, the mind generates various thoughts and produces all kinds of concepts and ideas, which in turn latch onto a variety of things. We need to realise that the empirical mind—which thinks, anticipates, and remembers—is empty of enduring essence. If we go beyond those thoughts, concepts and ideas, and look into the nature of mind, we will discover that it is also empty of inherent existence.

The *Dharmadhatu-prakrtysambheda-nirdesa* of the *Ratnakuta* says:

> Buddha: 'Oh Noble Ones, you should analyse the mind to determine whether it has the characteristics or attributes of the colours white, red, yellow, blue, or green. Is it like a crystal? Is it by nature pure or impure, permanent or impermanent, material or immaterial, eternal or non-eternal?'
> Monks: 'Oh Venerable One, the nature of mind is immaterial. It cannot be reified with qualities, characteristics and attributes. It does not dwell anywhere. It cannot be grasped. It cannot be shown.

> It has no appearance, no origin. It is imperceptible.'
> Buddha: 'Oh Noble Ones, can this nature of mind—which is immaterial, unable to be revealed, groundless and imperceptible—be found within, without, or somewhere in between?'
> Monks: 'No sir, this is not so.'
> Buddha: 'Oh Noble Ones, because the nature of mind is devoid of these characteristics and attributes, it does not occupy space or time, is not material, does not dwell anywhere, cannot be perceptible, and is inseparable from ultimate reality. However, this does not mean it is divorced from ultimate reality, for they are identical.'

The *Ratnakuta Sutra* says:

> Whenever lust, hatred, or ignorance arises in the mind, you should relate them to the three times. If we probe further into the nature of these experiences, you see that you cannot understand these mental states in relation to the past, because the past is no more. You cannot pin down these present mental states, because this mind is unstable and elusive. You cannot understand them in relation to future experiences, because they have not occurred yet. The nature of mind cannot be perceived, determined or revealed, because it has no perceptible form, and lacks intelligibility.

As you pursue this exercise, you will realise that the past is insubstantial because it has ceased to exist and only remains in our fading memories. The future is insubstantial because it has not yet come to be and the present moment is insubstantial because it is fleeting and unstable. When you probe more deeply into the experiences of your deluded consciousness and realise their insubstantiality in relation to past, present, and future, your delusions of lust, anger, and ignorance will weaken. The *Ratnakuta Sutra* also says:

> Buddha: 'Oh Mahakasyapa, the nature of mind cannot be found within, without, or somewhere in between. It has no determinate characteristics. It is atemporal because it cannot be located within the three times. Something that is imperceptible and does not dwell anywhere cannot be shown to another person.'

Again, it says:

> Buddha: 'Oh Mahakasyapa, the nature of mind is not found when we look for it. It cannot be found in the five psychophysical constituents, eighteen elements, or six sense fields. When we examine our

> stream of consciousness, we may wonder where the mind comes from and think that it arises from perceived images. Contemplate those mental images and try to determine whether they are distinct from mind or the same as mind. If they are different, the holistic realm is divided into subject and object. If they are the same, the mind has objectified parts of itself and its overall subjectivity has been lost.'

The *Tzu gnas rin po che mdo* says:

> We cannot discover the nature of mind in a literal sense. If that were possible, the nature of mind could be found in the history of the psychophysical constituents or interactions between the senses and their inputs. We do not find the nature of mind in any of these places.

When you pursue this line of inquiry, you might think, 'The nature of mind exists because mental images exist.' Extend your inquiry further by looking at the relationship between that mental image and the nature of mind itself, to see what kind of relationship actually exists between them. Ask yourself whether they are the same or different. The *Vairocanabhisambodhi* says:

> Buddha Vajradhara: 'Oh Guhyapati, how should a seeker analyse and identify the nature of mind? Does it exist as an entity with shape, colour, or form? In what way is it related to the physical body, feelings, concepts and dispositions? What is the locus of mind? Is it mysteriously linked with the self, as a third party to self and other? We must analyse the mind in this way to determine how it arises in our existential mode.'

The same text says:

> Buddha Vajradhara: 'Oh Guhyapati, understand that not even enlightened beings or arhats who have overcome internal conflicts of mind have been able to apprehend the nature of mind and they never will. Why is this so? The nature of mind in its intrinsic purity is not something we can apprehend as this or that. It does not dwell anywhere or occupy time and space. Oh Guhyapati, the nature of mind has never been understood in the conventional sense, even by the enlightened ones and it never will. It cannot be understood in the sense of knowing, because it is not an entity, and has no determinable characteristics. The nature of mind is devoid of primary

> and secondary qualities; it is not yellow, red, white, long, short, round, square, and so on. It is not even partial to the concept of gender insofar as it has nothing to do with being male, female, or androgynous. It cannot be restricted to any type of sentient creature, in either the human realm or the realms of ghosts, spirits, demons, demi-gods, or angels. The nature of mind is all-pervasive and cannot be confined to one class of sentient creatures.
> Therefore, Oh Guhyapati, the nature of mind is not found in the sensual realm, form realm, or formless realm. It does not belong to this world or any higher order of reality. It is not revealed as better in one state of embodiment or another. The nature of mind cannot be found in any of these places because it is like space. It goes beyond the thinking mind and deluded consciousness. It cannot be found in the visual organs or within the body, consciousness, or even mental activities themselves. Why is this so? The nature of mind is like space, devoid of all characteristics and transcendent to mental activities, thought patterns, and conceptual notions.'

Statements such as these can be found in the Sutric and Tantric literature of Mahayana Buddhism. In brief, these quotations all emphasise that the nature of mind is indeterminate in the conventional sense. It has no characteristics, such as primary and secondary qualities of colour, shape, location, appearance, or temporal and spatial reality. After thoroughly examining the nature of mind in this way, you will determine the impossibility of defining it. When you realise the utter futility of trying to identify it, you will also understand that the nature of mind cannot be reduced to other entities or existent things. You must investigate the nature of mind in relation to what you perceive through your senses and through what you understand about the structures of consciousness. When you carry out this analysis, you will eventually realise that you cannot apprehend the nature of mind in the same way that you apprehend sensory objects or inner mental states. The nature of mind is more comparable to space. The *Bodhichittavivarana* says:

> Words like 'nature of mind'
> Are only verbal designations.
> They do not refer to anything in particular.
> There is nothing to refer to;
> Even the designation has no reality of its own.
> Even enlightened beings have not been able to
> Identify it its all-encompassing nature.

> It is devoid of any semblance of thinghood
> Beyond the notion of apprehender and apprehended
> And categories of male, female, and androgyny.
> In brief, since the nature of mind is devoid of all this
> It cannot even be intuited by the wisdom of the buddhas.
> The nature of mind has no identifying characteristics,
> So what mental faculty could enable
> Even an enlightened being to apprehend it?

The *Siksamuccaya* says:

> The nature of mind is difficult to grasp. It is not even an object of comprehension for buddhas. When we see that all external methods for gaining insight into the nature of mind are inadequate, we understand that the practice of analysing and contemplating this nature is in keeping with the practice of all enlightened beings. The nature of mind can be realised through this practice of inquiry but cannot be proven through empirical evidence, sensory validation, or reasoning.

It also says:

> Because the nature of mind does not resemble any of the things that we know of in the phenomenal world, we cannot identify it as this or that. It is devoid of all characteristics and attributes, having the same nature as space itself. While the nature of mind is not different from ultimate reality, a proper understanding of this is extremely difficult to grasp.

(iv) How to determine the nature of mind

As we examine the nature of mind, we will eventually arrive at the conclusion that it cannot be comparable to things in the external world or the workings of deluded consciousness. The nature of mind is recognised to be without definable characteristics, conceptual determinations, spatial position, or any dependence on anything else. We then perceive the nature of mind as equivalent to space. The *Mahakarunanirdesa Sutra* says:

> The nature of mind is like space
> Therefore, we should contemplate it
> As expansive as space
> And arising in the same way as space.

The *Maitreyaparipraccha Sutra* says:

> Maitreya: 'How should we examine the nature of mind?'
> Buddha: 'As devoid of all empirical determinations and attributes, just like space.'

The *Vairocanabhisambodhi* says:

> The nature of mind is like the nature of space because it is not polluted by the empirical determinations of mind.

Numerous textual references compare the nature of mind to space.

Saraha says:

> We should try to understand the nature of mind
> By regarding it as the same as space.

Savari says:

> Once the root of deluded consciousness has been severed
> The nature of mind will be revealed to be the same as space.

To say that the nature of mind is like space is to say that the probing, inquiry and analysis of insight meditation, when fully carried out, will make thoughts and concepts naturally cease. Up to this point, we have been using thoughts and concepts to discover the nature of mind, but when we exhaust all possibilities, non-conceptual insight will be the result. The use of thoughts and concepts in this context is called *prajna* or 'discriminating awareness' because it leads to insight. This process is compared to gazing into space, because everything within our visual field is undifferentiated expansive space, without any sensory objects. Tilopa says:

> When you gaze into the middle of space
> All sensory stimuli cease to impact on mind.
> When you use concepts and analysis
> To look into the nature of mind,
> Concepts will subside
> And give way to enlightenment.
> Mist and clouds do not go or dwell anywhere
> Because space has no position.
> Similarly, once the nature of mind has been determined,
> The thoughts and concepts that were part of analysis
> Naturally subside into that very nature.

He also says:

> Ordinary people say that space is empty
> But this is just a convenient expression.
> Space is neither empty nor non-empty
> Because it has no characteristics or attributes.
> The nature of mind is said to be luminous
> But this is also a convenient expression.
> Mind itself has no definable characteristics or attributes.
> Therefore, mind is said to be like space.

Savari says:

> If we try to understand space in relation to centre and periphery,
> We will soon realise such notions do not apply.
> When we look for the nature of mind
> We discover the same thing
> Because the nature of mind lacks definable characteristics.
> When we practise looking for the nature of mind
> But can discover nothing;
> That is the greatest discovery!
> We see that there is nothing to be seen.

We can therefore use thoughts and concepts to realise the nature of mind. This method is compared to using two sticks to start a fire. The *Kasyapa-pariprccha Sutra* says:

> When we rub two sticks together to produce sparks
> The resultant flames consume the sticks that gave them life.
> In the very same way, the concepts of discriminating awareness
> Lead to a non-conceptual realisation of the nature of mind.

If we employ concepts by applying discriminating awareness, it will eventually lead to the non-conceptual, intuitive, non-dual experience of the nature of mind. The analogy between the nature of mind and space should not be taken too far however, because there is a difference between them. Although the analogy is helpful, we cannot say the nature of mind and space are the same, because while the nature of mind is devoid of characteristics and attributes just as space is, it also has the quality of being luminous. This is known as self-cognising awareness. The nature of mind is apprehended through this self-cognising awareness because there is no difference between the nature of mind and self-cognising awareness. While the nature of mind is not an entity that can be apprehended through some faculty of mind, it can be directly realised as the discovery of self-cognising awareness. This discovery cannot be compared to our normal experience. It is inexpressible, incommunicable, and impossible to formulate. The *Samadhinirmocana* says:

> It would help us to realise that self-cognising awareness
> Is without characteristics or attributes.
> It is indefinable, beyond concepts, and intellectual formulations,
> And transcends the notions of existence and non-existence.

The *Samdhivyakarana Sutra* says:

> The nature of mind is all-pervasive,
> It cannot be located and therefore can't be understood
> As existing within, without or in between.
> Nor can we say it is permanent or impermanent;
> It can only be realised through self-cognising awareness.

The *Hevajra Tantra* says:

> Self-cognising awareness
> Can be realised directly
> But it cannot be formulated
> Or expressed through conceptual frameworks.

It also says:

> The realisation of self-cognising wisdom is great bliss.
> That is how we attain enlightenment.

The nature of mind is realised through self-cognising wisdom, which is identical with the nature of mind. We must understand that such an experience is inexpressible. It is also the source of unchanging bliss. When the phrase 'self-cognising wisdom' is used, we should be wary of any duality that may appear to be involved. When the nature of mind is probed, analysed, and discovered to be completely devoid of all characteristics and attributes, that realisation is called self-cognising wisdom. It is not other than the luminous aspect of the nature of mind. This experience cannot be compared to normal types of cognition, such as recognising something through the senses or apprehending something through conceptual categories. There is no difference between the cogniser and the cognised. Tilopa says:

> Self-cognising wisdom
> Is free from any empirical determinants.

You have to experience it for yourself through self-examination.
I, Tilopa, cannot reveal anything to you.

The dangers of misinterpreting your meditative experiences cannot be over-emphasised. For example, the experience of stability in tranquillity meditation can be mistaken for a realisation of the nature of mind. Various other experiences may also arise during meditation due to your karmic imprints and unconscious processes, and you may mistake these for a realisation of the nature of mind. You may also experience calm and lucidity during deep states of relaxation, where the mind is devoid of mental activities and rests in spaciousness and emptiness, and you might jump to the conclusion that this is the nature of mind. All these pitfalls have one thing in common; you have not developed sufficient understanding of what the nature of mind really means.

These experiences are all contingent upon causes and conditions. Certain meditative experiences are produced by causes and conditions and you either become attached to those experiences or conceptually classify them as something, such as the realisation of the nature of mind. When you have a genuine realisation of the nature of mind through self-cognising wisdom, it is not conditioned or dependent upon any experiences as such. Thus, the nature of mind must be viewed as devoid of all characteristics.

The expression 'perceiving the nature of mind' does not mean we can actually perceive anything, as we do in our meditative experiences. When we realise the nature of mind, there is no concept of a perceiver or perceived; there is no differentiation at all. There is no difference, even to the size of a hair tip, between the perceiver and perceived. The nature of mind is not contingent upon anything and so cannot be contingent upon meditative experiences. It would therefore be wise to keep the following advice in mind. The *Prajnaparamita-samcayagatha* says:

Ordinary people claim to have seen space.
We should reflect on this and ask ourselves:
'What does it mean to see space?'
We may also say, for the sake of convenience,
'I have perceived the nature of mind.'
But in reality there is nothing to be perceived.

Saraha says:

The nature of mind is pure, like space, from the beginning.
We should gaze upon it again and again,
Until we realise there is nothing to be seen.

Savari says:

> We find that all experiences
> Whether subjective or objective
> Have no essence once we look for them.
> That which cannot be found is ultimate reality.
> Unconfined by the concepts of past, present, or future
> Reality is unchanging and its nature is great bliss.

He also says:

> Seeing the nature of mind means seeing yourself
> When I'm left alone to look at myself
> Even I am nowhere to be seen.
> When there is no one to see and nothing to be seen
> That is inexpressible.
> Since it is inexpressible,
> No one can understand it.

Naropa says:

> The luminous nature of mind
> Is devoid of all essence.
> You will not find an essence,
> Even to the size of the tip of a hair.

Beginners should at least try to develop some understanding of the nature of mind through the practices of mindfulness, awareness, and confidence. The *Ting 'dzin dam pa'i mdo* says:

> When we let the mind rest in its own natural state,
> We will gain experiences that cannot be defined.

Tilopa says:

> The nature of mind is undifferentiable from ultimate reality.
> Our meditative experiences may be fleeting in the beginning
> But they should be cultivated further,
> Through the practices of mindfulness and awareness.

Maitripa says:

> According to the Tantric tradition
> The workings of mind are determined by the circulation of energy.
> Mind is without any substance of its own.

3. Mind's dynamic manifestations

(i) Realising all appearances are product of mind

Ordinary people, who are untutored in examining the nature of mind, instinctively cling to the notion of an objective world as something that exists independently of their minds. They believe the world and its contents have their own inherent existence, which is unaffected by our sensory impressions and quite distinct from the conceptual categories of our minds. This is a completely distorted view of the world, for in reality, the external world is nothing but a construction of our minds. The *Lankavatara Sutra* says:

> The coming together of our conceptual categories
> And latent karmic tendencies
> Constructs our perceptions of an autonomous world.
> In reality, the world is completely dependent on the mind
> And can be perceived and understood only through mind.
> No material world exists apart from mind.

The *Vajrapanjara* says:

> The sensory world of form, sound, taste, smell, and touch,
> All this is determined by the mind itself.
> Realise this world that we perceive through the senses
> Depends upon the mind.
> The Buddha did not say otherwise.

At this point, we may wonder, 'Why do we have this inveterate tendency to believe in an external world with an objective, independent, self-sufficient existence?' This instinctive belief is due to ignorance about the nature of mind. When that primordial comprehension of mind and its nature is absent, we give rise to the fundamental duality of subject and object. Once we have created this basic split, we cling to the notions of self and other with great determination. We view anything other than ourselves as completely different to and independent of ourselves. Because of this fundamental split, we react to our belief in an independent and objective world with extreme attraction or aversion and all kinds of psychic imprints and latent tendencies are created in the storehouse consciousness. The *Lankavatara Sutra* says:

> When the karmic imprints are violently activated
> Belief in the duality of subject and object is strengthened.
> Yet no external world exists independent of mind.
> To believe in such a world is to distort reality.

The *Vajrapanjara* says:

> Since beginningless time
> Ordinary sentient beings have clung to the notion
> Of an ordinary perceptible world.
> But the external world is a manifestation of mind
> And is dependent on the structures of mind.

Again, we may wonder, 'How does the physical appearance of the world seem to have such an enduring and impenetrable solidity?' As long as our ignorance continues we will think a material world exists of its own accord and independently of the mind, and that it has an enduring essence that is unchanging, immutable, and real. A combination of ignorance, delusion, and psychic imprints creates this belief. We cannot perceive the insubstantiality of the material world so we think that things like rocks and mountains exist of their own accord. But this is not the characteristic of the world as such. Saraha uses the following analogy:

> When cold winds gust over a river
> The river's surface gradually turns to ice.
> In a similar way, our ignorance
> And the violent activities of our karmic impressions
> Form a fixed and solid impression of the world.

Saraha's explanation employs a technique called 'marrying the example to the meaning.' In any case, just because something appears to be solid, that does not make it so. For example, a person suffering from cataracts may perceive strands of hair falling from the sky, but this does not mean there are actually any hairs in space. The mind creates the world in the same way. This is not an exact analogy however. A person's normal perception is restored when their cataracts are removed but the external world does not cease to exist when you realise it has no enduring essence.

The external world isn't completely created by individual minds. It also exists in relation to our collective karma and to that extent it must remain. Realisation of the nature of mind does not entail some revelation that the external world is non-existent. It entails realising that the nature of mind and the external world are inextricably bound.

You must develop a proper understanding of this relationship between the mind and the world, while reminding yourself that conceptual understanding alone will never rid you of your mistaken beliefs or eradicate your karmic traces and dispositions. Virupa says:

Simply having a conceptual understanding of how things are
Will not give rise to non-dual experience
Any more than knowing that a person has cataracts
Will make the disease go away.
The person must receive treatment.

An experience of non-duality will not make your perception of the external world cease; it will simply ensure you are no longer subject to the distortions and mistaken beliefs that afflicted you in the past. The *Vajrapanjara* says:

There is no such thing as external appearances,
They are all just manifestations of the mind.
You must realise the nature of mind.

The *Bodhichittavivarana* says:

The imaginary, the relative, and the thoroughly established
Are all imbued with the same reality.
To understand that is to understand the nature of mind.

(ii) Realisation that brings insight into all appearances

Saraha says:

Mind is the king of all creation,
Both samsara and nirvana are created by it.
So even they must be understood in relation to the nature of mind.

The root of all of our experiences in the conditioned world is mind itself. Everything that we can experience, both internally and externally, is a product of mind. He also says:

All experience arises from the space-like nature of mind;
Our experience of sublime nirvana
And our bondage in samsaric existence
Both arise from mind itself.

A sutra says:

To understand the nature of mind
Is to understand the mind's lack of enduring essence
Because the nature of mind is luminous and empty.

The nature of mind is the basis of all experience whether it is good or bad.

When we realise this we automatically realise the emptiness of the phenomenal world, because we will understand the nature of all that has arisen in the mind. Another sutra says:

> To realise the nature of one thing
> Is to realise the nature of all things.

Aryadeva also says:

> Someone that has insight into one thing
> Automatically gains insight into all things.

Aryadeva's *Catusataka* says:

> When we establish the right view about one thing
> We automatically have that view regarding everything else
> Because the emptiness we discover through insight into one thing
> Is the nature of every single individual thing.

When we realise the nature of any single form to be emptiness, we will automatically realise this to be the same nature that pervades everything. When we determine emptiness by seeing an object through the visual sense organs, we do not then need to go through the same experience with all the other senses one by one. That single visual experience of emptiness will be automatically transferred to all the other senses. Atisha's *Satyadvaya* says:

> There are no divisions in emptiness.
> It is undifferentiated and all-encompassing.

It is important to determine the nature of mind; once we have determined it there will be no further need to worry about all the things that arise in the mind and determine their nature one by one. The *Samadhiraja Sutra* says:

> When you understand the nature of mind
> And apply that understanding to everything in the mind
> All phenomena become pure like space.
> One single insight causes the comprehension of everything.

When we realise the true condition of one thing, we will understand the true condition of all things. The essence of emptiness is understood as the unceasing manifestation of the sensory world. When it is said, 'understanding the nature of mind gives rise to an understanding of everything that arises from the mind,' this does not mean that things will stop manifesting when the nature of mind is recognised. It means that the nature of the thoughts, concepts, and emotions that arise in the mind is inseparable from emptiness. There is the unity of appearance (what arises in the mind) and its nature (emptiness). The *Bodhichittavivarana* says:

> The nature of brown sugar is sweetness
> The nature of fire is heat.
> Just so, everything that arises in the mind,
> Has the nature of emptiness.

It also says:

> Emptiness is the same as the manifestation of the sensory world
> And the sensory world is the same as emptiness.
> We cannot have one without the other.
> Anything that is created must arise anew
> And is therefore impermanent;
> Arising and impermanence cannot be separated.
> There can be no ultimate truth without relative truth
> And no relative truth without the ultimate.

(iii) The actual stages of this meditation

Mahamudra insight meditation is similar to Sutric insight meditation except that the sutras advocate analysing the selflessness of things while Mahamudra analyses the internal workings of mind. Thoughts and emotions arise in the mind and dissipate back into the mind. Insight meditation makes it easier to determine their nature as they arise.

Begin by adopting the proper meditation posture and learning to stabilise the mind as described in the previous chapter. Then allow the mind to rest, so that it has the qualities of lucidity and spaciousness, and simply maintain that awareness. When you have attained a sufficient level of stability and tranquillity, give rise to a sudden violent anger, making sure the feeling is very strong, then observe that anger and try to determine its qualities. How does that anger manifest? Where does that anger dwell? What is that anger dependent on? How can that anger be identified? Is that anger a tangible thing? Analyse the way your anger appears in your mind in this way.

If your mind wanders, relax your attention for a while, and then try to generate that emotion again. If you have trouble generating anger and cannot pull your mind away from a state of tranquillity, visualise someone who has done you harm and try to generate a feeling of anger towards them. Then examine that emotion. You can do the same thing with other strong emotions, such as lust, jealousy, and desire, deliberately giving rise to them after dwelling in tranquillity for a time. You can do the same with thoughts that may not be as violent or intense. Generate one of the many thoughts that plague your mind and then analyse that thought and try to determine its dwelling place. Does it have any form or shape or support? Can it be identified, pinned down, or grasped? Examining the nature of thoughts and emotions as they arise, in this way, is very important.

Thoughts and emotions will gradually subside and be replaced by a sense of mental clarity and spaciousness during this type of analytical meditation. This is similar to reverting to tranquillity meditation. This should not be regarded as a problem, but you should try to prevent your thoughts from disappearing if you possibly can. You are trying to generate mental clarity while your thoughts are still active because it is much more difficult to determine the nature of those thoughts once they have subsided. You have to maintain your mental clarity while allowing thoughts and emotions to arise and disperse, then use that clarity to determine the nature of those thoughts and emotions. This is the secret of that particular practice.

Do not make any effort to eliminate or prevent your thoughts when they spontaneously arise in the mind. If you continue with this practice, you will gradually gain conviction in the fact that you do not need to eliminate them. When you can determine the nature of these thoughts and emotions, you no longer cling to them, and they reveal themselves to be insubstantial and elusive. You should not try to prevent violent thoughts or emotions from arising in the mind during insight meditation either. Simply observe whatever arises with awareness. When you can maintain mental stability and awareness and perceive the vividness of thoughts and emotions without distraction, those same thoughts and emotions will no longer have any hold over you. Their manifestation will be very different from ordinary experiences because you have now understood their nature. Success with this technique is tantamount to achieving an experience of insight in relation to thoughts.

Having examined the internal workings of mind, turn your attention to the sensory world and examine that. Instead of blocking out your sensory impressions because you are afraid of being distracted by them, use the senses to determine the nature of your impressions. We experience phenomena when our five sense consciousnesses encounter the five sense fields. This contact is largely determined by our karmic traces and dispositions. Do not try to prevent whatever encounters your sense organs from stimulating your sense consciousnesses.

At this point, it should be said that this type of insight meditation is comparable to the Sutric methods, but it is not quite the same as them. Some Madhyamaka techniques encourage us to employ a conceptual analysis that reduces gross physical objects to atoms and atoms to nothingness in order to develop a conceptual understanding of emptiness. This technique is not employed in Mahamudra. Our emphasis is on the perceiver rather than the perceived. We focus on our own mind rather than the phenomenal world.

Whenever you see or hear something, just remain in a meditative state and analyse how you are apprehending that sensory object, focusing your attention on the perceiver rather than the sensory object itself. Shift your focus to your mental processes or strong emotions such as lust, hatred, happiness, and unhappiness. Allow them to arise and manifest in your mind and then focus on the experiencer.

Meditators should be cautioned here about the correct way to focus on a sensory object. These objects may grow gradually fuzzy, even when the mind retains a sense of lucidity and spaciousness. This is tantamount to reverting to tranquillity meditation, which is something that you should not allow when you are practising insight meditation. Keep your focus on your mental phenomena and look at the apprehender of the things that are making contact with your senses. You will realise the nature of the perceiver by keeping your focus on these phenomena and examining the perceiver. Once you can remain in a stable state and focus on the phenomena, without feeling the need to block them out or be distracted by them, you have achieved a certain experience of insight in relation to phenomena. Such a state is hard to describe! You apply this dual analysis to the things you experience and to the experiencer because reality is inseparable from appearances. Reality is whatever appears to mind. This is an important concept to remember. The ability to let go of your experiences while maintaining clarity is regarded as an important sign of progress.

Some meditation manuals describe techniques that only deal with the stabilising aspect of meditation. They emphasise the importance of mental lucidity, which is cultivated by reducing concepts, thoughts, and emotions to attain a non-conceptual state. The Mahamudra approach regards this method as lacking in subtlety because it is also important to maintain a state of clarity when the mind is in a dynamic state, without allowing the mind to slide into a state of mental concentration. We need to be able to make use of the agitated mind, the mind in motion, and the mind that is actively engaged in the experience of phenomena.

It may initially be easier to remain in meditation if you follow techniques that are geared toward producing a stable state free from mental processes, but you cannot remain in a state like that forever. You will have no way of dealing with your experiences when thoughts and emotions re-emerge or when you are confronted by phenomena again. In fact, this re-emergence can become the cause of great anxiety. Mahamudra meditation is therefore applied to both the active mind and the mind at rest.

Meditation that encourages stability of mind is only useful for beginners; experienced meditators should incorporate techniques that deal with all mental states. Otherwise thoughts that arise in the mind and the phenomena that appear to the senses may be incorporated into the stability of tranquillity meditation but will not be amenable to the self-cognising awareness that arises in insight meditation. In Mahamudra, we use thoughts and phenomena to advance on the path, instead of viewing them as obstacles to meditation.

§ Attaining Certainty About The Root Of Samsara And Nirvana

1. Thoughts and appearances are of mental origin

The following exercise is quite different from the one described above. That exercise was meant to determine whether your mental processes and perceptions of the external world had any enduring essence. This exercise involves observing the origin, duration, and dissolution of thoughts and appearances to see whether the nature of mind and the nature of thoughts are the same.

Begin by stabilising the mind in tranquillity meditation and then give rise to a thought from within that state. When a thought arises, observe its origin, duration, and dissolution. When you look at the origin of thought, you should ask yourself where it comes from. What has given rise to that thought? If you automatically assume that it must have arisen from the nature of mind, you should question that assumption. Has the nature of mind caused that thought to arise? Is the arising of a thought from the mind a causal relationship, such as the relationship between a mother and her son, or more of a spontaneous manifestation, such as the sun and its rays? Determine the relationship between thoughts and the mind in this way.

When you look at the duration of a thought, ask yourself, 'Does that thought have any qualities?' 'What is the thought about?' If the thought is related to anger, examine the texture and quality of that anger. Is it vivid and violent in nature or is it there in a more gentle way? Is that anger intelligent? Can it be grasped or is it too elusive for that? Look at the qualities of a thought while it persists in these ways.

When the thought eventually dissipates, look into where it has gone. Did the thought cease because it was suppressed or did it cease naturally? Did it cease as a result of prior causes and conditions? Has the thought stopped? If the thought was suppressed, what agency was used to suppress it? Analyse all kinds of thoughts, both subtle and gross, and try to determine their nature. This exercise can gradually be applied to a wide range of human experiences.

In the next exercise, generate thoughts that give you pleasure and then generate thoughts that give you pain and try to determine whether pleasure and pain have any intrinsic nature. Really examine whether there is any real or essential difference between the two types of experience. Do they have any essential differences from the ultimate point of view? Can we say love is intrinsically good and hate intrinsically bad?

This exercise will break down dualistic notions that are well entrenched in your mind so that you can gradually come to see that thoughts and emotions are not bad, because they have the same nature as the mind. Without needing to abandon these thoughts and emotions, you can learn to maintain a sense of lucidity in your meditation, even when the mind is beset by myriad thoughts. This exercise will also help you see that thoughts lack any intrinsic quality of their own. They will then begin to reveal themselves as luminosity.

You need to recognise that thoughts and the nature of mind are like waves and the ocean. The nature of the waves and the nature of the ocean is water. In just the same way, the nature of mind and the nature of thoughts is luminosity and emptiness. Thoughts arise from the unobstructed nature of mind and when we examine them, they reveal themselves to be luminous in nature. When properly understood, the myriad thoughts that arise in the mind never go beyond the luminous and empty quality of the nature of mind. The nature of mind is what allows us to have experiences at all. Thoughts arise from the unobstructed openness of mind's own nature.

This practice can also be applied to phenomena. When you gaze at a visual object or listen to a sound, look at the origin, duration, and cessation of that sensory experience and determine whether sight or sound are registered independently of mind. Is the sound really in the external world or is it within the mind? In what way are the senses and the sense objects related? Do they exist independently of one another? If the senses and sense objects are different, in what way are they different? If mind and phenomena are the same, in what way are they the same? Has mind become the same as phenomena or has phenomena become the same as mind? If you examine the mind and phenomena in this way, you will gradually realise the unity of mind and phenomena.

You can extend this exercise by examining beautiful and repulsive things. Listen to sounds that are pleasantly musical and sounds that are jarring and disruptive, and then observe how the dualistic mind is constantly categorising things as intrinsically good or intrinsically bad. You need to examine whether these things really do have any intrinsic nature apart from the projections of mind. Your dualistic notions will loosen gradually through this practice and you will develop a conviction in the fact that there is no intrinsic difference between things that are beautiful and things that are ugly. The same can be said about sights, tastes, smells, and physical sensations.

This exercise is intended to dismantle the dualistic notions that compel us to view things as dichotomies. If you do this practice properly, you will begin to perceive the unity of all your experiences—the unity between mind and phenomena and the unity between phenomena and its nature. You will also come to see that phenomena and mind are inseparable. Our experiences of phenomena are like the experiences of a dream; all of its incidents and characters are no different from the mind that dreams them. You should realise that phenomena (which are regarded as external to mind) and the mind (which is regarded as existing within the body) cannot be separated from one another.

This does not mean phenomena will cease to appear once you realise this unity. Whatever manifests is a product of causes and conditions; the coming together of sense object, sense organs, and mind. Your mind will become relaxed and anxiety free when you experience the unity of mind and phenomena during insight meditation because it will no longer be afflicted by hope and fear. This realisation is sometimes called the experience of one-flavouredness. The notion of one-flavouredness will be elaborated upon in the final chapter.

2. The nature of tranquil and active mental states

Begin this practise by settling the mind in tranquillity meditation. You first look at the settled state of mind in terms of its origin, duration, and cessation and then you give rise to a particular thought and look at that in terms of its origin, duration and dissolution. You are trying to determine the difference between the mind in its tranquil state and the mind in its dynamic state. The point of this exercise is to realise that the nature of the settled and active states of mind is the same because neither state has any essence. There is no difference between their essential natures, they simply appear to be settled or agitated in your experience.

Examine these states of mind to see if there is any intrinsic difference between the two. Is the settled mind superior to the agitated mind in its essential nature? Is the settled mind really better than the agitated mind in its intrinsic properties? Probing into this question will lead you to realise that there is no essential difference in their nature because both are empty of essence. Nor is there any difference in terms of their intrinsic properties because neither one is better than the other. Entertain the idea that there is no intrinsic difference between the two states of mind and then examine what that means. Is there really no difference between the two states at all or do these two states of mind only appear to be the same? Examining the appearance of these two states leads to the realisation that their lack of difference cannot be understood in either of these ways.

Apart from our mental clinging to these two states of mind and the fact that you conceptually differentiate them, there is no essential difference. The nature of the tranquil state and the nature of the dynamic state are the same as the nature of mind. The mind settled in mental equipoise and the active mind should both be viewed as creative expressions of the nature of mind. Just as waves have the same nature as the ocean and sunshine has the same nature as the sun, the settled and agitated mental states in meditation should be viewed as the creative expressions of the nature of mind. Do not exercise any kind of acceptance and rejection during Mahamudra meditation by embracing the settled state and rejecting the agitated state. It is possible to remain in a state of meditation, regardless of our mental state, through this technique. If the mind is in an agitated state, simply remain in that state. If the mind is in a settled state, remain in that. The crucial thing is to understand that we do not always need to be in a state of meditative stability. We only need to maintain a sense of awareness and have a feeling of spaciousness and lucidity. It is important to develop confidence and certainty in the workability of this technique.

You might wonder at this point, 'How can the nature of mind give rise to two totally different mental states that result in two totally different experiences?' That can be explained by the karmic imprints of mind because these are responsible for our physical body and the subtle energies that travel through it. When body and mind encounter the external world, there is the interdependence of sensory object, sense organs, and mind. When these three operate in unison, we have the various experiences of mind. Saraha says:

> The manifestation of mind is like the movement of wind,
> It does not stay still for one second.

Maitripa says:

> The so-called activities of mind
> Are nothing more than the circulation of subtle energies.

A log tossed about on the surface of the ocean does not move because of any voluntary act of its own. Just so, the storehouse consciousness stirs up the subtle energies that travel through the body and gives rise to the involuntary movements of mind. The *Bodhichittavivarana* says:

> Just as a log in the ocean
> Is tossed about by waves
> The ocean of the unconscious,
> Which is located in the body,
> Gives rise to the movements of mind.
> If there were no body,
> There would be no movement,
> Only self-cognising awareness would remain.

I will conclude this section by mentioning the views of different masters. Some masters say there can be no meditative equipoise when the mind is active. Others say our agitated thoughts will naturally dissipate when we focus on them and our agitation will be transformed into the state of tranquillity. Most masters assume that we can gain some insight into the agitated state of mind when the mind is in a state of tranquillity and we can gain some insight into the state of tranquillity when the mind is in a state of agitation. According to Mahamudra, all of these approaches are incomplete.

The first approach is inadequate because it deals with the two states of mind separately. The meditator must either remain in a state of tranquillity or a state of agitation, so that there is no real understanding of the inseparability of these two states from the perspective of their intrinsic nature. The second approach also contains defects, because its emphasis on meditative tranquillity avoids the agitated state of mind and we cannot therefore gain any insight into it. The third approach is the best option of the three, but even that is incomplete because it fails to emphasise the common nature of both states of mind. The proper view, according to the Mahamudra tradition, is to not think of these two states of mind as any different at all in terms of their essential nature. This is why the example of the ocean and its waves is given. These two states of mind—which seem so different and are experienced so differently—have the same flavour. Only our experience and mental habits perceive them as different. Saraha says:

> When a gust of wind blows across a calm lake,
> Waves will appear on its surface.
> The nature of mind also gives rise
> To two very different states of mind.
> This is the view of the one who holds arrows.

This point will be elaborated upon further in the section on the practice of awareness in relation to mental agitation and meditative stability.

3. All appearances are non-arising

Having determined the nature of thoughts and internal phenomena to be the creative manifestations of the nature of mind, we will now turn our attention to the nature of mind and try to determine how it exists. It is important to develop confidence and certainty in the fact that the nature of mind is uncreated, unoriginated, and unconditioned.

Contemplate and examine the causes and conditions that could give rise to the nature of mind. You need to jettison any notion of the nature of mind as having the characteristics of a conditioned entity. The nature of mind has no duration precisely because it is not an entity. It is free from any primary and secondary qualities and not dependent on anything other than itself. Furthermore, the nature of mind does not arise or dissipate. Since it is not a conditioned entity, no causes and conditions can bring it into existence and no causes and conditions can end it. We must know with certainty that the nature of mind is not brought about by causes and conditions. It does not even exist in the present moment and so cannot be talked about in terms of coming into or going out of existence.

It is important to appreciate this atemporality of the nature of mind. If the nature of mind did exist in time, there must have been a time when it did not exist, a time when it will cease to exist, or a time when it had not yet come into being. We can't say that the nature of mind exists in the present moment because it cannot be apprehended in an empirical way. It does not reside in the past, it does not exist in the present, and it will not come into being in the future. The nature of mind does not fall into the extreme of eternalism because it is completely unconditioned and it does not fall into the extreme of nihilism because it is completely atemporal.

The nature of mind is unconditioned, not a product of causes and conditions and without existence in the way that other things exist. Nonetheless, it is the precondition for all our experiences, from samsaric bondage to nirvanic release, because the nature of mind is the indeterminate ground upon which all conditioned things arise. Being unconditioned, it has no definable characteristics and cannot be represented as this or that. It can't even be symbolised by anything else that exists.

The nature of mind has not come into being because it is uncaused from the beginning. It has no duration because it cannot be apprehended in the present moment. It cannot cease to exist because it is unconditioned and free from empirical characteristics. The nature of mind is not a product of any cause. It does not come into being because of certain causes and it cannot be brought to an end because of certain conditions. It is unceasing since it does not exist in time and cannot be apprehended in relation to origin, duration, or cessation. Whether the nature of mind has been understood or apprehended by sentient beings makes no difference to it; it does not become more worthwhile when it is recognised or less worthwhile when it goes unrecognised. Since it is atemporal and unconditioned, it is ever-present even if nobody recognises it. We cannot acquire it and we cannot lose it as a result of our personal achievements or failures.

The nature of mind is unchanging and can only be apprehended through discriminating awareness. We must make a concerted effort to have an intuitive and unmediated experience of it, an experience that cannot be expressed in words or conceptualised in any definable way. Discriminating awareness, which involves the use of concepts to determine the nature of mind, will eventually result in the dawning of non-conceptual wisdom. As Saraha says:

> If we gaze repeatedly into the nature of mind
> Which is pure and expansive like space,
> We realise there is nothing to be seen.
> The nature of mind is not an entity.

He also says:

> When mind goes looking for the nature of mind
> By using thoughts and concepts,
> It stabilises into a meditative state.
> Just as rock salt melts when it meets water,
> Thoughts and concepts are absorbed into the nature of mind.

The second *Bhavanakrama* says:

> When we look for the nature of mind using our discriminating awareness, we do not discover it as an entity. It is not found within, without, or in between. It is not found in the past, the future, or the present because it cannot be found in space or time. Mental processes don't originate anywhere or dissipate into anything as such. The nature of mind cannot be grasped or shown with concepts.

The *Bhavanakrama* quotes the *Ratnakuta Sutra*:

> Buddha: 'Oh Kashyapa, if we look for the nature of mind, we will

never discover it. What cannot be discovered cannot be perceived. What cannot be perceived cannot be said to have existed in the past, to exist in the present, or to come into existence in the future. What cannot be discovered and cannot be found in the past, present or future has no intrinsic properties. What has no intrinsic properties cannot come into existence. What cannot come into existence cannot go out of existence.'

The *Dharmaraja Sutra* says:

> Buddha: 'Oh sons and daughters of noble family, if you wish to attain liberation by severing the limb of grasping mind, abandon dualistic ways of thinking. Think of your mind as one, because the nature of mind is emptiness, which is not something we can either obtain or abandon. When you recognise the nature of your own mind, it will reveal itself to be enlightenment.'
> Student: 'How can you say that we can't acquire or abandon the mind when it is the source of our proliferating mental states and psychic processes?'
> Buddha: 'When mind is concentrated and gives rise to analytic mind, you will realise that the nature of mind is free from determining characteristics, origination, and dispersion.'

The *Saddharmaparigraha Sutra* says:

> Understand the nature of mind to be free from the extremes of existence and non-existence because it has no intrinsic properties. Anything that lacks intrinsic properties is not a conditioned phenomenon. We establish the middle way and the middle view by overcoming the extreme views of eternalism and nihilism. All conditioned things are devoid of essence. Realising that is the path to enlightenment. That is how I have revealed it.

Many similar statements that support the Mahamudra view of the nature of mind can be found in both the Sutric and Tantric literature.

THE CHARACTERISTICS OF EMERGING INSIGHT

To know whether we have successfully given rise to insight through the above meditation exercises, it might be helpful to hear what others have said about them. Some commentators say that we experience insight when we apply analysis with discriminating awareness during tranquillity meditation because that analysis subsides back into the state of meditative concentration. This is an erroneous interpretation of insight from the Mahamudra perspective. Other commentators say that the spaciousness we experience in tranquillity meditation is the realisation of insight. However, real insight has not occurred in this case either. We may have elevated experiences of tranquillity as an extension of our mental concentration but that is not the same as insight. We should overcome the meditative experiences that occur in tranquillity meditation and put our efforts into the practice of insight because it is only by employing the proper techniques of insight meditation that we succeed in attaining insight.

It can also be very difficult for some people to attain insight. No matter how often they meditate or how diligently they persevere with the techniques of insight, they fail to experience it. If that is true of your own situation, shift your attention to the following two primary methods and practise these for a while. The first method entails practices that generate merit and the second method entails practices that reduce the delusions and obscurations of mind. These are known as accumulation and purification practices. Continue with tranquillity meditation in conjunction with these practices and emphasise the lucidity and clarity of your mind. Even meditators who have difficulties in attaining insight will eventually succeed if these three methods are combined.

Other people have a genuine comprehension of what is involved in insight practice due to their innate intelligence, but may mistake this comprehension for real insight. It is very important to understand the difference between intellectual knowledge and actual insight. Another point to bear in mind is that some people are very eloquent and articulate, but their experiences may have nothing to do with real insight, while other people have no verbal skills but may have experienced true insight.

It is important to ascertain whether you have attained genuine insight and to be alert to the pitfalls cited here. If the 'true seeing' of insight meditation is not cultivated you will never transcend worldly states of meditation, no matter how long you practise tranquillity techniques. These techniques are also common to other religious traditions, such as Hinduism. Tranquillity meditation alone will not even lead to the realisation of the *arhats* or 'foe-destroyers' let alone the insight of the bodhisattva or of Mahamudra as the apex of the Tantric tradition. You should pursue the practice of insight relentlessly.

You may ask, 'How can we judge whether we have attained insight or not?' Genuine inconvertible insight is not attained until the third yoga of Mahamudra. However, even a beginner can have glimpses of ultimate reality. This is comparable to seeing the waxing moon. Even though it is not yet the complete moon, the waxing moon is still the moon. An element of insight can be present at the beginning stages of meditation in this way. Insight is attained through determining the nature of mind, recognising that thoughts and emotions are its creative activities, and realising that the sensory impressions are also its reflections. In brief, everything that comes within the realm of perceiver and perceived is unconditioned, because its nature is emptiness. The phenomenal aspects of reality come into being from conditioned things but the unconditioned aspect of reality can only be perceived through insight. We see through insight that the nature of conditioned entities does not come into being, does not dwell anywhere, and does not cease to exist. When you attain real certainty that things have no intrinsic essence and are therefore empty by nature, you have had a certain experience of insight.

If you cannot gain even that much certainty, you would do well to study what the past masters of the Practice Lineage have said. When meditators realise the nature of mind is empty and devoid of empirical characteristics, so that the experience of emptiness and self-cognising awareness come together, this recognition is 'beginner's insight.' Meditators who continue to practise this will evolve in their certainty until they eventually attain 'ultimate insight.'

The sutras claim that insight is not attained until we have attained pliancy of body and mind. We attain physical pliancy through tranquillity meditation and mental pliancy through insight meditation. Only this dual pliancy is regarded as proper insight in the Sutric system, all previous stages are only a provisional form of insight. According to the Mahamudra system however, this is not certain. As we said in the previous chapter, the attainment of one-pointed concentration without any pliancy of body and mind is regarded as a genuine experience of insight in the Mahamudra tradition. This is the view held by the lineage holders of the oral instruction system.

BLENDING MAHAMUDRA INSIGHT WITH OTHER SYSTEMS

The *Samadhinirmocana Sutra* lists four types of insight meditation. We can match the approaches of the Mahamudra system with those four methods. 1) 'Insight that discriminates all existent things' corresponds to the Mahamudra method that determines the creative activity of the nature of mind in terms of thoughts, emotions, and sensory impressions. 2) 'Insight of differentiation' corresponds to the Mahamudra method that determines thoughts, emotions, and sensory impressions as having no enduring essence. The first insight determines the conditioned aspect of things and the second insight determines the unconditioned or empty aspect of things. 3) 'Insight of understanding' corresponds to the Mahamudra method applied to the phenomenal aspect of what arises in mind as well as its nature.

This insight therefore arises when we develop a conceptual understanding of the relationship between the conditioned and the unconditioned aspects of reality. 4) 'Insight of examination' corresponds to the Mahamudra method that determines the relationship between the two aspects of reality in more refined ways. Asanga's *Sravakabhumi* says:

> In what way should analytical insight be applied to existing things? First, analyse the conditioned aspect of reality, then analyse its unconditioned aspect. Following that, use discriminating awareness with conceptual comprehension to analyse both aspects of reality to apprehend their definable characteristics. Finally, analyse the nature of these two aspects in more subtle forms.

The Mahamudra system can also be explained in terms of three types of Sutric insight that arise from the analysis of conceptual understanding. These are also listed in the *Samadhinirmocana Sutra*. 1) 'Insight with determination' applies concepts to determine the nature of phenomenal reality. 2) 'Insight of probing' examines the unconditioned aspect of reality to realise that everything on the empirical level has no enduring essence. This insight is accompanied by a sense of novelty because it is something new and unlike anything we have previously experienced. 3) 'Insight of discrimination' is applied once we gain understanding of these two aspects of reality because the realisation that nothing has enduring essence leads to liberation and the experience of enduring bliss. The *Samadhinirmocana Sutra* explains:

> What insight is dependent on determining the definable characteristics of phenomena? Once we attain meditative stability and engage in analysis, we gain a conceptual understanding of phenomena. What insight is dependent on probing and investigation? When we use discriminating awareness to analyse things in a very detailed way, we realise that the nature of conditioned phenomena is unconditioned emptiness. What insight arises from full comprehension? When we discern the relationship between the conditioned and unconditioned aspects of reality, we become liberated and attain enduring bliss.

These different forms of insights are included for your information only. The meditation manuals of the Practice Lineage do not usually refer to the

Sutric methods. However, I have included them here because the relationship between the Mahamudra and Sutric approaches might be of some interest to you.

In brief, Mahamudra meditators come to realise that the perceiver and perceived are empty of enduring essence through analysis. The Mahamudra emphasis on realising the nature of mind and overcoming deluded consciousness is comparable to the insight meditation of the sutras, which uses discriminating awareness to break down our concept of self in relation to the five psychophysical constituents. This is very similar to how Mahamudra practitioners come to realise the nature of mind. The difference is that the Mahamudra tradition understands mind to be hanging onto the notion of an indubitable immutable self, so the object of analysis in Mahamudra meditation is the mind itself rather than the concept of self.

There is a strong parallel between these two approaches. The Sutric method uses logic and reasoning to reveal the lack of inherent existence in all things. This is sometimes called the 'selflessness of phenomena,' because it refers to the lack of substance in phenomenal existence. The sutras speak of 'selflessness of persons' and 'selflessness of phenomena.' Mahamudra practitioners analyse the sensory impressions and mental processes to realise that nothing exists independently of mind and therefore that things have no inherent existence of their own. This is still comparable to the Sutric method, because both systems conclude that nothing has self-sufficient, independent, inherent existence. Dharmakirti says:

> Examine the material world
> To establish insubstantiality.

Aryadeva says:

> Realising that the material world lacks substantiality
> Will bring samsara to an end.

There is a difference in the order with which these two types of insights are practised in the Mahamudra and Sutric approaches. The Sutric method first focuses on an analysis of the external world to realise that phenomena have no enduring essence. Only then does it turn to an analysis of the mind. The Mahamudra method only analyses how phenomena appear to the mind, not the phenomenal world, because the so-called external world does not exist in its own right and therefore can have no enduring essence. Mind clings to the phenomenal world because it is mistaken about its nature, so if we can establish that mind has no enduring reality, it will be easy to establish that the external world has no reality as well. If we realise the nature of mind, there is no need to realise the nature of the external world as a separate insight, because mind is the root of everything. Tilopa uses the example of a tree to illustrate the importance of using the mind rather than world to attain insight. In the same way that cutting the root of a tree will cause the trunk, branches and leaves to all dry up, cutting the root of mind will cause the phenomenal world and everything in it to reveal their insubstantiality. If we analyse the nature of mind, everything else will become self-revelatory.

This completes the explanation on guiding meditators on the path of insight meditation.

5

Stages of Identification

HOW TO IDENTIFY THIS SYSTEM OF MEDITATION

This has two parts:

- Identifying the innate nature of mind
- The definitive meaning of coemergent wisdom

§ Identifying The Innate Nature Of Mind

1. The nature of mind

We have discussed the nature of mind at length but we have not yet dealt with the nature of mind as a whole. From the Mahamudra point of view, the nature of mind has to be understood in relation to three aspects: its nature, essence, and characteristic.[1] We can separate the nature of the mind into these three aspects from the conceptual point of view only. In reality, we can make no such differentiation. The nature aspect is emptiness. This empty nature pervades the aspects of the essence and characteristic, so they fundamentally all have the same nature. However, we can understand the mind in relation to these three aspects in relation to how mind manifests. We speak about the nature, essence, and characteristic of mind in that way.[2] The *Amnayamanjari* says:

> The nature of everything is emptiness. The essence of emptiness is no different to the nature of mind and how it manifests. However, we need to understand the way that mind manifests in relation to three aspects: nature, essence, and characteristic.

Gampopa says:

> What is the nature of mind? The nature is emptiness, because it has not come into being, does not endure, and cannot cease to exist. The essence is luminosity, which is non-conceptual. The characteristic is the unceasing flow of mental processes produced by mind, which manifest in both enlightened and unenlightened states.[3]

He also says:

> The 'nature' of mind is emptiness, which is all-pervasive and completely free of embellishments. It pervades both samsara and nirvana and is unconditioned. The 'essence' of mind is luminosity, which is unceasing. The 'characteristic' of mind is our mental processes, which are brought about by karmic traces and dispositions.

Phagmo Drupa says:

> The nature of mind is inseparable from Mahamudra
> And has three aspects:
> Nature, essence, and characteristic.
> 'Nature' is free from the concept of origin, extinction,
> And conceptual determinations.
> 'Essence' is unobtrusive and luminous.
> 'Characteristic' manifests
> As enlightened and unenlightened experiences
> In respect to nirvana and samsara.

There is not much difference between the nature and essence aspects of mind. The third Karmapa, Rangjungpa, says:

> The nature of mind is empty, the essence is luminous,
> The characteristic appears in whatever way it wants.

You should also realise that the nature of mind is completely free from the ideas of origin, duration, and extinction. It is atemporal. At the same time, the nature of mind is not confined to our psychophysical constituents. Free from the idea of self and other, it is the very condition that enables duality to exist. The *Guhyasamaja Tantra* says:

> Emptiness is unsullied by notions of individual existent things.
> It is not confined to the psychophysical constituents,
> Sense fields, or consciousnesses

Of the perceiver and perceived.
It is reality, free from any essence and all-pervasive,
Just like the nature of mind.

The *Bodhichittavivarana* says:

The mind of the enlightened ones
Is unsullied by the notions of self or skandhas,
And unvitiated by conceptual proliferations.
It reveals itself through emptiness.

When we engage in the types of exercises presented in the previous chapter, we come to realise the nature of mind is not something that can be identified or labelled as this or that. It is free from all conceptual determinations and is realised as emptiness itself. The *Satyadvaya* says:

When we examine relative truth
We realise that its nature is empty;
No abiding or enduring essence can be found.
That is the ultimate truth.

The nature of mind is the same as the emptiness that pervades the realities of both samsara and nirvana. Aryadeva says:

There is only one reality;
It is present in the multiplicity of phenomena.

Aryadeva's *Catusataka* also says:

The emptiness of one thing is the emptiness of all things.

The *Satyadvaya* states:

No differentiation can be found in emptiness;
Not even to the slightest degree.

2. The essence of mind

The *Astasahasrika-prajnaparamita Sutra* says:

The essence of mind is luminous.

The *Lankavatara Sutra* says:

The essence of mind is luminous.

> It is the same as the tathagatagarbha.[4]

Many other texts assert that the essence of mind is luminous.[5] To say 'the essence of mind is luminous' is the same as saying the mind's nature is unconditioned, has not come into being, is unvitiated by the psychophysical constituents, is free from conceptual proliferation, is unchanging, and lacks essence like space itself. This assertion does not ascribe any attributes to it. The *Upalipariprccha* states:

> To say that the essence of mind is luminous
> Is to say that mind is not intrinsically defiled or polluted.

The *Uttaratantra* says:

> The essence of mind is luminous and unchanging.

The *Jnanalokalamkara Sutra* says:

> Buddha: 'Manjushri, the mind of enlightened beings is naturally luminous. It is called "luminous" because mind is not corrupted by the emotional conflicts and so on. It is pure, expansive, and uncorrupted, just like space. Mind is naturally luminous.

The *Vairocanabhisambodhi* says:

> The essence of mind is luminous; it is completely unsullied, uncorrupted, and can't be found within or without the psychophysical constituents.

It also says:

> The essence of mind is the same as the essence of space. The essence of mind is the same as the mind of an enlightened being. Understand the essence of space and the enlightened mind to be the same.

The *Guhyasamaja Tantra* says:

> The essence of mind is luminous.
> It is pure right from the beginning, like space.

There are people, untrained in understanding Mahamudra practice, who automatically assume that they have experienced the natural luminosity of mind when they experience some spark of mental clarity. It is completely mistaken to imagine that luminosity is something that illuminates, something that dispels darkness, or something that can be perceived as a light. To say 'the essence of mind is luminous' is to say that mind is intrinsically undefiled and uncorrupted by emotional conflicts, desires, and passions. We only use the expression 'the essence of mind is luminous' for the sake of convenience so do not take this designation literally. This point was already made in the previous quotations. If we interpret 'luminosity' to mean something that has a white colour, some kind of light or spark, the mind would be white in colour or some kind of light or spark. That is tantamount to turning the essence of mind into an entity, which would contradict the understanding of the essence of mind as being uncorrupted, naturally undefiled, and intrinsically pure.

You may then ask, 'How we can attain self-awareness? If luminosity is not some kind of spark or light and if mind is free of any colour or defining characteristics, how do we experience luminosity and how is self-awareness realised?'[6] To understand this question, we turn to Naropa's *Drstisamksepta*:

> Everything we experience is dependent on mind.
> Every experience has a certain appearance
> But at the same time is luminous by nature.
> Luminosity, the essence of mind,
> Is no different to everyday experience.

He also says:

> Self-awareness is unvitiated by conceptual determinations.
> Whatever appears to the mind is empty,
> Whatever is empty appears to the mind.
> These two are inseparable
> Like the reflection of the moon on water.

For this reason, meditators who claim to have experienced the luminosity of mind when they have a meditative experience of clarity are completely mistaken. Such experiences of mental clarity are conceptual and conditioned. That is not a proper realisation of the essence of mind. The essence of mind has to be understood in relation to the nature of mind, which is emptiness. The *Vimalaprabha* says:

> What is the nature of self-awareness? Self-awareness is that which is luminous and free from conceptual proliferation. Its nature is empty and unchanging, it is unintentional, and it is unsullied but blissful. The notions of cause and effect are the same here, in the same way that heat and the light of a fire are one and the same thing.[7]

The *Manjusrinama-samgiti* says:

> That which is self-aware is the nature of mind;
> It transcends all conditioned things.

It also says:

> It comprehends everything including self and other.

Je Drikhungpa says:

> The so-called Mahamudra is nothing other than self-awareness.

We have to realise, in this way, that talking about awareness is the same as talking about luminosity. For these reasons, when a yogi has a certain meditative experience we cannot automatically assume it is the same as self-awareness or luminosity. The *Samadhinirmocana* says:

> Self-awareness isn't an object of conceptual understanding.

The *Guhyacintya Tantra* says:

> The luminosity of mind, which is self-awareness,
> Is free from ideas of permanence and impermanence,
> Origination and cessation, existence and non-existence,
> Because it is free from all conceptual determinations.
> Understand that it is not an object of conceptualisation.

3. The characteristic of mind

The 'nature' and 'essence' of mind are obscured in the sense that ordinary sentient beings have no understanding of them. 'Obscuration' simply means that we do not have a proper understanding of our true condition due to our adventitious conflicting emotions. This produces the causes and conditions for our continued wanderings in samsaric existence, where we experience pleasure, pain, and so on. However, it is possible to eliminate these adventitious defilements and obscurations through the practice of meditation. We will thereby realise that the nature of our own mind is the dharmakaya. Once we realises that, we become an enlightened being and can continue to work for the benefit of others in this world through our physical manifestation. This is all related to the characteristic of mind. The *Drstisamksepta* says:

> Emaho! The mind that is defiled and obscured
> Is the cause of our ceaseless wanderings in samsara,

Where we continually experience
Untold suffering and pain.

It also says:

Lo! When the mind becomes purified of defilement
We realise buddhahood
And work in the world for the benefit of others.
Everything we experience is transformed
With the absence of defilements.
And we experience untold joy!

Saraha says:

Mind is the root of all of our experiences;
Samsara and nirvana both arise from it.

The *Samputa Tantra* says:

When mind is bound by emotional conflicts
We wander in samsara.
When mind is purified and revealed as luminous
All defilements and obscurations fall away.
That is the attainment of nirvana!

A sceptic might say, 'If the essence of mind is luminous and uncorrupted, it should never have been defiled by conflicting emotions and obscurations in the first place. Even if it is possible to eliminate the defilements, what guarantee is there the defilements will not come back?' The word 'adventitious' is not meant to infer that the defilements somehow came onto the scene accidentally. Adventitious refers only to their removability. Because we can remove the defilements, they are not permanent and can therefore be seen as adventitious. The *Uttaratantra* illustrates this relationship between defilements and the essence of mind through the following analogies:

The essence of mind is like pollen in a lotus,
Wheat grains in the dirt,
A precious Buddha statue wrapped in rags,
A poor woman giving birth to a would-be monarch,
Or gold nuggets in the earth.
The essence of mind, which is luminous,
Is hidden in the defilement of conflicting emotions.

Even though mind is intrinsically pure, it is not pure in our current state because of the adventitious defilements. When these adventitious defilements are eradicated the essence of mind will reveal itself as luminous and undefiled. The *Hevajra Tantra* says:

> Ordinary sentient beings are buddhas.
> They are temporarily deluded,
> Due to adventitious defilements.
> But once those defilements are lifted;
> They become buddhas.

Nagarjuna says:

> As long as a precious stone is encased in rock,
> Its radiance remains unobserved.
> When the outer covering is chipped away,
> The stone reveals its lustre.
> So the essence of mind is luminous,
> But its luminosity is unable to shine
> Because it is clouded in defilements.
> Its full lustre comes when we attain buddhahood.

The characteristic of mind is related to our various mental processes and relevant to both enlightened and unenlightened states. This unceasing mental activity can be compared to a white cloth that can be dyed any colour. Even though the mind is intrinsically pure it becomes sullied by our karmic traces and dispositions and other forces.[8] As the *Lankavatara Sutra* says:

> The essence of mind is luminous but goes through various experiences due to our conflicting emotions and defilements in the same way a white cloth takes on colours.

To understand how the characteristic of mind really operates we would need to examine how the eight forms of consciousness interact with one another. However, time does not permit us to elaborate on that here.

§ The Definitive Meaning Of Coemergent Wisdom

1. The meaning of coemergent wisdom

Coemergent wisdom is nothing other than that which pervades both samsaric and nirvanic experience. Namely, the luminous nature of mind, which is empty and all-encompassing, like space itself. The *Hevajra Tantra* says:

> Coemergence is the great wisdom.
> Present within our bodies;
> It cannot be divided into subject and object,
> Is neither material nor immaterial
> And pervades both active and tranquil mental states.

This experience cannot be articulated or communicated in verbal or written form since it cannot be fully comprehended conceptually. However, it can be experienced through self-cognising wisdom. The *Matta-stotra* says:

> As indeterminate and undifferentiated as space;
> Emptiness cannot be verbalised,
> Conceptually entertained or communicated.
> But it can be understood through self-cognising wisdom.
> I prostrate to emptiness,
> The mother of all buddhas.

Tilopa says:

> Oh! This mind is self-cognising wisdom.
> It is beyond verbalisation and cannot be pondered.

The *Hevajra Tantra* says:

> That which cannot be articulated is coemergent wisdom.

Coemergent wisdom is explained in these quotations from various Tantric texts. The etymology of 'coemergent' comes from the inseparability of the phenomenology of mental events and various so-called 'external material things.' In other words, the nature of mind and the nature of the external material world is the same. The reality aspect and the phenomenal aspect are coemergent because we cannot say reality takes precedence over phenomena. They arise simultaneously. This simultaneity is conveyed by the word 'coemergent.'[9] There is no causal or logical priority in terms of phenomena or reality. The *Hevajra Tantra* also says:

> That which arises simultaneously is coemergent.

Dombipa's *Sahajasiddhi* says:

> That which arises together
> Is called coemergent wisdom.

Indrabodhi's *Shundur*, a commentary to the above text, says:

> When two things arise together they are called coemergent.
> 'Coemergence' therefore means temporal things
> And atemporal reality arise simultaneously.

2. Different meanings and their identification

Coemergent wisdom can be understood in relation to three aspects: ground, path, and fruition coemergent wisdom. The essence of mind, which is luminous and hidden within every sentient being, is called 'ground coemergent wisdom.' The proper view, which is developed through hearing, pondering, and meditating on the teachings until the realisation of emptiness occurs is called 'path coemergent wisdom.' The continual effect to acquaint ourselves with these practices results in the full realisation of the ground coemergent wisdom, which is called 'fruition coemergent wisdom.'

The *Hevajra Tantra* and other texts talk about three kinds of coemergent wisdom. According to their division, there is 1) coemergent wisdom that arises from the sublimation of libido, 2) coemergent wisdom of the ground, and 3) coemergent wisdom of the inseparability of bliss and emptiness. 'Coemergent wisdom of the ground' refers to the luminous and empty essence of mind. 'Coemergent wisdom that arises from the sublimation of libido' involves the transmutation of sexual energy, which is referred to as the melting of bodhichitta.[10] 'Coemergent wisdom of the inseparability of bliss and emptiness' is authentic coemergent wisdom.

This is not a Tantric text, so you should understand that in the Mahamudra tradition, coemergent wisdom refers to 'the inseparability of the nature of mind and the nature of the phenomenal world.' Je Gomchung understood coemergent wisdom in two different ways: (1) the coemergence of mental processes and the nature of mind, and 2) the coemergence of the phenomenal world and the nature of the phenomenal world. This divergence seems to be based on a slight difference between (a) experiencing the phenomenal world as an objective reality, and (b) experiencing the phenomenal world as the subject of mind. The essence of mind, which is luminous, non-conceptual and free of all empirical determinations, is the nature of mind. All the unceasing mental activities, in the form of samsaric and nirvanic experiences, arise from it. Coemergent wisdom refers to 'the coexistence of the essence and nature of mind' in this context and also 'the coemergent wisdom of appearance and reality.' Experiences that are precipitated by conflicting emotions are called 'the coemergent wisdom of conceptuality and emptiness.'

The definition of the term 'coemergent wisdom' is the same as above. 'Co-emergent' means that the nature of all things and the things themselves are inextricably bound, like brown sugar and sweetness or heat and fire. The nature of mind and phenomenal appearance are also inextricably bound, like the sun and its rays or sandalwood and its scent. Nagarjuna says:

> Just as the nature of sugar is sweetness,
> And the nature of fire is heat,
> The nature of all things is emptiness.

He also says:

> Relative truth is emptiness,
> Emptiness is inseparable from the relative world;
> We can't have one without the other.
> The emptiness of all phenomena is established
> By this fact: everything that is brought about
> By causes and conditions is impermanent.

Je Gampopa says

> The nature of mind is 'the coemergent wisdom
> Of dharmakaya and phenomenal appearance.'
> As such, it is the radiance of dharmakaya.

The 'coemergent wisdom of dharmakaya' refers to the nature of mind, which is emptiness. While the nature of mind is empty, that does not mean it is a total state of blankness. All the determinate and differentiated experiences of thoughts, concepts, and ideas arise from the nature of mind, which is indeterminate and undifferentiated. The relationship between experienced phenomena and the nature of mind is the same as the relationship between the sun and its radiance or sandalwood and its fragrance. Je Gomchung says:

> The nature of mind is dharmakaya.
> The experiences that arise in mind
> In the form of appearances,
> Are the radiance of the dharmakaya.
> The concepts, ideas and thoughts of mind
> Are the waves of dharmakaya.
> Their inseparability is coemergent wisdom.

You may well wonder, 'Does this mean that even ordinary people have the experience of coemergent wisdom?' It may not be understood by ordinary beings, but whether they understand it or not, coemergent wisdom is present and unceasing in their minds. For example, you cannot separate a lamp and its light. If you remove the lamp, the light will automatically be extinguished. However, even though a lamp emits light, we would not gain any benefit from it if we were blind. In the same way, even though coemergent wisdom is present within every one of us, we remain ignorant of its presence unless understanding dawns on us. Saraha says:

> A blind person in a dark house
> May light a hundred lamps,
> But it will be of no benefit.
> Coemergent wisdom is present in everyone;
> Though extremely close to our hearts,
> It remains distant because of ignorance.

Shavaripa says:

> Even when the sun is free from clouds,
> A blind person still lives in a world of darkness.
> Though coemergent wisdom is present in everyone,
> The ignorant remain quite distant from it.

Virupa says:

> When we realise that the phenomenal world
> Is devoid of enduring essence,
> And only exists nominally;
> This understanding is the same as coemergence.
> Coemergence is not found other than
> The coexistence of phenomena and its nature.

3. The significance of coemergent wisdom

What does it mean to talk about coemergent wisdom within the context of Mahamudra? How should we understand it? Gampopa says we understand coemergent wisdom when we realise that thoughts, concepts, and ideas arise from the nature of mind. This involves recognising that the phenomenal world, emptiness, mental events, and the nature of mind all coexist.

This knowledge has been unavailable to us so far and as a result, we have fallen victim to our dualistic ways of thinking that some things are good and other things are bad and so on. When we are introduced to these kinds of Mahamudra instructions, we come to understand the nature of our mind and realise that all our experiences are inseparable from the nature of mind. Phagmo Drupa says:

> Mind, thoughts, concepts, and the dharmakaya
> Have coexisted from the beginning.
> To understand this is to understand coemergent wisdom.

We can also speak about coemergent wisdom in specific terms. For example, 'the mind that manifests thoughts and concepts is coemergent with wisdom'[11] and 'the mind that thinks, wills, and strategises is coemergent with the nature of mind.'[12] In brief, coemergent wisdom can be understood in relation to the coemergence of luminosity and emptiness, appearance and emptiness, awareness and emptiness, bliss and emptiness, and so forth. This involves understanding the 'nature' of mind and phenomena is the same as the 'empirical determinations' of phenomena. That is the essence of coemergent wisdom.

HOW TO IDENTIFY COEMERGENT WISDOM

This has three parts:

- The coemergence of mind
- The coemergence of thought
- The coemergence of appearance

§ The Coemergence Of Mind

When the mind is free of the two obstacles to meditation and you are no longer disturbed by thoughts of good and bad, you can rest the mind in its natural condition of restfulness. When you gaze into this state of mind, you will realise that even without deliberately trying to stop thoughts or contrive mental states, your thoughts naturally disperse into that state of restfulness.

This state of restfulness is known as tranquillity meditation. In this state of tranquillity, which is not a neutral state, the mind appears to be luminous, unobstructed, and self-aware. We use this awareness to analyse the nature of mind. This is known as insight meditation. The *Sutralamkara* says:

> We first establish stability by learning to rest the mind.
> Having established that stability,
> We engage in the analysis of insight meditation.

The only difference between tranquillity and insight meditation belongs to our conceptual understanding of them. They are undifferentiable in terms of experience. When we rest our minds, we must make certain that we do not fall into an absorptive state or we will lose our awareness. We must vigilantly maintain the awareness of insight. When we are engaged in the analysis of insight meditation, our minds must be stable and concentrated. We therefore have to learn to practise tranquillity and insight meditation simultaneously. The *Samadhinirmocana Sutra* says:

> 'When do tranquillity and insight meditation become united?'
> 'When we attain one-pointed concentration.'

We do not need to elaborate on the way to identify tranquillity and insight meditation here, because this was dealt with extensively in earlier chapters. Now we must establish these two types of meditation in relation to the nature of mind. The nature of mind is the same as the dharmakaya. Many other terms are used to refer to the nature of mind and these will be explained presently.

Anyone with any understanding of the nature of mind is known as a yogi. This experience of the realisation of the nature of mind is called meditative concentration or samadhi. The *Jnanamudra Sutra* says:

> Phenomenal appearance is impressed with the seal of mind.
> We have to establish mind as devoid of substance.
> Anyone who understands this is a yogi.

The *Samadhinirmocana Sutra* says:

> Question: 'How long should we engage in meditation?'
> Buddha: 'Until we understand the nature of mind.'

The *Samadhiraja Sutra* says:

> Samadhi means to understand the nature of mind as originless.

It also says:

> When there is nothing to be conceptualised, nothing to be grasped, and nothing to be verbalised, we realise that the nature of mind is devoid of enduring essence. This is the attainment of samadhi. Through the blessings of our teachers, we come to understand that the nature of mind is like space. We attain samadhi by focusing on that meaning.

The *Nam mkha'i lta bu'i ting nge 'dzin gyi mdo* says:

> Through the elixir of the guru,
> We understand the mind to be like space.
> By focusing on the meaning of this state,
> We attain samadhi.

The importance of contemplating non-conceptual wisdom has been reiterated repeatedly in many sutras. The *Avatamsaka Sutra* says:

> If you want to follow the path of the buddhas,
> Train yourselves in understanding the nature of mind.
> Abandon any notion of conceptuality or non-conceptuality
> And understand the nature of space-like mind

The *Lalitavistara* says:

> The essence of mind is luminous and unconditioned.
> This is the elixir that enables
> An understanding of the reality of things.

The *Samputa Tantra* says:

> When conceptuality is transcended,
> We come to understand non-conceptuality.
> The sacred path of the buddhas
> Is to overcome the samsaric condition
> By remaining in a state of non-conceptuality.

The *Samvarodaya* says:

> We contemplate the nature of mind
> As being of one flavour, just like space.
> Do not engage in over-conceptualisation;
> The nature of mind
> Is omnipresent and all-pervasive, just like space.

These quotations from sutras and tantras make it amply clear how important it is to realise the nature of mind. This point does not need to be dwelt on any further. Many words have been used to refer to the same thing, as the *Drstisamksepta* demonstrates:

> The nature of mind, free from empirical determinations
> And conceptual categories, is intrinsically pure and unpolluted.
> This is called non-abiding nirvana.

> It is also called Vajrasattva,
> Vajradhara, the sixth buddha-family, Manjushri,
> The god of wisdom, Vairochana, great bliss,
> The great union, the dharmakaya, the fourth empowerment,
> Coemergent wisdom, and primordial purity.
> All these words mean the same thing.

It also says:

> Bodhichitta means the same thing,
> Buddha nature means the same thing,
> The family of the buddhas means this,
> One-flavouredness, and great bliss
> Mean this also.

It further says:

> Self-cognising wisdom awareness,
> Self-awareness, and non-conceptual self-awareness,
> Means the same thing.

Again, it says:

> The ground of samsara, the peace of nirvana,
> Spiritual attainment,
> The middle way, and the middle view;
> These are what we need to perceive.
> These are what we need to meditate on.

Words that refer to the nature of mind are to be found in numerous other texts. In brief, whether we call it the dharmakaya, great bliss, coemergent wisdom, spontaneously arisen wisdom, self-cognising wisdom, absolute bodhichitta, tathagatagarbha, or the nature of reality, we are talking about the nature of mind. The *Phyag rgya chen po rab tu mi gnas pa'i rgyud* says:

> The nature of mind is Mahamudra.
> It is unsullied,
> It cannot be accepted or rejected.
> There is no such thing as a path,
> And no such things as antidotes.
> It is the authentic being of the buddhas,
> The source of all positive qualities;
> Spontaneously self-established.

§ The Coemergence Of Thought

Begin by meditating on the nature of mind for a while. When your mind has become somewhat settled, give rise to an afflicted emotion such as lust or anger. When that emotion has arisen, gaze at it without conceptualisations. If you can maintain this nonconceptual gaze, your experience of the emotion will be different from the way you would normally experience it. Don't grasp at that experience, simply allow it to be there, until you realise the nature of the experience has no essence. That is the realisation of coemergent wisdom of thought, because you recognise the nature of mind and the nature of the emotion as indivisible and coemergent. Just as the ocean and its waves have the nature of water, the mind and its thoughts have the nature of emptiness. Allow thoughts and emotions to be there without obstructing or trying to suppress them. Perceive the inseparability of appearance and emptiness.

To understand that emotions have no intrinsic nature is to understand the nature of mind. We cannot find the nature of mind separate from that. From this point of view, not grasping at whatever arises in mind is tranquillity meditation, and realising that whatever arises in mind has no enduring essence is insight meditation. To realise that the nature of mind is empty when mind is in a dynamic state is to understand the coemergent wisdom of thought. It is also to experience the union of tranquillity and insight. This is what we mean when we say, 'realising thoughts as dharmakaya.' Kagyupas emphasise the importance of not rejecting thoughts because our path is to realise wisdom by realising the nature of thoughts.[13] Some people think the sutras do not support this view, but they are mistaken. The *Aksayamatinirdesa Sutra* says:

> We attain enlightenment by understanding the nature of emotional conflicts and then realising this nature.

The *Sagaramatipariprccha* says:

> Sagaramati: 'Oh Victorious One, I find it extremely difficult to understand the nature of mind.'
> Buddha: 'To understand the nature of mind is to attain wisdom.'

It also says:

> Buddha: 'All things should be understood in terms of equanimity. Do not think of enlightenment as something distant and superior to your own present mind.'

The *Savadharmapravrttinirdesa Sutra* says:

> The nature of desire is nirvana.
> You should also understand anger, ignorance, and so on in this way.
> Enlightenment resides in conflicting emotions.

It also says:

> There is no difference between lust and enlightenment.

The *Ratnakuta* says:

> Everything arises from that which has no origin.

The *Hevajra Tantra* says:

> Wisdom and conceptuality are the cause of samsara.
> There is no difference between the two in terms of their nature;
> They have the same nature regardless of their manifestation.

It also says:

> That which is said to be samsara is also nirvana.

Again, it says:

> The anger and afflictions of samsara are the same as nirvana.

The *Samputa* says:

> Samsara and nirvana do not exist in duality.
> To understand the nature of samsara
> Is to attain nirvana.

Saraha says:

> The wisdom that dispels ignorance is like the radiance of the sun.
> This inspires all things to be pacified and blissful.

Nagarjuna says:

> No difference can be found
> Between samsara and nirvana.
> They have the same nature.

Aryadeva's *Nirvikalpaprakarana* says:

> No nirvana can be attained
> Without abandoning concepts and conflicting emotions.
> Do not get caught up in dualistic notions.

Virupa says:

> If we follow our teacher's instructions properly,
> Whatever arises in mind is revealed as the seal of reality.

Tilopa says:

> The skandhas, sense-fields, and elements
> Are inseparable from Mahamudra.
> Everything arises from Mahamudra
> And everything disperses into it.

The *Tshig bsdus* of Naropa and Maitripa says:

> Conflicting emotions are wisdom.
> Wisdom is a fire that consumes a forest.

It also says:

> Thoughts that become self-liberated are the same as wisdom.

Maitripa says:

> Thoughts arise from that which is non-originated.
> The nature of thought is the nature of mind.
> There is no difference between them from the beginning.
> Understand the one flavour
> Of thoughts and the nature of mind.

Marpa says:

> The movement of mind
> Which manifests in the dualism of subject and object
> Dissolves into dharmakaya.

Milarepa says:

> When we do not realise the inner workings of mind,
> We wander in samsara.
> When we realise the nature of thoughts and concepts,
> We realise wisdom.
> This is how we become fully developed.

Gampopa says:

> When concepts and thoughts are understood,
> They are revealed as inseparable from the nature of mind.

More statements could be quoted from Kagyupa masters to reiterate this point but these are easily found in other texts so I will not elaborate further. Some people make incorrect assertions about how to practise the coemergent wisdom of thought, which should be brought to the reader's attention at this point. Some people believe thoughts and concepts dissipate when we gaze at them and this reveals the dharmakaya. Other people believe that we realise dharmakaya when we realise the nature of thoughts to be dharmakaya and that we fail to realise dharmakaya when we fail to recognise our thoughts. These views are both incorrect.

The first assertion is based on the idea that we have to abandon thoughts which do not have the nature of dharmakaya, in order to realise the nature of mind which does have the nature of dharmakaya. This approach obviously does not reveal the nature of thought to be dharmakaya. The second approach makes the nature of dharmakaya contingent on our understanding of it. It says the dharmakaya will suddenly appear on the scene when we understand its nature, but it is nowhere to be found when we are unaware of it. This is incorrect because the dharmakaya is omnipresent. It can make no difference whether we understand it or not. If this second assertion were valid, the dharmakaya would be conditional on our experiencing it.

What then is the correct view? Even if we have not realised the nature of thoughts to be dharmakaya, this does not mean the nature of thoughts is not dharmakaya before we come to realise it. The nature of thought is dharmakaya no matter what. For example, we cannot establish the existence of the sun based upon whether somebody has a pairs of eyes to perceive it. The presence or absence of our eyes is immaterial to the existence of the sun.

Others disagree that samsara and nirvana are inseparable and make a distinction between them. They claim that the peace of nirvana is real and the conditioned existence of samsara is illusory. However, if conditioned existence were unreal, there would be no object to call 'samsara.' We have to realise that samsara and nirvana are indivisible; nirvana is no more real than samsara. We could otherwise not speak of coemergence because there would only be nirvana and not samsara. 'Coemergence' means that samsara and nirvana are co-present.

§ The Coemergence Of Appearance

Our perceptions of the external world arise because of our karmic traces and dispositions. This is therefore not so different from the coemergence of thought. However, the emphasis is placed on what we perceive through our senses in this context. Begin by resting the mind in its natural condition by practising tranquillity meditation and then gaze at a particular object, concentrating more on the appearance of that object than on the mind itself. Hold that appearance in your mind without conceptualising about it. Simply focus on the phenomenon and do not make any inferences about whatever appears to your mind. You will gradually come to understand that the nature of appearances is also devoid of enduring essence.

You are focusing on the aspect of coemergence to realise that what appears to the mind and the nature of that appearance are inseparable. This is how we see the inseparability of appearance and emptiness. You realise coemergence when you realise that perceiver and perceived are by nature indivisible and empty. When you dream during sleep, your various dream experiences disappear upon waking. In just that way, the phenomenal experiences that appear to mind have no enduring reality. The only difference is that phenomenal appearances have continuity and they will persist for as long as our karmic traces and dispositions remain. Lingrepa says:

> The nature of mind is inseparable from phenomenal appearance.
> Do you understand that, Shivataro?

We can also apply these exercises to the objects of our other senses. As Nagarjuna says:

> When we understand the reality of one thing,
> We understand the reality of everything.

This whole notion of the 'coemergence of appearance and emptiness' is elaborated on more fully in the final chapter, in the section on the yoga of one-flavouredness. We are only going to briefly focus on it here. We should not judge or conceptualise about whatever appears to the mind; it should simply be allowed to appear vividly. To focus your attention on the object of appearance is tranquillity meditation and to realise that object of appearance to be devoid of enduring essence is insight meditation. Appearance is emptiness and emptiness is appearance. When you realise that these two are inseparable, you will experience the coemergence of appearance and emptiness. The Kagyupa masters have always said that appearances are inseparable from dharmakaya and dharmakaya is inseparable from appearances. This view can be validated by quotations from other sutras and tantras. It is not an original invention of the Kagyupas. The *Prajnaparamita-hrdaya Sutra* says:

> Form is emptiness; emptiness is form. Form is none other than emptiness; emptiness is none other than form.

The *Prajnaparamita Sutra* says:

> Emptiness and form are no different;
> They cannot be disassociated from each other.

The *Sarvadharmasvabhanasamatavipancita-samadhiraja* says:

> Even form reveals the nature of enlightenment.

It also says:

> Enlightenment and form are equal;
> They cannot be separated.

Again, it says:

> The nature of everything is the same as the nature of nirvana.

This sutra's commentary by *Manjusrikirti* says:

> The nature of form is enlightenment.
> Enlightenment is inseparable from form.

It also says:

> Sound is not separate from nirvana.

The *Samadhiraja Sutra* says:

> Form and the nature of form should not be viewed as separate.
> We should not think form is one thing and enlightenment another.

Those are Sutric quotations. The Tantric texts make the same point as the following extracts demonstrate. The *Hevajra Tantra* says:

> Grass, plants, and other vegetation
> Constitute static and active reality.
> The phenomenal world is inseparable
> From its own nature.
> We realise reality by meditating on this.
> This is the same as self-cognising wisdom,
> The producer of great bliss.

The *Vajrapanjara* says:

> The nature of the sense objects is the same as the nature of mind.

The *Samputa* says:

Looking at physical objects,
Listening to sounds,
Engaging in verbal exchanges,
Tasting different flavours,
Engaging in various activities:
If our mind is aware and undistracted
We become yogis.
That is the same as bodhichitta.
That is the diamond mind of Vajrasattva.
That is perfect complete enlightenment.

The *Lhan cig skyes pa bsam gyis mi khyab pa'i rgyud* says:

Coemergent wisdom of mind is dharmakaya.
Coemergent wisdom of phenomena
Is the radiance of dharmakaya.
Realise that mind and phenomena
Are inseparably coemergent.

Saraha says:

Earth, water, fire, wind, and space
Are inseparable from the one flavour of reality.
Nirvana and samsara are not two,
Because they have the same nature;
The nature of all-pervasive reality.

Shavaripa says:

All visual and auditory perceptions
Are like magical illusions or a mirage;
They have no enduring essence.
That which understands this is mind.
Pervaded by the reality of emptiness,
It has no centre or circumference.

Virupa says:

Whether we experience happiness or suffering
It is not outside Mahamudra.

Tilopa says:

The skandhas, sense fields, and elements

Are encompassed by Mahamudra;
Nothing is left outside it.

Naropa says:

The multiplicity of things that appear to mind
Cannot be differentiated from the nature of mind.

Naropa says:

Dharmakaya is established when appearance is self-liberated.
When you appreciate the full significance of appearances,
Everything will manifest as the great symbol.

The *Tshig bsdus* of Naropa and Maitripa says:

The self-arising nature of appearance is dharmakaya.

It also says:

If you realise the nature of reality,
You realise all external appearances
To be Mahamudra.

Maitripa says:

When you realise that the empty nature of what appears to mind
Cannot be spoken of in terms of coming together or separating;
You realise Mahamudra.

Marpa says:

When we realise that both the workings of internal mind and the appearance of external phenomena are unoriginated and empty, we realise Mahamudra.

Milarepa says:

As long as our minds are clouded by delusion,
We are bound to external phenomena
By clinging, grasping and fixation.
When we realise that appearances are devoid of essence,
The phenomenal world becomes our friend.

Gampopa says:

The manifestations of phenomena

Arise from our karmic traces and dispositions.
See them as inseparable from reality!

Many other such statements have been made by Kagyupa masters but there is no need to quote them here.

HOW TO ELIMINATE FLAWS IN MEDITATION

This has two parts:

- Incorrect approaches to meditation
- The flaws of partial meditation

§ Incorrect Approaches To Meditation

The previous chapters on tranquillity meditation stressed the importance of cultivating one-pointed concentration, free from the meditative obstacles of stupor and agitation, because that is how we maintain a blissful, lucid, and non-conceptual meditative state. However, while this meditative state might heighten our capacity to develop psychic powers, it will not lead to final enlightenment because it is not imbued with insight. A mind that has attained one-pointed concentration is not a mind that has generated insight or understood the reality of things. As Nagarjuna says:

Anyone who has not understood
That the nature of reality is emptiness,
Will not attain liberation.
They wander helplessly within samsara.

We must remember to cultivate insight. It is only through the cultivation of insight that we gain an understanding of the reality of things and recognise our own nature. We will never gain any insight if we do not practise insight meditation. Even if we practise tranquillity meditation diligently our meditation practice will not be Mahamudra meditation. The *Samadhiraja Sutra* says:

Many people engage in meditative absorptions
But this will never demolish the notion of an abiding self.
It is impossible to achieve liberation through this method.

Some people encounter difficulties in meditation because they have not received many teachings or spent much time with a teacher. They then fail to differentiate tranquillity and insight meditation and cannot maintain insight meditation if they are introduced to it. They are also vulnerable to meditative obstacles because they gradually abandon mindfulness and awareness. Some people even think they are in a meditative state when their minds are afflicted by these obstacles. I would therefore like to elaborate on these experiences.

Two primary obstacles arise when we engage in tranquillity meditation: dullness and mental agitation. We may be focused on a visual object, for example, and the image becomes fainter and more blurred until we eventually cease to perceive it. This can also happen with aural perceptions, where sound becomes increasingly faint until all awareness of it ceases. You may enter a total state of absorption where all six sensory functions cease. This is similar to experiencing a loss of consciousness. The mind loses its clarity, just like clear and translucent water that becomes very opaque and dense when frozen. That is one kind of experience associated with absorption.

At other times, your senses may still be operating, but your capacity to perceive sensations is greatly reduced because of your meditative concentration and your senses gradually become indistinguishable from one another. These states of mind are brought about by mental dullness. Avoid the experience of having your senses shut down in a state of mental absorption. Sometimes you might also lose all physical sensations so that there is neither feeling nor mental cogitation. This is almost like a total state of unconsciousness. You should not regard the absorptions as something to be cultivated; they are brought about by mental dullness and nothing more.

There are also meditative experiences where your mind has not become clouded. You may retain a sense of clarity but your mind still lacks perspicacity. That is a neutral state of mind and should not be cultivated either, because a neutral state of mind cannot bring positive results. Certain people have said a neutral state of mind leads to the formless realm, but this view does not withstand scrutiny. There is a huge difference between a neutral mental state and the formless realm. In any case, neither a neutral mental state nor the stages of absorption connected with the formless realm can be used to further your spiritual progress. Those states of mind do not have any understanding of the reality of things or the nature of the self. The *Bodhicharyavatara* says:

> A mind that fails to understand the nature of reality
> May be led to temporary states of absorption;
> But those states do not lead to liberation.
> An inactive mind cannot be the cause of enlightenment.

Other people believe that a real meditative state is the intermediate stage between our mental processes. For example, there is a gap between where one mental process has ceased and another mental process has not yet arisen. This is incorrectly regarded as the meditative state. This is not a real meditative state because it is devoid of the insight that arises from insight meditation. Such a state of mind is merely comparable to a loss of consciousness, drunkenness, or a shock within which all our mental functionings have temporarily come to cease.

Even if these states of mind are accompanied by an element of mental clarity this does not mean that proper insight is present. You must have a real understanding of the reality of things for proper insight to be present. These states of mind lack that understanding. Even if you have a rudimentary knowledge of insight meditation, you must regard your mental processes as enemies if you cannot combine that with tranquillity meditation, because your mental processes will only disturb you more and you will have enormous difficulties resting your mind. This state may be acceptable for a beginner, but it is certainly not a state of mind to be cultivated. Gampopa says:

> When the mind is peaceful, at rest, and without gross mental activities, it will not reveal the true nature of things or mind. Do not attempt to prolong such a state.

He also says:

> Some meditators believe we should block all mental processes and remain in a state of non-discriminatory meditative equipoise. Such a mental state will never bring about real wisdom. It only gives rise to an incomplete state of awareness.

Meditative experiences may appear to be blissful when you rest in a mental state that is undisturbed by preoccupations with past, present, or future. You might think you are in a meditative state where everything is perspicacious and translucent and even perceive your mind at ease and without concepts for a moment. The three experiences of bliss, clarity, and non-conceptuality can be experienced successively or in combination during meditation. However, even if such experiences arise, you should not automatically assume that they are related to insight meditation. These meditative states still lack proper insight. They are vague, elusive, indefinite, and unclear.

Another meditation system encourages meditators to contemplate things as lacking in inherent existence and as empty of substance.[14] They are also told to contemplate the mind in this way. From the Mahamudra perspective, this approach is incorrect because it leads to the view that mind is emptiness, which will lead meditators to fall into a nihilistic mode of thinking and fail to give rise to proper insight. This approach also encourages meditators to fixate on the ideas of insubstantiality, lack of inherent existence, and emptiness, leading them to become very attached to these ideas. As Nagarjuna says:

> Those people who think that emptiness is a view,
> Do not understand what emptiness means.

He also says:

> Anyone who tries to understand emptiness as a view
> Has little intelligence and only brings misfortune upon themselves.

The Mahamudra approach must avoid the nihilistic view of emptiness. Another critic of Mahamudra has suggested:[15]

> The Mahamudra approach to meditation is extremely dull.
> It reduces your intelligence to the level of an animal.
> If you are lucky, you might end up an arhat.

This critic did not properly understand the Mahamudra position. If Mahamudra really led to the animal realm, nobody should practise it because it would become impossible to pursue the three trainings of listening, contemplation, and meditation. It would also mean that animals and arhats are the same, given the critic has grouped them together this way. He goes on to say:

> Accordingly, if you want to practise the system of Mahamudra;
> You must first receive the relevant empowerments.

If this were the case, people of dull intellect would not be the proper objects of empowerment, but that would contradict the following statement in the *Hevajra Tantra*, 'people of low intelligence and the mentally incapacitated are also the object of empowerment.' It would also mean that any dull people who practise Mahamudra and receive the relevant empowerments are laying the seeds for further mental dullness.

Such criticism is ill-founded. There is a real difference between practising Mahamudra improperly and suffering the consequences of doing so. If we engage in bodhisattva practices improperly once we embark on the Mahayana path, we may regress to become a follower of Hinayana path, but that does not mean the practice of Mahayana automatically leads to becoming a Hinayana practitioner. It simply means that we have failed to practise certain things properly and have suffered from certain consequences because of it.

This applies to an incorrect practice of Dharma in general. We will only have unpleasant experiences if we do not follow the instructions properly. However, no one in their right mind would say that spiritual practice causes unhappiness. We also need a rudimentary form of insight to accomplish the four stages of meditative absorption in the formless realm and we still need to cultivate insight to traverse the path of the arhats. To say that the practice of Mahamudra leads to an animal state is therefore completely off the mark. Shravakas that practise the cessations in their own meditation system, need to have an understanding of the insubstantiality of ego, which is associated with insight meditation. This critic contradicts the third *Bhavanakrama* where it says, 'We must have first achieved cessation if we are to attain the four stages of meditative absorption.' Certain stories are told about the cessation experienced by arhats, but these are merely stories, and do not correspond to the real spiritual development of an arhat. Other critics have made the claim:

> Some lamas believe Mahamudra experience
> Is about undergoing a conversion experience
> Where all gross mental activities cease,
> As a result of having faith in the guru.
> This approach to meditation just reflects
> Physiological or mental impairment.

Nowhere does the Mahamudra literature say that a non-conceptual state of mind is the same as Mahamudra meditation so it is complete nonsense to make this claim. If this were true, the blessings of the guru and the obstructing forces would be the same. The Mahamudra tradition has never accepted a state of non-discrimination to be Mahamudra meditation.

§ The Flaws Of Partial Meditation

Some people also claim that Mahamudra meditation consists of settling the mind into a state of non-conceptuality and clarity. This meditative method may be appropriate for the experience of tranquillity meditation, but it is not correct for Mahamudra meditation. Just because we have an experience of mental clarity and non-conceptuality does not mean we have attained any kind of insight. Meditative experiences that are free from any dualistic perceptions can be regarded as the first stage of Mahamudra meditation, but consciously trying to suppress thoughts and concepts while cultivating a non-conceptual state of mind is not Mahamudra meditation. That approach also makes it very difficult to maintain a clear perspective during post-meditation.

Other people believe we must first settle our mind and then rid it of all mental activity before we can gradually cultivate a state of mental clarity. Yet others believe we should maintain mindfulness and grasp each thought and concept as it arises so that we can truly understand it. However, our approach to meditation should not be too deliberate or require too much effort. We need to learn how not to make an effort to attain a meditative state. If we fail to clear away our doubts and assumptions about the nature of thought and appearance, we will never learn to loosen our minds naturally and will continue to create problems through over-exertion.

You can use these methods at the beginning if you are aware of the dangers, but you should gradually learn to let them go. Thoughts and appearances will start to subside by themselves if you learn to eliminate your doubts and to recognise their nature. If you fail to gain a deeper sense of that nature, on the other hand, you will find it difficult to maintain this meditative approach.

It is therefore very important to recognise three things: the non-conceptual state of mind, the conceptual state of mind, and the state of mind that engages in phenomenal perceptions. You should be able to recognise the nature of mind in all three states and not assume that it is only a recognition of the non-conceptual state that matters. To regard the non-conceptual state as the archetype of all your meditative experiences will greatly restrict your meditative practice. The Mahamudra view says it is far more important to be introduced to mind in its dynamic state through variegated experiences than to cultivate a non-conceptual state.

RECOGNISING FLAWLESS MEDITATION

This has three parts:

- The nature of mind is ordinary mind
- Distinctive characteristics of ordinary mind
- Contemplating ordinary mind

§ The Nature Of Mind Is Ordinary Mind

Some uninformed people fail to understand the meaning of the term 'ordinary mind' or *tha mal gyi shes pa*. They mistakenly think this Mahamudra term is a reference to the mind of delusions and defilement. 'Ordinary' is *prakrti* in Sanskrit and *tha mal* in Tibetan, both of which have a dual meaning: a 'natural state' and a 'common state.' In the Mahamudra context, *prakrti* should be understood in the first sense.

Ordinary mind therefore refers to the natural condition of mind, which is luminous and untarnished by defilements arising from emotional conflicts and so on. The masters of the Kagyu tradition are not the only ones to call this incorruptible nature 'ordinary mind.' Similar statements have also been made by other masters. The *De kho na nyid rab tu mi nges pa'i rgyud* says:

> Ordinary mind is the source of all our spiritual boons.
> If you let your mind be in its natural condition;
> The three aspects of Buddha's being will arise.
> Allowing the mind to rest without restraint
> Gives rise to the natural emergence of wisdom;
> Mind left alone without conditioning
> Is the indestructible nature of mind itself!
> This same natural state
> Is the mother of the buddhas of the three times.

Sharipa says:

> Ordinary mind is pure when left in its natural condition.
> Do not corrupt it through interference,
> Do not try to grasp onto it,
> Do not try to release it;
> Simply leave it in its natural state.

Kotali says:

> Ordinary mind is the essence of all mental activities.
> Once the six sensory impressions are purified
> And mind ceases the mental imputations
> That creates our suffering and anxiety;
> We can let the mind be in its natural state without meditation.

Milarepa says:

> Meditators who try to grasp ordinary mind are deluded.
> Ordinary mind will elude them.

Gampopa says:

> To cultivate ordinary mind is supreme amongst all practices.
> Ordinary mind is buddha embodied in human form.

Many other quotations could be cited to illustrate the importance of understanding ordinary mind.

§ Distinctive Characteristics Of Ordinary Mind

People have begun to employ this notion of ordinary mind indiscriminately so that it has become quite a common expression. However, very few people understand what it actually means. Gampopa's *Tshogs chos chen mo* says:

> Anyone who wishes to cut through the root of cyclic existence must cultivate a proper understanding of ordinary mind. This so-called 'ordinary mind' is mind that is unvitiated by conditioned phenomena. It is untarnished by mental activities and free from mental dullness and agitation. To recognise this ordinary mind is the same as realising the wisdom of self-awareness. People who do not realise ordinary mind are called 'sentient beings.' A failure to understand ordinary mind is the same as being bereft of wisdom and will ensure that our minds are governed by ignorance. To let the mind rest in its natural condition and recognise this ordinary mind is called *rig pa* or 'intrinsic awareness.' It is also known as actuality, coemergent wisdom, the natural condition, being devoid of conceptual proliferation, luminosity, and so forth. These are all synonyms for ordinary mind.

When Gampopa says ordinary mind is not vitiated by conditioned phenomena, he means that ordinary mind has nothing to do with philosophical views, such as what mind is or what mind is not. Nor does it have anything to do with a philosophical understanding of the triadic aspect of mind, in terms of its nature, essence, and characteristic.

To say that ordinary mind is 'untarnished by mental activities,' means that it is uncorrupted by mental phenomena, such as desire, aversion, and other delusion-forming mental processes. Ordinary mind is also 'free from mental dullness and agitation,' which implies that it is never distracted and remains intrinsically aware at all times. Letting the mind rest 'in its natural condition' does not mean we need to make the mind rest, because the mind's natural tendency is to rest. Je Yanggonpa says:

> The traditional term for this natural condition of mind is
> 'non-conceptual wisdom,' but meditators refer to it as
> 'ordinary mind.' In essence, they are the same.

Some people take the words they read or hear from previous Kagyu masters out of context and thereby have an insufficient understanding of what these masters actually meant. They think 'ordinary mind' refers to the aspect of mind that is non-conceptual. However, this is incorrect. Gampopa and his nephew Gomchung maintain that ordinary mind means 'mind that is unstained by ordinary perceptive forms.' Cultivating non-conceptuality and rejecting conceptuality in meditation is not what we mean by the ordinary mind in its natural state. As Gampopa says:

> The aforementioned term, 'unstained by ordinary perceptive forms,' means that, in its intrinsic nature, ordinary mind is uncorrupted by dualistic concepts. Ordinary mind does not therefore refer to the non-conceptual aspect of mind. It should be understood as unvitiated by conceptual proliferation, but that does not mean it is the opposite to the conceptual activities of mind. If that were the case, ordinary mind would be conditioned in one form or another.

He also says:

> Ordinary mind should not be understood through conceptual categories such as existent or non-existent, empty or not empty, conceptual or non-conceptual, wholesome or unwholesome, and so forth. Ordinary mind is nothing other than the mind that we already experience in its various forms. Not trying to condition this very mind is to understand the nature of mind.

Again, he says:

> The term 'ordinary mind' means being free from any conceptual or philosophical views of mind. 'Unconditioned' means that mind is not affected by our efforts to make it rest, to place it in a meditative state, and so on.

Yanggonpa says:

> The 'nakedness' of ordinary mind means allowing it to rest in its own natural condition without conceptual interpretations is the same as understanding the nature of mind.

Understanding the nature of mind in its nakedness is the same as giving rise to non-conceptual wisdom. We have to realise that ordinary mind is not separate from the various activities of mind. We can understand it through its manifestation in concepts, thoughts, and emotions. As Yanggonpa again says:

> In brief, ordinary mind refers to that mind left in its own natural condition. Meditating on that leads to realisation of Mahamudra.

As stated earlier, you should not think that ordinary mind has anything to do with non-conceptuality. Ordinary mind must be understood in relation to three things: the nature of mind, conceptuality, and the appearance of the phenomenal world. We have to understand ordinary mind in relation to all three, rather than assuming it can be understood in relation to non-conceptuality alone. If you fail to understand it in this expansive way, you will never properly grasp that ordinary mind is the same as the natural condition of mind.[16] You have to approach ordinary mind from this perspective because you need to avoid holding onto ideas of acceptance or rejection. If you approach ordinary mind only from its aspect of non-conceptuality, you will be ignoring the aspects of conceptuality and appearance, which constitutes an exercise in acceptance and rejection. It must be said, however, that a full understanding of ordinary mind is extremely difficult to attain.[17] Yanggonpa says:

> Many competent meditation masters can elaborate on the intricacies of meditative experience, the stages of meditative absorption and so forth, but very few are competent enough to introduce the experience of ordinary mind.

Recognising ordinary mind is the same as realising our own nature. We will understand ourselves and obtain self-knowledge. Once ordinary mind is recognised, any mental activities that arise in the mind will all be self-liberated. Even thoughts that are not spiritually orientated, which would normally bind us to samsara, become liberating because we now understand the very nature of the mental factors that bound us to the samsaric condition. Gampopa says:

> Understanding the nature of whatever arises in the mind
> Is the same as perceiving the form of the buddha.

Je Gomchung says:

> Understanding the nature of mind,
> Understanding ordinary mind,
> And understanding the activities of mind;
> Constitutes self-understanding.
> This understanding is the same
> As the dawning of wisdom.

When you possess such understanding, you will no longer be disturbed, perturbed, bound, or victimised by your various mental activities. Ordinary mind is something special. When it is understood, the mind of an ordinary person becomes the mind of a buddha. Tsangpa Gyare says:

This mind of an ordinary person
Is the essence of dharmakaya;
No guru needs to show you this.
You can recognise its true nature,
Through your own efforts.

Many such statements can be found in the texts of the Kagyu tradition, but as space is limited, I will not elaborate upon them any further here.

§ Contemplating Ordinary Mind

The ability to recognise ordinary mind and contemplate it without distraction is meditation. Gampopa says:

There is no meditation other than simply resting
In the natural condition of mind.
This is ordinary mind.

We should meditate by cultivating mindfulness. If you become distracted, patch it up by reinforcing your mindfulness. The *Amrtaguhya-tantraraja* says:

This self-luminous mind
Cannot be found by meditating
Nor can it be found by not meditating.
Meditation involves discrimination,
Non-meditation involves discursive thought.
There is really nothing to meditate on
And nothing to distract us, even for a moment.

Sharipa says:

Do not view anything as negative or deficient
Use everything as part of the spiritual path.
Do not crave signs of progress in meditation.
Even though you are not trying to meditate,
In the conventional sense;
Never become victim to laziness and complacency.
Maintain your awareness at all times.

Sharipa's *Bhavanarthasiddhi* says:

When in a state of meditation
Do not meditate on anything in particular.

It is only by convention
That we call this practice 'meditation.'

Whatever meditative experiences you have while meditating—a sense of emptiness, a sense of bliss, a sense that concepts are settling by themselves, or a sense that you perceive various impressions—neither allow yourself to get drawn into them or pull away from them. Remain in an undistracted state and try to recognise the nature of these things, without conditioning them, without interfering with them, and without trying to interpret them. Meditation techniques that encourage blocking sensory impressions or suppressing mental activities are described as 'meditation with hook' by Sambojara, a Drukpa Kagyu master, who says:

Such meditation lacks profundity.

Instead of trying to block out your sensory impressions or suppress your mental activities as they manifest, view them as the radiance of the sun or waves on the ocean. Just as the sun and its radiance or the ocean and its waves are intimately related, the various activities of mind and the natural condition of mind are intimately connected. Instead of viewing mental activities as negative and something that needs to be eradicated, view them as the creative activities of mind. Simply allow them to pass and dissolve into the natural state of mind. In the Mahamudra view, nothing is intrinsically good or evil, so there is no need to view disturbing experiences as negative. You can use any experience as part of your meditation, it does not have to be a restful or peaceful state of mind. When your mind is in a dynamic state, with various thoughts, concepts, and emotions arising, meditate on that. When mind is at rest and feeling peaceful, meditate on that. When certain sensory impressions arise in the mind, incorporate that into your meditation. Nothing should be avoided or regarded as an obstacle to meditation.[18] Gampopa says:

Whether we are in a non-conceptual state
Without accepting or rejecting anything,
Or a dynamic state with proliferating thoughts;
Try to maintain a tranquil state
Without any regarding either state as good or evil.
This is non-conceptual wisdom,
This is resting in the natural state of mind.
You no longer need to make any effort.
Meditation will arise automatically
Without our being able to stop or abandon it.

Just as thoughts and concepts arise
Without your being able to stop them,
Non-dual wisdom will naturally arise.

Gomchung says:

We can never be separated from
Our intrinsic and luminous awareness.
Every thought, idea, and concept
Has the same nature as the nature of mind.
When we recognise mental phenomena to be ordinary mind,
What was binding becomes liberating.
It is seen as the expression of ordinary mind itself.
Do not view mental phenomena as negative.

You may wonder whether a beginner should simply pursue this practice of focusing the mind on each emerging thought, instead of practising the various stages of meditation. Some people have the innate ability to awaken through the instantaneous path, but most of us do not have the requisite talent for that approach. We need to be led through the various stages of meditation or we will never eliminate our doubts and assumptions about mind, thought, and appearance. We will not gain insight into the nature of these things, let alone gain certainty in their real nature. As Gampopa says:

> From the Mahamudra point of view, a yogi does the same thing as an ordinary meditator. Both a yogi and a beginner are encouraged not to control the mind. You just allow your mind to rest by not employing ideas of acceptance or rejection. It does not matter whether your mind is already in a state of rest, in a disturbed and agitated state, or engaged with various sensory impressions—all these things can be used to further your meditative state. If you do that, you will eventually experience the dawning of understanding with respect to non-dual wisdom, which arises from insight into the ordinary nature of mind. At this point, you will no longer need encouragement to practise meditation. You will not be able to stop practising!

This completes the discussion on the stages of identification.

6

Integrating Meditation and Post-meditation

WHY WE MEDITATE AFTER RECOGNISING THE NATURE OF MIND

You may have gained proficiency in meditation but if you cannot integrate meditative experiences with experiences in post-meditation you will regress to the state of any other ordinary person. As Saraha says:

> Meditators who understand something
> Of the nature of mind,
> Yet continue to behave in habitual ways,
> Are like a king who abandons his throne
> To sweep dirt in the market place.
> Do not abandon the inexhaustible bliss of spiritual experiences
> For the sensory pleasures of the world.

Tsangpa Gyare says:

> Meditators who have meditative experiences
> But cannot maintain them in everyday life
> Are like a rich man who scatters his wealth in a cyclone,
> A lion who roams with stray dogs,
> Or a precious stone in a swamp.

You must avoid this aberration. Another aberration to avoid is an excessive concern with the virtuous deeds you perform with your body, speech, and mind. If you apply yourself too ardently to the accumulation of merit through virtuous deeds, you will fail to bring an understanding of ordinary mind into everyday life. Saraha says:

Alas! Glimpsing the unconditioned nature of mind,
Yet remaining caught in conditioned phenomena
By cultivating virtues and abandoning vices,
Is like chasing after mere stones
When you already possess a precious gem.
The real nature of mind is not found
Through excessive exertion.

Tilopa says:

That which is transcendent cannot be understood
Through mental cogitations and discursive thoughts.
The meaning of non-doing cannot be understood
By becoming entangled in activities.

Atisha says:

When we come to understand the nature of mind
We will no longer have to exert ourselves
By accumulating virtue
Through the actions of body, speech, and mind.

Milarepa says:

When a mind free from discursive thoughts arises;
Do not get distracted by conventional discourses,
Or you will get mired in the eight worldly dharmas.

He also says:

When meditating on Mahamudra,
Do not get too obsessed with the virtues of body, speech, and mind.
This may lead to losing non-conceptual wisdom.
Learn how to remain in the natural state of mind.

Such statements were made by the great masters, to show us that we must learn to free ourselves from the prison of discursive thoughts, if we hope to understand that which is non-conceptual.[1] Virupa says:

If you wish to create a fire
By rubbing two sticks together;
You must rub them without interruption.
If you wish to integrate the meditative and post-meditative states,

> You must engage in meditation without interruption.

The *Abhisamayalankara* says:

> We attain insight
> By engaging in analysis,
> Becoming acquainted with the path,
> And engaging in repeated contemplation.

THE GENERAL PRACTICE OF MEDITATION

To maintain this meditation, apply mindfulness, awareness, and vigilance at all times. A sutra says:

> Meditators who constantly possess mindfulness and awareness will never be harmed by erroneous views.

The *Bodhicharyavatara* says:

> Meditators who wish to guard their minds
> Must practise mindfulness and awareness,
> Even at the cost of their lives.

The definition of mindfulness is 'the mental faculty that does not forget the object of attention.' The *Ratnakutaparipeccha Sutra* says:

> Meditators who possess mindfulness
> Will never be harmed by emotional conflicts
> Or be vulnerable to internal or external negativities.
> Mindfulness also prevents their going astray
> Or losing track of the proper spiritual path.
> Mindfulness is the door that prevents
> Unwholesome mental events entering consciousness.

In brief, mindfulness turns our mind to what is wholesome and creates the conditions for positive mental states. There are many categories of mindfulness. The *Dharmasamgiti Sutra* says:

> There is mindfulness that discriminates between entities, mindfulness that understands things individually, mindfulness that comprehends things, and mindfulness that sees the nature of things.

The *Aksayamatipariprccha Sutra* says:

> Mindfulness stabilises the mind by freeing it from its mental deceptions. Mindfulness reveals the deficiencies in the samsaric condition, steers us toward the path of nirvana, and ensures that we adhere to the path of the holy ones.

The *Dharmasamgiti* says:

> Oh, sons and daughters of noble family, mindfulness practice enables bodhisattvas to understand the nature of all things as being empty and unborn. Oh, sons and daughters of noble family, the practice of mindfulness enables bodhisattvas to realise that which is difficult to comprehend through ordinary means. Understanding the expanse and depth of reality enables bodhisattvas to realise the nature of things in a way that ordinary people, shravakas and pratyekabuddhas cannot.[2]

Understand that the sutras present mindfulness in many different contexts and with many different meanings. Bearing that in mind, we understand mindfulness in this way in the present context. Aryadeva's *Catusataka* says:

> Mindfulness is that which brings the mind back
> To the object of attention,
> When the object of attention has been temporarily forgotten.

Chandrakirti says:

> Mindfulness is the ability to focus the mind without illusions
> And connect our present mental state with the past.

The *Abhidharmasamuccaya* says:

> Mindfulness stops the mind from forgetting the object of attention and thus prevents mental distractions.

We come to understand how to cultivate virtue, based on the mindfulness of body, speech, and mind. The *Bodhicharyavatara* says:

> When we can maintain mindfulness
> And remain vigilant,
> Awareness will arise quite naturally.

It also says:

> Awareness is that which repeatedly examines
> The aspects of body and mind.

In this particular context, the most important thing is to apply mindfulness and awareness to mental phenomena. If you fail to maintain that mindfulness and awareness, you will leave yourself open to all kinds of obstacles. The *Bodhicharyavatara* says:

> Even if we engage in the three trainings,
> We will not gain much benefit from them
> If our mind is devoid of awareness.
> A pot with a hole in it cannot retain anything.
>
> Even if we are learned, have unshakeable faith,
> Complete devotion, and apply exertion;
> We will make little spiritual progress
> If we lack awareness.
>
> People who have no awareness
> Get robbed of all their merit.
> Their lack of vigilance
> Make them regress on the path.

We become immune to the attacks of delusion and the emotional conflicts if we maintain our mindfulness, awareness, and vigilance. Positive spiritual qualities will then develop and flourish in our minds. As the *Tathagatacintyaguhyanirdesa Sutra* says:

> Anyone who possesses mindfulness can tame their own mind, watch the minds of others, dispel mental processes that increase delusions, and cultivate wholesome mental qualities.

It also says:

> Maintain mindfulness and awareness and your mind will not get caught up in unwholesome patterns of thought.

The *Candrapradipa Sutra* says:

> The practice of virtues such as ethics, generosity, and patience
> Rests on the foundation of mindfulness.
> Regard mindfulness as a magic pot of treasure.

Nagarjuna's *Suhrllekha* says:

> Through mindfulness, we perceive the vices
> Of miserliness, deviousness, deception, pride, desire, and anger

The narcissism of physical beauty, knowledge, youth, and power;
And through mindfulness, we overcome them.
Mindfulness is the nectar of immortality
And the rope that binds us to samsara.
For this reason, great king,
You must strive to increase virtue,
By practising mindfulness with reverence.

These words of wisdom are reflected in the words of past Kagyupa masters:

> Revulsion is 'the foot' of meditation, interest is 'the crown' of meditation, mindfulness is 'the essence' of meditation, love and compassion are 'the activities' of meditation, and shame and conscientiousness are 'the armour' of meditation.

Therefore, abandon various distractions and practise mindfulness.

THE VITAL ROLE OF MINDFULNESS

This has six parts:

- The importance of mindfulness
- Identifying meditation and post-meditation
- Maintaining a meditative state
- Resting the mind in meditation
- Maintaining post-meditation
- How to integrate meditation and post-meditation

§ The Importance Of Mindfulness

Mindfulness is important in the three trainings of hearing, contemplation, and meditation. It is particularly important in the practise of meditation because the meditative state will go to waste without it. The *Suhrllekha* says:

Mindfulness is the highway
Travelled by the buddhas of the three times.
Practise mindfulness with great diligence,
For its loss will undo all previous effort.

Gampopa says:

> Mindfulness is the sovereign approach to developing the right view.

Instead of immersing yourself in a variety of techniques,
Concentrate on cultivating mindfulness.
Do not look for any spiritual practice apart from this.
Without mindfulness, no other practice will do any good.

Phagmo Drupa says:

If you do not apply the guard of mindfulness,
Lack of awareness will be the result.
You will be robbed of the precious jewel of wisdom
By the four negative forces.[3]

Je Drikhungpa says:

Mindfulness is the highway
Travelled by the buddhas of the three times.
Maintain mindfulness at all times,
Or nothing you do through body, speech, and mind
Will produce any results.

There are different kinds of mindfulness: 1) mindfulness that directs your attention to the relevant object of meditation, and 2) mindfulness that rests with the object of meditation. The first kind of mindfulness is for beginners learning to direct their minds towards an object of meditation. The second kind of mindfulness is for meditators who have developed some proficiency in maintaining mindfulness without distraction for a short time. At the beginning, these two types of mindfulness arise successively but as time goes by they become integrated. The ability to direct the mind to the object of meditation and the ability to rest the mind with that object of meditation will then arise simultaneously.

The mindfulness that rests with the object of meditation can be divided into two kinds: 1) mindfulness with effort, and 2) spontaneous mindfulness. Mindfulness with effort has two aspects: (i) the ability to rest the mind during certain meditative experiences, and (ii) awareness that comes from realising emptiness. Spontaneous mindfulness has these two aspects: (i) transcending any effort to apply mindfulness because awareness has given rise to wisdom so that mindfulness can now arise spontaneously, and (ii) realising that the distinction between meditation and meditator is an illusion and there is never a time when we are not meditating. At this point, meditation has become completely integrated and mindfulness occurs spontaneously without any thought of its generation.[4] Orgyenpa applied these four types of mindfulness to each of the Four Yogas of Mahamudra, and thereby multiplied them into twelve types of mindfulness. He considered the meditation on each successive type to be an extremely effective way of giving rise to increasing levels of mindfulness.[5]

Beginners should concentrate on the mindfulness that directs their attention to the relevant meditation object. Once they attain an awareness of the unborn nature of appearances, they can apply the mindfulness that rests with the object of meditation. They begin with the intensive application of mindfulness and progress to a type of mindfulness that stabilises itself naturally. Je Gotsangpa says the first type of mindfulness is an intensive form of concentration and compares it to a kingfisher catching a fish. As the preceding moment of mindfulness fades, it is revitalised by applying renewed effort.

You may wonder why mindfulness is emphasised in this way when the commentaries repeatedly speak of 'lack of recollection' and 'lack of mental fabrication.' Those references apply to meditative absorption. The *Sagaramatipariprccha* says:

> A meditator must practise mindfulness
> That is without recollection or mental fabrication.

The *Arya-Buddhasamgiti* says:

> Question: 'Oh Manjushri, what is meant by "settled in mindfulness"?'
> Manjushri: 'All things are memories or mental fabrications.'

The *Smrtiyupasthana* and the *Anumusmrti* contain many references to mindfulness without memory or mental fabrications. For example:

> Meditate on the mindfulness of the buddhas,
> Which is devoid of memory or mental fabrication.

Another reference says:

> Focus on the mindfulness that is undisturbed, direct, uncompromising and retentive, and that remembers the path of the Aryas.

'Lack of recollection' refers to the pacification of discursive thoughts. It does not signify forgetfulness, mindlessness, unconsciousness, or sleep. Similarly, the term 'lack of mental fabrication' does not signify an absence of thought. The *Avikalpapravesa-dharani* says:

> Buddha: 'Oh, son of noble family, why is it said "the meditative state of non-conceptuality lacks mental fabrication"?'
> Student: 'Because meditators transcend all dualistic thoughts.'

The *Bhavanakrama* quotes the *Avikalpapravesa-dharani* to say:

> By disengaging from mental fabrications, we abandon all the cognitive marks of form, and so forth.

The phrase 'disengaging from mental fabrications' means we stop investigating and analysing after we have seen the inconceivable nature of mind through wisdom. The same text explains that this term does not include mental activities as a whole. It refers to a specific stage of meditation where we disengage from all discursive thoughts and conceptual activity. Saraha says:

> Oh yogin, settle into the nature of mind.

Savaripa says:

> Master the process of realising
> The state of simplicity.

The *Sravakabhumi* says:

> From the beginning, meditate
> With a lack of recollection and mental fabrication
> So that you neither fixate on cognitive marks
> Or become distracted by them.

Thus, the terms 'lack of recollection' and 'lack of mental fabrication' are here used to mean 'the absence of dualistic thoughts' and 'the absence of discursive thought.' The third *Bhavanakrama* says:

> If we were to equate a lack of recollection and a lack of mental fabrication with mindlessness and mental blankness, the meditative process would be called into question. A lack of memory and thoughts can never be the cause of insight. If we were simply to seek a state of non-discrimination, even fainting could be the cause of insight, for it too lacks memory and mental activity.

To summarise, 'lack of recollection' and 'lack of mental fabrication' refer to remaining in the flow of non-conceptual mindfulness, which has been discovered through wisdom. The third *Bhavanakrama* says:

> You should therefore understand, analytical meditation precedes the contemplative state, which lacks recollection and mental fabrication. Analytical meditation is sufficient for bringing about this state of non-conceptuality. When yogins investigate through analytical meditation, they do not consciously cognise emptiness

> in the present moment, past, or future. Yogins must enter a meditative state described as 'without recollection or mental fabrication,' because you can only realise emptiness and eliminate all conceptual confusion by attaining that state.

You would do well to learn how to eliminate dualistic thinking, recollection, and mental fabrication, as well as how and when to maintain the flow of non-conceptual mindfulness. To think that mindfulness and other mental activities should be rejected is to go to the extreme.

§ Identifying Meditation And Post-Meditation

You may wonder how to establish the difference between meditation and post-meditation at this point. In the context of the Four Yogas of Mahamudra, it is difficult to attain a proper sense of meditation and post-meditation during the yoga of one-pointedness because meditation is heavily influenced by meditative experiences at this stage. Nevertheless, we can have a certain experience of meditation and post-meditation even here. Meditation is defined as a state of mind that is free from mental dullness and agitation and which is able to rest in its own natural condition. When the ordinary mind rests in its own natural condition, all of its gross mental activities will decrease and thoughts that are related to egocentricity and other conceptual activities will dissipate. For as long as that state persists, we can say we are maintaining a state of contemplation. Atisha's *Madhyamakopadesa* says:

> Meditation is attained when the mind
> Is free from mental agitation, dullness, afflictions, and memory.
> The mind will not be victimised by discursive thoughts,
> Those thieves that rob the mind of peace
> As long as it remains in meditation.

You should not understand the terms 'lack of recollection' and 'lack of mental fabrication' to mean getting rid of all mental activity. Ending mental activities is about maintaining mindfulness so that mind is no longer distracted by or caught up in discursive thoughts. As long as you can maintain mindfulness, distractions will not occur and cause the mind to wander. However, as soon as even a slight distraction arises in mind, you will be disturbed by discursive thoughts. When mind is completely distracted, it will be robbed of its calm and perceive images while grasping after conceptual thoughts. These are all related to your previous experiences and are delusion-creating mental activities. You must generate mindfulness and bring your attention to the object of concentration before it has become distracted. Noticing that mind is distracted and bringing it back to the object of concentration is related to post-meditation. For this reason, it is said, 'meditation is like space' and 'post-meditation is like illusory experience.'

From this point of view, meditation and post-meditation do not necessarily correspond to the meditative and post-meditative states. If the mind becomes distracted, but you refocus it immediately, this should be regarded as meditation even if you are not doing formal sitting practice. If the mind becomes distracted, you notice it and then bring your attention back to the object of meditation, this should be regarded as post-meditation even if it occurs during formal practice. Je Zhang says:

> When you can maintain mindfulness
> And stay in a translucently open and spacious state,
> You are in a state of meditation.
> If various discursive thoughts arise in that state,
> It becomes a post-meditative experience,
> Even if you are sitting in formal practice.
> For this reason, meditation
> Is maintaining translucency of mind,
> Whether you are walking, sitting, or lying down.

In Mahamudra, it is important not to discriminate between conceptual and non-conceptual states. There is no such distinction in reality, so you must not prefer one state of mind over the other.

There are meditation masters who teach students by first introducing the practice of meditation and then introducing post-meditation experience until the students experience coalescence of the two. These students can then incorporate whatever they experience in daily life into their meditation practice so that meditation and post meditation are integrated and reinforced. That is the intention of the Practice Lineage and we are following that approach here.

§ Maintaining A Meditative State

Gampopa said we must be skilled in three things to maintain a meditative state. The first skill is the correct physical posture, which was explained in the chapter on tranquillity meditation. The skill is dealing with the experiences of mental agitation, dullness, and whatever arises in the mind without letting them condition our experiences. The skill is about fostering your meditation by beginning with short sessions and increasing the number of sessions until you are proficient. Gampopa says:

> At the start, maintain a correct physical posture because it is difficult to stay in the meditative state without it.

Do not apply too much effort to maintain your posture; simply loosen your body and mind. To refrain from holding your physical posture too intently or too tightly is not enough; you must loosen your mind as well. Allow your body and mind to rest in the natural state by not applying too much effort. This is the first stage in maintaining a meditative state. Gampopa continues:

> In the middle, allow your mind to rest in the natural condition without restlessness.

Once you have developed the correct physical posture, make sure your mind is not afflicted by doubts such as, 'Am I doing this correctly? or 'Am I doing this incorrectly?' Instead of disturbing the mind by thinking such things, let your mind rest in its natural condition. Gampopa concludes:

> In the end, understand that all experience lacks substantiality.

No matter what experiences arise, in terms of your physical sensations or mental experiences of a comforting or disturbing nature, they are empty of inherent existence. Their nature is emptiness. If you can realise that the nature of these physical and mental experiences lacks substance, your physical and mental disturbances will dissipate automatically into their own natural condition.

Furthermore, Gampopa says, 'meditate like space,' which means that you should try to expand the mind until it has a sense of complete openness without obstruction. There should be a complete absence of stuffiness in your experience of mental spaciousness. Then he says, 'expand mind like the earth,' which means that the application of mindfulness and awareness should be all-encompassing and embrace every domain of mind without exclusion. Next he says, 'rest the mind like a mountain,' which means the mind should be immovable in the face of distractions. Then he says, 'light the lamp of mind,' which means you should try to increase your awareness so that your mind becomes illuminated. Finally, he says, 'mind should be like a crystal,' which means that mind should be free of the obscurations and defilements that normally obscure its pristine nature.

These methods for maintaining the meditative state are applicable to both meditative and post-meditative stages.

§ Resting The Mind In Meditation

1. Resting the mind in its natural state

(i) Six methods for resting the mind

According to Tilopa:

> Not engaging in retentive thoughts, non-cogitation,
> Non-projection, non-meditation, non-examination,
> While letting the mind rest in its natural state.

1) 'Not engaging in retentive thoughts' means to not dwell on past events. 2) 'Non-cogitation' means to not dwell on thoughts that condition the mind as they arise, by elaborating on them. 3) 'Non-projection' means to not anticipate certain things in the future. These three aspects of resting the mind are extremely common. Saraha says:

> From the perspective of the nature of mind,
> There is nothing to meditate on;
> So remain like an infant.

He also says:

> The mind cannot be viewed as an internal or external entity.
> So abandon thoughts and the object of thoughts
> And dwell in the mind's natural state.
> The nature of mind is free from hope and fear.

Again, he says:

> We cannot talk about a meditator or meditation,
> So what is there to meditate on?

Shavaripa says:

> Since the nature of mind is non-conceptual,
> There is nothing to meditate on.
> In just the same way, we cannot picture space.

4) 'Non-meditation' means not deliberately trying to put the mind into a meditative state by using visualisations or other methods, because this only gives rise to the dualism of subject and object. Saraha says:

> Ah! Do not try to contemplate the mind's natural state.
> By reinforcing the duality of meditation and meditator,

You will abandon the enlightened state
And only bring affliction on yourself.

He also says:

For a mind detached from inherent existence,
There is neither meditation nor meditator.
The ultimate freedom from hope and fear is inseparability.

Savari says:

An ignorant mind has nothing to meditate upon,
While a realised mind has no duality of meditation and meditator,
Space does not conceive of space.

Virupa says:

The nature of mind is free
From duality of meditation and meditator.
Mind should be free from dualistic notions of any kind.

5) 'Non-examination' means not indulging in discursive thoughts once you can rest your mind without the concept of subject and object. Saraha says:

The nature of mind is free from extremes and defilement.
Intrinsically pure, it cannot be the object of analysis.
To make it so would be like stirring a nest of poisonous snakes.

He also says:

If we engage in the analysis of conventional insight meditation,
Using the negation of one and many;
Mind will only be distracted by discursive thoughts
Instead of becoming translucent and clear.
Like rushing toward an abyss in broad daylight;
This is certainly a very pitiful state.

Again, he says:

The nature of mind cannot be understood
Through concepts or labels.
It is spacious, entityless,
And beyond conventional definitions.
The nature of mind
Is devoid of empirical determinations,

So what's the point in analysing it?
It will not be revealed as this or that.

Shavaripa says:

Through analysis the mind becomes bound.

Virupa says:

Ordinary mind is beyond expression.
It cannot be fully grasped by conventional categories.
It is not an object of conceptual analysis.
It cannot be represented as this or that.

6) 'Letting the mind rest in its natural state' means that the mind should not be interfered with but allowed to rest automatically. Saraha says:

When we allow the mind to rest in its natural state
Spiritual fruition arises spontaneously.
Spiritual fruition has been present from the beginning.

He also says:

The naturally pure nature of mind,
Should not be interfered with;
Even by practising samadhi.

Sharipa says:

The mind, which is pure, does not need any alteration.
Allow the mind to be as it is,
And you have already attained buddhahood.

Virupa says:

Ordinary mind is the same as ultimate truth;
We do not need to establish it.
We cannot abandon, analyse, or annihilate its existence.
Just allow the mind to rest in its natural condition,
And you will attain enlightenment.

Maitripa says:

Do not try to condition the nature of mind.

In this way, many different methods of maintaining the meditative state have been presented. They are all wonderful methods for determining ultimate reality. Tilopa says:

> Without mental cogitation, conceptual analysis,
> Meditation, hope, or fear,
> Allow the mind to function in its own natural process.
> That is the supreme method.

(ii) Well-known methods for resting the mind

Gampopa's *Tsog chos chen mo* elucidates four ways of resting the mind:

> Watch the nature of mind and 1) rest the mind loosely, 2) rest the mind in its natural condition, 3) rest the mind comfortably, and 4) rest the mind in a relaxed manner.

To 1) 'rest the mind loosely' means to understand that mind has the ability to rest quite naturally when left alone so we do not have to force it to remain in a state of meditation. Gampopa says:

> Meditators who can really rest the mind loosely
> Experience an excellent meditative stability.
> Meditators with less ability to rest the mind loosely
> Experience meditative stability according to their looseness.
> Meditators with no ability to rest the mind loosely
> Have no ability to experience a meditative state.

You may wonder, 'Why does the mind remain in its natural condition when it is not interfered with?' and 'Why is our meditation better the more we are able to rest the mind loosely?' When you do not react to the experiences that arise in meditation with either attraction or aversion, but allow your thoughts and emotions to loosen and settle, obsessive mental processes naturally come to cease and mind automatically enters into a restful state. This is called 'the integration of tranquillity and insight meditation.' Mahasiddha Zhang says:

> When mental activities are allowed to rest loosely,
> And you clearly perceive mental events
> Without entertaining discursive thoughts,
> There will be a sense of total expansiveness, like space itself.
> This experience is none other than dharmakaya;
> The embodiment of luminosity.

Saraha says:

When you allow mind to rest during meditation
When in an agitated state;
Mind will free itself
And agitation dissipates automatically.

He also says:

If you apply concentration with too much pressure
Mind will only become more agitated.
If mind is allowed to rest in a loose manner,
You will achieve a contemplative state.
The things that shackle ordinary people,
Become the cause of liberation
For meditators skilled at letting mind be.

Tilopa says:

When mind is unconditioned and loose,
It automatically settles in a restful state.

He also says:

The nature of mind is like space itself.
We cannot entertain it with discursive thoughts.
If you can rest in that natural state of spaciousness
Without trying to make the mind rest,
That is the same as attaining Mahamudra.
By becoming acquainted with this
You will achieve supreme liberation.

To 2) 'rest the mind in its natural condition' means that since the nature of mind is devoid of empirical determinations and free from any perceivable attributes or characteristics, you will come to realise that it cannot be understood. To rest the mind in its natural condition simply means remaining in the natural state of mind. Just like a gold nugget the has not yet been moulded and processed by a goldsmith, the natural state of mind is undisturbed by thoughts, concepts, and emotions. Some meditation masters call this, 'letting the mind rest without any uncertainties,' like a thriwa bird entering its nest. Saraha says:

When we can engage in the meditation of non-cogitation,
We have truly understood the pith instructions of masters.

He also says:

> Contemplating non-conceptual wisdom
> Which is beyond discursive thoughts,
> Is the attainment of fruition.

Savari says:

> Being trained in understanding the nature of mind
> Is the supreme of all meditation caves.

Virupa says:

> Coemergent wisdom cannot be found externally.
> To realise that the nature of mind is devoid
> Of all characteristics and determinants
> Is to realise Mahamudra.

To 3) 'rest the mind comfortably' means allowing your mental processes to rest in their natural condition without desiring, grasping or applying effort. Just as a prisoner longs to escape when he is imprisoned but has no such thoughts of escaping when he is free, mind becomes increasingly agitated when you make an effort to rest it. Simply let it rest comfortably without any pressure. Saraha says:

> A man in shackles wants to escape in the ten directions,
> But when released, remains in a state of immovability
> Like a stubborn camel fastened to a post.

To 4) 'rest the mind in a relaxed manner' means resting the mind without entertaining any thoughts of reality or unreality, good or evil, acceptance or rejection, clinging or detachment. Simply let the mind go, like straw that lies loosely on the ground when you sever the rope that binds it. As Saraha says:

> Whatever your mind fixates on is what you should relinquish.

He also says:

> Think not of thingness or nothingness, samsara or nirvana,
> Or any aspiration to attain nirvana or abandon samsara.
> Oh yogin, just try to rest in a state of equanimity.

Elsewhere, Gampopa describes three ways of resting the mind: 1) without modulation, 2) with relaxation, and 3) in its natural condition. Resting the mind without modulation is like resting the mind comfortably and involves not trying to condition or modulate experiences as they arise. Whatever mental disturbance arises during meditation, it is dissipated by itself, without the need for antidotes. Hold your mind in the manner of a child, with a sense of mental clarity but without grasping after anything. Savari says:

> Ordinary mind is the same as the natural state.
> There is no reason to make the mind rest in its natural condition;
> The mind's natural tendency is to do so.
> There is no need to modify or modulate the mind at all.

He also says:

> Do not hold your breath intensely or concentrate too hard.
> Allow mind to be unconditioned yet aware, like a child.

Maitripa says:

> When mind remains in an unmodulated state,
> It is the same as dharmakaya.
> As long as we try to condition the mind
> Through the techniques of meditation,
> We will not attain full realisation.

He also says:

> Meditation involves remaining in an undistracted state.
> Do not try to meditate by conditioning your mind or speech.
> The proper state of meditation is not attained
> By distinguishing between meditation and non-meditation,
> Or by applying antidotes.

(iii) Other methods for resting the mind

Nagarjuna says:

> Do not engage in mental cogitations,
> Entertain discursive thoughts
> Or modulate your experiences;
> Let the mind rest in a relaxed manner.
> The unconditioned mind is the nature of mind.
> This is the attainment of non-dual wisdom.

He points out these four ways of resting the mind: 1) resting the mind in non-cogitation, 2) resting the mind through non-meditation, 3) resting the mind through non-modulation, and 4) resting the mind in a relaxed manner. Longchenpa's *Sems nyi ngal so* says:

> Listen, my son, meditators wishing to find rest
> Should maintain a non-distracted state
> By not modulating the mind
> And resting the mind comfortably.

Three different kinds of resting the mind are elucidated here: 1) maintaining a non-distracted state, 2) not modulating the mind, and 3) resting the mind comfortably. Gampopa says:

> Rest your mind like the sky free from clouds!
> Rest your mind like the ocean free from waves!
> Rest your mind like a lamp undisturbed by wind!

These images represent three methods of resting the mind: 1) resting through cultivating the state of non-conceptuality, 2) resting through cultivating the state of stability, and 3) resting through cultivating the state of unvitiated intrinsic awareness. The *Caturaksamahamudra* says:

> Rest the mind as if it were a garuda, effortlessly soaring through space. Rest the mind with total stability, like the ocean free from waves! Rest the mind in its intrinsic state of awareness, like the sun unobscured by clouds! Rest the mind as if it were waves on the ocean, so that whatever arises is the pure creativity of mind itself! Rest the mind as if it were a child admiring frescoes on a temple wall, so that it is clear but non-grasping! Rest the mind like a bird soaring through space, so that it leaves no traces in the sky!

The meditation master Khendrup Chegompa lists the following methods for resting the mind: 1) resting the mind in the pristine non-conceptual state without agitation or effort, 2) resting the mind in an unmodulated state without vitiation, and 3) resting the mind in its natural condition. A second set of three consists of the following: 1) resting the mind in its authentic condition, 2) resting the mind in a relaxed manner, and 3) resting the mind in total clarity. He discusses two further methods: 1) resting the mind in non-meditation, and 2) resting the mind in non-distraction.

As we can see, many different methods for resting the mind have been enumerated. I will not elaborate upon them all here. What has already been said should be enough to learn how to rest the mind. These methods will also become clearer as we proceed with the text.

Previous Kagyu masters have said that we can learn to rest the mind through its aspect of rest or through its clarity. You let the mind rest through its aspect of rest by letting it remain soft, quiet, serene, and loose. You let the mind rest through its clarity by allowing it to be clear, lucid, vivid, fresh, lustrous, and distinct.

You can learn to rest the mind in these two ways. Beginners must first learn to cultivate one-pointedness, because that will help to develop a certain level of mental clarity. Gampopa says:

> You must train in one-pointedness
> Until you develop the ability
> To resist distractions.
> The ability to recognise the innate clarity of mind
> Arises from that.
> When you accomplish these things,
> You have successfully established yourself in meditation.

Nonetheless, even if you have firmly established yourself in meditation practice, this does not mean that you have gained any realisation. These are only meditative experiences, which are quite distinct from meditative realisations.[6] Gampopa also says:

> Experiencing the mental clarity associated with meditative experiences and remaining in that state without distraction is meditative restfulness. Realising the nature of things as empty of inherent existence through prajna or insight is realisation.

In brief, until we gain proper realisation, we should regard the meditative experiences of bliss, clarity, and non-conceptuality as quite uncertain and transient. These are not the same as meditative realisations.[7] Even if you attain a sense of one-pointedness in meditation, your experience of the intrinsic nature of mind will only be an intellectual exercise, if you have no meditative realisation. Milarepa says:

> One-pointed concentration is not real awareness.
> The trunk of the tree, not the fruit;
> It is not genuine non-conceptuality.

We need to attain the union of mental clarity and mental stability, which comes from the practices of tranquillity and insight meditation. These two must be practised conjointly, not separately.

2. The condensed explanation

(i) Maintaining a state of non-meditation

The error of applying intellectual processes or trying to condition the mind so that you can cultivate a meditative state has already been explained from the Mahamudra perspective. However, I will elaborate a little more on it here to bring out the essential points of those discussions.

The natural condition of mind is free from all extremes and partialities so your attitude towards that natural condition should also be impartial. Do not judge anything that arises in mind as inferior to your experiences of emptiness and luminosity. Do not entertain thoughts of reality or non-reality, what should be abandoned or cultivated. Simply meditate without any discursive thoughts.

Since the nature of mind is spacious and devoid of direction, do not focus with too much focus or deliberation on an object of meditation. Since the nature of mind does not increase or decrease, do not approach it with any hope of realising it or any fear of losing it. Nor should you cling to the nature of mind as some sort of concept. Since the nature of mind transcends any notion of good or evil, do not approach it with the idea of acceptance or rejection. Since the nature of mind is devoid of all attributes and characteristics, don't approach it with any mental image or visualisation nor apply any excessive effort.

In brief, meditate without meditating. This means that you meditate without any conscious effort to apply techniques because that kind of meditation only gives rise to discursive thoughts and mental images and you start to cling to these as characteristics of mind. This approach to meditation won't lead to the proper view or meditation. A sutra says:

> The meditation of the prajnaparamita is nothing other than non-meditation.

The *Guhyasamaja* says:

> Since the nature of mind is empty
> And lacks characteristics,
> There is nothing to meditate on,
> No meditator and no act of meditation.
> Reality can't be described
> In terms of existence or non-existence.
> A mental image can't serve as the object of meditation.

The *Vajrapanjara* says:

> We should not meditate on the notion of emptiness
> Or the notion of non-emptiness.

Saraha says:

> Relinquish everything you are conceptually attached to.

He also says:

> Whatever you hang onto conceptually
> Will prevent your entering liberation.

Again, he says:

> Even if we cling to something as small as a sesame seed
> In our meditation;
> It will only give rise to suffering.

Savari says:

> When we meditate on Mahamudra
> Do not meditate on anything.
> There is nothing, even the size of an atom
> To be meditated upon.

Virupa says:

> When you conceptualise the nature of mind,
> You become attached to that meditative experience.
> If you think meditative experience
> Is the same as realising the nature of mind,
> You have gone astray.

Tilopa says:

> Gaze into reality
> Without entertaining discursive thoughts.

Maitripa says:

> As long as we maintain awareness without distraction
> We do not need to condition body or speech.
> Do not entertain thoughts of meditation or non-meditation;
> There is no need to apply antidotes.

(ii) Maintaining a state of non-distraction

We cannot apply techniques that condition the mind, but we must maintain our awareness at all times. The mindfulness that allows us to remain in an undistracted state is a progressive thing. It begins with the ability to maintain mindfulness in a feeble way, progresses to the practice of mindfulness through the Four Yogas of Mahamudra, and culminates in the realisation of the nature of mind. In this context, maintaining mindfulness and awareness simply means remaining in a state of awareness of the nature of mind. However, this is impossible for a beginner, so we must first learn to remain with whatever arises in the mind by applying mindfulness. This will help to resist distractions. Saraha says:

> The mind should observe itself without distractions.
> When the mind becomes distracted
> The opportunity to realise the nature of mind
> Is lost in a forest of discursive thoughts.

Sharipa says:

> Undistracted mind should watch itself.

Virupa says:

> Maintain mindfulness without thinking
> about existence or non-existence.

Tilopa says:

> A mind free from distractions is the king of meditation.

Maitripa says:

> Remain in a state of non-distraction.

There are different levels of non-distraction. The ability to maintain a certain level of mindfulness or awareness does not automatically mean you are meditating properly. You may have a sense of being present and aware at the beginning, but on closer examination, you will see that distractions are occurring on a very subtle level. A similar distraction may occur in relation to the nature of mind. Since the mind is devoid of any direction, subtle mental processes may give rise to the meditative experiences of bliss, clarity, and non-conceptuality, but simply regard this as a very subtle form of distraction.

In brief, recognise that even subtle forms of conceptual understanding about the nature of mind are to be transcended. You may have a subtle understanding of the nature of mind in relation to mind's characteristics or lack of characteristics but even the idea of not entertaining discursive thoughts can become a discursive thought. All of this must be gradually left behind. Saraha says:

> When mind is purified of all defilements,
> No emotional conflicts can arise.

He also says:

> When mind becomes empty of discursive thoughts,
> We attain enlightenment.

Virupa says:

> As long as we engage in discursive thoughts,
> We are bound to the dualistic condition,
> Which will force us to remain caught in cyclic existence.
> We must ascertain the nature of discursive thoughts.
> When we realise their empty nature,
> They will disperse and become liberated.

He also says:

> The notions of emptiness, non-origination, and ultimate reality
> Are very remote from a direct experience of emptiness.

Sharipa says:

> Look! Look! But do not look at anything.
> Meditate! Meditate! But do not meditate on anything.

Learn to cultivate a meditative state from the beginning. There has to be an object of meditation, the application of effort to remain with that object of meditation, and so on. Start with the meditative techniques outlined in the previous chapters and gradually gain an understanding of the nature of mind. You can then move slowly and progressively through the Four Yogas of Mahamudra until you realise the nature of mind is devoid of all characteristics and empirical determinations. This progressive blooming of the enlightened mind is conveyed by examples of the waxing moon, cub of a lion, and so on.[8]

(iii) The vital points of Mahamudra meditation

We can see that the methods of non-meditation and non-distraction cover all aspects of our meditative states. Non-cogitation, not entertaining discursive thoughts, not conditioning the mind, and not analysing our thoughts are all aspects of non-meditation. Resting in the natural state of mind, resting the mind in a relaxed manner, and resting the mind in its own condition are all aspects of non-distraction.

In the Mahamudra system, the ability to let the mind rest without an object of meditation is tranquillity meditation. The ability to maintain awareness without distraction while in that state of rest is insight meditation. Non-meditation and non-distraction conjoin in this way because the qualities of tranquillity and insight are present when these two methods are integrated.

This state is described in many ways, depending upon the literature that you consult. For example, it is described as 'non-conceptual wisdom' or 'non-deluded awareness' in Sutric literature. Sometimes it is even described as 'emptiness.' This same state of mind is described as 'coemergent wisdom' in Tantric literature. Sometimes it is referred to as 'luminosity' and also as 'emptiness.' In Mahamudra literature, it can also be referred to as 'the coemergent nature of mind,' 'the actuality of mind,' 'the nature of mind' and so on. This mind is described in various ways in the different teachings of Buddha. The *Prajnaparamita-samcayagatha* says:

> Though ordinary people talk about seeing space
> When asked to describe it,
> They have not seen space at all.
> When we perceive the nature of mind,
> We realise that there is nothing to perceive.
> When we perceive 'nothing to be perceived,'
> We have realised the real nature of things.

The *Samputa* says:

> Remaining in a state of non-conceptual samadhi
> Is like a sky free from clouds.

The *Bodhisattvabhumivrtti* says:

> Perceiving space and perceiving emptiness are the same.

The *Dharmadhatustotra* says:

> When we abandon discursive thoughts
> And realise the nature of mind,
> We realise that the nature of all things is empty.
> That is to realise the dharmadhatu.

The *Bodhicharyavatara* says:

> When mind does not think discursively
> About existence or non-existence,
> All proliferating thoughts subside.
> We realise the nature of emptiness.

Atisha says:

> Since the dharmadhatu is devoid of empirical determinations,
> The mind that apprehends it is free of defilements.

At this point, certain warnings must be given to beginners of meditation. An over-emphasis on non-meditation during tranquillity practice can lead to mental dullness. An over-fixation on non-distraction during insight meditation can lead to mental agitation. The way to deal with dullness and agitation has been dealt with extensively in the relevant chapters so you should consult those chapters again to refresh those details. Briefly stated, the right approach to these distractions is to allow your mind to rest and then maintain awareness without being too tight or too loose, just like a brahmin spinning his yarn. Gampopa says:

> Allow your mind to rest in a relaxed manner
> So it is free from dullness and agitation.

Phagmo Drupa says:

> When we meditate on the dharmakaya,
> Do so as a brahmin spinning yarn;
> Without conditioning and without modulation.
> Simply let the mind rest in a relaxed manner,
> Unvitiated by mental dullness or agitation.
> Apply Mahamudra techniques if it becomes so.

Critics have objected to the 'brahmin spinning yarn' example, saying:

> Some say, 'let the mind rest in its natural condition'
> And call this Mahamudra, using the example
> of a brahmin spinning yarn.
> While wool is unconditioned in its natural state
> It becomes something else once spun
> And no longer corresponds to an unmodulated state of mind.
> Therefore, this example is incorrect.

These critics have failed to appreciate the significance of this example. The yarn a brahmin spins is used to illustrate the tautness of the yarn not the substance of the yarn. We have to learn to let the mind go in a relaxed manner, so that it is not too tight or too loose; it can be compared to a brahmin's thread. If the thread is spun too fast and too tight, it will break, if it is spun too slow and too loose, it will fray. In the same way, the mind should rest in a moderate manner, without being too uptight or too distracted. These critics seem to have also misunderstood what it means 'to rest in the natural state of mind.' Just resting the mind is not the same as resting the mind in its natural condition. Je Gotsangpa says:

> The way to maintain the meditative state
> Is to gaze into the depths of the nature of mind
> Where nothing is revealed.
> The nature of mind is not an entity
> To be revealed as this or that.
> Resting in non-cognition is meditative equipoise.

The nature of mind is not an entity that can be grasped through having certain attributes, qualities, or characteristics. However, when we allow the mind to rest loosely in its natural condition, we can experience its non-substantiality. We rest in this natural state by maintaining mindfulness and awareness. We do not rest by deliberately focusing on anything or by clinging to notions of cultivation and abandonment. That summarises the vital points of Mahamudra meditation.

§ Maintaining Post-Meditation

1. Maintaining the attitude of mindfulness

You may wonder at this point, 'Now that I have some idea of how to remain in equanimity by resting in the natural state during meditation, what attitude should I have during post-meditation?' Your attitude during post-meditation should be the same as your attitude during formal meditative training. Begin by learning to apply mindfulness and awareness in everyday life and do so consistently.[9] Je Drikhungpa says:

> If you are skilled in applying mindfulness, you are skilled in meditation. Oh, my son, cherish the practice of mindfulness.

There is no difference between meditation and post-meditation as far as the cultivation of mindfulness is concerned. You must apply the same mindfulness in both mental states. While there is no difference in terms of mindfulness itself, there is a difference in the way mindfulness is applied. When you engage in wholesome activities during everyday life, you may precipitate certain sensory impressions through various circumstances. You must learn to stay with your sensory impressions when this occurs.

Whether it is a visual, auditory, olfactory, gustatory, or tactile sensation, you must try to remain in a purely phenomenological mode without becoming immersed in the conceptual activities of acceptance and rejection or believing what you perceive to have inherent existence. This phenomenological way of viewing the world is comparable to an infant perceiving a temple. Whatever appears to the infant's mind is vivid and clear but it doesn't give rise to an impulse toward craving, clinging, and so on. You must maintain this sense of mental spaciousness while experiencing sensory impressions.

In brief, this involves the application of two practices that were previously outlined: 1) realising the nature of discursive thoughts, and 2) realising the nature of sensory impressions. Try to apply what you learned from these two practices in meditation when you go about your everyday affairs. The *Bodhicharyavatara* says:

> It is not seeing or hearing things
> That needs to be negated.
> It is our inveterate tendency
> To believe in the reality of things
> Which needs to be negated;
> This is the cause of our sufferings.

2. Practising mindfulness in everyday experience

You may wonder how to apply this mindfulness to everyday experience. This can be illustrated by the way a herdsman looks after his cattle. A herdsman does not try to lead his herd nor constantly crack his whip; he allows the cattle to wander quite freely within certain limits. As long as they remain in his sight, he does not try to round them up or put pressure on them. In the same way, we should not try to block or chase after the sensory impressions that arise during post-meditation. Just as the herdsman allows his cattle to wander about on the grass, you should allow your six senses to operate without clinging to their impressions. Try instead to perceive the inseparability of phenomena and emptiness. Whatever appears is empty of inherent existence. Whatever lacks inherent existence will manifest.

You need simply to be present with whatever sensory impressions you have. Je Gotsangpa says:

> When you are in a state of meditation
> Remain with your discursive thoughts,
> Then relax into that state,
> And discursive thoughts will dissipate by themselves!
>
> When you are in post-meditation
> Gaze at your sensory impressions,
> Without engaging in discursive thoughts,
> And try to see that everything lacks inherent existence.
> Without clinging to impressions, they are vividly perceived.
> Discursive thoughts will arise in peaceful and dynamic states,
> As long as mind does not cling to them,
> It is 'discursive thoughts turning into meditation.'
> You don't need to cultivate peaceful mental states,
> Or abandon discursive thoughts.
> Pure meditation is an undistracted state;
> Remain in an undistracted state without meditating.

Je Gotsangpa gave these relevant instructions in these simple terms. Learn to apply mindfulness to all activities during everyday experience, whether it be eating, walking, or sleeping. At the beginning, your mind will be distracted, but if you engage in formal meditation consistently, you will learn to carry that mindfulness into post-meditation. Just as you learnt to apply mindfulness through effort in meditation, you must learn to apply mindfulness through effort during post-meditation. You will then gradually develop the ability to stay with your sensory impressions without distraction and to perceive phenomena as inseparable from emptiness.

If you find it difficult to apply mindfulness in everyday life, return to the practice of introducing the 'inseparability of discursive thoughts and emptiness' and the 'inseparability of phenomenal experience and emptiness,' as outlined in previous sections of this text.

The following exercise will help to improve your practice of mindfulness in everyday life. When your mind has settled peacefully in a state of meditation, deliberately give rise to a particular discursive thought and then observe the origin, persistence, and dissipation of that thought. This exercise will help you to realise the inseparability of discursive thought and emptiness and the inseparability of phenomenal appearance and emptiness. Saraha says:

The discursive thoughts that afflict mind
Are free from inherent existence,
Their nature is emptiness;
Because they are devoid of any notion of causes and conditions.
Discursive thoughts will be self-liberated
If you realise this; there is no greater insight than this.
Such insight cannot be generated
Simply by perceiving or hearing things.

He also says:

Normal consciousness sees things dualistically
As perceiver and perceived.
Realise that the nature of perceiver and perceived is the same
Then remain in that state of non-distraction;
And you will achieve liberation.
Not to realise this is the cause of all anguish.

Savari says:

All the rivers in India, the Ganges and the rest,
Merge into the ocean and become salty.
The deluded mind and its discursive thoughts
Merge into the undifferentiated state of dharmakaya
And exhibit the flavour of emptiness.

Virupa says:

None of the empirical determinations of mind
Have any enduring substance.
They are dependent upon our mental
imputations and conceptual apparatus.

3. Recognising the nature of discursive thoughts

(i) Recognising the nature of objects

We learn to recognise the nature of phenomenal appearances without discursive thoughts in post-meditation as a result of arduous meditative training in mindfulness. Like two friends accidentally meeting in the street who immediately recognisie one another, we recognise the empty nature of an object as soon as we apprehend it. Saraha says:

The nature of reality is present in all things,
In front and in back, to the left and to the right.

He also says:

Whatever arises in mind is an expression of emptiness.
Can anyone separate the water from its waves?

Maitripa says:

All the various mental processes
That arise in the mind
Are expressions of mind's nature.
As soon as we realise their nature
They are revealed to be the nature of mind.

(ii) Recognising the state of awareness

Practitioners not fully trained in meditation may become temporarily distracted, but are then able to catch themselves within that state of distraction because of their rigorous meditative training in mindfulness, and rest with whatever has arisen in that moment. This ability to bring the mind back to a state of awareness is comparable to snow falling on a rock or lake; where snow melts as soon as it lands. Saraha says:

Just as a bird that flies from a boat
To wander about in the sky
Must eventually return to that boat;
The mind that wanders must eventually return to itself.

Sharipa says:

A bird that soars in the sky above a boat
Must eventually return to its perch.
A mind that becomes distracted
Must eventually return to its natural condition.

(iii) Remaining undisturbed by activities of mind

Meditators fully trained in the practice of meditation will not be disturbed by their mental processes in the way beginners are disturbed. For example, if it starts to storm when a forest fire is small, the flames will be easily extinguished. If it starts to storm once a forest fire has gathered strength, the flames will only spread and grow. The mind of an experienced meditator is equivalent to the first analogy, because mental agitation, mental well-being, and other meditative experiences automatically reveal themselves as expressions of the nature of mind. Saraha says:

> Everything that manifests in the mind
> Arises as an expression of the nature of mind,
> Just as a spark gives rise to a forest fire.

Maitripa says:

> Emotional conflicts cause great wisdom.
> They aid the meditator,
> Like a forest fuels a fire.

He also says:

> When we realise phenomenal appearance
> Lacks inherent existence;
> It is revealed as the dharmadhatu.
> Discursive thoughts reveal themselves
> To be expressions of wisdom.
> The inseparability of these two is dharmakaya.

Phagmo Drupa says:

> Discursive thoughts enhance your spiritual growth
> If we meditate in the four sessions of a day.
> Regard meditative experiences
> As the meeting of old friends,
> As snow falling on rocks,
> As the spreading of a forest fire,
> As the experience of inner bliss and emptiness.
> The 'meeting of old friends' refers to
> Bumping into an old friend by accident
> And immediately recognising them.
> When discursive thoughts arise,
> You recognise their nature immediately
> And realise the emptiness of the nature of mind.
> This is the same as 'recognising the nature of objects.'
>
> 'Snow falling on rocks' refers to
> The way snow melts when it lands on a warm rock.
> When you realise the nature of mind

In the very moment of distraction;
Whatever arises in mind is inseparable from dharmakaya.
When you can realise this automatically
This is the same as 'recognising the state of awareness.'

The 'spreading of a forest fire' refers to
The way a fire spreads and consumes everything
Without discriminating about location or purity.
Even should it start to rain or hail,
This only helps a raging fire to spread more quickly.
Meditators who are firmly established in their practice
Realise the nature of their mental processes
No matter what is taking place in their mind.
Whatever discursive thoughts arise, be they good or evil,
Notions of perceiver and perceived, attraction and aversion,
Will be consumed without cultivation or abandonment.
You simply need to recognise their nature.
The more discursive thoughts you have,
The more conducive for your meditative progress.
This is the same as 'remaining undisturbed by activities of mind.'

Once you arrive at this final stage of meditation,
It no longer matters what discursive thoughts arise;
They will no longer disturb your mind in any way.
You will now only have meditative experiences
Of bliss, clarity, and non-conceptuality
Even being pricked by a needle gives rise to bliss.
When you engage in walking, sitting, or lying down,
Your experiences will be pervaded by bliss and clarity.
These experiences should be regarded
As signs of meditative development.

4. Realising post-meditative perception is a magical display

(i) How to perceive everything as illusion-like

There are many ways to understand the concept of a magical display. Some people think that realising everything to be like an illusion occurs when we see everything that arises in the mind or that appears to the senses to be unreal. Other people think it is when we attain meditative equipoise, we have a certain understanding of emptiness and can contemplate the amorphous vision of whatever appears to the senses. Yet others think it is when we rest with whatever arises in the mind and see it as amorphous.

All three understandings are mistaken. To assume that seeing everything as without reality is sufficient to realise everything as illusion-like is an extreme view, because it leaves no provision for understanding dependent origination. This understanding of illusion falls into the extreme of nihilism. To assume that simply being able to contemplate the vision of phenomenal appearances is also incorrect, because it fails to appreciate the significance of being able to determine the nature of phenomenal appearance. To understand how to perceive everything as illusion-like, you need to understand the nature of phenomenal appearances. The third assumption is also incorrect because it regards everything that arises in the mind as illusory. This only involves seeing everything as illusory, nothing more.

To understand what the ability to perceive everything as illusion-like in post-meditation actually means, the question of illusion must be examined in relation to two aspects of emptiness: 1) emptiness as it is in itself without reference to the empirical world, and 2) emptiness in relation to the empirical world. Emptiness as it is in itself obviously cannot manifest literally because emptiness does not possess the characteristics of an entity and therefore has no attributes. Emptiness in relation to the empirical world is revealed through existing things. We will examine the latter aspect of emptiness. How then is illusion to be understood in relation to the empirical world? The *Prajnaparamita-samcayagatha* says:

> To perceive the five skandhas as without inherent existence
> Without separating the skandhas or their illusory nature;
> Is to understand emptiness in relation to empirical characteristics.

The *Samadhiraja Sutra* says:

> The nature of illusion can be understood
> By the examples of tricks, dreams, mirages,
> The city of the gandharvas, and so on.
> Understand all things this way.

Many different examples of illusion are given in other texts. To make this more comprehensible, I will present only one example: the tricks of a magician. A magician can conjure up various objects, such as a horse or elephant. These objects have no existence of their own, but people in the audience will nonetheless be fooled into thinking the horse and the elephant are real. There is a discrepancy between how the magician views the phenomena he has given rise to and how the audience views it. The magician does not take the apparitions seriously while the audience does. The *Samadhiraja* also says:

> A magician may conjure up forms
> Such as a horse or an elephant,
> But they are devoid of reality.
> In the same way, regard all things
> To lack inherent existence.

(ii) How to perceive the post-meditative state as illusion-like

To appreciate the concept of perceiving all things to be illusion-like, we have to understand how a magician views his own tricks. The magician perceives the phenomena he has manifested, but he does not get taken in by his own tricks. There are two things involved here: perception of the phenomena and belief in the reality of the phenomena. Meditators continue to perceive the empirical world in the same way as ordinary beings, but they no longer believe that phenomenal appearances have any enduring essence. They understand that phenomena arise due to causes and conditions, due to having functioning sensory organs, and so on. It is the same phenomenal world that is perceived by advanced meditators and by ordinary people, but meditators do not believe that it has any kind of inherent existence. This is called, 'perceiving all things to be illusion-like in post-meditation.' Savari says:

> When we probe into the nature of things
> We realise that they are like a dream;
> They have no enduring essence.
> That frees us from attachment and clinging.
> Our minds will become peaceful
> When we realise that the entire phenomenal world
> Is like an illusion.

He also says:

> Every sensory impression should be regarded as an illusion, a mental image, a reflection; the mind that perceives this is like space.

To understand the inseparability of the phenomenal world and emptiness, it is easier to begin by understanding that the nature of mind is empty. This is achieved by remaining in a state of meditative contemplation during post-meditation and then consistently reflecting on the notions of inseparability, discursive thoughts, phenomena, and emptiness. Regard all phenomena as illusions, but do not become so obsessed with those illusions that you disregard causal dependency.

Some people become so obsessed with the notion of emptiness that they disregard dependent origination and thereby fail to understand the real meaning of illusion. This is a nihilistic view and totally incorrect. Such people should seek to remedy this view by gaining a correct understanding of karmic cause and effect. In brief, it is essential to realise two things simultaneously: 1) the cause and effect of actions, and 2) the insubstantial nature of all things. The *Bodhisattvabhumivrtti* says:

> When we are fully aware of the intrinsic emptiness of all things, we abide by the principle of karmic cause and effect. Oh, how wonderful! Oh, how marvellous!

By investigating the assumed inherent existence of all things, we develop an awareness of non-discrimination. Despite being devoid of essence, emptiness manifests as form, sound, and so on. These two aspects—insubstantiality and the appearance of phenomena—are characterised by the Kagyu masters as 'space-like emptiness' and 'illusion-like emptiness.' Following from this, the current exponents of this system describe these two aspects as 'space-like equipoise' and 'illusion-like equipoise.' They sometimes also refer to them as 'transcendent awareness' and 'awareness of phenomena.'

The teachings of the Practice Lineage often refer to methods that maintain an awareness of the nature of mind without trying to reduce mental agitation. This is because the nature of mind is always steady and unmodulated, while mental agitation is only transitory. However, some people misunderstand this instruction, taking it to mean that we must sustain agitated consciousness as spontaneous experience. Other people misunderstand this instruction to mean we must maintain even a deluded awareness without interference. Both understandings fail to differentiate between mind and meditation, between what should be rejected and what should be accepted. The real instruction is about how to allow agitated thoughts to come and go without acceptance or rejection, at a particular level of meditative attainment. It should only be practised after you have gained some insight into the nature, essence, and characteristic of mind. Only then can you maintain awareness amidst agitated thoughts without attempting to alter anything.

It has been said that if you fail to realise the mind's innate clarity through analytical meditation, in the manner of someone examining a bone by crushing it, you will be distracted by the various meditative experiences that arise. You must be able to purify the experiences of bliss and clarity, and maintain your awareness, without becoming emotionally attached to the experiences. Otherwise, you will simply reinforce your deluded awareness and create further causes for rebirth in cyclic existence. Je Drikhungpa says:

> To rest in defiled consciousness is to remain in samsara.
> To become attached to meditative experiences
> Is to create the cause for rebirth in the god realm.
> To realise the nature of mind is to attain nirvana.
> To realise the inseparability of samsara and nirvana
> Is to attain union on the path of transformation.
> If you realise that which transcends concepts:
> The unmodulated, ultimate, self-arising,
> Spontaneously accomplished state;
> You will fulfil the wishes of self and other without effort.
> Real accomplishment is the state that transcends all accomplishment.

What is meant by 'unmodulated'? It means resting the mind in its natural state without alteration. The phrase 'not altering consciousness,' means not being reflexively aware of the nature of reality. The phrase 'to blend mind and sensory appearances' is to gain a genuine intrinsic awareness of the nature of mind. The phrase 'to release yourself into the arising sensory impressions' refers to resting in the nature of mind without seeking affirmation or rejection.

In brief, if you can maintain uninterrupted mindfulness of the nature of mind during post-meditation, everything that appears to mind will be seen as illusion-like. This ability to maintain an awareness of the natural state during post-meditation will ensure that you will be able to maintain your perception of the insubstantial nature of sensory appearances without altering anything. It is crucial to maintain this awareness of the insubstantiality of thoughts and appearances. Gampopa says:

> To meditate on reality with unwavering mindfulness
> Is the king of all meditation.
> Guard the mind against fleeting diversions.
> Seek nothing but undistracted mindfulness!

He also says:

> As long as the peg of clinging is not removed,
> Our thoughts will create karma.
> Guard the mind with undistracted mindfulness!

§ How To Integrate Meditation And Post-Meditation

It is extremely difficult to know how to integrate meditation and post-meditation because much depends on the different dispositions of meditators. It is therefore extremely problematic to generalise about the integration of meditation and everyday experience. There is also a lack of documentation on how blending these two methods is actually accomplished, possibly because of this difficulty. When asked how meditation and post-meditation are to be blended, Gampopa replied:

> When you engage in everyday activities without wavering
> And maintain a sense of clarity in whatever you do;
> You achieve the blending of meditation and post-meditation.

He also says:

> Student, 'Have we failed to integrate meditation and post-meditation if we lose mindfulness?'
> Gampopa, 'Yes, the integration of meditation and post-meditation is lost if you fail to apply mindfulness.'

Je Drikhungpa says:

> Anyone who masters meditation and post-
> meditation on separate levels
> Is called a bodhisattva.
> Anyone who masters the union of meditation and post-meditation
> Is called a buddha or mahasiddha.

As this last quote indicates, subtle differences exist between experiences gained in meditation and experiences gained in post-meditation, depending on the meditator's level of realisation. For example, there are subtle differences between a bodhisattva and a fully enlightened buddha, because the former will experience a slight sense of separation of meditative and post-meditative states. No such distinction exists for a fully enlightened being.

If we apply this gradation to the so-called Four Yogas of Mahamudra, real integration may take place on the final stage of the yoga of non-meditation.[10] It will still be very difficult to maintain mental clarity in post-meditation; even if you have attained the yoga of non-conceptuality. For example, it is said that with experiences at the intermediate stage of one-flavouredness, the meditator's experience in post-meditation will still be vitiated by subtle discursive thoughts. Gampopa's nephew inquired:

> Je Gomtsul: 'How do we integrate meditation and post-meditation?

> Can we engage in post-meditative activities without being separated from one-pointed concentration? Is post-meditation identical to a dream or an illusion? Is there any integration with the meditative state if we lose our mindfulness in post-meditation through overwhelming discursive thoughts?'
> Gampopa: 'There are different levels of integration. For example, you can engage in everyday activities in the state of one-pointed concentration and use discursive thoughts as they arise in post-meditation. To engage in post-meditative activities without losing one-pointed concentration is excellent, but it is rarely done. However, if you can identify your post-meditative experiences as dream-like, this is all right. If you lose your mindfulness because of overwhelming discursive thoughts, you will fail to integrate meditation and post-meditation.'

It is possible to integrate meditation and post-meditation, even on the yoga of non-conceptuality, because it is not essential to integrate the two to have a complete experience of luminosity. It is sufficient to have an understanding of everything as illusion-like. If you can bring your mind back to the object of concentration, even if distraction arises, this is also part of integrating the two. The *Prajnaparamita-samcayagatha* says:

> Understand the integration of meditation and post-meditation
> To mean that you can apply the insight gained in meditation
> To your everyday experiences
> And realise that all things lack inherent existence.

Savari says:

> If you realise the nature of mind,
> Even distractions arise as expressions of Mahamudra.
> Once you realise the nature of mind,
> There is no such thing as real distraction;
> Everything becomes an extension of the meditative state.

We can apply this to the Four Yogas of Mahamudra. On the yoga of one-pointedness, meditators are not completely free of the pleasant meditative experiences that arise at the initial level of that yoga. Their experience will still be slightly vitiated by these experiences and they will not be able to completely integrate meditation and post-meditation. However, a certain level of integration can still be achieved, even at this stage. Once you make some progress on this path and attain the intermediate level of one-pointedness, your discursive thoughts are more subdued and can be self-liberated as they arise. This leads to an increased ability to integrate meditation and post-meditation. However, you will only achieve a proper level of integration once you attain the final level of one-pointedness.

On the yoga of non-conceptuality, the integration of meditation and post-meditation becomes more of a reality. Once you attain the intermediate level of this yoga, any discursive thoughts will no longer obscure your mind, because they are seen as an expression of the nature of mind. You will thereby experience everything that arises in the mind as empty. Your experience of mental clarity and your perception of the phenomenal world will be revealed as inseparable from emptiness. When you attain the final level of non-conceptual yoga, there will be no difference between meditation and post-meditation even during asleep, because your mind will no longer yield to unruly mental states.

On the yoga of one-flavouredness, deluded thoughts decrease even more and a further integration of meditation and post-meditation takes place. You will begin to perceive whatever arises in post-meditation as pure presence, which manifests without inherent existence. For this reason, the Kagyupa masters have said that real integration can only be achieved on this yoga. This is the view of Gampopa and his disciples, as well as Phagmo Drupa and Tsangpa Gyare. These Kagyu forefathers have all stated that the real integration of meditation and post-meditation can only be achieved at the level of one-flavouredness. However, there are subtle differences between the levels of one-pointedness, non-conceptuality, one-flavouredness, and non-meditation in relation to our meditative experiences and how we apply them. You must also bear in mind how important it is to have a proper understanding of each of the meditative levels within each of the Four Yogas. You should know how to cultivate them and how to deal with obstacles when they arise. This will be dealt with in the final chapter.

7

Eliminating Meditative Deviations

HOW TO RECOGNISE MEDITATIVE DEVIATIONS

This has two sections:

- Four deviations associated with emptiness
- Three deviations associated with meditative experiences

§ Four Deviations Associated With Emptiness

1. Identifying primordial and temporal deviations

Four types of deviation can occur when you are practising meditation and trying to realise emptiness, each of which has two parts: (i) primordial deviations, and (ii) temporal deviations. You experience a primordial deviation when you apprehend emptiness as an object of conceptual understanding, instead of having a direct and immediate experience of emptiness. You experience a temporal deviation when you cultivate your practice in accordance with this conceptual understanding. Whichever of the two occurs, they are vitiated by an emptiness that is an object of conceptual thought.

(i) Mistaking the emptiness of appearance

Mahamudra literature emphasises the unity of phenomenal appearance and emptiness. We have to realise that phenomenal appearance (produced by the coming together of causes and conditions) and emptiness (ultimate reality) coexist in the state of non-duality. Meditators who fail to understand non-duality, mistake ultimate reality for a universal object of conceptual understanding. This is one type of primordial deviation.

Since ultimate reality is devoid of all empirical determinations such as good and bad, meditators who take emptiness as an object of conceptual understanding abstract the concept of emptiness from their immediate experience of the phenomenal world. They deny the validity of karma because of this misunderstanding. They think ultimate reality must go beyond our normal concepts of good and bad, since it is empty and therefore, anything goes. This delegitimises the whole notion of morality. This fixation on the concept of emptiness leads to a denial of relative reality in the empirical world. This is another type of primordial deviation.

These meditators may be able to explain this concept of emptiness eloquently to others as an object of conceptual thought, but they will never translate their understanding into direct experience. The failure to translate that understanding into immediate experience is the cause of temporal deviations.

(ii) Mistaking the ground, path, and fruition

According to the Mahamudra teachings, we must understand the ground, path, and fruition as unitive rather than separate because they all relate to the nature of mind. Even though we may make a conceptual distinction between three aspects of spiritual experience, they are united from the perspective of the nature of mind. They are indivisible because the nature of mind embodies all the qualities of the dharmakaya. When you regard emptiness as an antidote to be used on the path, you fail to realise that dharmakaya is inherent within the nature of your mind. You think the path of emptiness leads to the realisation of the three aspects of buddha's being and the five wisdoms of the enlightened mind, at some point in the future, and regard them as extrinsic rather than intrinsic to the nature of mind. This is a primordial deviation.

You may feel tempted to turn to other meditative methods and practices, thinking that the practice described here is somehow deficient. However, all the necessary methods for realising buddhahood are present in Mahamudra meditation. Only a lack of confidence in yourself causes you to seek methods that may appear to be superior or more effective. You may also be tempted to manufacture the meditative experiences of bliss and clarity and become engrossed in the experiences of bliss and emptiness. These are temporal deviations.

(iii) Mistaking emptiness for an antidote to delusion

Some meditators regard emptiness and mental delusions as completely separate and independent from one another and conclude emptiness must be the antidote to delusions. These meditators have failed to appreciate the fact we do not eliminate delusions, we transform them into wisdom through self-understanding.

Transformation is the antidote. No such duality exists between delusion and wisdom. Thinking that you need to eradicate delusions through emptiness is to understand things dualistically, seeing delusions as something you need to abandon and emptiness as something you need to cultivate through insight. This is a primordial deviation.

You try to deconstruct the experiences, thoughts, and concepts that arise during meditation and remain in a state of contemplation instead of exercising mindfulness and trying to gain insight into what is going on in your mind. This is a temporal deviation.

(iv) Mistaking the inseparability of form and formlessness

Some meditators believe that karmically wholesome deeds only apply to relative reality and that we have to go beyond relative reality by understanding emptiness. They reduce everything to emptiness, including the compassionate activities of the six paramitas, and remain in the contemplation of a manufactured concept of emptiness. You can do this through Tantric practice for example, by reciting the mantra of emptiness, which is OM SVABHAVA SHUDDHA SARVA DHARMA SVABHAVA SHUDDHO HAM.[1] This is a primordial deviation.

You may fail to understand the order and coherence of your practice, by creating a particular mental state, and then trying to remain in that state during meditation. If your mind has become distracted and you are able to detect that distraction, you try to cut through it deliberately and then remain in a state of thoughtlessness. This is a temporal aberration.

The primordial and temporal deviations occur in relation to these four situations, depending upon your understanding. Your practice follows from that understanding. It is therefore essential to be alert to and aware of these four deviations so that you can identify and eliminate them.

2. Guarding against these deviations

The above comments clearly demonstrate that misunderstanding the nature of emptiness is the fundamental error here. Of the pair of deviations described above, the primordial and the temporal, the first deviation has the most drastic consequences. To suffer from primordial deviations is to fall into the wrong view. Saraha says:

> Clinging to the concept of emptiness
> Is more foolish than believing in substantial existence.

Nagarjuna's *Mulamadhyamikakarika* says:

> Those with little intelligence fixate on the concept of emptiness
> And thus endure much suffering.

To think of emptiness as a negation of the relative reality of the world is to fall into the extreme of nihilism, the view that nothing exists at all. Entertaining this nihilistic view does not lead to liberation. On the contrary, it is the cause of falling into lower states of existence. Gampopa says:

> Meditators with a conceptual understanding of emptiness
> Will not attain proper understanding
> Even if they are not attached to or fixated on it.

If your deviations are of a temporal rather than primordial nature—meaning they are meditative deviations—they will not necessarily lead to the formation of wrong views. Since they are an indication that you have not undertaken your practice with a proper understanding, it will be quite difficult for you to make any noticeable progress on the path. It is therefore extremely important for meditators to be alert and aware lest they fall victim to these temporal deviations.

An understanding of the term 'Mahamudra' can help you gain a proper understanding of reality from this point of view. Mahamudra embodies both the unconditioned and conditioned aspects of reality. If you view reality from the unconditioned perspective, you cannot say anything has come into existence or not come into existence, is permanent or impermanent, true or false, because reality in itself is devoid of all empirical determinations and cannot be conceptualised.

From the conditioned perspective, everything arises in an unceasing manner due to causes and conditions. If the appropriate causes and conditions come together, certain effects will inevitably come about. We do not need to negate relative reality to understand ultimate reality. Meditators who understand that emptiness is the essence of conditioned phenomena and that conditioned phenomena are the nature of emptiness will develop a proper understanding of reality as a whole. Such a view will not lead to any misconceptions about reality. Nagarjuna says:

> There is nothing that is not created by causes and conditions.
> Therefore, there is nothing that is not empty by nature.

The Mahamudra emphasis is on seeing the inseparability of relative and ultimate aspects of reality. The *Bodhisattvabhumivrtti* says:

> Conditioned phenomena are emptiness and emptiness is essentially

no different from conditioned phenomena.

We must understand emptiness in relation to conditioned phenomena and relative truth in this way. Furthermore, the Mahamudra teachings say that ordinary mind contains all of the attributes of the ground, path, and fruition, because they are ultimately all united in having the same essential nature. Emptiness does not become an obstacle to understanding the path. It is very common for people to think of emptiness as an antidote on the path, but from this perspective, the ground, path, and fruition all have the nature of emptiness. Saraha says:

> All Buddhist concepts of paths, stages, and fruition
> Have the same flavour.
> Try to imprint that indelibly in your mind.

He also says:

> When we contemplate self-originating awareness
> Everything is naturally complete within itself, including the fruition.

Again, he says:

> Fruition is already present in the continuum of consciousness
> So do not get bogged down by the afflictions of hope or fear.

Aryadeva says:

> Everything that exists is imbued with one reality.

Gampopa says:

> Self-cognising awareness, which is empty and luminous
> Is no different from dharmakaya;
> Fruition is not something to be attained at a future time.
> The qualities of fruition are present in the mental continuum.
> How wondrous! The effect is already present in the cause.
> This self-cognising awareness is like a precious jewel.

A Mahamudra commentary says:

> Everything that exists has one flavour; the flavour of emptiness. If we realise this, we realise even the delusions we regard as something to abandon and the wisdom we regard as something to cultivate have the same flavour.

If we understand that the ground, path, and fruition do not exist as discrete and independent phenomena, but are embodied in the same reality of the nature of mind, we will no longer view emptiness as an antidote to certain obstacles on the path. The *Hevajra Tantra* says:

> There is no gap or discontinuity
> Between the immaculate wisdom of a buddha
> And the deluded mind of an ordinary being.
> Both mental states are imbued with the same reality.

It also says:

> Emotional conflicts, such as hatred,
> That perpetuate the samsaric condition
> Are the very things that can lead to nirvana.

Nagarjuna says:

> There is no difference between samsara and nirvana.

Maitripa says:

> Conflicting emotions, when understood, are the same as wisdom.

Furthermore, meditators with a proper understanding of Mahamudra automatically understand that practices associated with the accumulation of merit on the relative level are imbued with the nature of emptiness. In other words, the wholesome deeds that you perform on the relative level are not performed outside the sphere of Mahamudra. Meditators who understand this will not fall into the error of conceptualising emptiness, with only a vague idea of what emptiness might be, because this deviation involves the separation of emptiness and positive actions. Virupa says:

> Whatever we experience as a result of previous actions,
> Whether pleasant or unpleasant,
> Does not exist outside the realm of Mahamudra.
> Nothing can happen outside the sphere of emptiness.

Savari says:

> Conditioned phenomena are inseparable
> From ultimate reality.

Maitripa says:

> If you understand the ultimate nature of things

You will experience everything as Mahamudra.
That is actualising the dharmakaya!

It is important that we develop a proper understanding of the relationship between ultimate reality and the phenomenal world as well as the relationship between ultimate reality and the spiritual path.

Furthermore, Gampopa says that most deviations on the spiritual path come from two sources: 1) mistaking your meditative experiences for realisation, and 2) reducing your realisation to the level of mere meditative experience. Firstly, you might employ techniques to induce the meditative experiences associated with bliss, clarity and non-conceptuality and all three of these might arise as extremely inspiring and uplifting. Therein lies their seductive nature. These experiences have the potential to trap you and make you imagine you have attained realisation. Meditators can become extremely attached to these experiences. Secondly, deviations can arise when you attain a genuine realisation, after receiving and following the instructions of your teachers, while simultaneously having the meditative experiences of bliss, clarity, and non-conceptuality. Instead of dwelling in the state of realisation, you may fall victim to the allure of those meditative experiences, attempting to recapture them as they fade instead of remaining in the state of understanding.[2] Je Drikhungpa says:

Meditators that get swayed by the temporary experiences
Of bliss and clarity, which are sometimes there and sometimes not,
Only increase their expectations.
They become like children chasing rainbows.
The more they run, the further away it becomes
Until it dissolves into space!

If you chase after meditative experiences, you can potentially become frustrated. The more you try to manufacture or recreate those experiences, the more elusive and unobtainable they are. You need to be attentive to ensure you avoid those pitfalls. A critic made the following comments about the deviations listed in Mahamudra literature:

You must make use of concepts
If you wish to abandon these deviations;
That is not Mahamudra.
If you really hope to abandon them,
You must already understand Mahamudra.
But if you could abandon these deviations

Without having an understanding of Mahamudra
Then anybody could realise mahamudrahood.
Therefore, if Mahamudra has been attained
There can be no question of going astray,
And if you do go astray
It cannot be Mahamudra.[3]

This criticism is unjustified for the following reasons. As Maitripa and other past masters have emphasised, the key point is the inseparability of concepts and self-cognising awareness. When the nature of concepts is understood, they can lead to the realisation of mahamudrahood. These past masters have shown a way to understand concepts, where they do not need to be pitted against Mahamudra. We can have a unitive understanding of the totality of things rather than a divisive understanding of it. Nonetheless, it has never been said that the mere thought of avoiding the four types of deviations mentioned above is the same as having the Mahamudra experience. Maitreya's *Sutralamkara* says:

If intelligent people make the effort to understand reality
They will acquire non-conceptual wisdom.
All defiling tendencies of mind then subside
The way a powerful potion cures the poison of snakebite.

Shantideva's *Bodhicharyavatara* says:

Anyone who wants to eliminate the darkness of ignorance
And quickly attain enlightenment;
Should meditate on emptiness.[4]

If we were to take the previous criticism seriously, we would have to say it is in conflict with the prominent Mahayana masters just quoted. Meditators must have some kind of conceptual understanding to steer them in the right direction. Almost all systems of insight meditation make use of concepts at a preliminary level because these concepts enable meditators to gain non-conceptual direct insight. The function of analytical meditation is to eliminate a lot of erroneous beliefs and conceptions. If that were not the case, we would have to say that no sentient being can make use of concepts in a constructive manner and therefore everything that we experience is the same as Mahamudra. The very criticism levelled against our system of meditation doubles back on the critics themselves.[5] These critics are thus commenting upon their own assertions when they say:

> Ignorant people who follow the Mahamudra system sow the seeds to be reborn as cattle.

Furthermore, if the deviations described above are not possible within the context of Mahamudra practice, they would not be possible in any of the other Buddhist systems either. That is blatantly contradictory; it is well-known that practically all the Buddhist teachings contain detailed descriptions of the Paths and Stages. We would then have to say there is no such thing as a deviation on the Paths and Stages of other Buddhist traditions. The above critic's views are therefore in conflict with both reason and textual authority.

§ Three Deviations Associated With Meditative Experiences

1. Why meditative experiences are possible grounds for deviation

Meditators whose minds are not given to distraction and who have the ability to distinguish lucid states of mind from dull states of mind will have various meditative experiences during meditation. This is particularly true for meditators with some experience in harmonising the psychophysical energy pathways and the movements of that energy. This skill will ensure their meditative stabilisation is undisrupted by distractions and they will pursue their meditation with great diligence and enthusiasm.

You will experience various overwhelming, uplifting, and wondrous states of mind as your latent psychic imprints are activated and the five sense objects appear before the five sense faculties as mental images. Quite peculiar, quasi-sensory experiences may arise, such as seeing physical objects when there are none, hearing things when there is nothing to be heard, or smelling things when there is nothing to be smelt. All kinds of psychic material will be drawn directly from the mind but the way such experiences arise depends greatly on the psychological make-up of each individual.[6] We cannot generalise about this. Nonetheless, it can be said that everyone who experiences these things does so within the context of the meditative experiences of bliss, clarity, and non-conceptuality. While it is not known how or in what manner these experiences will arise, it is safe to say they will arise in association with one or all of these meditative experiences.

The experience of bliss might give rise to bodily sensations of well-being or pleasure; a feeling that may become so pervasive, the existence of the body is forgotten entirely so that only the feeling remains. The experience of bliss might also overwhelm you mentally with feelings of joy so that you cannot resist the urge to burst out laughing. You might also simply have a sense of mental well-being. Sometimes the experience of bliss can persist for some time. These experiences have been described in this way by some masters.

For example, you may become unaware of the passage of time so that day and night pass by without your noticing. The experience of bliss can be experienced in this kind of psychosomatic way. The experience of clarity might make you perceive the mind to be translucent like crystal and there may be a general sense of light around everything you see. When you go to sleep without a light in your room, you might sometimes imagine you are able to perceive objects near and far. You may also experience images of flashing lights and have some kind of intimation that you possess supernormal cognition.

The experience of non-conceptuality has to be understood in relation to clarity. You may feel that everything is empty and the objects of your senses become blurry and indistinguishable. You may even have the experience of being non-existent or feel that nothing in the world exists. Your very subtle thoughts, which are normally very hard to detect, may cease to function. Your mind will become completely empty of any activity and you will perceive it like the sky, free from clouds.

Those experiences all arise in relation to the aspects of bliss, clarity, and non-conceptuality. Others say that these meditative experiences can occur in relation to body, speech and mind. They teach that before you can actually attain proper realisation, you will experience the blessings of the three vajras as signs of things to come, because these portentous experiences influence what will occur on the level of your body, speech, and mind. It is said that before the onset of ultimate realisation, there are portentous signs that indicate the onset of actual realisation, such as very unusual and peculiar dreams. When you experience the vajra blessing of the body, your body may shake or move with violent force, or you may levitate or be compelled to run involuntarily. All these physical reactions happen automatically and spontaneously, without any volition on your part. When you experience the vajra blessing of speech, you may experience the urge to chatter, laugh, or wail and be overcome by the urge to express yourself in various unconventional ways. When you experience the vajra blessing of mind, you will experience various levels of concentration, supernormal cognitions, and so on.

Many such experiences are mentioned in other texts, but do not conclude that these experiences will happen to everyone. It just means that such things can happen. You should therefore have some familiarity with them so that you understand what is going on if they do. Anyone with some skill or talent in harmonising the body's psychophysical energies will be particularly susceptible to these experiences.

According to our Practice Lineage, meditative experiences can be classified according to different meditation techniques. There are meditative experiences obtained through tranquillity meditation, meditative experiences obtained through a combination of tranquillity and insight meditation, and meditative experiences that arise from understanding. Gampopa says, 'meditative experiences obtained through tranquillity meditation arise when you channel your psychophysical energy into the central energy pathway,' at which point you may experience bliss in relation to your body and mind and you 'experience mental clarity from the ability to enjoy the experiences of bliss and non-conceptuality, while remaining in the state of meditation without any mental processes.' In the practice that combines tranquillity and insight meditation, the psychophysical energy activates various physiological changes where the five elements dissolve into each other when it enters the central energy pathway. Gampopa goes on to say:

> Simultaneous with this process is the appearance of various quasi-sensory mental images, such as mirage, smoke, fireflies, flames, a clear sky, and so on. This devolution of the essential qualities of the five elements is called 'the five signs.' Meditators will also go through various other mental states, referred to as 'the eight beneficial qualities.'[7] These physical and mental changes relate to experiences that arise through combining tranquillity and insight meditation. This will only occur to people who have been able to adopt the proper meditation posture and engage in the practice properly. Meditators who have only managed to focus on the object of meditation at a very basic level are very unlikely to have these experiences.

Meditative experiences will always be attached to the occurrence of realisation to some degree. Realisation refers to the naked recognition of self-cognising awareness for what it is, without the embellishment of conceptual thinking. For example, when a teacher introduces a student to his or her mind by saying, 'this is it' and the student is able to recognise it, this recognition will be something familiar, not something novel or new. This realisation is about recognising what we already know, right from the beginning.

The bliss we experience coterminous with realisation is not a bliss associated with pleasurable experiences that arise from our karmic traces and dispositions as it is with meditative experiences. It is a transcendental bliss.

Similarly, mental clarity is the experience of translucency and immaculateness completely devoid of defilement. Non-conceptuality is the absence of any subtle under-currents of mental activity. The difference between meditative experiences and meditative realisation is that the latter is transcendent. It is important to know that realisation will still be accompanied by certain meditative experiences, even though those experiences are no longer vitiated by delusion and defilement. According to Gampopa, this comes from the correlation between three types of meditative experiences and three types of meditation: tranquillity meditation, the combination of tranquillity and insight, and realisation.

2. How we turn meditative experiences into deviations

We have to investigate how these different meditative experiences can lead to deviations. Deviations can occur either in relation to the three types of meditative experiences collectively or individually. The fundamental causes of deviations are your own responses. The main cause for any type of deviation is responding to meditative experiences with elation when they arise and disappointment and frustration when they do not arise. Even though the objects of meditation are generally very useful and important, any fixation that develops in relation to those objects has the potential to obstruct enlightenment.

If you fixate on the experiences of bliss, clarity, and non-conceptuality, those experiences may contribute toward the production of further karmic causes and conditions, instead of directing you to enlightenment. They create the karmic causes and conditions for pleasurable experiences in the future and may cause you to be reborn at a higher level of being, but they will not lead to enlightenment. If you feel frustrated, resentful, and despairing in the absence of meditative experiences, that may contribute to the production of karmic causes and conditions for degeneration and regression and may cause you to be reborn at a lower level of being. In brief, you should always beware of fixation and attachment to your meditative experiences.[8] Saraha says:

> The meditative objects we fixate on
> Become obstacles to liberation.
> To view meditative experiences as good
> Will not lead to enlightenment,
> It becomes a seed for the continuation of samsara.
> Karmic imprints born of frustrations and despair
> Result in further suffering and pain.

He also says:

> Oh, do not be attached to blissful experiences,
> That only reduces them to pleasures.
> If you are attached to desirable things,
> The pure and immaculate nature of mind
> Becomes poisoned by clinging.

Again, he says:

> If you cherish meditative experiences
> As something to hang onto,
> Even if that thought be small as a mustard seed,
> It will cause interminable problems and pain.

Virupa says:

> When we conceptualise the nature of mind
> And become attached to meditative experiences,
> We mistake those experiences for actual realisation.
> If we pursue meditation along these lines,
> We have deviated from the proper course.

The meditative experiences that arise from bliss, clarity, and non-conceptuality can be the cause of continual wandering in samsara. When taken individually, they can lead to different forms of existence. For example, if you become attached to the experience of bliss, it will degenerate into the experience of pleasure and compel you to dwell in the sensual realm. If you become attached to the experience of clarity, you will be compelled to dwell in the form realm. If you become attached to the experience of non-conceptuality, you will be compelled to dwell in the formless realm. Even though meditators can attain psychic states that correspond to these realms of existence, they will not produce enlightenment.[9] Attaining these higher states of consciousness will only temporarily allay our experiences of suffering. They are therefore only regarded as resting places, not the ultimate goal, because while various levels and intensities of pleasure are experienced in these higher realms, sooner or later we have to experience all the discomforts of samsaric existence all over again. Gampopa says:

> If attachment arises to these three meditative experiences, it will leave positive karmic imprints on our mental continuum, which gives rise to the potential experience of three realms of existence. If you become attached to the physical and mental well-being

associated with bliss, you will be reborn in the sensual realm where certain pleasures may be enjoyed, but when that positive karma is exhausted, you will have to re-experience all the suffering and dissatisfaction of the samsaric condition. If you become attached to clarity, which can be enjoyed by avoiding mental agitation and drowsiness, you will be reborn in the form realm, where you dwell in a joyous state for a time. When that karma is exhausted, you will have to descend into lower forms of existence once again. If you become attached to non-conceptuality, you will be reborn in the formless realm, but the same fate awaits you. Sooner or later you will be thrown back into lower forms of existence and endure suffering and pain again, just like everyone else.[10]

Je Phagmo Drupa says:

When you practise your teacher's meditation instructions
You will experience meditative bliss in due course.
If you become attached to that experience,
You will be propelled into the sensual realm.
Clarity, like the moon in a cloudless sky, arises
Where you transcend distinctions between outer and inner.
If you become attached to that experience,
You will be propelled into the form realm.
When the experience of non-conceptuality arises
Even subtle levels of thoughts subside.
If you become attached to that experience,
And think it has to be regenerated or maintained
You will be propelled into the formless realm.

Je Lingrepa says:

Meditative experiences can be very colourful and dramatic
And are compared to rainbows.
Meditators with little intelligence are overwhelmed by them
And therefore lose themselves.

Comments such as these could be quoted extensively, but that is unnecessary. Suffice to say all the leading masters of the Practice Lineage agree that to become attached to meditative experiences can have drastic consequences. Je Barawa says:

The highest levels of meditative absorption

Are called 'infinite space,' 'infinite consciousness,'
'Nothingness,' and 'neither existence nor non-existence.'
When we meditate on the nature of mind
As inseparable from empty space without boundaries;
This can lead to the 'samadhi of infinite space.'
When we regard consciousness
As some kind of boundless cosmic state;
This can lead to the 'samadhi of infinite consciousness.'
When we think emptiness means that nothing exists;
This can lead to the 'samadhi of nothingness.'
When we think that everything
Neither exists nor does not exist;
This can lead to the 'samadhi of neither existence nor non-existence.'

This is the classic Buddhist formulation of the highest samadhis. According to this same exposition:

Meditative absorptions can be attained
In direct relation to these samadhis.
When we fixate on the experience of bliss
And attach to a conceptual understanding of it,
Even the experiences of joy, bliss, and one-pointed concentration
Can lead to the first level of absorption.
When we fixate on the lucidity of mind
Meditating one-pointedly on joy and bliss,
This can lead to the second level of absorption.
When we cease to apply analysis and investigation
And fixate on the experience of neutrality,
Applying mindfulness and awareness,
This can lead to the third level of absorption.
When we attain a meditation of complete equilibrium
And fixate on this practice of perfect mindfulness,
Experiencing neither pain nor pleasure,
This can lead to the fourth level of absorption.

If we block out all sensory impressions
And remain in a state of non-conceptuality,
Without entertaining any thoughts whatsoever,
So that not even consciousness remains,
This level of absorption is known as 'unconsciousness.'

If we are not careful we may get lost
Within the various levels of meditative absorption
And fail to achieve the desired goal.

If we practise concentration,
Block the sensory impressions,
And remain in a state of thoughtlessness
Where all mental events have ceased,
This is known as 'the cessation of non-cogitation.'
If we enter a state of complete non-differentiation
Where everything becomes fuzzy and indistinct,
This is known as 'the state of neutrality without mindfulness.'
If we are pervaded by a sense of dullness and stupor
Where no conscious mental activities are present,
This state of mind is comparable to an animal.
All of these states of mind should be seen as deviations
From a proper meditative state.

These deviations have been examined in relation to the levels of consciousness we can tap into through tranquillity meditation. This is known as 'common meditation.' Deviations can also occur in relation to the 'uncommon meditation' of insight. Je Phagmo Drupa says:

Even if you attempt to avoid attachment
To the experiences of bliss, clarity, and non-conceptuality,
It is still possible to drift into the states of an arhat or pratyekabuddha
And fail to secure final realisation.

Je Yanggonpa says:

If you are attached to the experience of bliss,
Fixated on the experience of clarity,
And conceptual about the experience of non-conceptuality;
You will not go beyond levels of consciousness
Accessible within the three realms of existence.
Even if you refrain from attachment to these experiences,
You will still be in danger of falling into the mind set
Of either an arhat or a pratyekabuddha,
If you do not give birth to insight into the nature of ultimate reality.

It is clear from this, that if we do not have sufficient compassion and insight into emptiness, understanding born of conceptual discrimination will never lead to full buddhahood and our development may be arrested at the stage of an arhat or pratyekabuddha. Gampopa seems to be saying as much in his exposition, but I myself have some reservations about this, because even arhats and pratyekabuddhas must have attained the results of both tranquillity and insight meditation. Tranquillity stabilises the mind and insight arises from the realisation of the non-existence of an abiding immutable ego. Furthermore, arhats and pratyekabuddhas would have abandoned all kinds of conflicting emotions. Anyone who lacks attachment to meditative experiences but has no still insight cannot go beyond the levels of concentration and absorption described above. Arhats and pratyekabuddhas must therefore have experienced insight and gained a level of attainment that goes beyond what can be achieved through these different levels of consciousness according to common meditation practices.

Someone might query this with the following quote by Gampopa, 'If meditators have a certain experience, but are unable to determine the nature of that experience, it can still lead to the state of cessation.'[11] How is that to be explained? Cessation refers to the meditative experience of the arhats and pratyekabuddhas. Gampopa's *Tshogs chos bkra shis phun tshogs* says:

> When a meditator who embodies the eye of Dharma understands the nature of mind and encounters the experiences of bliss, clarity, and non-conceptuality, he or she should determine that the nature of those experiences is empty. An inability to do that is called not being able to determine the presence of phenomena. This failure will lead to cessation without discrimination. A meditator who drifts into that state of mind has not gone beyond the samsaric condition at all and is still confined within the parameters of common meditation.

The meaning of 'cessation without discrimination' is explained in the *Abhidharmakosa* of Vasubandhu:

> The cessation without discrimination is a cessation that prevents things from arising, not a cessation without any cogitation.

The auto-commentary on this text says:

> The other type of cessation is 'cessation without discrimination', which means when certain causes and conditions are not present, certain positive or negative mental states no longer arise.

The effect of cessation with discrimination is indeterminate. Cessation without discrimination has to be differentiated from cessation with discrimination. The *Bodhicharyavatara* says:

> The cessation of mental activities
> Obtained by not realising emptiness,
> Only leads to a state of absorption
> Where all mental activities have ceased.

The state attained here is therefore cessation without discrimination. The same point is made in the Sutric teachings. As one sutra says:

> If meditators practise worldly forms of meditation and attain various altered states of consciousness, they will not overcome clinging to the notion of an unchanging, immutable self. If clinging is not abandoned, you will not uproot mental agitations caused by conflicting emotions.

It is important to combine insight and tranquillity meditation for this reason. Even if altered states of consciousness are attained through worldly types of meditation, this will not lead to enlightenment. It will bring all mental events to an end so that all cogitations cease, but the end result will only be the attainment of mind sets associated with the three realms of existence. These altered mental states correspond to the mind set of the formless realm because the absorption obtained through the cessation of mental activities is comparable to the fourth level of absorption on the formless realm. When you attain these altered states of consciousness, your mind ceases to function and your primary and secondary mental activities cease to operate. When all conscious sensations, feelings, and activities are absent, it is very easy to imagine that you are experiencing the state of ultimate peace.

All of these mental states are regarded as deviations, because no altered state of consciousness can produce the insight that the nature of the self is empty of inherent existence. Since the belief in an unchanging, permanent self is the root of the samsaric condition, all the defilements will sooner or later re-emerge unless that belief is uprooted and you will never transcend the samsaric condition. Dharmakirti says:

> If you believe in an unchanging, permanent self
> The belief in an unchanging, permanent other will arise.
> All misfortunes come from this dualism of self and other.

Even if you enter the various trance-like, altered states of consciousness, you can only reach the peak of samsaric existence through them. You cannot go beyond it. Whatever you attain fails to go beyond cessation without discrimination.

Cessation with discrimination is the product of discriminating awareness, which is developed in insight meditation by using the Four Noble Truths as the object of meditation. Most defilements are eradicated by this insight, which means cessation is attained by using discrimination. This attainment is called 'cessation with discrimination' to distinguish it from 'cessation without discrimination.' Much confusion has been generated from the failure of some commentators to distinguish the two. As mentioned, some commentators say the meditative experiences that arise when we have not properly established their nature lead to the deviation of 'cessation without discrimination.' Other people misunderstand the point of this comment because they fail to understand which cessation is attributed to the shravakas. They attribute 'cessation without discrimination' to the shravakas, when in fact arhats and pratyekabuddhas attain 'cessation with discrimination.' Even learned ones, who should know better, keep repeating the mistake made by their predecessors and cast aspersions on shravakas by saying they have only attained 'cessation without discrimination.'

When even learned ones do not rectify mistaken interpretations about the teachings, other people will follow them until that interpretation becomes the norm. Shravakas have attained 'cessation with discrimination' because they have attained the level of a non-returner or foe-destroyer (*arhat*), which is the optimum attainment of a shravaka. When saints on the shravaka path attain cessation, they must do so through insight into selflessness. The above-mentioned commentators have not understood this point. They would not disparage the attainments of arhats or view their achievements as comparable to the animal realm if they could appreciate the difference between these two types of cessations. It is therefore very important to realise that the cessation attained by shravakas is very different to the cessation attained by someone who manipulates their consciousness on the worldly path.[12] The *Saddharmaekacitta* says:

> Even without attachment to the pleasurable experience of bliss, meditators face the danger of becoming lost in the sensual realm. Even without fixating on the experience of clarity, meditators can go astray in the form realm. Even without conceptualising the experience of non-thought, meditators may wander into the formless realm.[13]

There are still the dangers of deviation, even if we do not fixate on our meditative experiences. Implicit within the above quotation is the acknowledgement that an attachment to the experience of bliss, a fixation on the experience of clarity, and conceptualising about the experience of non-conceptuality are to be automatically abandoned. The failure to determine the empty nature of these experiences can give rise to the nihilistic concept of non-existence, which is a misinterpretation of emptiness and can therefore only lead to lower forms of existence.[14] Meditators must be aware of the dangers involved in failing to understand the emptiness of meditative experiences even when no attachment or fixation is present. These dangers were mentioned at length in the previous section so there is no need to repeat them here. Gampopa elaborated on the importance of a proper understanding of the emptiness of meditative experiences in the statement, 'We can only make constructive use of meditative experiences when we have an understanding of emptiness.' In other words, we cannot attain realisation without gaining insight into emptiness and without that insight our meditative experiences will only become corrupted.[15] Gampopa says:

> It is possible to misunderstand
> The non-duality of subject and object.
> Even if we have no attachment to the concept of duality
> And have certain experiences when meditating on non-duality,
> We can lack insight into the nature of those experiences.
> Even if we develop a view free from conceptualisation
> And think it the ultimate view free from all extremes,
> It may still be the product of conceptual formulations.
>
> Even if we dwell with great confidence in contemplation
> And think it is transcendental meditation,
> It may still be a worldly meditation.
> Even if we engage in various wholesome deeds
> We will not progress beyond the attainment of the shravakas,
> If we fail to develop compassion.
>
> Always be alert and wary of your own experiences
> Never become too reliant on them.
> Ensure your understanding is genuine.
> It should not be something you have manufactured.

3. Methods for preventing these deviations

These deviations will arise if meditative experiences are not understood and handled correctly. Such deviations are only possible because we lack insight into the nature of reality. When meditators fail to realise that their experiences are devoid of essence, different experiences will arise on the phenomenal level. There can be no concept of origination or cessation in terms of our experience because experiences cannot be identified as this or that; their nature is empty and emptiness cannot be spoken of as coming into being, persisting, or dissipating. Experiences come about through the interaction between the energy pathways, the flow of energy, the mind and its impressions, and karmic tendencies. If meditators are lured by the intensity of these experiences and grasp onto them as if they had some kind of essence, they fail to realise their nature is emptiness. That is why deviation occurs. It is of paramount importance to engage in meditation and allow meditative experiences to arise without becoming fixated or attached. This is how we prevent ourselves from going astray.[16] Gampopa says:

> When meditators experience bliss, clarity, and non-conceptuality, they should determine the nature of those experiences to be originless. An inability to determine the nature of these experiences is called 'not being able to determine the presence of phenomena.'

This was explained in the previous section. When certain experiences manifest and the nature of those experiences remains undetermined, it will lead to confusion. In summary, these deviations can take place on two levels: the worldly level and the supramundane level. We discussed the eight altered states of consciousness on the worldly level: the four stages of concentration in the realm of form, the four stages of absorption in the formless realm, and the deviations that occur on the supramundane level when emptiness is not properly apprehended. Some people make spiritual progress but are arrested temporarily on the level of shravakas. However, if meditators do not get fixated on anything and develop the understanding that all experiences have the nature of emptiness, there will be no room for deviations.

The fundamental root of deviation is the tendency to grasp, cling, fixate, and become attached to experiences. Meditators should simply let their experiences rest in their own natural state, without allowing them to become polluted by the elements of grasping or clinging. Remaining effortlessly in the natural state of equilibrium, without entertaining thoughts of acceptance or rejection, is 'meditation,' from a conventional point of view. This is also how meditation must be practised according to the Mahamudra teachings.[17] The

Pradipoddyotana says:

> If you can let the mind be in its own natural state
> Even when various experiences are arising;
> Meditation is not other than this.

At this point, one might raise a very relevant question, 'If the fundamental point of meditation is to realise emptiness and not simply rely on experiences, does that mean realisation should be completely free of meditative experiences?' That is not the case. To completely separate meditative experiences from realisation is to go to the other extreme and is also incorrect. As Gampopa says:

> Realisation has to be accompanied by the experiences of bliss, clarity, and non-conceptuality. Milarepa says, 'To remain in the contemplation of emptiness without experiences is not quite complete. It is like the tree trunk without the fruit. This is a particular quality of mind but it is not realisation.' To be attached to meditative experiences at the expense of realisation is one extreme, to think realisation has to be completely disassociated from meditative experiences is the other extreme and should also be avoided.

Atisha says:

> Remaining in the contemplation on emptiness
> Is comparable to deriving enjoyment
> From the nectar of a flower in space.

The realisation of emptiness should be enriched by meditative experiences. Therefore, we must endeavour to embody both realisation and experiences. How do we combine these two? Firstly, we constantly remind ourselves of the importance of insight and the apprehension of ultimate reality. Emptiness is no different from the nature of mind. The nature of mind is empty; it is totally devoid of characteristics and attributes and transcends all forms of description. We will gradually gain some intuitive apprehension of that reality with this understanding. Reality will be revealed as ineffable precisely because reality has no attributes or qualities and we cannot apply the distinction of subject and predicate to it. That type of realisation has to be translated into direct experience.[18] When direct experience occurs, it will be accompanied by meditative experiences. Both realisation and meditative experiences must be embodied because an embodied realisation is also a form of experience.

Gampopa says:

> When meditators begin to practise, right from the beginning, they should focus their mind on awareness. As that awareness develops it will turn into unwavering attention. That unwavering attention is what will lead to the realisation of self-cognising awareness.

He also says:

> The experience of mental clarity is awareness;
> The maintenance of attentiveness is mental stability;
> The realisation of self-cognising awareness as emptiness is insight.

If we can maintain that understanding of emptiness in relation to meditative experiences, our meditative experiences will never become corrupted. According to the Mahamudra literature, realisation is also sometimes present within meditative experiences, in which case they are called 'natural meditative experiences' or 'authentic meditative experiences' because meditative experiences and realisation are joined as one. This is an important point for understanding how deviations can be avoided or prevented. Gampopa says:

> When meditative experiences are not separate from realisation and realisation is not separate from meditative experiences they are called 'existential meditative experiences,' 'the meditative experience of coemergent wisdom,' 'authentic meditative experiences,' 'the meditative experience of Mahamudra,' and so on. They are called 'genuine' and 'authentic' because such experiences are accompanied by an understanding of the nature of mind. The relative aspect and the ultimate aspect of mind are conjoined. The relative aspect of mind provides the richness of the experience and the ultimate aspect of mind provides insight into the authentic condition of reality. From the perspective of the nature of mind, there is no such thing as existence and non-existence and no mental attributes can be identified. From the perspective of the relative aspect of mind, various meditative experiences will emerge, be enjoyed, and then dissipate. Meditative experiences arise as bliss, clarity, and non-conceptuality. From the ultimate perspective, all these experiences are empty by nature and they are inseparable from the nature of mind. Realisation and meditative experiences are brought together by combining the relative and ultimate aspects of mind in this way.

Some people say:

> Meditative experiences of bliss, clarity, and non-conceptuality are the causes of deviation and the meditative experiences of bliss, clarity, and non-conceptuality are the apexes of meditative realisation.

People who say such things reiterate the point that meditative experience without realisation leads to deviations and meditative experiences combined with realisation leads to self-realisation. The first type of experience is polluted by desire, longing, grasping, and attachment while the second type of experience is imbued with understanding and insight. Certain commentators, who do not follow this system of meditation, have criticised this by saying:

> The mere avoidance of deviations
> That relate to the three aspects of meditative experience;
> Will bring about 'cessation through non-discrimination.'
> That defines an arhat.

It has never been said that the mere avoidance of deviations will lead to realisation of mahamudrahood. That criticism is therefore untrue. As far as deviations are concerned, we can deviate on a worldly level as well as the level of the shravakas. To single out the shravakas and speak about their type of cessation in this context seems unnecessary. Anyone who has been able to attain the level of shravaka sainthood has secured the realisation of a non-returner or foe-destroyer and has thereby rid themselves of the defiling tendencies of mind.[19] Certain followers of Sutric practice, who regard analytical insight meditation to be the most effective means for realising emptiness, have also made objections to Mahamudra meditation. Other teachers have made the following comment:

> We should analyse emptiness
> But not engage in the contemplation of emptiness.
> The latter will not produce a realisation of emptiness
> Or will only produce a false realisation,
> Equivalent to the cessation through non-discrimination
> That is attained by shravakas.

This again is incorrect. We cannot become familiar with emptiness if we do not contemplate it and the *Prajnaparamita sutras* actually emphasise the importance of such contemplation. The emptiness contemplated in Mahamudra is called 'ever-perfect emptiness.' It does not lead to a vacuity of mind. This vacuity can occur if we contemplate voidness rather than emptiness. As a matter of fact, we can turn this argument around and use it against the critics' own position.

Their own approach is most vulnerable to leading meditators to the concept of emptiness as a form of vacuity, because they believe the only way to realise emptiness is through the analytical method that uses negation to reduce everything to emptiness. This type of negation does not involve affirmation. It is called the logic of reductio ad absurdum. This type of negation is actually cautioned against in the *Kalachakra Tantra*, which points out the danger of a systematic use of negation without affirmation being the cause of others falling into a nihilistic view of emptiness. It might be advisable to avoid that. The logic of reductio ad absurdum has been used in two different ways: negation without affirmation and negation with affirmation.

The Kagyu and Nyingma teachings use negation with affirmation, while some other systems use negation without affirmation. We should be aware of that subtle distinction.

HOW TO ELIMINATE THE OBSTACLES TO MEDITATION

This has two sections:

- Removing general obstacles to meditation
- Removing internal and external obstacles

§ Removing General Obstacles To Meditation

There are many approaches to meditation and the objects of meditation. There is no one way to practise it. In spite of this diversity, we can attain the meditative state by ensuring that the object of meditation is vividly present while keeping the mind from wavering through the influence of defilement. That sense of a vivid clarity has to be present. You must also ensure that the aspect of stability is present so that you do not lose this mental clarity. Whatever type of meditation you are practising, it must involve the cultivation of clarity and stability. Their presence automatically deals with the fundamental obstacles to meditation. Mental clarity leaves no room for the obstacle of mental dullness, and stability does not allow the obstacle of mental agitation to rob the mind of its equilibrium.

If we were to describe the subtle differences between the obstacles of dullness and agitation, we could say dullness includes mental states such as stupor, drowsiness, and lack of clarity while agitation includes mental disturbances, regret, doubt, longing, and ill-will. Beginners deal with these obstacles in different ways to advanced meditators.

The method for beginners was explained in great detail in the general descriptions of tranquillity and insight meditation in Book One so there is no need to elaborate further here. More advanced meditators should not view dullness and agitation as obstacles in an ultimate sense. You should no longer regard them as something to be overcome or abandoned. You should instead learn to use them as part of your meditation. If you are practising Mahamudra meditation and have gained a degree of understanding from your practice, you need to understand the nature of these obstacles, instead of investing time and energy in trying to overcome them. Milarepa says:

> Skilled meditators should not try to eradicate
> The obstacles of dullness and agitation.
> Applying that kind of effort is like
> Lighting a lamp when the sun is shinning.

Milarepa is saying that when properly understood, the nature of these obstacles is already luminous and there is no need to illuminate that which is intrinsically pure. Gampopa says:

> If either obstacle arises,
> Do not try to eradicate it.
> Look instead into its nature!

You should deal with the general obstacles to meditation in this way. You have to be skilful however, so always remember that the way you relate to these obstacles should depend on how advanced you have become at practising meditation. That has to be kept in mind.

§ Removing Internal And External Obstacles

The *Vairocanabhisambodhi* says:

> There are two kinds of obstacles to meditation;
> Those that originate in our psychophysical constituents,
> And those that originate in the environment.

It also says:

> Obstacles from our psychophysical constituents
> Consist of the things that go wrong:
> Nausea, infections, viruses, gonorrhoea,

Hot and cold flushes, depression, and so on.
They have their origin in our psychosomatic condition
And thus arise internally.
Other obstacles arise in relation to our environment
And the people we deal with daily.
They are like the thorns of a bush that constantly prick us.
And cause various external difficulties because of this.

Relatives and friends can also be great obstacles to your practice because contact and intimacy with them can have a destructive influence on your commitment to meditation. Your practice can also be disrupted by people who maintain ill-will toward you or who want to do you harm. You might start harbouring a desire to retaliate and these preoccupations will disturb your mind and disrupt your practice.

It is also possible to encounter obstacles that have no apparent or natural cause and seem to originate from supernatural sources. Your body can also suffer from all kinds of diseases that are contracted from the environment. The harmony of the five physical elements may become upset, which can be traced to three types of ailments: diseases that come from bile, diseases that come from hypertension, and diseases that come from phlegm. All diseases can be traced to these fundamental ailments, which in turn are the product of disharmony in the physical elements and mind.

Certain environmental conditions can cause the mind to produce an uncontrollable proliferation of concepts and an increase in worries, anxieties, and fears. These obstacles sometimes do not seem to settle down, no matter what methods you use. If you fail to handle them with the proper understanding, your mind will get completely lost in the 'eight worldly concerns.'[20] Meditators should always be aware of these obstacles. If and when they arise, you must make the effort to overcome them by using the appropriate and relevant methods, rather than yielding to them and allowing yourself to become completely overwhelmed.

Furthermore, it is said that all kinds of other obstacles can arise in our body, speech, and mind when we are trying to cultivate our meditation practices. You will experience obstacles in relation to mind when your consciousness is dim and dull and your experiences become diluted. You will experience obstacles in relation to speech when you are compelled to verbalise whatever you experience in meditation indiscriminately, thus failing to resolve these experiences. You will experience obstacles in relation to body when your mental tendencies become fragmented, your physical energies are restless, and you do not want to remain in one place to pursue your practice.

You should take decisive steps to deal with these things when they arise. Do not just leave them alone or become discouraged by them. One method of dealing with them is to invoke the blessings and energies of past lineage masters. Visualise them at the appropriate centre and imagine that you are actually receiving their blessings and that their energy is being transmitted directly from them to you and pacifying all of your obstacles.[21]

Try to imagine this as vividly and realistically as possible. We do not only encounter obstacles when undesirable things happen, even positive things can turn out to be obstacles, if we reflect on them, because they lead us astray and cause us to lose focus in our practice. It is essential to be aware of all the obstacles that may arise in relation to your own psychophysical constituents and your external environment and to learn to deal with them appropriately.

That ends the chapter on how to eliminate meditative deviations.

8

Determining the Originless Nature of Mind

THE ORIGINLESS NATURE OF MIND

This has five parts:

- Determining the nature of mind through lada
- The nature of mind is empty from the beginning
- Observing the nature of mind in relation to what arises
- Recognising that whatever arises in mind is originless
- Regarding the mind both day and night

§ Determining The Nature Of Mind Through Lada

The teachings of Mahamudra contain a technical term called *lada*, which means 'the ability to determine the nature of mind so precisely there is no room for uncertainty.' This word is to be understood as meaning the establishment of the conviction that the nature of mind is free from origination, persistence, or dissipation and it does not dwell in any linear concept of past, present, or future. It is devoid of all spatial and temporal determinations. The word *lada* describes the attainment of meditators who have developed real conviction in the reality of the nature of mind. They are freed from uncertainty through determining its existential condition. Tilopa says:

> Meditators should not entertain thoughts of this or that
> But contemplate matters relating to lada.

Saraha says:

> Receive the instructions of your meditation teacher
> And contemplate the nature of mind as completely baseless.

> This is supreme meditation.

He also says:

> The nature of mind has been originless right from the beginning.
> We establish confidence in this
> Through the encouragement and instructions of our teacher.

Savaripa says:

> Meditators must remain in the natural state of mind,
> Free from the extremes of existence and non-existence
> And the concept of the three times.

Tilopa says:

> Mahamudra is nothing other than remaining in the natural state without an intentional object.

Maitripa says:

> To contemplate the nature of all things as comparable to space
> Is the practice of Mahamudra.

Many different practices have been formulated that relate to the cultivation of lada according to the Practice Lineage. The experience of lada is produced of these practices and occurs when you endure very lucid experiences of bliss, clarity, and non-conceptuality because of the diminution of your pollutants and defilements. When meditative experiences give way to a feeling of spaciousness and mental clarity, your experience assumes a quality of non-duality with a sense of emptiness and luminosity. When this sense of emptiness and luminosity is very persistent, so that the thoughts and concepts that arise in your mind cannot disturb your mental stability, you will be able to maintain both clarity and stability. The vividness of your experience of emptiness and luminosity will now be present no matter what kind of mental processes occur in your mind. This also applies to experiences associated with sensory impressions. No matter what appears to the senses, it will not distract you. On the contrary, you will perceive phenomenal appearances and emptiness to be co-present.

In brief, to attain lada is to gain conviction in the indivisible nature of thoughts and emptiness and the indivisible nature of phenomenal appearance and emptiness. It won't matter what state of mind you are in, what mental process you give rise to, or what is present to your senses, you will not waver from that understanding of non-duality. To arrive at that kind of conviction is lada.[1]

This is the proper result of Mahamudra meditation. Nonetheless, novice meditators should be forewarned of certain pitfalls at this point. Some meditators mistakenly develop false confidence based on a manufactured conviction. Without actually having any real and direct experience of self-cognising awareness or any relevant meditative experiences, they fall victim to a false confidence based on a familiarity with the practice and its teachings and claim various spiritual attainments that they have not actually acquired. These meditators have come under the influence of all kinds of illusions. Other people might possibly be impressed by their claims and believe them. Even if the response from others is positive, the welfare of those actual meditators will be in grave jeopardy, because they have made it impossible for themselves to properly determine the nature of mind. They are merely indulging in an elaborate form of self-deception.

On the other hand, genuine and sincere meditators, with sufficient meditation experience, but who do not make the effort to develop lada, will also hamper their own progress. It is important for experienced meditators to develop lada properly. It can also happen that a meditator's innate temperament might make it possible to develop lada automatically, even without their deliberately trying to, when they eradicate subtle forms of attachment and fixation in relation to their meditative experiences. This can occur during visionary experiences of certain lineage masters and so forth. However, this happens only to a very few fortunate ones. For the majority of us, it is extremely important to develop the experience of lada once we have sufficient meditation experience. This is the best way to deal with the judgemental mind that views certain experiences as good and other experiences as bad, as worthy of cultivation or worthy of derision and rejection. You only become more and more entangled in judgementalism about meditative experiences if you follow the latter path and will fail to attain liberation. Tsangpa Gyare says:

> Many meditators know the techniques of meditation,
> But very few know how to meditate properly,
> Without fixation on meditative experiences.

Anyone following the instructions and practices of the Mahamudra teachings must keep the experience of lada in mind. The development of lada speeds up progress for all meditators. Lada is very relevant for those few fortunate ones who have the ability to attain enlightenment rapidly on the instantaneous path. It is even more relevant for meditators who need time to mature on the path by progressing through the Four Yogas of Mahamudra until they eventually attain the yoga of non-conceptuality. This understanding of lada is one of the pith instructions to help meditators make rapid progress. Meditators who are not informed of it might spend years in practice, while meditators with knowledge of the benefits of this experience achieve progress in a very short time; in a matter of days in fact. You must learn to determine the nature of mind properly by developing lada.

§ The Nature Of Mind Is Empty From The Beginning

The experience of lada is essential for determining the nature of mind, but it is especially so in terms of determining the locus of that experience. That locus of the nature of mind is the nature of ultimate reality. This is inseparable from the nature of mind. This was quite extensively explained in the previous chapter. However, to refresh your memory, the essential points will be summarised here. The fundamental insight all meditators must attain is that all their experiences, both internal and external, are dependent on mind. The nature of mind cannot be encapsulated in any of these experiences, because it is free from the concepts of existence and non-existence. It is also free from any dualistic notion of perceiver and perceived. Furthermore, the concept of change or fluctuation is quite foreign to the nature of mind so we cannot say it comes into being or goes out of being. The nature of mind is therefore permanent, unlike the experiences that occur within mind as mental or sensory events, because it does not go through temporal change and the concept of the three times cannot be applied to it.[2] The only analogy that indicates anything about the nature of mind is space. Saraha says:

> Coemergent wisdom, the nature of mind,
> Cannot be said to be tangible or intangible,
> And cannot be symbolised as this or that.

Savaripa says:

> From the purview of the nature of mind,
> Movement and non-movement,
> Existence and non-existence, do not apply.
> Its nature is like space;
> Permanent and unaffected by the passage of time.
> Though we conventionally speak about 'space'
> It has no properties or attributes
> That contrast to physical entities.
> The nature of space is empty.

To say that space is existent or non-existent is irrelevant;
Space cannot be symbolised.
It is comparable to the nature of mind.
Failure to see that is to misconceive the nature of both.

Virupa says:

The nature of mind is empty,
Devoid of attributes and properties
And known as Mahamudra.
Just as space cannot be said to have properties,
The nature of mind is atemporal,
Has never come into being,
Is free of all empirical determinations,
And is all pervasive and changeless,
Just like space.

To realise the nature of mind this way is not about seeing it as empty of empirical determinations through recognition, it is about seeing that it has been so, right from the beginning. The nature of mind has always been devoid of attributes and properties. This is why it is unchanging. Even though we speak about space or lack of space you have to understand this is only conventional language; it does not actually refer to anything. Space is devoid of properties, so we cannot talk about its properties or about different kinds of space, and so on. Tilopa says:

Though we speak of space as empty,
Space is not something we can describe in a satisfactory manner.
We say that the nature of mind is empty and luminous,
But from the ultimate perspective
It cannot be said to have any characteristics.
The nature of mind is just like space;
Nothing can be predicated about it.

You have to realise that the nature of mind is empty in this way. If you can realise that, you will perceive everything that arises in relation to mind as imbued with the same reality. Remain in the natural state, free from the concept of coming into being, persisting, and dissipating. When this is done properly, you no longer need to concern yourself with mindfulness or distraction, meditative stability or mental agitation. Everything that arises in the mind will be naturally self-liberated by settling into mind's natural state. Savaripa says:

> The nature of mind gives rise to all experiences
> Both in mind and phenomenal appearance.
> If there were no nature of mind,
> Nothing at all could be experienced.
> Meditators must remain in the natural state;
> For anything that arises in mind
> Will then settle back into the nature of mind.
> If you try to examine the mind and its processes
> You will find no intrinsic nature to be discovered
> And no agent trying to discover it.
> If you remain in meditation
> Through the Mahamudra method,
> Everything will settle into the nature of mind
> Free from the concept of the three times.

He also says:

> To remain in that state means
> Being in the state of unchangingness.
> Natural bliss arises from that state.

Meditators should realise that lada experiences arise in relation to their understanding of the nature of mind itself. From the viewpoint of the nature of mind, nothing needs to be abandoned or cultivated. The following quotation makes this clear:

> The nature of mind has been pure and immaculate right from the beginning. Just like space, which is unaffected by cloud formations and weather, the nature of mind contains nothing that needs to be cultivated or abandoned. The nature of mind is quite unaffected by anything that goes on in the mind in terms of what is wholesome or unwholesome.

§ Observing The Nature Of Mind In Relation To What Arises

1. The inseparability of the nature of mind and appearances

The Mahamudra lineage is called the Practice Lineage and the blessings of its spiritual masters are an essential part of our development as practitioners. We must be open-minded and humble to be proper vessels to receive and contain the blessings that flow from these masters. All the great past masters unanimously emphasised the importance of humility because you can progress much more rapidly in your meditation if you have this attitude. Je Drikhungpa says:

> Whether your Mahamudra practice flourishes or not,
> Will depend on whether you feel humility
> In the presence of the lineage masters.

He also says:

> The four aspects of a lama's being
> Are like snowy mountain peaks.
> When the radiance that emanates from sincere humility
> Shines on these snowy peaks,
> The snow melts and flows downstream as a river of blessings.
> Do not forget to cultivate humility!

Saraha's *Queen Doha* says:

> The nature of all things is emptiness;
> Only the kindness of the lineage masters
> Will help us develop this realisation.
> The stream of blessing that emanates from the masters
> And the stream that flows from our humility,
> Must meet and join together as one stream.
> You must develop humility toward the past masters!

We can find many other comments that emphasise the importance of blessing and the attitude of humility. Before you embark on the practice outlined in this section, you must undertake the usual preliminaries of refuge, arousing bodhichitta, and so forth and then engage in guru yoga. Generate a strong desire to know ultimate reality and the nature of your mind. Then develop a very deep and intense feeling of humility and request the blessings of the lineage masters so that you can have this realisation.[3]

Once you have practised the general and specific preliminaries, allow your mind to rest in its natural state. Try to maintain a sense of awareness without distraction, but without directing the mind toward any specific object. Just maintain a sense of spacious openness and then give rise to a subtle thought. By 'subtle thought,' we mean a thought that is uncontaminated by strong positive or negative emotions; a simple thought without any emotive embellishments. Simply be aware of that thought, without fixation and without distraction and then suddenly give rise to a gross level of thought, meaning a thought that is contaminated by an intense positive or negative emotion. Try to switch back and forth between these two states of mind and determine whether there is any difference between them. Can you detect a difference between a state of total contemplation, the experience of a subtle thought, and the experience of gross thought with its accompanying layers of mental agitation and strong emotion? This technique can be applied to all kinds of experiences; experiences that generate pleasure, pain, or lust. In short, anything that gives rise to your innumerable delusions can be incorporated in this exercise.

You should sometimes prevent the rising of thoughts, sometimes encourage them, and sometimes simply follow their evolution and try to determine the nature of these different types of thoughts. You can do the same thing in relation to your sensory impressions of the external world. Focus your mind on things you find beautiful and then focus it on things you find immensely repulsive. You can also look at objects of different sizes, colours, and types. The same approach can be taken to the objects of the other senses. Pay attention to sounds that you find beautiful, sounds that you find disturbing, sounds that are loud, soft, or faint, and sounds that are pitched differently and try to determine whether there is any essential difference between them. Apply this discrimination to all the other sense impressions as well.

Gaze intently at objects with your eyes wide open and then close your eyes. Focus your attention on objects to your left and then to your right. Try to experience things from different perspectives and angles and examine the various ways that things are experienced. Spend several days repeating these exercises and look at the relationship between mind and sensory experiences. How does the world avail itself to the mind through the senses?

The purpose of these exercises is to determine a fundamental absence of duality between emptiness and appearance or between emptiness and the mental processes. Whatever arises in the mind internally and externally can't disturb it once you determine the nature of all experience.[4] The inseparability of phenomenal appearance and emptiness was explained in some detail in a previous chapter so you should refer back to that. Saraha says:

> Determine the nature of what appears to your sense organs
> As no different to the nature of mind.

Savaripa says:

> The Ganges, and all the rivers of the world,
> Flow down to the salty ocean and assume the same taste.
> Our sensory impressions of the external world
> And our mental events also have the flavour;

The flavour of ultimate reality.
Understand this!

Virupa says:

When you realise that your memories and thoughts
Are like a mirage of water;
You will be freed through having realised,
You are unbound from the beginning.
The very nature of thoughts and emotions
Has never been different from the nature of mind;
So you have never strayed from your own natural state.

Tilopa says:

Just as mist or clouds in space
Don't dissipate anywhere and nowhere dwell,
If you can determine the nature
Of everything that arises in mind in this way
You will remain completely undisturbed.
The nature of mind is like the depths of the ocean
And mental events are its waves.

Maitripa says:

When we realise the nature of thoughts is unoriginated
Just like the nature of mind itself
Those very thoughts dissipate into the natural state.

He also says:

The causes and conditions experienced by mind
Have the same nature as the nature of mind.
That is what is meant by Mahamudra.

By applying the techniques described in this section to the inner workings of mind and the sensory impressions, you will be able to determine with certainty the non-duality of the nature of mind and what occurs in the mind.

2. Overcoming the dualism of meditation and meditator

In Mahamudra, we meditate on the nature of mind to attain the kind of realisation that is genuine, immediate, and uncontaminated by conceptual understandings.

A conceptual understanding of the nature of mind as something that is free from the concepts of origin, persistence, and extinction is not real Mahamudra insight. Your insight must be born from direct experience. Direct experience is the authentic experience of a yogin. The following method will help to overcome the dualistic conception of meditation and meditator and to enhance your experience of the nature of mind.

Begin with the same practice as before. Allow your mind to rest in its natural state with a sense of open spaciousness and then maintaining an awareness of that. Look at your chosen object of meditation for a while and then turn your attention inward to your mind to see if there is any gap between meditation and meditator. You will gradually realise there is no separation between the two. They simply merge into one another when you cannot find a meditator as something separate from meditation. The unceasing experience of awareness is obvious, but even that awareness has no substantial reality.

This is how we learn to determine the nature of mind in relation to the experience of meditation and the subject engaged in that experience. For example, when you look at your experiences, you can distinguish between past experience, present experience, and possible future experience, but from the purview of the nature of mind, there is no difference between past, present, and future whatsoever. When you realise that, all of your experiences will dissipate back into the nature of mind, just as clouds and mist naturally dissolve into space.

You can also focus your attention on the notion of self and other. If you persist with this contemplation, you will realise that even these concepts have arisen from the baseless and unoriginated nature of mind. The concepts of self and other are not supported by anything, because the nature of mind is not dependent on anything. It is completely free right from the beginning. You will develop conviction that the nature of mind is devoid of all empirical determinations, even though it is the source for everything that arises through this method, and gradually realise that all of these dualistic notions—meditation and meditator, past, present, and future, self and other—are products of mind. They all arise from the nature of mind itself, which is not polluted by the activities of mind, because the concept of delusions and liberation, loss and gain, coming together and separating do not apply to the absolute aspect of mind.

You should spend several days practising these contemplations, without thinking about prohibiting certain experiences or discouraging others. Allow all kinds of things to arise in the mind and then rest in a relaxed manner without contrivance and without conditioning anything. You will then realise the non-duality of the nature of mind and what arises from it.[5] Saraha says:

> When you really think about it
> There is no meditation and no meditator;
> Genuine yogins must divest themselves of such thoughts.
> Failing to do this only causes further mental affliction;
> Dualistic notions must be overcome.

He also says:

> The aspect of mind that does not entertain
> Thoughts of meditation or meditator
> Is known as indestructible mind;[6]
> Free from the tendencies of hope and fear.

Again, he says:

> To realise the non-duality of self and other,
> Back and front, and all other dualistic notions;
> Is the source of all blissful experiences.
> Once understood, nothing that arises in mind,
> Is divorced from its original source.

Savaripa says:

> Those with genuine understanding
> Are not afflicted by the duality of meditation and meditator.
> Just as space cannot be split in two,
> Meditators and the objects of meditation cannot be divided.
> Dualistic thoughts and concepts merge together
> As when mixing milk with water.
> If we understand this,
> Multiple experiences may arise
> From the inner workings of mind
> And the perceptions of the external world,
> But everything will have one flavour.
> Once unity in multiplicity is perceived
> The experience of great bliss is unceasing.[7]

Virupa says:

> The nature of mind is open spaciousness,
> It cannot be identified as this or that.
> Meditation and meditator do not apply.

He also says:

> When you realise the inseparability of seer and seen,
> All concepts are self-liberated naturally.
> When you demolish the concept of a meditator,
> You become free from effort.
> When you relinquish the attainment of a goal,
> You become free from hope and fear.
> When you expose the deception of an unchanging self,
> You become victorious over internal conflicts.
> When you drop fixation on the perception of things,
> You transcend both samsara and nirvana.

You will be able to determine the nature of mind in relation to whatever arises from it through these contemplations.

§ Recognising That Whatever Arises In Mind Is Originless

The recognition of the originlessness of what arises in mind comes from divesting mind of any thoughts of an object of meditation. You have to dismantle your fixation on an object of meditation. You also need to relax your concepts about a meditator, abandon any longings for meditative experiences and stop making an effort to produce certain meditative states. Relinquish any notion of attainment and any notion of a subject who attains anything.

In brief, all of your concepts about what to practise or how to practise must be discarded. Even subtle forms of desires that are directed toward the development of mindfulness, meditative equipoise, and meditative experiences must be abandoned. You should even let go of the notion of letting go. You can then let the mind rest in its natural state without trying to transform or condition it. Allow your mind to rest in a relaxed way and maintain a sense of ease by not trying to prevent or follow the thoughts or concepts that arise. The mind can simply wander about without interference if you do not try to control or follow your thoughts. If distraction arises from time to time, this should not be a cause for worry or anxiety. There is no need to examine your mind by asking, 'What caused this distraction?' Even those thoughts should be relinquished. When you don't experience distraction and can maintain a sense of pure awareness, don't think of meditation, meditative experience, or the application of techniques. Simply experience it and leave the experience alone.

You should gradually develop the ability to maintain this awareness in post-meditation, at least during retreat situations. When you engage in the three basic actions of eating, walking, and sleeping while on retreat, do not entertain conceptual proliferations about your actions, thinking that you must do this or that. Just perform actions with a sense of awareness and spontaneity. Apart from these three basic actions, do not get involved in anything. Even any Tantric commitments you may have should be stripped down to a minimum. Temporarily suspend any engagement in pujas, daily prayers, and so on and simply practise silence. When you go to sleep, do not concern yourself with what you should do tomorrow. Drift off to sleep and let the mind be—with thoughts or the absence of thoughts—just as it is. Try to abandon ideas of wholesome or unwholesome actions, or of wholesome or unwholesome thoughts and feelings, and remain in a state of ease. That sense of ease should be undisturbed, no matter what happens. If your meditation sessions go well and you have encouraging experiences, do not get attached to them or feel elated. If your meditation sessions go badly and you have disturbing or disconcerting experiences, do not give rise to anxiety. If you can rest in the natural state at all times, without being swayed by the activities of mind no matter what occurs, you can remain in a state of meditation.

This state of naturalness without artificiality is the nature of mind. The nature of mind does not come into being or cease to be; it cannot be acquired, lost, cultivated, or transcended. It makes no difference whether you are aware of this or not. It doesn't matter whether the mind is distracted or not. Even your ideas about having or not having meditative experiences, having or not having realisation, should settle within the nature of mind. When you are in that state, whatever arises in the mind manifests as pure presence. Thoughts, concepts, and feelings all dissipate back into nature of mind and everything that gives rise to experiences becomes naturally liberated within it. Everything happens within the meditative state, nothing happens outside of it. You will develop conviction that meditation is all-encompassing and have the ability to stay in a meditative state regardless of what you are doing or thinking. Everything becomes part of meditation.

It would be appropriate at this point to alert anyone who engages in this advanced level of practice to certain dangers about it. It is important not to turn the technique of resting in the natural state into a subtle way of preventing thoughts from arising in the mind. This is the technique used by Hwashang Mahayana and places a subtle emphasis on the stability aspect of mind. It is possible to become so self-absorbed within this practice, that instead of letting the mind rest in its natural state, you plunge yourself into deep and distressing states of depression as a result of the circulation of psychophysical energy within the mind and body. You must employ methods to uplift yourself and make sure you don't fall into that state again. Remind yourself of the importance of practising 'letting the mind be in its own natural state' and allow your mind to wander about with a sense of ease. Depression and other forms of mental distress are often caused by a failure to develop that sense of ease.

Practise this approach for a number of days during retreat to see if your meditative state is disrupted. If you can say, 'I experience interruptions from distraction or sleep, which cannot be incorporated into the meditative state,' look more carefully at your experiences. Ask yourself, 'What is the nature of distraction?' 'What is the nature of sleep?' Even those states of mind can be incorporated into meditation. As Saraha says:

> When you meditate without the thought of meditation
> You will experience its fruition very quickly.

He also says:

> To develop positive qualities,
> There is no need to look other than
> The nature of mind;
> They are already present.
> This cannot be discovered through Sutric or Tantric teachings.
> It is discovered within the mind itself,
> When we relinquish all forms of clinging.

Again, he says:

> The essence of mind is free from virtue and vice;
> We do not need to do anything.
> Abandoning thoughts of doing,
> We discover great bliss.

He also says:

> When mind entertains no thought of itself;
> We realise enlightenment.

He furthermore says:

> When mind is at rest in its own natural state,
> Undisturbed by thoughts of this or that;
> We achieve liberation from the samsaric condition.

He also says:

When we realise that the things
We think, perceive, and do in body, speech, and mind
Come from the mind itself;
We are freed of all constraints.

Savaripa says:

When yogis realise that
The nature of samsara and nirvana is essenceless,
They don't get bogged down by hope and fear.
What is there to cultivate or abandon?

He also says:

Lo! The yogi who realises non-duality
Renders the concepts of acceptance and rejection irrelevant.
Just as I have never become fixated or had to abandon anything;
You, my son, must realise,
There is fundamentally nothing to be done.

Virupa says:

Without concepts of things to be understood
Or agents to understand them;
We realise there is no such thing
As being or not being free from delusions,
And remain in a state of equilibrium.
If you understand that
You need no techniques from someone else.
Everything that arises is undifferentiable from dharmakaya.
How can you think of acceptance or rejection?
Since you no longer need to worry
About meditation or non-meditation,
You are untouched by conventionality.
Everything you experience is independent
Of what does or does not appear to you,
And you become free from fixation on appearances.
Since you are not afflicted
By the dilemma of doing or not doing,
You become free from intentionality.
Since you are devoid of hope and fear,
You dissipate all forms of clinging.

He also says:

> When you stop entertaining thoughts
> Of meditation and non-meditation,
> And your mind is free of such defilement;
> You establish real conviction.
> You perceive ultimate reality
> Where there is no knower and known.

Again, he says:

> The best method is to be unconcerned
> About abandonment or achievement.
> Your mind will no longer be contaminated,
> By attachment to ideas or deeds
> And you will have no fear of what arises in mind.
> Establishing proper contact with ultimate reality
> Will give you the ability to remain in the natural state
> Without being inauthentic or artificial.
> And you will act in an authentic
> And spontaneous manner without constraints.
> This is the most supreme method.

Tilopa says:

> You should not give rise to concerns about
> transforming or not transforming mind.
> If you can remain in an authentic state of being,
> Nothing can disturb you.

He also says:

> Have no concept of meditation or examination,
> Do not engage in meditation with effort,
> Do not engage in action with deliberation,
> And remain free of hope and fear.
> If you let be and act in this manner,
> All subtle and gross mental fixations
> Will be naturally liberated,
> Without the use of antidotes.
> Nothing can arise outside
> The existential condition of ultimate reality.

Again, he says:

> Fixation of any degree or kind
> Obscures the naturally luminous quality of mind.
> Corrupting notions of this or that
> Cut off the authentic state of being.
> If you can remain natural
> Without entertaining these notions;
> And just allow thoughts and ideas to rise and fall,
> Like huge waves that crash back into the ocean
> Without disturbing the ocean's depths.
> Nothing that occurs will disturb the mind.
> This attitude is the lamp that illuminates ignorance.
> If you can free yourself from the preoccupations
> That normally follow people,
> The secret of the sutras and tantras will be revealed.

These extensive quotations from the songs of the mahasiddhas emphasise the importance of remaining in the natural state. They clearly demonstrate that all the Tantric yogis and yoginis make the same point. Gampopa says:

> When yogis and yoginis abandon
> The notion of the spiritual path,
> And no longer concern themselves
> With what to cultivate or abandon;
> They become free of anxiety
> About the results of practice,
> And extinguish hope and fear.
> Thus they see through the falsity
> Of their perception of existent things;
> And realise that self-sufficiently existing entities
> Are dependent on conceptual constructions.

He also says:

> When we rest in the nature of mind
> We retain our awareness,
> Whether mind is stable or agitated.
> All manner of things may arise in mind,
> But none can dilute its unsullied nature;
> Like mist and clouds, they dissipate into space.
> When we meditate without intentionality,

Without thoughts of a knower or a known,
And without concern for the meditative state,
We become completely carefree.
We can live our lives just as we wish.

Again, he says:

When you cease to worry about maintaining your awareness
Distractions cannot arise
And your state of mind will not transition
Between meditative and post-meditative states.
Wherever you dwell,
Everything becomes a part of meditation.
Dualistic notions are seen as mind's creations,
Not something that exists independently of mind.

He further says:

To realise that the nature of mind is essencelessness
Makes this very world a liberating experience.
If there is no fixation the thoughts and concepts that arise
Liberate, rather than bind.
If there is no attachment or longing
We can maintain a state of equilibrium
In all situations, at all times.
If you realise this, meditation becomes unceasing.
That is the attainment of non-meditation.

Gampopa says:

For those who realise the unreality of mind
All appearances are the dharmadhatu.
For those who cease to discriminate
All thoughts are spontaneously liberated.
For those who relinquish fixation and longing
Everything exists in equilibrium.
For those who realise all this
Meditation becomes non-meditation.

Many comments of this nature can be found in the writings of realised Tantric masters. If you have the wish to gain more inspiration, you should consult their works.

§ Regarding The Mind Both Day And Night

As the previous section explains, the ultimate aim of Mahamudra practice is to maintain the meditative state. We need to mix meditative and post-meditative experiences until there is no qualitative difference between them. You will achieve this by regarding the mind both day and night. When you apply lada, you should make sure your awareness does not become too intense or you may become fixated upon it. Simply let whatever arises in the mind alone, without imposing judgements on it and without any clinging or grasping. Just try to see thoughts and concepts for what they are. Even the thought of seeing your experiences as empty by nature should be relinquished. Do not make distinctions between meditative experience and post-meditative experience during practice and refrain from the tendency to transform, change, or contrive your experiences in any way. Je Zhang says:

> When engaged in Mahamudra meditation
> Don't try to develop any specific state of mind.
> There should be no thought of beginning, middle, or end.
> Let go of whatever arises in the mind without judgement.

At this point, some readers might ask, 'Isn't there a danger of losing our awareness if we practise like this?' There is no such danger. When we become aware of whatever is in the mind and then relax and let it go, that in itself will dismantle our tendency to cling and grasp. This is the form of awareness that you need to develop and apply. This is the ultimate form of awareness, because it is completely divorced from clinging and grasping and it enables realisation of the nature of mind and ultimate reality. This type of awareness has to be distinguished from the awareness we normally apply in meditation. That awareness simply means becoming aware of our mental processes and events or placing our attention on the object of meditation. The awareness that we are cultivating here is far superior to those everyday awarenesses, although we do need to use everyday awareness during meditation, if we want to arrive at this ultimate form of awareness. Savaripa says:

> Mahamudra is none other than the state,
> Where mind is no longer afflicted with the ideas
> Of attainment, abandonment, mental activity,
> Lack of mental activity, and so on.

This type of continuous meditative state is called 'non-meditation' because you no longer have an object of meditation. Everything is incorporated into the state of meditation so that there is no distinction between meditation and post-meditation. This is the fruition of Mahamudra practice. This meditation, which is totally inseparable from your being-itself, is the best form of meditation. It should be mentioned, at this point, that you will still be subject to intervals of disruption in post-meditation at this stage. However, if you can become aware of those distractions, realise their nature and let them go, you will not deviate from the method of Mahamudra. This is the same as mixing the mental states of meditation and post-meditation.

This method can also be used to mix your experiences of day and night. Beginners at meditation may need to apply a degree of effort to clear their mind of its usual preoccupations and concerns, but when mind is stable and clear, you should drift off to sleep in that state. The ability to go to sleep with this attitude and maintain it when you start to dream is a wonderful achievement. However, this will not come easily for most practitioners, so if you find yourself drifting into slumber, becoming completely unconscious and starting to dream without any sense of awareness at all, do not be overly concerned. If your first thought upon awakening is to look into the nature of your dream experiences, this is sufficient for mixing daytime experience with dream experience. Gampopa had the following exchange with a student about this practice:

> Student: 'What happens when the mind drifts into sleep and experiences arise, but there is no sense of awareness in the mind? Can we actually purify those experiences by reflecting on them later? Is it really essential to be aware of experiences at all times to determine their nature?'
> Gampopa: 'It is not necessary to be aware of your thoughts at all times. Just try to determine the nature of thoughts as soon as awareness has risen. They will then become naturally liberated and purified. It does help if you are able to maintain a sense of awareness at all times, but it's of no real significance if you are unable to do so, because you can still realise the nature of those thoughts and naturally and spontaneously overcome delusions and defilements. When you go to sleep and dream without being able to detect luminosity in the midst of your dreams, you should still look back on those dreams when you awaken, and realise that the luminosity of your mind and your dream experiences are inextricably bound. They cannot be separated.'

You need to develop the confidence to realise that luminosity does not exist elsewhere. It is already present in those very dream experiences, even though you may not be aware of it while dreaming.[8] Many such exchanges between teachers and students make similar points about mixing these two experiences. However, even when you come to this point in the practice, if there is still the nagging thought in the back of your mind that you need to acquire certain states of mind and transcend others, it may be a sign that you should stop this practice. The application of lada may be premature for you. Go back to more fundamental practices and give this one a rest. Gampopa says:

> I do not entertain notions,
> Of acquiring certain mental states and transcending others
> And thus discriminate between mental distractions and awareness.
> As long as you entertain such thoughts,
> You have not gone beyond the dualistic notions
> Of acceptance and rejection.

He also says:

> To think you attain meditation through awareness
> And give rise to delusions through distraction
> Is just another creation of mind.
> There is no such thing in actuality.

You should apply lada and try to develop real confidence without concerning yourself with anything else for a continuous period of five days.[9] Follow that with a one-day break and then repeat the practice continuously for seven days. Follow that with another one-day break and then repeat the practice for ten days. Follow that with a one-day break and so on. Once the whole notion of lada is established, you will gradually become free from the notion of meditation and meditator, of experience and experiencer, of understanding and someone who understands. All these dualistic notions will subside and you will no longer be separated from what is real.[10]

There is no doubt that you will attain some form of realisation if you pursue this practice, but how you attain it or what type of realisation you attain will depend on your own capacity, psychological make-up, and other associated factors. It would also depend upon how much practice you have done. If you are unable to attain realisation through this approach, go back to the practice of mixing meditation and post-meditation, then gradually work through your dualistic notions until you can even transcend your fixation on the concept of emptiness. If you follow this practice properly, have no doubt that you will become established in the uncontrived, authentic state of being. There is no method more profound than this; no transmission that contains better instructions than this. That is how you should regard this practice.

9

Transforming Adversity on the Path

HOW TO TRANSFORM ADVERSITY

This has three parts:

- How and when to use the methods of transformation
- How to understand what we are transforming
- Six methods for transforming adversity onto the path

§ How And When To Use The Methods Of Transformation

We now turn to the methods that transform the adverse circumstances and situations that we encounter in meditation and in everyday life and make them a part of our spiritual path. You should be able to treat anything that happens, whether good or bad, as an aid for meditative and spiritual progress. We tend to regard adverse circumstances and situations as obstacles and fail to deal with them appropriately or to incorporate them into our spiritual life.

This instruction on how to deal with adversity differently, immediately precedes the explanation of the Four Yogas of Mahamudra, which is the goal of Mahamudra practice. I have explained all the techniques that you will need to apply in relation to tranquillity and insight meditation and examined all the ways that you should deal with various meditative experiences. However, difficulties may still arise, in spite of your proficiency in tranquillity and insight meditation and you will have to come to terms with them. You will therefore need to become familiar with this section of the text before you can turn your attention to the Four Yogas of Mahamudra.

What is the appropriate time to resort to techniques that transform adverse circumstances and situations onto the path? You must have achieved some grounding in the practice and be acquainted with the notion that disturbing thoughts and emotions are inseparable from ultimate reality. You must also understand that the way we perceive the world through our sensory apparatuses is not completely separable from how things actually exist in reality. In other words, you need to have recognised the unity between appearance and reality to some extent. Furthermore, the memory of your meditative experiences must frequently intrude on your everyday experiences of the world and your engagement in it. If you do not have this minimal foundation to your practice, it will be practically impossible to use adversity as part of your spiritual path. Anyone wishing to employ methods of transformation must meet these criteria.

The appropriate time for employing these methods is after you have had a direct experience of the nature of mind and attained the understanding that arises from wisdom. Your habituated mind will still be susceptible to the influences of delusion and emotional conflicts, despite this fundamental understanding of reality and this insight into your true condition, so that excessive clinging, grasping, and intense feelings of aversion may still arise. Even advanced meditators are not insulated from the internal disturbances that arise from the habitual workings of the mind. They may still become disturbed by what they see, hear, taste, smell, and touch from time to time. When your mind is disturbed by the sensory impressions, and the techniques of tranquillity and insight meditation seem ineffective, you should turn to the methods of transforming adverse circumstances and situations on the path.

Another appropriate time for employing this method is when you have grown a little complacent, self-assured, and confident because your practice has been fairly consistent for a while. That confidence may deprive you of the ability to look more deeply into your own mind. If you could look deeper, you would see various unacknowledged and unconscious psychic tendencies, which have the potential to cause all kinds of mental disruptions if they remain unresolved. Sooner or later, these unresolved and unacknowledged psychic conflicts will emerge and cause all kinds of disruptions in your mindstream. These are examples of how and when to make use of the methods of transformation.

In brief, you should use this method when you are practising mindfulness and awareness to deal with mental agitation or dullness and you are having difficulty employing your unsettled or disturbing thoughts and emotions in a constructive and creative manner. You should also use this method when you are constantly bogged down by the tendencies of hope and fear, expectation and doubt. Hope arises when we have the perception, either real or imagined, that our meditation is progressing according to plan. Doubt arises when uncertainty pops up about our general meditation or spiritual practices. If this twin tendency of hope and fear, expectation and doubt, keeps resurfacing, you must employ the methods of transforming adverse circumstances and situations onto the path.

We generally use the methods of transformation under two circumstances: 1) when mindfulness and awareness fail, and 2) when the obstacles of hope and fear, expectation and doubt, keep appearing. You will sometimes practise meditation in the wilderness, as will be explained shortly, and must be prepared for the circumstances and situations that you may encounter there. Nonetheless, it is very possible that your emotions will overwhelm you under such circumstances, so you fail to deal with them in a spiritual, constructive, or beneficial manner. It is important to use the methods of transformation in this situation also.

One last scenario where this method is useful is when you are actually able to maintain mindfulness and awareness to a substantial degree even in post-meditation, but you remain habituated to the use of antidotes, even now that you have no need for them. You feel the urge to employ some method out of fear and uncertainty, even when your mind is stable and aware. The benefit of the methods that transform adverse circumstances and situations cannot be over-emphasised, even here.[1]

When should we actually apply this method? The appropriate time is after we have experienced 'spiritual heat' or wisdom.[2] Wisdom is often metaphorically compared to the sun. When the heat of wisdom makes itself known, we can use the methods of transformation. The *Hevajra Tantra* says:

> Only when you have felt the heat of wisdom,
> Are you qualified to use methods of transformation.

In our Practice Lineage, it is very important to apply these methods at the appropriate time, precisely because there are meditators who may have attained a degree of experience in the stability of tranquillity meditation, but have not enjoyed a real experience of the nature of mind. They use whatever arises in the mind to transform their mind and lack full understanding. Other meditators are misled into thinking they are engaged in transforming adverse circumstances onto the path, when they have not even managed to stabilise the mind, let alone gained any insight into the nature of mind. They spend prolonged periods in solitude or frequent cemeteries and so forth, imagining they are dealing with their own fears of mortality and death when their real motivation is to gain the recognition of others. They want to be regarded as saints or someone who has advanced on the spiritual path when no such progress has occurred. The importance of knowing the appropriate time and appropriate methods for overcoming adverse circumstances and situations without self-deception is extremely important.

We must be true to ourselves, or we will fail to understand what we need to transform. We will never be able to discern undesirable and loathsome situations and circumstances or know how to make use of them as part of our spiritual path, if we do not have a certain level of fundamental insight. That is the precondition for these methods. The mind, by nature, feels a lack of fulfilment and constantly grasps after this and that. In so doing, it eliminates any possibility of going beyond that grasping to establish a certain level of stability through meditation. This method also becomes relevant when we want to go beyond stability and make use of both the stable and distracted states of mind. Although mind is constantly directed outwardly so that it grasps after this and that, when it settles into itself and has attained a degree of stability, we can use these methods of transformation to go beyond both states of mind. There is no real difference between a mind in motion and a stable mind and these methods of transformation deal with both states. The *Hevajra Tantra* says:

> Whether the mind is agitated or stable,
> Both states can be part of meditation.

The Tantric system presents many methods that deal with adversity. For example, the father tantras mention three methods for transforming negative thoughts, emotions, and situations: 1) the extremely elaborate method, 2) the simple method, and 3) the very simple method.

The mother tantras mention another three methods: 1) the secret method, 2) the rigorous method, and 3) the victorious method.

Other Tantric literature mentions four methods for transforming negative situations, environments and experiences: 1) the method of Samantabhadra, (2) the secret method, 3) the method of concealment, and 4) the rigorous and victorious method.

Yet another four methods are mentioned in Tantric literature: 1) the method for beginners, 2) the method for gaining power over wisdom, 3) the method for internalising that wisdom, and 4) the method of complete freedom.

While these methods relate to the Tantric teachings and not necessarily the Mahamudra teachings as such, they are still relevant aids for Mahamudra practice. These Tantric methods of transformation relate to the creative imagination and fulfilment stages of Tantric practice.[3] There is no incompatibility between Tantric methods and Mahamudra practice. Certain Tantric methods can be incorporated into the Mahamudra system and used to enhance and develop our Mahamudra practice. This view is shared by the Practice Lineage and prominent Indian teachers such as Saraha, Savarisvara, Virupa, Tilopa, and so on. Their biographies and teachings clearly state that certain Tantric methods can be incorporated into Mahamudra practice.[4]

The *Kalachakra Tantra* is also clear that practitioners who have matured to the point where they can work with methods for turning adverse circumstances and situations onto the path must still adhere to the prohibition that celibate monks and nuns cannot employ sexual techniques to transform lust. Monks and nuns must be content to use the elaborate method, the simple method, and the victorious method; they mustn't engage in secret methods that affect their vows of celibacy.

It is easy to fall victim to laziness and complacency when you engage in these methods, so that very little is gained from them, even if you practise them for a long time. Instead of always trying to practise in the most comfortable way possible, you should sometimes place yourself in undesirable situations, such as going into the wilderness. These more difficult circumstances require you to extend yourself and your resources so that you will then begin to develop. If you remain content with your current situation and just try to deal with it as best you can, you cannot expect to attain any fast or unexpected growth. Many past masters have gone to places that are eerie and frightening for this reason. They spent time in the mountains, in cemeteries, in places haunted by ghosts, spirits, and so forth. They even spent time with corpses. We engage in these practices precisely because they give rise to fear, aversion, and anxiety and we would really much rather avoid them. If you do this you will be able to develop very quickly by confronting your fears.[5]

The Kadampa masters of the past also made use of methods of transformation. They emphasised the following five practices: 1) observing moral precepts while remaining in solitude, 2) using antidotes, 3) internalising the received instructions, 4) gaining conviction in the practices, and 5) dealing with adverse circumstances and situations.

Gampopa lists the following four achievements from practices of this nature: 1) gaining confidence in the content of the oral instructions, 2) gaining confidence in the methods of self-transformation, 3) gaining certainty in our meditative experiences, and 4) gaining confidence in our world view.

Mahasiddha Zhang lists five results from the methods of transformation: 1) we gain the key that unlocks the treasures of mind, 2) freedom from fear of internal and external disturbances, 3) no more susceptibility to self-deception, 4) no gap between how we see ourselves and who we really are, and 5) we can deal with adverse circumstances and situations by spending time in solitude.

There are five methods for dealing with adverse circumstances:

1) Seeing ourselves as a wounded deer. A wounded deer does not seek companionship, but yearns to be left alone. You should also spend time in solitude and avoid everyday concerns, such as protecting your loved ones and attacking your enemies. Avoid thoughts of your own livelihood and of being good practitioner so that you can cultivate sponsors and practise in comfort. You must be single-minded in your intentions with this practice so that no external factors can sway your mind.

2) Adopting the posture of a lion. Lions symbolise majesty and are the kings of the animal kingdom; all other animals submit to them. Lions symbolise fearlessness because a lion has power over all the animals but they have no power over it. You must display a similar kind of fearlessness toward the external environment and the inner workings of your mind and feel no apprehension, uncertainty, or fear about what occurs around or within you.[6]

3) Being like the wind in space. The wind is always in motion and does not remain anywhere even for a second. Similarly, don't fixate on anything; not your work, self-perception, possessions, pleasurable indulgences, or the recognition or acknowledgement you receive from others. You must learn not to fixate on such things. Instead, be like the wind that touches everything but never sticks to anything. You encounter different situations, possessions, and experiences, but just like the wind, don't become stuck to anything.

4) Developing the quality of space. Just as space has no centre or periphery, you should not think of yourself as an agent with a fixed identity. Do not think, 'I must do this, I must do that,' and give rise to all kinds of thoughts about what you should and should not do in meditation. We tend to think about what we should concentrate on in post-meditation and what we should not concentrate on in meditation, and then fixate on that. Free yourself from these preoccupations, and be like space, which has no centre or periphery.

5) Emulating the mind of a mad person. Just as a madman loses all judgement about what he should be thinking or how he should be behaving and spontaneously embraces whatever occurs in his mind, you should learn to become less judgemental and moralistic. Don't think something is intrinsically good and something else is intrinsically bad and we need to develop the good and incorporate it into our being and abandon that which is bad and discard it from our being. Instead, allow yourself to experience whatever arises in the mind, without becoming fixated on it, just like a mad person.[7]

These methods are ways to deal with adverse circumstances and situations as part of the path and will enhance our view of reality.[8]

§ How To Understand What We Are Transforming

We need to transform all of the psychic tendencies we have so far been unable to deal with due to ignorance and to the implicit belief in the duality of subject and object. This fundamental misunderstanding is the cause of our continuous wandering in samsara. The *Vairocanabhisambodhi* says:

> When we have no control over our minds,
> We are the victims of our proliferating thoughts and concepts.
> This generates all kinds of mental afflictions
> And perpetuates the samsaric condition.

In the context of this teaching, proliferating thoughts and concepts are not intrinsically evil or impure in themselves; the harm comes from our failure to understand their nature. The proliferation of thoughts and concepts that contribute to our delusions and defilements can therefore be used to enhance our practice through the methods of transformation. The source of wisdom lies in understanding these thoughts and concepts. It does not lie in getting rid of them. In other words, the cessation of the samsaric condition is not attained by overcoming or discarding the unceasing activities of mind, it is overcome by understanding them. The *Hevajra Tantra* says:

> Conceptual proliferations lead to liberation
> From conceptual proliferations.
> The samsaric condition leads to the purification
> Of the samsaric condition.

Saraha says:

> To understand conceptual proliferation is to have wisdom.
> That is how you empty the ocean of samsara.

Naropa and Maitripa also say:

> Self-liberated thought is no different from wisdom.

Readers might still argue at this point, 'Shouldn't we just be introduced to the nature of thoughts by being told they are no different to dharmakaya, and just leave it at that? The insight meditation section of this text has already explained the nature of thoughts to be dharmakaya. How come that is not sufficient? How come the methods of transformation have to be introduced for dealing with conflicting emotions and conceptual confusion?'

The simple answer is while some exceptional people can benefit directly from insight meditation instructions and understand the nature of thoughts in an instantaneous and unmediated fashion, for most people this is unfortunately easier said than done. Most people will gain much more benefit from learning to transform their negative emotions as part of the spiritual path. These people do not get the real point of the practice at first so just to think 'the nature of thoughts is dharmakaya' and 'the nature of conflicting emotions is dharmakaya' may not be very helpful. They do not have the ability to understand what this actually means. This is why they need to engage in methods of transformation. Furthermore, most people can deal with their thoughts and emotions during meditation, when they are not too intense or overwhelming, and will thereby gain some understanding of their nature and that gives rise to wisdom. However, when violent thoughts and emotions occur, these meditators do not have the ability to deal with them. Just saying, 'the nature of these experiences is dharmakaya' will not help very much. These meditators need to transform their violent thoughts and emotions so that their experiences can become part of meditation.

Unless you can apply the methods of transformation properly, you may experience deviations and aberrations in your meditation. Just thinking 'the nature of thoughts is dharmakaya' may actually mislead you into thinking that thoughts are somehow okay and a part of meditation. You will rarely be in a meditative state if you regard arising thoughts and subsiding thoughts as dharmakaya. In any case, if you can use mindfulness and awareness to be in a meditative state and can see the nature of thoughts and emotions when they are minor, that does not mean you will not be overwhelmed again when really disturbing thoughts and emotions arise. Intense lust, attachment, anger, or hatred deprive you of the opportunity to understand their nature.[9] This will continue to be a problem, even at the level of the second yoga, because of the difficulty of looking into the nature of thoughts and emotions when the mind is disturbed.

Even meditators who are comparatively advanced should use the methods of transformation. Many people who have attained some degree of success and who have practised meditation for many years still fail to grasp the essence of meditation. This happens when you have not given sufficient thought to the practices of transformation.[10] It is therefore very important for both beginners and advanced meditators to be familiar with the methods of transformation. It is not just beginners who can be naive and ignorant of the relevant methods and teachings, even advanced practitioners often fail to see the significance of transformative methods. The fundamental essence of transformation is still the practice of mindfulness; it has nothing to do with other meditative techniques. Being mindful while being present is all that is required. Je Drikhungpa says:

> If there is mindfulness, there is meditation;
> Without it, there is no meditation.

He also says:

> An unceasing flow of mindfulness
> Means the meditative state has been secured.

It is essential to realise that mindfulness constitutes a very important part of these transformation methods. When you have the intention to employ transformation and you understand that mindfulness is the foundation of this practice, there is one other important thing to remember. All kinds of transformation are talked about, but in this context, the important thing to understand is that all of them can be subsumed under 'the method that transforms conceptual proliferation.' All the other forms of transformation are just elaborations on this. Realising that conceptual proliferations are no different to dharmakaya is central to this practice. You will not deal effectively with disturbing thoughts and emotions through the methods of transformation if you do not have this understanding.

Six methods of transformation are commonly found in the Mahamudra teachings. It is very important for the reader to know that these six methods were used by the forefathers of the lineage. Gampopa did not formulate them clearly in his writings, but they are nonetheless to be found in a fragmentary way within them. These six methods are: 1) transforming disruptive situations, 2) transforming physical and mental illness, 3) transforming the fear of death, 4) transforming disturbing emotions, 5) transforming disturbing thoughts, and 6) transforming fear of possessions.

Tsangpa Gyare, of the Drukpa Kagyu school, rediscovered some hidden texts left behind by Rechungpa.[11] These texts emphasise the method of one-flavouredness and are now a very important part of Drukpa Kagyu practice. There are three central points to remember with these six methods.

1) Recognising the nature of thoughts: you must not allow yourself to get entangled in thoughts of good and bad in terms of what arises in your mind. We usually judge every thought to be either good or bad, so to begin the practice of transformation, you must stop judging your thoughts. The nature of those thoughts will be recognised when you cease to judge them.

2) Abandoning clinging to self: this is about the middle of the practice and goes beyond the question of judgement, to deal with the emotional reac-

tions that follow those judgements. Do not follow your emotional reactions when they arise so that you become completely overwhelmed by them nor resist your emotional reactions so that you are constantly fighting with them or trying to deny them. You can suspend your emotional reactions more effectively, if you stop thinking of yourself as having an enduring identity. Stop saying, 'All these emotions are happening to me and harming me.' When you pay more attention to your emotions as they arise and less attention to who you think is experiencing them or how you think they are affecting you, your experiences will become more open. The possibility of transformation will then become a reality. This is the only way the mind can automatically remain in the subtle condition.

3) Becoming free of hope and fear: at the conclusion of this practice of transformation, this is what will allow the real changes to occur. When you can free yourself from thoughts of hope and fear, expectation and doubt, you will cease to think of your meditation as a waste of time when you experience mental agitation or to think that you have had a wonderful experience and latch onto it if your mind remains calm. The idea is to free yourself from these mental tendencies in the practice of meditation.[12]

You have to apply this attitude to the method of transformation itself. Instead of thinking, 'How do I know I am using this method properly?' and becoming completely bogged down in fearful and anxious thoughts, just stick to the practice. Nor should you think, 'This technique works, I have to do more of it,' when you have positive experiences during this method. That will only leave you open to disappointment and you will just go back and forth between hope and fear. These three stages of meditation must be employed, but not necessarily in a linear way. They are really three different experiences that can be had during meditation. It is nonetheless essential that you identify your thoughts at the beginning, identify and deal with your emotions in the middle and relinquish your hope and fear at the end.

§ Six Methods For Transforming Adversity On The Path

1. Transforming disturbing thoughts and concepts

The *Hevajra Tantra* says:

> When your ear is filled with water
> You can only get it out by injecting something else.
> You can only free yourself from disturbing thoughts and concepts
> By understanding their nature, not by getting rid of them.

Thoughts are liberated by making use of thoughts. How then are disturbing thoughts and concepts transformed? You should not think you need to vigorously and vigilantly get rid of them, but shift your attention to the nature of those thoughts. Instead of paying too much attention to specific or concrete experiences of a thought as it arises, shift your attention to the nature of that thought. When you constantly pay attention to disturbing thoughts, your mind can become more disturbed. If you shift your attention to the nature of those thoughts, the thoughts themselves become transformed. This is called making use of disturbing thoughts and concepts as part of the spiritual path. Gampopa says:

> Don't think of abandoning disturbing thoughts and concepts; view them as very beneficial and helpful. They are quite indispensable and essential to your growth, not something to be eradicated. You cannot do without them. Learn to love your thoughts; they are no different from their nature. Disturbing thoughts and concepts are our companion and friend. There is no other path apart from disturbing thoughts. They are the wood for the fire of wisdom.[13]

Gampopa made numerous references to methods of transforming conceptual proliferation as part of our spiritual path.

However, in the present context, you should make use of disturbing thoughts and concepts in the following manner. Right at the beginning, when you experience a disturbing thought in association with moral concepts of good or bad, whether it be intense or subtle in nature, do not judge it as either morally praiseworthy or morally condemnable or you will give rise to an emotional reaction such as pride, disgust, shame, and so on. Apply mindfulness, remain with the thought and try to recognise what is actually going on. If you fail to do this, experiences may take place in your mind, but you will fail to recognise them and deprive yourself of the opportunity to make use of them as part of the spiritual path.[14]

Try not to become fixated on the experiencer who seems to be affected by these activities of mind. Here, the method for transforming proliferation of thoughts is quite different to the methods in insight meditation. In insight meditation, you deal with your proliferating thoughts by slowing down your thinking and then observing the origin, persistence, and dissolution of a thought to see that it has no inherent reality of its own. Another common insight method is to allow the mind to wander and then give rise to mindfulness and awareness and follow your stream of thought. In this context, we do not pursue either of those methods, not because they are not valuable, but because they may not always work. That was mentioned at the beginning of this section.

The essence of this practice is to make use of thoughts and concepts as they arise. Do not regard disturbing thoughts and concepts as things that contain some inherent reality of their own so that they are capable of harming you. Do not try to prevent disturbing thoughts arising in the mind, follow them, or generally condition your experiences in any way. When you no longer view disturbing thoughts and concepts as a problem, they will become more vivid, more lucid, more spacious, and less upsetting. They can become a part of your meditation without your having to accept, reject, or condition them in any way. This is called 'transforming thoughts into the spiritual path.' Just thinking about your disturbing thoughts in this different way is enough to liberate them. Maitripa says:

> Thoughts originate in the unborn state;
> Inseparable from the beginning.
> To transform disturbing thoughts
> Is to understand the nature of one-flavouredness.

Gampopa says:

> When disturbing thoughts are understood
> To be inseparable from our authentic state,
> They are unconditioned in their full creative expression
> And become self-liberated.

Je Gotsangpa says:

> When a disturbing thought arises;
> Look at its nature instead of fixating on its manifestation.
> If you can rest in the nature of that thought,
> It will be transformed.

He also says:

> When you realise that you can detach
> From the way mind classifies and judges things
> And cease to fixate on these activities,
> While retaining a sense of recognition;
> Disturbing thoughts will be transformed
> And become part of your meditation.

You must recognise that the nature of disturbing thoughts is free from the notions of abandonment and cultivation. You do not need to cultivate or abandon thoughts to transform them. This first method of transformation is associated with disturbing thoughts and you may initially experience ups and downs because you lack confidence in this unfamiliar method. This can lead to difficulty in relating to your disturbing thoughts and concepts and you may be unable to see how they can be part of your spiritual path. However, no matter what you experience, you must realise that whatever takes place on the cognitive and emotional level is intimately related with your body. When the psychophysical energies and the energy pathways are not working in unison, all kinds of mental disruptions occur, and vice versa. Nonetheless, despite these difficulties, it does not mean no benefit has been gained from this method, even if it is not perceptible to you. It is important to know that. The benefits will become more obvious in due course, if you persist with it. Simply stick with the practice, instead of indulging in hope and fear, wondering, 'Am I getting something out of it?' 'Am I doing it the right way?' 'How do I know this is working?' It is also important to not become too complacent or confident when you have an intimation the practice has been beneficial.

Adopt the fundamental attitude of complete openness and be ready to embrace and accommodate all potential thoughts, experiences, and emotions that will arise in the course of your meditation. This openness comes about through letting go of whatever arises, without dwelling on past meditative experiences. If you experience a so-called bad meditation, you should not allow that to influence your thinking so that you expect the same thing to happen in the future. If you experience a good meditation you should not expect that to recur either. Have complete openness. This will free you from hope and fear in relation to potential meditative experiences.

These approaches are very important for all methods of transformation. They address the intellectual judgements we make about our experiences, the emotional reactions we have that reinforce these judgements, and the experience of hope and fear that further serves to solidify and reinforce our judgements and reactions.

2. Transforming the five poisons into ambrosia

Our negative emotions are usually associated with the 'five poisons' of excessive lust, anger, jealousy, pride, and ignorance. The traditional teachings advise us that we must abandon these if we hope to develop spiritually, but even these negative emotions can be used as part of our spiritual practice according to this method of transformation. The *Hevajra Tantra* says:

> When someone suffers a burn,
> It can be alleviated by applying heat.
> When the fire of passion arises,
> It can be quelled by the fire of passion.

The *Samputa* says:

> Only passion can purify passion,
> Only anger can purify anger,
> Only ignorance can only overcome ignorance;
> It is the same with pride and jealousy.

It is possible to transform these five poisons into five wisdoms. The five wisdoms are not realised independently of the five poisons; they are present in the very nature of the negative emotions. This is why the practice of transformation is so important. The Tantric teachings say lust can be transformed into the wisdom of discrimination, anger can be transformed into the wisdom of the authentic state, ignorance can be transformed into mirror-like wisdom, pride can be transformed into the wisdom of equanimity, and jealousy can be transformed into the wisdom of accomplishment. This is how we embody the qualities of the Five Wisdom Buddhas.

The Five Wisdom Buddhas and their wisdoms do not exist as transcendental entities that are removed from our ordinary condition; they are present within the mindstream of ordinary sentient beings. We transform the five poisons into the five wisdoms by actualising potentials that are already immanent within our own condition. What was not obvious is made manifest. Wisdom appears to be radically different from the poisons, precisely because it is the source from which all delusions and confusions arise. However, if we can go to the depths of our delusions and confusions, we will find that wisdom is contained within them.[15] Wisdom is contained in the depth of the poisons, which is why the poisons can be transformed into ambrosia. The *Samputa* says:

> Wisdom and conflicting emotions travel together.
> There are five poisons and five wisdoms.
> These are not different from the five buddha-families.

If we are willing enough and skilful enough to deal with the disturbing emotions in this context, we will not be touched by them, even while we live in the world and enjoy its sensual pleasures. We will know how to make use of our emotional poisons and transform them into ambrosia. The *Hevajra*

Tantra says:

> Foolish people indulge in certain activities
> Motivated by deluded thoughts and disturbing emotions,
> But they only become bound by them.
> Wise people who practise methods of transformation
> Engage in the same activities,
> And find the source of freedom.

Saraha says:

> A liberated and wise person
> May live in any environment,
> Without it affecting the purity of their character;
> Just as the utpala flower is untouched by muddy waters.
> This ability to transform disturbing emotions
> Is like the ultimate cure for poison.

He also says:

> Just as the rain that arises
> From the evaporating ocean,
> Loses all its saltiness when it falls from the clouds;
> Disturbing emotions have the capacity to benefit others
> Because those very poisons can be turned into ambrosia.

Desire arises in relation to the external world and the sentient beings that inhabit that world. Many material objects give rise to attachment or desire and then clinging and grasping arise in relation to them. The same applies to other sentient beings, particularly human beings, in relation to sexual desire and so forth. You must recognise it when you are compelled by a very strong urge to posses the object of your desire. This is the kind of desire that you need to transform. You succeed in that transformation by recognising the nature of desire itself. The other disturbing emotion that arises in our mind-stream is anger or hostility. This originates from a feeling of aversion, where we wish another person ill so that our mind becomes afflicted by rage, anger, and hostility. The method of transformation is effective when we can recognise that emotion and try to identify the experience. The conflicting emotion of ignorance may make its appearance in relation to depression. Your mind becomes dull, inactive, lethargic, and given to episodes of drowsiness and stupor that deprive it of clarity. You must identify, recognise, and acknowledge each conflicting emotion so that you know exactly what is occurring.

The conflicting emotion of arrogance is no different. Arrogance comes from an unrealistic attitude toward yourself, where you think you are superior in some way. Haughtiness arises from arrogance. You must be very clear in your mind when arrogance has arisen and recognise it without self-deception. The conflicting emotion of jealousy should be dealt with in the same way. Jealousy manifests in the mindstream when you perceive someone in possession of material wealth, personal gifts, or a relationship that you envy and your mind becomes extremely disturbed by what that other person is able to enjoy.

The best way to deal with conflicting emotions is to not think they are happening to you. Once you recognise the emotion, without lying to yourself in any way, and have the courage and determination to appropriate that experience, you have to realise that these things are not 'happening to you.' Whatever goes on in the mind and the person who experiences it are not different. Instead of thinking, 'I am being harmed by this experience; I must reject it,' you need to say, 'I am this experience; this experience and myself are not different.' You will cease to be bogged down by hope and fear if you do this. The importance of overcoming hope and fear has already been mentioned.

Once you master this method of transformation, you should from time to time deliberately direct your mind to a situation or person that you find either extremely appealing or completely reprehensible, and then allow the appropriate emotions of lust or anger to arise. When that emotion is manifest, maximise its intensity until it is almost unbearable, so that you suffer breathing irregularities or your body starts to shake and tremble, and then try to identify that experience. This is how disturbing emotions are used as part of the spiritual path. The more intense the emotional experience, the deeper the resultant insight or understanding will be. Maitripa says:

> Wisdom is no different from the disturbing emotions.
> Just as fire can consume a forest
> Wisdom can consume the five poisons.

3. Transforming the adverse effects of ghosts and evil spirits

When mind is disturbed, it is easy to imagine that you are hearing voices or talking to ghosts. Instead of thinking that you are communing with supernormal beings, you should recognise this experience to be the product of your own conceptual proliferation. A Tantric text says:

> Demons are no different to conceptual proliferation.

Naropa says:

All disease and illnesses are caused
By the proliferation of thoughts and concepts.
Demonic possession and your experience of being harmed
Are all conditioned by your thoughts and concepts.
Even your experiences of death and birth
Are conditioned by thoughts and concepts.
In brief, experiences of happiness and unhappiness
Have their basis in thoughts and concepts.
If you can cut through disturbing thoughts and concepts
All sicknesses and demonic possessions will dissipate.

Milarepa says:

The vision of ghosts and the thought of ghosts,
Arise within the mindstream of the yogi
And dissipate back into the mindstream of the yogi.
Evil spirits, ghosts, and demons
Have their origin in the agitated mind.
When yogins do not realise their mind's capabilities,
They fail to understand that its projections
Have no inherent reality.
They then become paranoid
And invest those projections with objective reality.
That is one source of delusions for yogins.

In the same collection of songs, Milarepa returns to his cave after fetching water from the river, and meets an apparition of demons, which he then engages in a song. The lead demoness says:

If you had not opened your mind to delusions
And viewed disturbing thoughts as your enemy
I would not be here.
You only see me because of the mental habits
Enshrined in the karmic traces and dispositions of your mind.
If you fail to understand your own mind
Simply telling me to disappear will have no effect.

Realise that whatever thoughts you have about gods and demons, they are the creation of our own mind. It is like mistaking a striped rope for a snake. The disturbing experience of seeing a striped rope is real enough; thinking the rope is a snake is an illusion. Similarly, the disturbing thoughts and emotions are real enough, but objectifying them and investing them with a reality that is independent of your mind is to indulge in an illusion. Even when you are convinced that you hear voices or have made contact with supernatural beings of a benevolent or malevolent kind, you must recognise this to be a product of your own karmic traces and dispositions. They are caused by the conflicting emotions of excessive desire, anger, and ignorance.

When a mutual influence between the body and mind arises—disturbances of mind causing the body to malfunction and dysfunctions of the body causing mental disturbances—the mind will create all kinds of illusions and apparitions. Tantric texts therefore say, 'Apparitions and the experience of nagas are caused by the distortions of ignorance.' Anger creates the apparitions of evil spirits with a ferocious and malevolent character, and lust creates all kinds of seductive demons. To overcome this type of delusional experience, you should accommodate these apparitions, instead of indulging in them or being fearful of them. The apparitions will subside if you can accept them. They will only become neglected if you try to push them away or pretend that they are not there. You should understand that these seemingly real, supernatural beings have no inherent existence; they are simply the creation of our own mind. Much of your fear and apprehension will be allayed through that understanding.

When it comes to actually transforming the adverse effects of ghosts and evil spirits, Gampopa spoke of a method for understanding that they have no intrinsic reality at all. However, this method is not completely compatible with the understanding of one-flavouredness. The method most in keeping with our discussion is quite different. The best way to transform the conceptual proliferations and emotional reactions associated with ghosts and evil spirits is by building confidence in ourselves by understanding that they are no different to the nature of our own mind. In other words, do not alter the apparitions of mind in any way.

Gampopa also mentioned another method for using ghosts and evil spirits as an aid to the spiritual path. However, when you engage in this method, you may think you are being taunted or harmed by an evil spirit. Even when you are not afraid of being harmed by them, it is still very common to suffer from a level of depression and anxiety from being afflicted by doubt, lack of confidence, and a fear of being overwhelmed by external forces. Nonetheless, it is important to persist with this method.[16]

One way to deal with this fear is to imagine the most ferocious, awesome and fearsome demon you can and then imagine the most fearful thing it could do to cause you harm. You might imagine being crushed between the earth and sky or an army of demons bearing frightening weapons and making threatening gestures advancing toward you and then cutting you open and piercing you. You might imagine being burnt alive by evil spirits or being thrown into a fast flowing river. In brief, give rise to the most horrific forms of demonic activity, generate a fear toward them and then try to increase that fear. This method of transforming fear of demons is about trying to increase rather than decrease your fear.

4. Transforming our suffering by developing bodhichitta

Gampopa's *Tshogs chos chen mo* mentions several ways of dealing with the suffering of human beings: 1) seeing the benefits of hardship and pain instead of regarding them as something to avoid or run away from, 2) seeing that the nature of suffering has no origin, and 3) realising that the spiritual qualities of love and compassion are developed through suffering because there would be no opportunity, need or use for such qualities without it.

These ways of dealing with suffering are compatible with certain methods of transforming adverse circumstances and situations in the context of Mahamudra practice. However, I would like to explain this method in a way that fits better with the transformation methods mentioned above. To understand this method of transformation properly, you need to understand something about suffering itself. Three general types of suffering pervade the lives of ordinary sentient beings: the suffering of suffering, the suffering of change, and the suffering of conditioned existence. Everyone experiences these kinds of suffering; no one is spared.

There are specific types of suffering that we should see with our own eyes; we should pay attention to how people kill, exploit, and enslave one another and the plethora of suffering that is produced from these actions. This is a specific suffering that we can actually observe directly and is caused by an external agent or another sentient being. There are also other specific types of suffering that people experience because of themselves, because of their own psychological makeup, tendencies, predilections, and so forth. Even when no one is causing us pain or inflicting harm on us, we can experience all kinds of mental suffering because of our own unruly minds. We often have no control over karmic traces and dispositions caused by our own mental habits. You should also pay close attention to this and try to see exactly what is going on.

Some people do not feel love and compassion when they see or hear about the suffering and pain of others. Instead, they feel compelled to change their own conditioned thinking and to eradicate the karmic habits of mind that are governed by their uncontrolled emotions, for fear of experiencing that suffering themselves. They may decide to embark on the spiritual path from the Hinayana perspective so they can eradicate their own karmic history and free themselves from suffering. Other people do give rise to love and compassion when they see or hear about the suffering of others. They do not just want to free themselves from suffering; they have the desire and intention to free others from the causes and conditions that give rise to suffering. This is the Mahayana perspective. From the Mahamudra perspective, the best way to deal with our own suffering is to think of the suffering of others and then develop love and compassion toward them. When we shift the focus from our own suffering to the suffering experienced by sentient beings in general, our own suffering can be transformed. Nagarjuna says:

> If you want to attain enlightenment
> And to overcome the suffering of samsara,
> You can only do so by adopting bodhichitta.
> Bodhichitta is as solid as an unwavering, majestic mountain.

You will no longer be swayed this way and that or feel overwhelmed by mental activities once you have established stability of mind, which is why you must develop love and compassion. The kind of compassion that you need if you want to deal with suffering comes from thinking about and observing the suffering of others. Look into the nature of that compassion before it subsides and try to see that it is no different from ultimate reality. This is called 'the inseparability of compassion and emptiness' in the Mahayana teachings. For this reason, emptiness is sometimes called 'the heart of compassion.' The word bodhichitta simply means 'compassion that is not divorced from ultimate reality' or 'compassion that embodies ultimate reality as its core.' References to the inseparability of compassion and emptiness are not only found in Sutric Mahayana teachings; the Tantric teachings also make the same point. The *Hevajra Tantra* says:

> True compassion cannot be separated from ultimate reality.
> The inseparability of emptiness and compassion
> Is described as bodhichitta.

The *Vajrapanjara* says:

> Compassion cannot be separated from emptiness.
> Anyone who can meditate on that point has found real refuge.
> Buddha, dharma, and sangha are embodied in that.

The *Samputa* says:

> To perceive the ultimate nature of reality
> As devoid of conceptual proliferation is to give rise to wisdom.
> Like a jewel that can satisfy the needs of the poor,
> Compassion works for the benefit of all sentient beings.

Saraha says:

> When your understanding of emptiness
> Becomes separated from compassion,
> You have already gone astray.
> If you meditate on compassion
> Without understanding emptiness,
> You will never find liberation.
> When you appreciate the need for both,
> You will neither remain in nirvanic quietude
> Nor become entangled in samsara.

It is important to realise that suffering is transformed by love and compassion. The kind of love and compassion that we need to develop isn't ordinary; it is the embodiment of ultimate reality. Savaripa says:

> When we overcome conceptual proliferations
> By seeing emptiness and the suffering of beings,
> Our eyes will be filled with tears
> And we will be prompted to benefit others.
> The best way to overcome our own suffering
> Is to direct our attention to the misfortune of others,
> Give rise to love and compassion within,
> And then try to see their nature.

5. Transforming disease through one-flavouredness

The Buddhist healing traditions generally understand disease and illness to be tied up with its own causes and conditions. The causes of disease are potentially present at all times within ignorance, which fails to understand our true condition and our proper relationship to ultimate reality. The other causes of disease are our emotional afflictions. The conditions for disease lie within the violent movements of our psychophysical energy, which disrupts the harmony of the five elements that normally keep our bodily activities within manageable limits.[17] When this harmony between the energy pathways and the five elements is disrupted, we suffer from various physical ailments and disturbances of mind. There are many kinds of physical illness, but they are all included within these four main divisions: 1) illnesses causes by prana, 2) illnesses caused by bile, 3) illnesses caused by phlegm, and 4) illnesses caused by a combination of two or all three of these.

The most relevant factor in treating your specific illnesses is how you view illness itself. You must look at illness within the context of your spiritual practice and recognise its real cause to be ignorance and the conflicting emotions. Then you need to develop insight. The most effective way of dealing with the symptoms of illnesses caused by blockages in the energy pathways, which disrupt the flow of psychophysical energies, is to use the breath to settle the mind because breathing meditation will help to channel the psychophysical energy more efficiently through the energy pathways. The best way to deal with actual illnesses themselves is by understanding emptiness. The most beneficial way to deal with an actual disease is by making use of that disease as part of your spiritual practice. You will then transform that adverse situation into part of your spiritual development.

Gampopa mentions three stages in the method for transforming disease into the spiritual path: 1) the method of expansion, 2) contemplating the phases of illness, and 3) realising the experience of illness is inextricably bound to our mental attitude. We often imagine our particular illness to be far worse than it actually is and exaggerate the agony and pain associated with that illness. When you contemplate the phases of your illness, you examine where the illness originated, where it resides, and how it eventually comes to dissipate. When you realise that your experience of the disease is inextricably bound up with your mind, you can make an effort to understand the nature of mind. The disease will then be transformed into spiritual experience.

These three stages are compatible with the method we shall present here, except we do not practise the second stage. The important thing, within the Mahamudra context, is to go beyond our ordinary ways of conceptualising disease, illness, health, and well-being. Having an aversion to illness and a craving for health is a fundamental obstacle. The dualistic association of joy with health and suffering with illness will not lead to a proper understanding of health and disease.[18]

You transform disease and illness by focusing your mind on whatever pain you are experiencing—your physical discomfort and your mental response to that discomfort—and by trying to incorporate that into your meditation practice. When you have a particular experience of pain, simply try to be with that pain, without conceptualising about it and without following your emotional reactions to it. If you can do that, a sense of mental clarity will arise even when pain is present. You should also dispense with the thoughts, 'I am suffering' and 'I am afflicted by this disease.' Do not think about the experiencer of the physical discomfort or the nature of the illness and how it is affecting you. The final attitude to adopt toward your illness is relinquishing any hope for signs of improvement by thinking, 'When am I going to get better?' or allowing yourself to be gripped by fear or uncertainty about whether you are going to improve by thinking, 'What if I don't get better?' or 'What if I start to deteriorate?' Try to maintain an attitude of equanimity. That will prevent your being swayed by these thoughts and apprehensions.

The suggested method for acclimatising yourself to illness and disease and for gaining a taste for this practice is to focus on the pain you experience when you have been sitting in meditation for a long time. You can use the aches and pains that start to appear in your joints, legs and back.[19] Do not conceptualise about that pain or react to it emotionally by thinking, 'This pain is happening to me' or 'I am being harmed by this experience.' Simply focus on the pain and employ the method described above. Another method for acclimatising yourself to illness and disease is to invite discomfort, instead of trying your best to avoid it, and then employing this method to transform that experience.

Obviously, you will not be able to do this straight away, but some of the conventional conceptual categories we use to understand our experiences will begin to break down, if we persist with this method. We will no longer view ourselves or our body in quite the same way. We will gradually stop viewing physical and mental discomfort as harmful, destructive, negative, and to be avoided at all costs. Experiences that we currently view as very negative, harmful, or traumatic can become part of our meditation practice until the experiences become the meditation.

If you become proficient in this method, you will gradually develop the ability to harmonise the elements through sheer force of will, without needing to resort to medication or other forms of treatment. Meditators who attain the experience of one-flavouredness that comes from rising above these preoccupations with illness and health may no longer need to resort to external forms of treatment at all. Their treatment can be effected from within. This method was employed by the mahasiddhas of the past, not just of India, but even great meditators like Drikhungpa, Gotsangpa, and so on are said to have cured themselves of illnesses through this practice of one-flavouredness, without needing to seek any other forms of treatment.[20]

This is something you should aim for in your own practice. Approach it with skill and intelligence and try to become familiar with these methods. This does not mean you can become complacent about your body or treat it casually. The body is a very important vehicle, because without a properly functioning body, you will be unable to engage in the spiritual practice effectively and enlightenment will be less accessible. You should never become indifferent to whether you live or die or start to regard your life as inconsequential. That would be to misunderstand this practice.

Furthermore, if you are really ill, you should seek medication and other conventional forms of help. There is no conflict between that and adopting this method. One method treats the body through conventional medicines and the other deals with illness through spiritual means. From the absolute point of view, we are emphasising the need to gradually rise above an excessive concern with avoiding illness and cultivating health as much as possible. That is what we need to understand. This attitude is not in conflict with the relative approach, which is to seek conventional medical help. Even with the stories of past masters, you must gauge your own capabilities and use caution and intelligence when applying these methods to your own life. The relative and absolute points of view must also be taken as a complementary way of looking at health and illness. You should not see them as alternative ways of looking at the reality of health and illness. They are quite compatible and not in conflict at all.

6. Transforming the fear of death

The essence of this approach is using the whole gamut of our experience during post-meditation, from the inner workings of mind to the world we perceive through our sensory apparatuses, to enhance our spiritual practice. That is the purpose behind all of these transformative methods. However, it especially underlies this last method, which is concerned with self-transformation during sleep and death. We apply this transformative method to the experiences of sleep and death by activating the intrinsic luminosity of mind.

The best way to transform the experience of death is by recognising that the intrinsic awareness of mind has two aspects. These are known as 'mother luminosity' and 'son luminosity.'[21] There is the possibility these two aspects of awareness may come together at the time of death. That is our aim. You must use your intrinsic awareness on a daily basis while alive, no matter what occurs in relation to your internal and external experiences, or whether your mind is dim or perspicuous.[22] Your experience should be transformed into spiritual development through intrinsic awareness. It is not a question of what experiences you have or do not have, it is a question of whether you have that awareness or not.

It is very important to let go of your attachments to places, people, and possessions at the time of death and not latch onto anything. If you happen to be wealthy, donate a portion of that wealth to Dharma activities so that your spiritual teacher can make use of it in a beneficial way. Allocate another portion for the appropriate rituals at the time of death to aid your departure. Some of your wealth should also be allocated to the ganachakra puja to be performed by your vajra brothers and sisters. If you have the ability, go to a place free from harmful characteristics when your time of death arrives and either lie down in the lion posture or sit in meditation. Visualise your primary teacher as the primordial Buddha himself and apply the method for transforming the fear of death with a sense of great devotion.

You are trying to transform the fear of death itself. You can feel so much terror at your imminent demise that your heart becomes frozen. When the time of death arrives, the body will go through various stages of dissolution in correspondence to the four elements. Different hallucinatory experiences may accompany that. The fundamental point of this method is not to allow yourself to get caught up in negative attitudes, such as fear or anger about your experiences. Try to allow your mind to naturally free itself from its obsessive fixation on the self, where you are thinking, 'death is happening to me' or 'something terrible is about to happen to me.' Nor should you worry, 'Will I be able to maintain luminosity of mind in the post-mortem state?' These are all fundamental obstacles that stand in the way of using this method of self-transformation effectively.

How should you deal with death? Try to recognise any understanding or experiences that relate to your death, which might arise in meditation, and then determine whether they are based on fear and apprehension or a feeling of self-assurance. Whatever understanding or experience you have, confront that in the given moment, then try to make use of it as part of your spiritual growth. Even if your experience is negative, use whatever manifests in your mind as part of your spiritual progress. In other words, concentrate on the value that is inherent within those experiences, rather than perceiving them as obstacles or hindrances that you must overcome. Then, just as you did in the other methods of transformation, leave the mind completely open and spacious, without allowing it to become corrupted by judgements or thoughts about things you desire or loathe. There is no doubt that you will begin to progress with this method, if you can leave your mind open in this way.

Even the Sutric teachings on the seven points of mind training contain a section on how to deal with the time of death and recommend methods in the context of that practice. Various texts recommend transference of consciousness practice as a preparation for death. However, according to the Mahamudra teachings, practices that deal directly with the negative thoughts and emotions that are associated with death are more direct and profound.

As a result of this practice, when the body goes through the stages of dissolution at the time of death, you will experience mother luminosity coming into contact with the son luminosity. Son luminosity is so-called because it is associated with the notion of development. We develop more and more insight and gain increasing confidence in the maintenance of awareness and so forth. Mother luminosity, on the other hand, is intrinsically pure and incorruptible.

The mother and son luminosity are not separate; the mother luminosity provides the opportunity to activate our awareness so it can give rise to son luminosity in our meditation practice. When the time of death arrives, mother and son luminosity are reunited. Water and its surface are not different; we can sometimes see a film on the surface of water, but this is not substantially different from the water that lies beneath it. In a similar way, mother and son luminosity are not different. Just as the space inside a jug is not damaged when the jug is broken, but merges completely with the space outside the jug, the son luminosity merges seamlessly with the mother luminosity at the time of death. This is synonymous with attaining the authentic state of our own being. A tantra says:

> Death results from conceptual proliferation.
> If we understand our own true condition
> We will travel to the state of ultimate reality.[23]

The *Manjusrinama-samgiti* says:

> Enlightenment and confusion
> Are differentiated by a moment.
> One moment we are confused
> The next moment we become awakened.

Gampopa says:

> When one thought follows another,
> Where can we find ultimate death?
> When the nature of dharmakaya is pure and uncorrupted,
> How can we find death there?
> We would not lament a rainbow vanishing into thin air;

Where can we really find death when the nature
of mind has no beginning or end?
How can we think of death in relation to that?[24]

We may fail to secure enlightenment by not realising the inseparability of emptiness and luminosity in this way for a variety of reasons. Most often, because we have not really worked hard enough in our meditation or still lack some familiarity with the practice. However, if you do the practice, even if you have not perfected it nor done it as well as you might have, it is very likely you will attain enlightenment in the post-mortem state soon after death. If you don't attain it at that point, you will become enlightened at the beginning of your next rebirth. If even that is impossible, there is no doubt whatsoever that you will inherit some of the tendencies and predilections of your practice in the next life. The principle of dependent origination will give rise to the causes, conditions, and effects of your practice through the impressions left in your mindstream from past actions and experiences.

That ends the chapter on how to determine the originless nature of mind and the transformation of adverse circumstances and situation on the path.

10

Four Yogas of Mahamudra

DIFFERENT TYPES OF REALISATION

This has two sections:

- Three types of accomplishment
- Understanding, experience, and realisation

§ Three Types Of Accomplishment

This text contains a systematic explanation of Mahamudra meditation. If you follow these instructions without going astray in various deviations you will automatically develop some kind of understanding. The same understanding will not necessarily be attained by each individual even if everyone followed exactly the same practice. Understanding manifests differently in practitioners precisely because we all have our own unique propensities, predilections, and characteristics. The type of understanding we develop will be largely determined by and contingent upon our own psychophysical factors and conditions.

Nonetheless, each meditator will essentially progress through four stages of understanding, called the 'four yogas' of Mahamudra. You will attain one of three types of understanding when you progress through these Four Yogas depending upon your level of past familiarity. These are known as great, medium, and small levels of understanding. These levels correspond to the accomplishments of three kinds of individuals. Great understanding corresponds to the instantaneous-type of individual, medium understanding corresponds to the intermediate-type, and small understanding corresponds to the gradual-type.[1] The latter type of understanding is attained in a very systematic and deliberate manner.

The understanding of instantaneous-type comes about when a meditator acquires both discernment and experience without much effort, after they are introduced to tranquillity or insight practices. In the context of the Four Yogas, such people gain an initial understanding of each of the yogas of one-pointedness, non-conceptuality, one-flavouredness or non-meditation. The level of initial understanding really depends upon the individual. It may only correspond to the first yoga or it may correspond to any one of the remaining three yogas. An example from the traditional literature might help to clarify this properly. When the sun penetrates a deep mountain gorge, the stones are heated the moment they are touched by the light; illumination and warmth are simultaneous. Similarly, an instantaneous-type meditator will develop understanding as soon as the light of comprehension enters his or her mind.

The understanding of intermediate-type occurs when a meditator acquires discernment based on information he or she receives through hearing or reading about the relevant practices. Such people have a degree of experience, which is supported by understanding. Three factors must be present within their mindstreams: intellectual faculties, experience, and direct understanding of what needs to be apprehended. Based on these three factors, the levels of experience and understanding that such people endure on the Four Yogas of Mahamudra, might occur in a successive fashion or in more erratic leaps. The intermediate-type of understanding is different to the previous one because it is feebler, more fluctuating and not securely established. The traditional example given for this type of understanding also involves the sun. While the sun is always in the midday sky, its illumination can be weak or strong depending on the clouds.

When you have understanding but cannot stabilise it, it can be very helpful to go into retreat. It is also helpful to do a retreat when you lack confidence in your understanding and practice, and want to re-establish that confidence. You can also strengthen your commitment by thinking about past masters who experienced similar struggles and then invoking their blessings and seeking their guidance. An understanding that has arisen in an unstable or wavering way can be made stable and consistent in this way. Even if you have not managed to stabilise your understanding completely, by attaining full comprehension of the fourth yoga, you might still gain that understanding during the bardo if you follow this approach.

The understanding of gradual-type occurs when a meditator bases his or her practice on these three factors: intellectual understanding, meditative experience, and realisation.[2] An understanding of the first yoga is always followed by an understanding of its succeeding yoga at this level; the order cannot be reversed. In the case of the gradual-type, even when understanding is there, it has no depth and remains feeble. The practitioner does not have the skill to deal with obstacles and antidotes appropriately enough to practice Mahamudra. To use another simile, when the sun shines on a clear and frosty day, the stones do not immediately become heated. Similarly, it takes time for the warmth of insight to penetrate the mind of the gradual-type of meditator.

These three types of understanding are connected to the Mahamudra teachings and practice. This does not mean that gradual and intermediate types have no opportunity to gain understanding in an instantaneous way. The most important elements that you can have are courage, inclination, and humility. If you develop the qualities of intense interest, humility, and courage, it might transform a lesser type of understanding into an instantaneous one.[3] You must be vigilant and attentive at all times, because you cannot predict when or how understanding will pop into your mind. The possibility of gaining a spontaneous and unexpected understanding, where all doubts and uncertainties are laid to rest, can never be dismissed.

Conversely, when your mind is closed, lazy, or inattentive, understanding may become present in your mind, but you fail to appreciate it because of your mental preoccupations. You fail to pay this understanding sufficient attention because of your distractions and then view it as nothing special. It is important to always remain open and attentive for this reason. Furthermore, you should talk to fellow practitioners who may have more experience in the practice, and consult spiritual teachers about your own understanding.

§ Understanding, Experience, And Realisation

The differences between intellectual understanding, meditative experience, and realisation are as follows. Intellectual understanding relates to inference, meditative experience relates to uplifting or depressing mental states, and realisation is direct experience. Intellectual understanding comes about when you hear certain teachings and contemplate them until a universal mental image arises in your mind about which you have an inferential understanding. This is followed by practice, where experiences during meditation and post-meditation, whether they be good, bad, uplifting, or depressing are understood to be just experiences. Realisation follows when you have a direct experience of how things are in reality, without delusions.[4] Tsangpa Gyare says:

> Intellectual understanding comes
> From analysing what we need to understand.
> Meditative experience arises with fluctuations in bliss and clarity.

Realisation comes from fully recognising
How things are in their true nature.

The following example might make this clearer. A man wishing to go to Bodh Gaya would consult a guidebook or talk to someone who had already been there to develop a mental image about it. When he actually takes the journey, he will have an inadequate but nonetheless powerful impression of Bodh Gaya, which is not enough to give him a real overview of where he is living. After some time, he will gain a real understanding of what it means to live in Bodh Gaya and no longer entertain doubts or uncertainties about it.

Each of these three stages relates to the three factors that a gradual-type of practitioner must rely on when practising the Four Yogas. Intellectual understanding is comparable to hearing about Bodh Gaya and forming a mental impression of it. Meditative experiences are like actually going to Bodh Gaya and gaining vivid but incomplete impressions of it. Realisation is like actually living there.

Meditative experiences entail the ability to maintain awareness in various mental states. Realisation comes when we have enough stability in tranquillity meditation to apply insight meditation to the realisation that nothing has enduring essence and thus apprehend the nature of reality.[5] Gampopa says:

Meditative experience is awareness with mental clarity.
Tranquillity meditation is stabilised
When mind remains without distraction.
Ultimate reality is realised
Through the discriminating awareness of insight meditation.
This is the way to generate genuine understanding in meditation.

That is the fundamental difference between our meditative experience and realisation. As Gampopa explains in this exchange with a student:

Student: 'What is the difference between meditative experience and realisation?'

Gampopa: 'Meditative experiences don't go beyond our ordinary frame of reference, conceptual understanding, or imagination, which is why they are not totally reliable. Meditative experiences are comparable to the light of the sun obstructed by clouds. Just as clouds are always shifting and never remain the same, the meditative experiences of bliss, clarity, and non-conceptuality are unsteady. If you become too fixated on them, your meditation will only become more complicated. If you pay no attention to

> them and let them go, your mind will become more open and free. Realisation is developed when you do not distinguish between the experiences that appear in your mind and their true nature. You realise that whatever arises is an expression of the luminous aspect of mind. Insight is developed when you relinquish any kind of distinction between meditative object and meditating subject.'

It may be relevant to look at what some other people say about intellectual understanding, meditative experiences, and realisation. Some say:

> Meditative experience is insignificant and negligible,
> Intellectual understanding is slightly better,
> While realisation is superior to both.

This is not quite correct. I have never seen it written anywhere that meditative experience is insignificant and intellectual understanding is superior. If meditative experiences were negligible, we wouldn't talk about experiences of past masters. We would also have to say there is an essential difference between meditative experience and realisation. There is a difference between the two, but that difference is not essential. Our Practice Lineage accepts the unity of meditative experiences and realisation.

The people who deride meditative experiences and present intellectual understanding as more in tune with realisation say, 'Intellectual understanding can lead directly to realisation.' This is preposterous. The teachings distinguish between *lung*, 'written and spoken transmission of the teachings,' and *rtogs pa*, or 'realisation.' Realisation is developed through personal experience, which in turn relies upon the written and spoken forms of transmission. If realisation were not that different from intellectual understanding, we would have to substitute 'intellectual understanding' for 'realisation' when coupled with the written and spoken transmissions. Even the meditative realisation developed from traversing the Paths and Stages would have to be reinterpreted as a form of intellectual understanding.

Such a contention is highly dubious and quite unacceptable. Look at past interpreters and translators of Buddhist texts and you will see how careful they were to find the precise words and terminology for their writings. They wanted to be very clear that the Tibetan words corresponded to the original Sanskrit ones. These translators clearly employed two different words to refer to two different things when they translated the original Sanskrit terms for 'realisation' and 'understanding.'[6] Other people also seem to be unable to distinguish between realisation and understanding and claim:

> Realisation can be clear or unclear
> And can be called either comprehension or understanding.

This is also totally mistaken. This problem is similar to the previous one. To say 'realisation can be clear or unclear' is to suggest that it can fluctuate, but that is a completely unacceptable understanding. If the insight developed through wisdom was somehow contingent upon our conceptual apparatuses we would indeed have to say there is no real distinction between realisation and intellectual understanding. However, that is not the case. Realisation is unmediated by conceptual referents. Realisation must be regarded as something that remains steady while intellectual understanding is dualistic, prone to fluctuation, and totally unreliable.

HOW TO UNDERSTAND THE FOUR YOGAS OF MAHAMUDRA

This has three sections:

- The Four Yogas in the Sutras and Tantras
- General identification of the Four Yogas
- Identifying their unique nature

§ The Four Yogas In The Sutras And Tantras

Implicit references to the Four Yogas of Mahamudra can be found in the Mahayana sutras. For example, the *Lankavatara Sutra* says:

> Buddha: 'Mahamati, those bodhisattvas endowed with the four qualities of enlightenment should be called great yogis. What are these four qualities of enlightenment? They relate to the following four attributes: 1) meditating on mind and what appears to mind, 2) meditating on how things come into being, persist, and dissipate, 3) meditating on the external and objective reality of things and their lack of enduring essence, and 4) meditating on discriminating wisdom. Mahamati, anyone in possession of these four qualities of enlightenment is called a mahasattva. They are mahasattvas precisely because they are great yogis.'

We could say Buddha was talking about the Four Yogas when he mentions these four attributes of enlightenment. You might ask, 'How can you say the Mahayana *Lankavatara Sutra* has any real connection with the Four Yogas in the Mahamudra teachings?' This connection will become clearer if we match each of the four attributes of enlightenment to the Four Yogas. The sutra's reference to 'meditating on mind and what appears to mind' is comparable to the first yoga of Mahamudra. The *Lankavatara Sutra* makes this clear in the following statement:

> Mahamati: 'How do bodhisattvas and mahasattvas excel in meditating on the mind and the things that appear to the mind?'
> Buddha: 'Bodhisattvas and mahasattvas realise that everything which exists in the triple world is dependent on mind by thinking, "Everything I experience in relation to the triple world is dependent on mind". They gradually become free of the idea that "me" and "mine" have some intrinsic reality of their own and realise the "I" is dependent on the notions of cultivation and rejection. They understand that their psychological makeup and their perceptions of the world and themselves are all conditioned by their own karmic inheritance and the habits it generates. Bodhisattvas and mahasattvas come to realise that their bodies, possessions, environment, and actions are all conditioned by and dependent upon their own conceptual categories and frames of reference.'

The Buddha's description here is essentially the same as the first stage of Mahamudra; the yoga of one-pointedness. The *Lankavatara Sutra* also expounds on the ultimate nature of reality as completely free of conceptual categories or frameworks. Our minds are separated from any notion of coming into being, existing for a time, and going out of being. The *Lankavatara Sutra's* reference to 'meditating on how things come into being, persist and dissipate' is therefore comparable to the second yoga of Mahamudra. The *Lankavatara Sutra* says:

> Mahamati: 'How do bodhisattvas and mahasattvas get rid of thoughts about things coming into existence, enduring for a time, and then going out of existence?'
> Buddha: 'That will depend on how bodhisattvas and mahasattvas view reality. When they understand that everything that arises is illusory and dream-like, they will realise that, in reality, nothing has come into being. Reality itself is not dependent upon causes and conditions. It can never come into existence, precisely because there was never a time when it was not in existence. The unexamined mind continuously constructs and conditions the world. When we do not understand this fact, we imagine that the external

> world exists of its own accord, independently of mind. Even mind itself lacks enduring essence. The psychophysical constituents and various experiences of the triple world are dependent upon causes and conditions, which are in turn dependent on mind. The self-sufficient, independent, inherent existence that we project onto phenomena has no reality. Bodhisattvas and mahasattvas fully understand their relative perception of the world because they can see that there is no enduring essence to anything whatsoever.'

The Buddha's description here is essentially the same as the second yoga of Mahamudra. When we understand the nature of ultimate reality through this insight, the notion of coming into existence becomes completely irrelevant. The *Lankavatara Sutra* states that, 'meditation on the external and objective reality of things and their lack of enduring essence' is comparable to the third yoga of Mahamudra. As the *Lankavatara Sutra* says:

> Mahamati: 'How do bodhisattvas and mahasattvas acquaint themselves with understanding that there are no such things as self-existing, discrete entities in the external world, even though we normally refer to such things?'
> Buddha: 'Bodhisattvas and mahasattvas become acquainted with this understanding when they realise that physical entities have as much reality as dreams and optical illusions. We perceive physical entities to be self-existing entities because of our karmic inheritance, which has conditioned our minds to perceive some kind of inherent discrete autonomy in things. That autonomy is only an illusion. Bodhisattvas and mahasattvas free themselves from these mistaken perceptions when they perceive this lack of inherent existence.'

The Buddha's description here is essentially the same as the third stage of Mahamudra, the yoga of one-flavouredness. The *Lankavatara Sutra's* reference to 'meditating on discriminating wisdom' is comparable to the fourth yoga of Mahamudra. As the *Lankavatara Sutra* says:

> Mahamati: 'How do bodhisattvas and mahasattvas come to possess discriminating awareness?'
> Buddha: 'Bodhisattvas and mahasattvas come to possess discriminating awareness when they understand that reality itself is transcendental. It is not affected by the concepts of space and time and is therefore uncaused. Even the notions of mind and

> consciousness lack substance. Bodhisattvas and mahasattvas give rise to discriminating wisdom when they realise the non-duality of subject and object.'

The Buddha's description here is essentially the same as the fourth stage of Mahamudra, the yoga of non-meditation.

We can therefore see the Four Yogas of Mahamudra are elaborations upon basic Mahayana concepts. The *Lankavatara Sutra* also alludes to the Four Yogas in terms of these four attributes of enlightenment. As the sutra says:

> Bodhisattvas and mahasattvas must understand
> That perception of the external world is conditioned by mind.
> They invert that by focusing on their own mind,
> Until they recognise it lacks self-sufficiency
> And gain complete understanding of ultimate reality.
> Reality cannot be identified as external or internal;
> It is all-encompassing and cannot be imagined,
> Because that would exclude what has not been imagined.
> Only this is true understanding of the Mahayana.

Kamalashila's *Bhavanakrama* and the *Prajnaparamitopadesa*, which relate to the Prajnaparamita teachings, both show that the Four Yogas must be understood in relation to the Sutric and Tantric teachings. In other words, the Mahamudra teachings have to be placed within the superstructures of Mahayana Buddhism. Even the Tantric teachings refer to the Four Yogas. The *bSam gyis mi khyab pa'i rgyud* for example, is quite unique in its presentation of the Four Yogas, and compares the Sutric version on the four types of meditative concentration with the corresponding four types of spiritual attainment:

> First, the samadhi known as 'the poise of a lion'
> Leads to the attainment of one-pointed concentration.
> You mind becomes lucid and clear
> And experiences the awakening of wisdom.
> This is the spiritual attainment of warmth
> Where you gain control over your own rebirth.
>
> Second, the samadhi known as 'illusory perception'
> Leads to the attainment of non-conceptuality.
> You will have greater experiences through this practice
> And achieve rarefied experiences and realisations.

This is the spiritual attainment of peak.
Third, the samadhi known as 'heroism'

Leads to the ability to see unity in diversity.
You will now be able to work for the benefit of others
And become sons or daughters of the enlightened ones.
Your powers will no longer be confined to time
But operational in past, present, and future.
This is the spiritual attainment of patient acceptance.

Fourth, the samadhi known as 'diamond-like'
Leads to the realisation of a fully evolved being.
You now realise meditation is not meant to attain anything
And that striving to attain a goal is no longer necessary.
This experience is equated with buddhahood itself.
It is not attained through rigorous practice,
But through being natural and spontaneous.
This is the most supreme dharma we can secure.

These meditative concentrations correspond to the yogas of one-pointedness, non-conceptuality, one-flavouredness, and non-meditation respectively.

This Tantric text matches different experiences within the Sutric and Tantric teachings to the Four Yogas of Mahamudra. The four types of meditative concentration, the four spiritual attainments, and the Four Yogas of Mahamudra are all compatible. The teachings on the Four Yogas of Mahamudra are not completely novel and don't conflict with the Sutric teachings. There is continuity rather than a discontinuity in these teachings. The *Hevajra Tantra* says:

Just as a waterfall maintains it continuity,
And a lamp maintains its flame;
Maintain your awareness day and night
If you wish to attain one-pointed concentration.

This corresponds to the yoga of one-pointedness. It also says:

No form to be perceived and no one who perceives it.
No sound to be heard and no one who hears it.

Again, it says:

When you have total experience

> There is no thought of origin, endurance, or cessation.
> No concern with abandoning samsara or attaining nirvana.

These total experiences correspond to the yoga of non-conceptuality. As the *Hevajra Tantra* also says:

> Meditation is not other than seeing the evenness
> And one-flavouredness of everything that exists.

This corresponds to the yoga of one-flavouredness. The *Hevajra* says:

> Discard any notion of deliberately practising meditation,
> You cannot speak of meditation or meditator.

This corresponds to teachings on the yoga of non-meditation. Saraha says:

> Abandon the object of thought and thought itself,
> And remain natural and uncontrived, like an infant.

This reveals the qualities of the yoga of one-pointedness. He also says:

> The thoughts and emotions that arise in mind have no essence or root.

This corresponds to the yoga of non-conceptuality. Again, he says:

> Whatever we experience internally and externally
> Is imbued with the same flavour.
> This cannot be captured by discursive mind.

This corresponds to the yoga of one-flavouredness. Finally, he says:

> When we free ourselves from samadhi
> What is there to meditate on?

This is a reference to the yoga of non-meditation. In brief, instead of thinking the Four Yogas of Mahamudra should be understood without reference to sutra and tantra, understand that the Sutric and Tantric teachings implicitly refer to the Four Yogas in their teachings. They implicitly refer to the yoga of one-pointedness when they emphasise concentration. They implicitly refer to the yoga of non-conceptuality when they elaborate on the concept of emptiness. They implicitly refer to the yoga of one-flavouredness when they say everything that exists, whether sacred or profane, is imbued with the same reality. They implicitly refer to the yoga of non-meditation when they say that non-acceptance and non-rejection lead to non-fixation.

Je Yanggonpa claims the Four Yogas of Mahamudra originated within

Gampopa's own personal experiences. They were formulated to make the practice of Mahamudra more accessible to meditators and Gampopa must be given the credit for this. Nonetheless, you can see that the essence of the Four Yogas is implicit in the body of Sutric and Tantric teachings, amongst the many references to the different phenomena that originate in and manifest from meditative experiences. This is well-known, while the systematisation of these meditative experiences within the Mahamudra teachings, where the spiritual journey is stratified in relation to Four Yogas, is quite unique and novel.

Besides these obviously oblique references to the experiences of the Four Yogas in the Sutric and Tantric literature, there is also a transmission that refers to Four Yogas that originated with Atisha. The songs of Milarepa contain numerous allusions to the experiences of the Four Yogas. In any case, tranquillity and insight meditation are common to all Buddhist traditions. Many practices, both old and new, relate to these two fundamental meditative approaches. This fact would be quite apparent to any keen observer. When it comes to explaining the experiences that arise from these meditative techniques and giving them form, we have to admit that our Kagyu tradition has paid more attention to details than other traditions. It has devoted a great deal of time and effort into grading and classifying the inner experiences of meditators. This should be seen as a unique characteristic of the Dakpo Kagyu tradition.

§ General Identification Of The Four Yogas

Many different lines of transmission are involved in the teachings on the Four Yogas. Gampopa transmitted these teachings to his disciples Gomtsul, Gomchung, and Phagmo Drupa.[7] Gomtsul in turn transmitted them to his own disciple, the Drugpa Kagyu master Lingrepa, who transmitted them to his disciple Tsangpa Gyare. Readers should therefore bear in mind that there are different transmission lineages when studying and identifying the Four Yoga teachings. I will present the Four Yogas in a general way, so that the gist of the teachings that originated with Gampopa and his disciples can be drawn upon to identify the yogic experiences. Je Gomchung says:

> Mind in a state of non-agitation
> Is the yoga of one-pointedness.
> Mind with a sense of certainty
> Is the yoga of non-conceptuality.
> Mind undisturbed by thoughts of acceptance or rejection

Is the yoga of one-flavouredness.
Meditative experience completely purified of adventitious elements
Is the yoga of non-meditation.

Gampopa says:

We realise the yoga of one-pointedness
When we maintain a lucid state of mind
Without preventing its unceasing mental activities.

We realise the yoga of non-conceptuality
When mental lucidity is revealed as self-present
And we cease to be concerned
About its existence or non-existence.[8]

We realise the yoga of one-flavouredness
When we are no longer concerned
With diligently trying to remove disturbing influences
From our sensory impressions or mental events.[9]

We realise the yoga of non-meditation
When we see reality consists of the empirical world
And the emptiness that is its nature.
Reality is these unceasing and inseparable aspects.

In brief, we have quoted Gampopa and one of his disciples, both of who were very much concerned with systematising meditative experience. They achieved that aim through the schema of the Four Yogas. Should you consult the extensive literature on the Four Yogas, you would find many different descriptions of them. However, to make them more succinct and accessible here, we could say that the yoga of one-pointedness simply means that your initial experiences of mental clarity and mental activity start operating together, instead of operating against each other. In other words, our intrinsic awareness is not something that gets aroused when the other functions of mind cease to operate or vice versa. The mind is completely open and all-encompassing by nature, like space itself, so there is no need to rid mind of its mental states and processes. Awareness can be developed and maintained coterminous with the normal functioning of mind.[10] Other masters also make this point. As thoughts and emotions don't act as obstacles to our goal, all we need to develop in meditation is a spacious attitude. Phagmo Drupa says:

When one-pointed concentration is developed
Meditators experience a sense of release
Just like gazing into an open sky.

Je Zhang says:

When one-pointed yoga first makes its appearance
Self-knowledge dawns and all barriers are broken;
A sense of enormous mental space and relief arises.
Mind that is without centre or periphery
Maintains a sense of awareness and emptiness.
Great openness is realised when these two factors are present
And all shutters are broken and left behind.
This is the yoga of one-pointedness.

The yoga of non-conceptuality is about rising above concepts of perceiver and perceived by realising that concepts apply only to things on the empirical level. The ultimate reality of emptiness has no origin, does not persist, and does not cease to exist. That which is empty cannot exist in time. Yet ultimate reality is present in the empirical world of space and time. When you realise this and thereby come to understand that subject and object lack essence, you attain the yoga of non-conceptuality. Phagmo Drupa says:

The yoga of non-conceptuality will dawn
When you see that conceptual categories
Do not apply to ultimate reality.
The actuality of ultimate reality is what makes
Both samsara and nirvana possible.
We may distinguish between ordinary and enlightened beings
But that is only because
We lack this understanding of samsara and nirvana.
Ultimate reality is all-pervasive;
Samsara does not have one nature and nirvana another.
This is not something that we can
Conceptualise in the ordinary sense
Saying that ultimate reality is permanent or impermanent.
We cannot even talk about acceptance or rejection
Where samsara is to be abandoned and nirvana to be actualised.
This is why the second yoga is non-conceptual.
That which enables insight into ultimate reality
Is a state that contains no differences.

Je Zhang says:

> When the yoga of non-conceptuality reveals itself,
> You will suddenly attain self-recognition.
> Ultimate reality has no differences;
> Differences only exist at the level
> Of the sensory organs and conceptual mind.
> Ultimate reality has no origin or cessation;
> Something without an origin
> Cannot come into being or cease to exist.
> You cannot apply concepts to originlessness
> As you do to the objects of the sensory world.
> When you realise that the ultimate aspect of mind
> Is no different from ultimate reality;
> You realise your own mind as dharmakaya.

The yoga of one-flavour is more concerned with our actions. Once you develop the above insight into ultimate reality, you will understand that your moral choices are based on contingent moral principles and avoid indulging in the idea that your moral options are either acceptable or unacceptable. You realise this state of one-flavouredness by remaining totally natural in your authentic way of being. Phagmo Drupa says:

> When phenomena reveal themselves
> To be endowed with one reality;
> Emptiness reveals itself.
> Thoughts of existence or non-existence,
> Emptiness or non-emptiness,
> Cease to play a significant role.
> Thoughts of understanding or not understanding,
> Meditation or post-meditation,
> Samadhi or non-meditation
> Reveal the same flavour.
> The flavour of ultimate reality.

Je Zhang says:

> When you understand the yoga of one-flavouredness
> You will understand yourself.
> Once you understand your true condition
> You will see that samsaric and nirvanic experiences
> have the same origin.[11]

You no longer need to worry to yourself:
Am I conceptualising or not?
Am I distracted by sensory experiences or not?
Are things empty in their nature or not?
Are things intelligible to the mind or not?
When you understand your own true condition,
It is an immediate experience;
There is no further need to indulge in rationalisation.

To attain the yoga of non-meditation is to arrive at the terminus point. You will have overcome all of the endemic problems associated with ordinary delusions and conceptual confusions. You will have freed yourself from meditative experiences and their associated problems and no longer distinguish between meditative and post-meditative experience.

This is called the yoga of non-meditation because a person who is fully enlightened is always present. There is never a time when an enlightened being is not present. The process of meditation might have involved deliberation, but you will now be able to be present naturally. Phagmo Drupa says:

Through training and acquainting yourself with practice
You become completely in tune with yourself.
Everything that you do or experience comes naturally
Because awareness is always nakedly present.
Naked awareness is now meditation;
Ordinary concepts of meditation no longer apply.
Transcending meditator and object of meditation,
Actualising the innate quality of the lucid nature of mind;
That is the essence of meditation
Through which we go beyond ordinary meditative experiences.
This is the yoga of non-meditation.

Je Zhang says:

When the yoga of non-meditation dawns
Your awareness suddenly has no reference point.
There is nothing to meditate upon and no meditator.
The fundamental qualities of an enlightened being,
Such as the three kayas and the five wisdoms,
Now make their appearance.

This is a very general way of identifying the Four Yogas of Mahamudra.

The Kagyu tradition has many meditation manuals that you can refer to but it's unnecessary to quote them further. There are no conflicting interpretations of the Four Yogas; I have just provided a sample of the interpretations of Gampopa and his disciples in an effort to identify them.

§ Identifying Their Unique Nature

1. The nature, essence, and characteristic of mind

The Mahamudra teachings ascribe three aspects to mind; nature, essence, and characteristic. Je Gomchung says:

> The nature of mind is realised in one-pointedness.
> The essence of mind is realised in non-conceptuality.
> The characteristic of mind is realised in one-flavouredness.
> Non-conceptuality is realised in non-meditation.

A great deal of space has already been devoted to these three aspects of the mind in previous chapters, so please refer to the relevant sections to enliven or regenerate your understanding of this topic. Our present discussion is confined to these aspects in relation to meditative experience and realisation.

According to this, we gain insight into the nature of mind as we continue in the yoga of one-pointedness. To recognise the nature of mind means to realise mind as luminous, clear, and undisturbed by thoughts and emotions.

We gain insight into the essence of mind as emptiness in the yoga of non-conceptuality. We realise that while thoughts and emotions may come and go, their nature is not subject to the same law of causality, precisely because the nature of thoughts and emotions has no origin, persistence, or cessation. How so? Thoughts and emotions may be a product of causes and conditions but their nature is uncompounded. To recognise the essence of mind means to realise that the mind's essence is emptiness. It is uncompounded, unconditioned, and not dependent on causal relationships.

It is unnecessary to abandon thoughts and emotions in the yoga of one-flavouredness. There is no need to think that positive mental qualities have a different reality. Everything we experience as human beings is the product of our own karmic tendencies and dispositions. The experiences we perceive as positive and therefore relate to nirvanic states and the experiences we perceive as negative and therefore relate to samsaric states have the same flavour. To recognise the characteristic of mind means to realise that thoughts, concepts, emotions, feelings, imaginings, memories, and so on are unceasing.

We realise there is no experiencer and nothing to be experienced in the yoga of non-meditation; there is no cogniser and nothing to be cognised. This is known as 'understanding the authentic condition.' Gampopa says:

> The mind has three aspects: nature, essence, and characteristic. The nature of mind is emptiness because it reveals the absolute non-origination, non-persistence, and non-cessation of mind. The essence of mind is luminosity. The characteristic of mind reveals a dual aspect: a vulnerability to deceptions and delusions, and the potential to be awakened. Meditators realise the empty nature of mind in the yoga of one-pointedness, gain insight into the luminous essence of mind in the yoga of non-conceptuality, and realise the characteristic of mind in the yoga of one-flavouredness.

An additional remark can be made to dispel a potential misinterpretation of the Four Yogas in relation to these three aspects of mind. Je Phagmo Drupa and Je Zhang for example, have reversed the order somewhat. According to them, we realise the essence of mind on the yoga of one-pointedness and understand the nature of mind on the yoga of non-conceptuality. You should therefore not be alarmed if you come across such variations in the teachings. There is no essential difference between the essence of mind and the nature of mind as they exist within themselves. The difference only exists in relation to the way we think about them.

You might then ask, 'If we don't really need to worry about whether we need to realise the essence of mind or the nature of mind first, is there any fundamental difference between the yoga of one-pointedness and the yoga of non-conceptuality?' The simple answer is that there is actually a big difference between these two yogas, experientially speaking. There is a similarity between them, in that we are talking about the presence or absence of awareness, but these two meditative stages are also very different. The difference involves the kind of experiences you can enjoy on these levels, so it is more a difference of degree than of kind. For example, you cling less to enjoyable meditative experiences on the yoga of non-conceptuality. There would also be a difference in how well you understand ultimate reality in relation to the inner workings of your mind and your perceptions of the external world.

2. The specific misunderstandings of each

We now turn to experiences that might arise in relation to the Four Yogas and to discussing their intensity. Meditators can very easily become disorientated and lose track of things because of these experiences. Je Gomchung says:

> If misunderstood, the yoga of one-pointedness
> Can lead to mental darkness.
> The yoga of non-conceptuality
> Can lead to fixation on emptiness and dissociation from the world.
> The yoga of one-flavouredness
> Can lead to vagueness and introversion.
> And the yoga of non-meditation
> Can darken our insight, like the sun obscured by clouds.

To elaborate, you should never become too confident in your realisation on the yoga of one-pointedness. You can have fleeting moments of insight into the essence of mind and glimpse the nature of mind to be emptiness, but the important thing is really how you relate to those experiences. It is more important for meditators that are unskilled in dealing with experience to look carefully at how they are relating to them rather than worrying about the experiences themselves.

Once you are caught up in such preoccupations, your original awareness will be lost and you will lose any real confidence in yourself. You will find that you have lost whatever experiences you did enjoy and have become subject to all kinds of confusion. Like a person groping around in the dark, you will not find what you are looking for, even if it is right there before your eyes.

You may divert your attention from the empirical world in the yoga of non-conceptuality if you exaggerate the importance of the realisation of ultimate reality. You may no longer be feeling that you belong in the world and disregard your moral responsibilities toward others. In other words, you can develop the extreme view of nihilism, which is essentially about concluding that everything is emptiness and therefore nothing matters.

If you fail to gain genuine understanding of the yoga of one-flavouredness, you will only develop a vague sense of the equality of things but you will have no enthusiasm for engaging in life or helping your fellow human beings. You will enter into a state of total introversion or self-absorption where you are oblivious to everything going on around you. The consequence of this is complete ignorance of skilful means.

Even with the yoga of non-meditation, the occasional experiences that you have of genuine non-meditation will always be disrupted if you fail to understand non-duality. Although non-meditation may be fully present in your mind, you will fail to perceive it, just as you fail to see the sun when it is obscured by clouds.

3. The yogas and post-meditative experience

In terms of post-meditation Je Gomchung says:

> Having risen from meditation on the yoga of one-flavouredness,
> There is a feeling of freedom or release.
> Having risen from meditation on the yoga of non-conceptuality,
> Everything is seen to be like an illusion.
> Having risen from meditation on the yoga of one-flavouredness,
> Everything is seen to be lacking enduring essence.
> Having risen from meditation on the yoga of non-meditation,
> Everything is the full expression of compassion.

To elaborate, do not cling to or conceptualise experiences on the yoga of one-pointedness and your mind will become free of fixations.

To say 'meditation reveals everything as illusion-like' on the yoga of non-conceptuality means we recognise all our experiences to have originated in the state of originlessness. When we encounter things in post-meditation, we no longer hold onto the idea of subject and object, perceiver and perceived, experiencer and experienced as totally independent of one another. We realise instead that neither subject nor object are endowed with enduring essence and are thus like an illusion.[12] We might fail to appreciate the inseparability of mental and sensory experiences and ultimate reality on the yoga of one-flavouredness, so we have to realise that they cannot be separated. We will then directly perceive that everything we experience lacks enduring essence.

On the yoga of non-meditation there is no longer any difference between meditation and post-meditation. You have advanced to the terminus point of the spiritual path where such distinctions can no longer be spoken. That insight that you have gained at this level will guarantee compassion is the natural expression of post-meditation. This is not the compassion expressed by ordinary people; it is compassion without an object. To say 'compassion is expressed during post-meditation at the level of the fourth yoga' is just a manner of speaking. In reality, we cannot make any distinction whatsoever between the meditative or post-meditative states for a fully awakened person. That is exactly the state we attain on the fourth yoga. The *Prajnaparamita-samcayagatha* says:

> The psychophysical constituents are empty of enduring essence.
> Even without meditating, a person who realises this,
> Would show spontaneous compassion to others
> And never be short of enlightened qualities!

Saraha says:

> Finding security within the nature of mind
> Is like a tree-trunk firmly rooted in the ground.
> Its branches reach out and pervade the triple world
> Bearing the flowers of compassion
> That affects everyone beneficially.

Tsangpa Gyare says:

> From the first stage of the yoga of one-flavouredness
> To the second stage of non-meditation,
> You will retain some form of clinging to your perceptions;
> Even though you see everything to be illusion-like.
> When you fully realise the yoga of non-meditation
> Not even the thought of illusion will arise.

A fully enlightened being must remain in contact with the normal world even though he or she no longer perceives the world in the same way as an ordinary person. A fully enlightened being still lives and works with the world, which is why the spontaneous expression of compassion comes into being.

4. The specific meditative deviations of each

Je Gomchung says:

> On the yoga of one-pointedness
> Meditators can fall into the trap
> Of clinging to experience as real.
> On the yoga of the non-conceptuality
> Meditators may misperceive their experience
> And fail to appreciate its true significance.
>
> On the yoga of one-flavouredness
> Meditators are still in imminent danger of being overwhelmed
> And their experiences are robbed of vividness and clarity.
> On the yoga of the non-meditation
> Meditators who cannot distinguish between
> Conceptual understanding and immediate realisation
> May be subject to the delusions of the knowable.

On the yoga of one-pointedness you may compensate for a lack of real confidence by fixating on your experiences and substantialising them.

On the yoga of non-conceptuality, you can distort experience by paying exclusive attention to mentally generated notions of emptiness. Instead of generating openness and acceptance to your mental events and attitudes, you mistakenly associate emptiness with things that you consider positive, wholesome, and pleasant, and disassociate emptiness from things that you consider negative and unpleasant.[13] However, a real experience of non-conceptuality comes from developing total openness.

On the yoga of one-flavouredness, you may find it very difficult to understand how to properly approach your attitude and practice. It is very easy to fall victim to preconceptions and habits and very difficult to develop a holistic attitude. You need to accomplish the integration of all polar concepts, experiences, attitudes, and behaviours because these are all grounded in your established dualistic notions and conceptual categories.[14] Meditators still find it really difficult to achieve this integration on the yoga of one-flavouredness. Even meditators lucky enough to have an inkling of integration, may fail to experience it completely, because they do not understand the true meaning of illusion-like reality.[15]

On the yoga of non-meditation, you need to be alert to the fact certain experiences of non-conceptuality during meditation may simply mean your mind is in a state of passivity without much activity. It is very easy to mistake this passivity for non-meditation, but it is nothing more than resting in the storehouse consciousness, which is only a temporary experience.[16] To do so would be to fail to gain a genuine perception of your true condition. Your natural state is not a state of passivity; it is complete mental clarity and alertness.

5. The yogas and post-meditative mindfulness

Je Gomchung says:

> Distractions occur on the yoga of one-pointedness,
> Which make it difficult to remain in an engaged state.
> Mind occasionally wanders on the yoga of non-conceptuality,
> But we can easily bring it back to its original state.
> Once we secure the realisation of one-flavouredness,
> The possibility of disengagement does not arise.
> On the level of non-meditation,
> Even the concepts of engagement or disengagement do not arise;
> Their relevance has been rendered useless.

To elaborate, you can become distracted and scattered when practising one-pointedness because you are unable to maintain mindfulness and will disengage from meditation. Even if you succeed in maintaining mindfulness for a time, this is more the result of habit than any real insight into your mental states.[17]

You may develop various types of clinging if you fixate on the application of mindfulness on the yoga of non-conceptuality and will again disengage from meditation. However, you have the ability to maintain mindfulness fully at this point in your spiritual development and may develop insight into your true condition. The possibility of both engagement and disengagement can occur during this yoga, unlike the previous one.

When you realise the yoga of one-flavouredness, you may lose mindfulness during post-meditation, but you will not lose your understanding. You can no longer become completely disengaged from the meditative state. True disengagement does not take place even when mindfulness is absent, because that underlying understanding is always present. Meditators at this level have the ability to reactivate their mindfulness almost at will. That accomplishment gives rise to insight into the unity of impressions, appearances, and emptiness. That insight equates with uninterrupted engagement.

When you attain the yoga of non-meditation, you will have developed mindfulness to such a degree, it will give rise to the full expression of wisdom. It is no longer possible for you to become disengaged from the meditative state. Whatever arises in the mind will become part of your meditative experience, instead of causing distractions and diversions in your mindstream. The very idea of engagement has now become irrelevant.

6. Integrating meditation and post-meditation

Je Gomchung says:

> On the yoga of one-pointedness
> We can distinguish between meditation and post-meditation.
> On the yoga of non-conceptuality
> The difference between meditation and post-meditation is less clear.
> On the yoga of one-flavouredness
> No distinction can be made between meditation and post-meditation.
> On the yoga of non-meditation
> There is only meditation.

To elaborate, there is no wisdom in the yoga of one-pointedness so you cannot have a genuine experience of meditation or perceive the sensory impressions to be illusion-like in post-meditation. Nonetheless, you will have a real experience of the meditative state through the proper application of mindfulness.

Your experience of meditation and post-meditation is quite different in the yoga of non-conceptuality insofar as you have now overcome the dualistic notion of subject and object. You will now have a genuine and authentic experience of the meditative state for the first time. Even though you still experience a difference between meditative and post-meditative states, you will see everything as illusion-like. You may still entertain dualistic thoughts of subject and object, but they will intermingle with your perception of everything as illusion-like.

In the yoga of one-flavouredness, there is no longer any separation between the meditative and post-meditative states. You now recognise that what is present to your senses and what arises in mind has the nature of emptiness. This insight will pervade both your meditative and post-meditative experiences, because you see the inseparability of current experience and ultimate reality. There will be a genuine coalescence of these two experiences.

In the yoga of non-meditation, various impressions will continue to make their appearance, but you will no longer be disturbed by them. Everything you experience has become part of your meditation. In other words, whatever you experience or enact is meditation. There is no further need to speak about meditative and post-meditative states. Je Zhang says:

> Once your mind has been arrested
> By a genuine understanding of your true condition,
> You can jump, run and shout
> And still maintain the meditative state.
> If a genuine understanding is absent,
> You might make the effort to meditate,
> But you will only have post-meditative experience
> Even if you are deliberately sitting in meditation.
> The ability to be present has not yet arisen.

He also says:

> Even if you have a deep understanding
> Of the teachings and methods of meditation
> And your view is profound and high,
> Without a true experience of meditation,
> You will be continuously haunted

By the gap between meditative and post-meditative states,
By the presence or absence of mindfulness,
And by the existence or non-existence of distraction.
Only when you give up any thought of deliberate meditation
Will you realise the meaning of non-meditation.

The real question that all Four Yogas raise is, 'How do we maintain awareness so that we can recognise and identify what is going on?' If you can do that, even physical activities such as jumping, running, and communicating will become part of meditation.[18] On the other hand, if you cannot be present, a real experience of meditation will remain elusive, even if you sit on the cushion very diligently. The real issue then, is not whether you are meditating, but whether you are present or not. Once you attain real presence of mind, you will understand the lack of real separation between the meditative and post-meditative states, between mindfulness and forgetfulness, between distraction and non-distraction. Pursuing your practice in this way will lead to the yoga of non-meditation. This last yoga corresponds to the fifth of the bodhisattva paths, namely the path of no more learning.[19]

7. The yogas and their stages of integration

Je Gomchung says:

On the yoga of one-pointedness,
We settle the mind in its natural state without contrivances.
On the yoga of non-conceptuality,
We bring meditative realisations into post-meditation.
On the yoga of one-flavouredness,
We integrate the meditative and post-meditative states
By employing meditative experience in everyday situations.
The yoga of non-meditation is the culmination point,
Meditation and post-meditation become one.

To elaborate, the first yoga is where you repeatedly employ mindfulness to settle your mind in its own natural state. You must maintain an element of exertion if you wish to stay in meditative equipoise and post-meditative mindfulness, using all of your activities to develop the power of mindfulness.

On the second yoga, you become well established in mindfulness and must remain in a state of meditation as open and wide as space itself. The sensory impressions are then seen as illusory displays in post-meditation because you clearly perceive their lack of enduring essence. The space-like contemplation of meditation and the illusory-like experiences of post-meditation merge until they become completely and fully integrated.

On the third yoga, you dismantle all dualistic conceptions and experience everything that you encounter in its unity. Relative reality (which reveals itself to consciousness) and ultimate reality (the nature of what is revealed) are perceived non-dualistically as inseparable.[20]

On the fourth yoga, you will obtain complete spiritual fulfilment as a result of the previous stages of integration. Gampopa says:

> The yoga of one-pointedness
> Creates the opportunity for spontaneity.
> The yoga of non-conceptuality
> Provides the opportunity for non-dualistic apprehension.
> The yoga of one-flavouredness
> Lends itself to direct non-conceptual realisation.
> The yoga of non-meditation
> Provides complete freedom from defilements and obscurations.

8. Some other characteristics of the four

Tsangpa Gyare says:

> The yoga of one-pointedness is not a transcendental state.
> It is a meditative state
> And only a worldly attainment.
> The yoga of non-conceptuality
> Is the first dawning of the transcendental,
> Where we perceive things directly for the first time.
> The yoga of one-flavour
> Reveals the empirical and transcendental
> To be coextensive and inseparable.
> The yoga of non-meditation is firmly established
> In the true authentic condition of the dharmakaya.

The yoga of one-pointedness is only realisation of a worldly meditative state. The yoga of non-conceptuality is where you glimpse ultimate reality for the first time. The yoga of one-flavouredness is where you perceive all sensory and mental events to be identical with ultimate reality, which thus nullifies their ability to disturb your mind.[21] The yoga of non-meditation is established in the true and authentic state of being, which can only be realised without conceptual meditation. Tsangpa Gyare says:

> If you persist in the practice of one-pointedness
> Your obsession with things will automatically cease.
> You might also develop various psychic powers
> Comparable to those of the Hindu system.
> When you realise the yoga of non-conceptuality
> You gain insight into ultimate reality.
> Whatever arises in mind or appears to the senses
> Is a theatrical performance or energy display.
> Different changes to your perception
> Will also take place contingent on your faculties.
> There will be other changes as well,
> Such as an increased capacity for compassion.
>
> When you attain the yoga of one-flavouredness
> The world and all its contents
> Becomes the realm of the buddhas.
> It will no longer matter what you are doing;
> You may be leaning backwards,
> Or sitting on your own head,
> You will always be in a deep state of stillness.
> Like a king seated majestically on his throne,
> Nothing will sway your inner strength and calm.
> You will see things as the product of causes and conditions
> Because you are not clinging to thinghood
> Or grasping onto their essence or substance.
> Just like an elaborate brocade cloth
> Shimmering in the midday sun
> You will see the full splendour of the world.
> Benefiting others and leading them on the path,
> You possess the proximate qualities of buddhahood.
>
> When you attain the yoga of non-meditation,
> You will be a fully enlightened being.
> There is nothing further to learn or overcome.

The qualities and characteristics of the Four Yogas have been described in the Mahamudra literature in this way. Je Yanggonpa says:

By familiarising ourselves with the Four Yogas
We can perceive their relationship to the practice
And use them to understand our own identity.

On the yoga of one-pointedness,
We become detached from our physical body
And pacify the five sensory impressions.

On the yoga of non-conceptuality,
We become detached from feeling and instinctual drives
And pacify consciousness.

On the yoga of one-flavouredness,
We sever all the conceptual categories
And pacify egocentric mind.

On the yoga of non-meditation,
We sever consciousness
And pacify the storehouse consciousness.[22]

In this way, the Four Yogas work on the five psychophysical constituents, which include the constituents of the individual self and the eight forms of consciousness. Je Yanggonpa says:

On the yoga of one-pointedness,
We learn to stabilise the mind but that mind is still sullied.

On the yoga of non-conceptuality,
We learn to differentiate meditative experience and realisation.[23]

On the yoga of one-flavouredness,
We integrate two types of meditative attainment:
Feeling based experience and insight based realisation.

On the yoga of non-meditation
There is no qualitative difference between
meditation and post-meditation
And no need to engage in formal practice.

These verses describe the Four Yogas in relation to the distinctions between meditative experience and realisation. These four types of yoga, which correspond to different levels of meditative experience and realisation during meditation, should be understood in relation to cause and effect. Je Yang-gonpa also says:

> On the level of one-pointedness,
> We are still subject to consequences,
> Because we believe in the reality of things.
>
> On the level of non-conceptuality,
> We understand that causality is not fixed and mechanical,
> But relational and interdependent.
>
> On the level of one-flavouredness,
> We see that causal relationships lack enduring essence,
> And begin to see that their nature is emptiness.
>
> On the level of non-meditation,
> We realise nothing has independent existence;
> Everything is subject to the law of interdependence.

The Four Yogas are here described in relation to the consequences of cause and effect in the mental domain. If you understand how cause and effect operate within the mind, you will understand the law of karmic cause and effect. Certain Buddhists say, 'If we understand the nature of mind through meditation, we won't have to concern ourselves with the law of cause and effect, because our mind will be completely pure and incapable of creating further karmic impressions.' This statement has no basis. Gaining a glimpse into the nature of mind will not automatically free it from the workings of karma.

The yoga of one-pointedness retains all the conditions for creating fresh karma, because we are still clinging, grasping, and fixating on our meditative experiences. It is still possible to create fresh karma once we have understood the nature of mind on the yoga of non-conceptuality, because we are still distinguishing between meditative and post-meditative experiences. It is even possible to become temporarily distracted and to create fresh karma on the yoga of one-flavouredness. In brief, as long as mind still grasps and clings to objects, there is the possibility of perpetuating our karmic tendencies. The *Ratnavali* says:

> If we believe in self-existing and fixed entities
> We will perceive an immutable and unchanging self.

> Until we can relinquish these mistaken notions
> We will continue to perpetuate karmic cause and effect.

Gampopa says:

> Until you purge yourself of clinging
> You will continue to create new karma
> Through conceptual confusion and delusion.
> Therefore, keep relying on mindfulness.

The karmic law of cause and effect operates on many different levels, depending on the degree or intensity of your clinging and fixation. Without gaining insight into ultimate reality, you will go on accumulating karma through mental clinging, despite your continuing meditation practice. The way you experience that karma may change as you progress on the path, but karma will by no means cease to operate. Even if you gain insight into the nature of reality, the illusory-like experience of karmic consequences will continue until you are firmly established within that realisation.[24] Gampopa says:

> You may ask, 'Where is the demarcation line between the domain of karma and the domain that goes beyond karma?' The law of karma will continue to operate in your mindstream until you will gain a genuine realisation into the ultimate nature of things and can perceive the empirical world as illusion-like. Even if you gain an insight into the nature of reality, a vestige of your karmic tendencies will remain until you become properly established in that realisation, but you should regard the karmic consequences of your experiences as illusion-like. In brief, karmic cause and effect will not be nullified until you attain a full realisation of your authentic condition. Only when you actualise your authentic state will you be completely free of the notion of karma.

This is how Gampopa delineates our karmic condition and our transcendental condition. Some people might find these comments disturbing and think, 'The teachings say that people with high spiritual attainments do not endure sickness, ill health, old age, and other kinds of suffering. How can we say such people endure karmic experiences?' This question could only be raised by someone who has failed to understand that there are many kinds of karmic experiences.[25] Certain types of suffering must be experienced, precisely because of our lack of insight. We fail to act with wisdom when our minds are governed by ignorance.

There are also types of suffering that are not a product of our immediate actions, but of our latent tendencies. Once we have become acquainted with ultimate reality, we no longer grasp after and fixate on things and therefore cease to perform any new karmic actions. Nonetheless, our latent karmic traces and dispositions have not yet been completely eradicated. Illusion-like karmic experiences and even more subtle karmic manifestations continue to function in our mindstream for this reason. Shantideva's *Bodhicharyavatara* says:

> As the mind becomes familiar with ultimate reality
> The gross tendencies of mind are overcome.
> Once insight into the nature of reality is fully established
> The last remaining traces of our karmic inheritance will vanish.

It also says:

> How can this happen?
> A magician conjures up a beautiful woman
> Then becomes attracted to his own illusion
> While knowing it is only a trick.

In a similar way, the karmic tendencies produced by our own conflicting emotions and conceptual delusions gradually become weakened and are eventually overcome by a realisation of emptiness.

THE DETAILED EXPLANATION OF THE FOUR YOGAS

This has two parts:

- How the Four Yogas were divided into twelve stages
- How to understand each of the twelve stages

§ How The Four Yogas Were Divided Into Twelve Stages

If you look into Gampopa's *Collected Works*, you will not find the Four Yogas divided into twelve stages. These divisions were passed down from master to disciple in the oral transmission, which is evident in the instructions of Je Gomtsul, and so on. Je Gomtsul's meditation instructions describe the yogas in twelve divisions, each yoga divided into three stages: initial, intermediate, and final. Phagmo Drupa, another great Kagyu master, also spoke about the initial, intermediate, and final stages of each of the Four Yogas.

This oral transmission was passed down by great masters such as Tsangpa Gyare and his disciples. It was also passed down by Rangjung Dorje, the third Karmapa, Je Khachopa, and the twelve yogis. It is important to preserve this tradition, which subdivides the Four Yogas into twelve stages, because it presents a very appropriate way of appraising our meditative experiences and realisations within the context of Mahamudra practice. Khachopa, who transmitted the teachings on these twelve stages, also mentions an alternative division of twenty-four stages. However, we will follow Phagmo Drupa's system of twelve stages here, as this is the most prevalent system in the literature on the Four Yogas of Mahamudra. This system divides the yogas in the following manner.

- The yoga of one-pointedness

1 Initial stage: a distinct experience of bliss and clarity
2 Intermediate stage: being fully established in concentration
3 Final stage: total integration of bliss, clarity, and concentration.

- The yoga of non-conceptuality

1 Initial stage: realising that mind is baseless and not grounded in anything
2 Intermediate stage: recognising that mind is rootless
3 Final stage: full comprehension of outer and inner phenomena.

- The yoga of one-flavouredness

1 Initial stage: recognising that samsara and nirvana are the same
2 Intermediate stage: a proper understanding of the perceiver and perceived
3 Final stage: seeing the equality of everything because everything in the empirical world is imbued with the same reality.

- The yoga of non-meditation

1 Initial stage: the realisation that there is no meditation or meditator
2 Intermediate stage: spontaneously establishing the meditative state
3 Final stage: joining the luminosity cultivated through meditation with the innate luminosity of mind itself.

You should be aware that these twelve stages are not like a ladder, where each rung leads to the next. There is no certainty the experiences that arise in Mahamudra meditation will occur in an orderly fashion. You might experience many different stages of the Four Yogas during the course of your practice. For example, when you reach but do not fully realise the final stage of one-pointed yoga, you might simultaneously experience the initial or intermediate stages of non-conceptuality.

Similarly, if you don't fully realise the final stage of non-conceptual yoga, you might experience aspects of the initial or intermediate stages of the yoga of one-flavouredness. Also an incomplete realisation of the final stage of one-flavouredness may simultaneously occur when you reach the initial or intermediate stages of the yoga of non-meditation. You need not concern yourself too much with a rigid and fixed interpretation of these twelve stages, because they will not necessarily occur in a strictly linear fashion.[26]

These Four Yogas are presented according to the direct meditative experiences and realisations of the forefathers of our Practice Lineage who erected the victory banner of meditation practice. Their structured presentation is reflective of the graduated path of practice because that is the relevant path for most people. However, you should bear in mind that these Four Yogas are not necessarily traversed or actualised in this order.

Those rare individuals with an ability to embark on the instantaneous or intermediate paths will especially not experience them in this order. Nowadays, many people who claim to be meditators show no sign of such extraordinary abilities. They seem instead to spend their time lazing about or indulging in distractions. The experiences these people have will be uncertain, to say the least. However, it is definitely possible for someone with a propensity for meditation, who has received the proper instructions from a lineage master, to make distinct progress in the manner described here, even in our own time.

For this reason, it seems important to provide guidelines for assessing our meditative progress. I have therefore extracted the following essential points about the Four Yogas from the existing body of traditional literature.

§ How To Understand Each Of The Twelve Stages

1 The yoga of one pointedness

(i) Differentiating the three stages

In this context, one-pointedness does not refer to any kind of concentrated meditative state. It is a special kind of meditative state. You can only attain this special kind of one-pointedness on the first yoga because certain meditative qualities are a prerequisite for it. The kind of one-pointedness that you need to establish at this level consists of resting the mind in its natural state without distraction. You must also be able to use your awareness to blend the mind in motion with the mind at rest.

You might raise the following objection, 'If a meditator can remain in the natural state in the yoga of one-pointedness, what could be so special about the yoga of non-conceptuality?' It is generally agreed that a real intimation of the nature of mind is gained for the first time at the level of the second yoga. You only attain a proximate realisation of the nature of mind on the level of one-pointedness. The object of meditation is restricted to mental events because you have not yet developed the ability to integrate your inner and outer sensations and experiences and you still tend to cling to your meditative experiences. This clinging is not overcome until subsequent yogas.

Certain commentators and practitioners have mistaken one-pointedness of tranquillity meditation for one-pointedness of Mahamudra meditation. Your mind may occasionally become passive in the one-pointedness of tranquillity meditation, because your thoughts, concepts, and ideas have settled and your mind can remain in concentration. You may also experience awareness in conjunction with that sense of mental illumination. However, this is not the same as the one-pointedness of Mahamudra meditation. Other people have mistakenly assumed an understanding of emptiness can be used as a supplement for tranquillity meditation and will produce a state of one-pointedness. This is also based on an erroneous assumption.

The first assumption is incorrect because a proper cultivation of tranquillity will not give rise to insight. The second approach is incorrect because it is one thing to develop an understanding of emptiness, but quite another to embody that understanding by being in the authentic condition. You will never gain the fundamental confidence of insight through tranquillity. Insight can only come from experiencing one-pointedness through the proper methods.

To establish yourself in the genuine state of one-pointedness, you need the awareness that stems from insight into your authentic condition as well as a stabilised mind. You also need the ability to equalise the restful state of mind and the mind in motion. In other words, we use mindfulness and awareness to perceive the nature of our thoughts and emotions when they arise and disperse in the mind. This is how we remain in the natural condition on the first yoga. Je Yanggonpa says:

> Transforming conceptual proliferations into understanding
> Is the gateway to your natural condition.
> The secret point of meditation is self-recognition.
> Coming into contact with your own true condition
> Leaves no separation; nothing stands in the way.
> Everything is seen as an expression of yourself.
> Apart from your own true condition,

Nothing is extrinsic to it;
Not even mindfulness, insight, and so on.
When you fully comprehend this
You realise that the meditative state is maintained
Between mind at rest and mind in motion.

This is how to cultivate the yoga of one-pointedness. The initial stage of one-pointedness is the meditative experiences of bliss, mental clarity, and non-conceptuality. It encompasses the point when these experiences are unstable and hard to maintain to the point where you need exert little effort to induce them. This is followed by the intermediate stage, where you may naturally fall into a meditative state from time to time, without the thought of doing so. As you meditate further, the stability of your meditation practice will make you feel more empowered. At the onset of the final stage, your meditative experiences become more continuous and flow into post-meditation. You can now maintain a sense of awareness throughout the four actions of eating, sitting, walking, and sleeping; sometimes for twenty-four hours in a day. That awareness has the element of clarity and emptiness and epitomises the final stage of one-pointedness.[27]

Tsangpa Gyare lists six pairs of criteria for assessing success in the Four Yogas of Mahamudra.[28] These are:

1 Has ultimate reality been perceived or not?
2 Has dexterity in practice been developed or not?
3 Have deluded thoughts been revealed as meditation or not?
4 Have the necessary qualities been developed or not?
5 Has full comprehension of empirical reality been attained or not?
6 Have the seeds for actualising the rupakaya been sown or not?

These six criteria for assessing our spiritual progress are very appropriate and I will now explain them in the context of each of the yogas.

- Has ultimate reality been perceived or not?

The nature of mind is unconditional emptiness, a state that gives rise to an unobstructed mental clarity. When you can remain in the state of emptiness and clarity, like a cloudless sky of space and light, you will experience self-awareness. Developing full confidence and certainty in the physical and mental well-being that comes from self-awareness is to perceive your natural condition. On the other hand, failure to develop full confidence and certainty in that experience is to remain within the usual experiences of your samsaric mind. You will be like a child looking at the reflection of the moon in a pond and being unsure whether it is a really the moon or only a reflection.

- Has dexterity in practice been developed or not?

You develop dexterity in the practice when you experience well-being, mental clarity, and a reduction in your conceptual proliferations while maintaining self-awareness with full confidence. When this awareness begins to pervade all aspects of your life, both day and night, it is a sign that you have developed the necessary dexterity. On the other hand, dexterity has not developed if there is an interruption in your awareness between the meditative and post-meditative states.

- Have deluded thoughts been revealed as meditation or not?

When you have the mindfulness to use whatever arises in your mind or is presented to your senses as part of meditation, those very mental and physical elements become meditation without your needing to abandon anything. Even your dreams may turn into experiences of luminosity. Deluded thoughts can become meditation in these ways. On the other hand, needing to consciously enforce mindfulness to stay in a meditative state when thoughts and sensory impressions impinge on your mind, means that deluded thoughts have failed to become part of your meditation.

- Have the necessary qualities been developed or not?

When you cease to concern yourself with the eight worldly dharmas and develop the psychic powers of exhaustion and overpowering, you have developed the necessary spiritual qualities. On the other hand, you do not have the necessary qualities if you cannot channel your mental powers properly, if you lack peace of mind, and if you cannot feel the presence of spiritual heat.

- Has full comprehension of empirical reality been attained or not?

If you regard the world seriously and take full responsibility for your actions as your meditative concentration becomes pure and clear, you will have full comprehension of the principle of interdependent origination. Following the norms of conduct without going against the world is a sign of attaining full comprehension of empirical reality. On the other hand, if your practice and understanding of emptiness do not lead you to taking the world seriously and you are capricious and irresponsible, this indicates a failure to comprehend empirical reality.

- Have the seeds for actualising the rupakaya been sown or not?

The seeds for the actualisation of the enlightened body have been successfully sown if you take the world seriously and can give rise to compassion because you feel impelled to benefit others when you see their suffering. On the other hand, if you remain completely engrossed in your private meditation and have become addicted to meditative experiences, you have failed to sow those seeds. When your mind is obscured and self-engrossed, it is difficult to give rise to a caring attitude for others. You will simply discard any altruistic thoughts and concentrate on accumulating our own experiences.

(ii) Dawning of inner experience

At the initial stage of one-pointed yoga, you will experience physical and mental well-being, mental clarity, and a reduction in conceptuality, but you will find it very difficult not to fixate on these experiences. All of your realisations and experiences will be coloured by these sensations, but the deluded thoughts and emotions that arise during meditation will dissipate of their own accord most of the time.

You will occasionally develop conviction in your meditation, but at other times you will be lost in deluded thoughts. You might also relate to everything with a sense of cheerfulness and joy during post-meditation. If you can maintain your mindfulness, the mental spaciousness and clarity you cultivate during meditation will be transferred to your daily life, providing you with the basic understanding that everything is a product of causes and conditions and that all experience is contingent on the mind.

Your dreaming will often decrease and you may even have lucid dreams from time to time, but there will be no fundamental difference between your dreams and the dreams of ordinary people. Some people's dreams may actually increase in number and their ability to have lucid dreams will become even more difficult.

You might also experience greater difficulty with your meditation and your mind may be disturbed by anxieties and you think, 'It is impossible for me to be in a meditative state.' You may become concerned you are making no progress whatsoever. However, at other times, your experiences will be encouraging and you think, 'That was a good meditation session!' You will experience many such fluctuations in your practice. Whenever you are swayed this way and that by either encouraging or discouraging meditative experiences, you should generate a feeling of connection to the lineage and develop pure vision about the authenticity of the teachings.[29] It will also help to generate a compassionate and a caring attitude toward others.

At the intermediate stage of one-pointedness, you will become more stable and experience fewer fluctuations in your meditation. Your meditative concentration will be imbued with the triple experience of bliss, mental clarity, and non-conceptuality or spaciousness. You might also enter into a meditative state quite naturally, even when you are not formally meditating, and whatever arises in your mind will be self-liberated in that state.

There will be a distinct reduction in your mental activities and whatever does arise will naturally disperse. You will retain a sense of spaciousness and mental clarity during post-meditation and experience everything in a very spacious and open way. However, you might occasionally revert to your old ways, perceiving everything as having enduring essence or fixed reality. Still, it will be much easier to apply mindfulness during post-meditation and easier to remain in a meditative state. You will be able to utilise your dreams as part of your meditative experience but your dreams will not always arise as part of meditation. You might also dream less and find you can practise meditation with a sense of cheerfulness that you do not need to grapple with.

At the final stage of one-pointed yoga, the meditative experiences of well-being, mental clarity, and non-conceptuality will become continuous. They will accompany everything that you experience, think or feel and all your deluded thoughts will dissipate into these meditative experiences. Whatever presents itself to your senses in post-meditation will also be liberated into those meditative experiences and all your dreams will be imbued with them.

There is still a vestige of clinging at this point however, because you may still hang onto these experiences as desirable. This kind of clinging is nonetheless far healthier than the earlier fixation. Your meditative experiences will gradually become transformed as you progress with the practice and you can expect to experience bliss and emptiness, awareness and emptiness, deluded thoughts and clarity, sensory impressions and clarity, and sensory impressions and emptiness. You will gradually see everything that exists as illusion-like because of these meditative experiences. Various experiences may arise during the final stage of this yoga, including the acquisition of certain psychic powers, humility, and pure vision. Some people even mistake this final level of one-pointedness for the ultimate state of meditation, imagining that there is nothing above or beyond it.

(iii) Maintaining this yoga

The yoga of one-pointedness should be practised in mountain solitudes or at least in isolation, while maintaining a vow of silence. If your mind becomes contaminated, you will not be able to use your mind properly and it may become quite dull. Even when the afflictions are not severe, you may still experience problems, such as the object of meditation becoming hazy and unclear. It is therefore very important to exercise extreme caution and avoid being afflicted by contaminations.

As you continue with the practice, you might encounter the obstacles of drowsiness and mental agitation and should apply the antidotes described earlier in this text. If your mind becomes extremely dull, resort to auxiliary methods of purification, such as confession. Receive further instructions and empowerments connected to your meditation from your teacher. This should be done in conjunction with offerings and the practice of generosity.

If the relationship with your teacher or other friends gets disrupted, you will need to make appropriate restorations to repair those relationships. If personal reasons prevent this resolution, regard this situation as a spiritual obstacle and try to remedy it by going for refuge, generating revulsion for superfluous things, and cultivating humility, pure vision, and compassion.[30] These things should all be done prior to your meditation.

After you engage in these preliminaries, remain in meditation. If thoughts or emotions arise or your mind automatically latches onto something, make sure awareness is also present. Just as a kingfisher waits for a fish and then catches it as soon as it leaps from the water, your awareness should be there to catch a thought or emotion as soon as it arises.

Maintain one-pointed concentration; not following your thoughts, not becoming distracted when deluded thoughts arise, not becoming fixated on the restful mind, and not being overwhelmed by sensory impressions during post-meditation. This is how we train ourselves not to fixate on pleasurable or unpleasant meditation experiences.

No matter what thoughts or experiences arise in your mind, refrain from cultivating, following, suppressing, or preventing them. When heavy meditative experiences arise, the true nature of your mind is covered over, so it is important to learn to separate yourself from the moisture of inner experiences. This can be done by maintaining awareness without conditioning the mind.

In post-meditation, familiarise yourself with the life stories of the past masters of the Practice Lineage to see how they practised and what they went through. You should also read the doha songs about the realisation of these spiritual masters and think, 'I will do similar things and practise in a similar way.' It is important to develop courage in this way.

If you do not attain the yoga of non-conceptuality even after you have practised one-pointedness for a long time, you must practise the three abandonments: abandoning attachment to the self, abandoning attachment to this life, and abandoning attachment to the people we love and aversion for the people we hate. Offer your body to the lineage masters so that you can let go of clinging to the physical body. Practise generosity by giving things away to your vajra brothers and sisters so you can detach yourself from worldly possessions and turn away from thoughts of indulging in the good life. Minimise food consumption, reduce spending on clothes, restrict conversations with others, and spend time in solitude.

It is much easier to avoid disturbances from the objects of your conflicting emotions and to limit your more extreme forms of craving, aversion, and resentment when you are in solitude. It is also less likely that your mind will wander if you leave your familiar surroundings. Even if you are unwilling to do this for a long time, you should make the effort to do it for at least a few years and practise silence.

We attain the yoga of one-pointedness by utilising the above methods. You will overcome clinging to the meditative state when you can dismantle your overly exaggerated attachment to positive meditative experiences. You will also realise that the manifestations of mind, which you usually perceive to be either good or bad, are in reality no different. The conviction that nothing arising in the mind is intrinsically bad or intrinsically good is borne in your mind. Your mind will thereby become free of disturbances from meditative experiences and remain in an undiluted and unconditioned state.[31] You should remain in that state without wavering. As Gampopa says:

> As a beginner, you must learn to cultivate mental awareness and to stay with that awareness. You will eventually realise that this awareness has been there right from the beginning. You have developed full certainty when you become familiar with that.

Tsangpa Gyare says:

> When one-pointed yoga is fully attained,
> Meditative experiences will be transcended
> By practising meditation without an object.

It is important to reflect constantly on the dangers of mistaking meditative experiences for realisation. It is easy for meditators who are undisciplined or who have limited contact with a meditation instructor to mistake certain meditative experiences for realisation. If you become mistaken in this way, you might meditate for a whole lifetime, but it will be practically impossible to realise the nature of mind. Even if you gain a glimpse of the nature of mind, it would be too easy for you to lose it again or to go astray. Gampopa says:

You can say that your view is free from extremes,
But if that view is not based on realisation,
It is just a construction of your conceptual mind.
Without developing full confidence in the view,
You may experience good meditation,
But it will not free you from samsaric bondage.

Je Drikhungpa says:

Clinging to meditative experiences,
Will enable you to take a higher rebirth. Nothing more.

It is therefore important to transcend meditative experiences and let them go. You should not even hold onto your authentic condition. Saraha says:

Even clinging to the nature of mind
Should be relinquished.

Gampopa says:

The dualism of experiencer and experience
Will prevent recognition of the authentic state;
Despite extensive meditation experience.

You will attain non-conceptuality when you can avoid these pitfalls and let go of your experiences. Dualistic notions, such as emptiness (as the object) and mind (as the subject), will disappear and your meditation will be revealed as the yoga of non-conceptuality.

2. The yoga of non-conceptuality

(i) Differentiating the three stages

The word 'non-conceptuality' implies that the natural state of mind is unconditioned, just like space. For this reason, we cannot speak of the natural state in terms of coming into being, persisting or going out of being. This nature of mind is known as non-conceptual because it is devoid of empirical characteristics. As Nagarjuna's *Mulamadhyamikakarika* says:

The ultimate condition of all things
Does not come into being or cease to exist.
There is no falling into the extremes
Of existence or non-existence,
No coming or going,

No unity or diversity;
It is free from all empirical characteristics.

Some people say non-conceptuality means 'the cessation of dualistic thoughts,' while other people say it means an 'understanding of emptiness.' Both of these views are incorrect. If the first assertion were true, the meditative state of tranquillity, where all thoughts are temporarily suspended, would be regarded as a state of non-conceptuality. If the second were true, the view that everything is emptiness would be equated with non-conceptuality. But neither of these scenarios is possible. As you persist in the yoga of non-conceptuality, you will eventually have a direct experience of the nature of mind, which is unconditioned like space and not contingent on anything for its existence. There is neither increase nor decrease. A popular sutra says:

It is profound, tranquil, free from conceptual proliferations,
Naturally luminous, and unconditioned.

The *Mahayanuttaratantra* says:

The nature of mind is luminous
Unconditioned like space, and resistant to change.

The yoga of non-conceptuality is therefore related to the realisation of the nature of mind. This yoga also has three stages of realisation: the initial, intermediate, and final. The onset of the initial stage is characterised by a realisation of non-conceptuality. You see that the nature of mind is free from empirical characteristics. Your mind will nonetheless remain contaminated by subtle forms of fixation on the concept of emptiness at this stage. You may also suffer from occasional anxieties, such as the fear that you will never escape from samsara and the hope for the peace of nirvana. The intermediate stage is realised when you fully comprehend that the nature of mind has no enduring essence. This comprehension is not polluted by thoughts of emptiness so you are no longer disturbed by anything that arises in the mind. You have not yet gained mastery over your sensory impressions and may still cling to them. You may also still experience emotional disturbances in the form of hope and fear. The final stage is attained when you realise that everything you can experience or conceptualise in the realms of samsara and nirvana is imbued with emptiness. You are then no longer afflicted by thoughts of hope or fear.

We can use the same six criteria employed in the yoga of one-pointedness to evaluate and assess our realisations in the yoga of non-conceptuality.

- Has ultimate reality been perceived or not?

If no fixation accompanies your realisation and no thought separates subject (the realiser) and object (that which is realised), you have perceived the nature of mind. On the other hand, if you have only achieved certainty in an intellectual understanding of the emptiness of the nature of mind, you will still experience a subtle form of clinginess to that experience. These experiences do pertain to the yoga of non-conceptuality, but they are not the same as actual realisation, so you have not yet truly perceived the nature of mind.

- Has dexterity in the practice been developed or not?

The sign of dexterity in this practice is that you no longer entertain thoughts of hope and fear, while the thoughts and emotions that do arise disperse back into a state of non-conceptuality. On the other hand, if you can realise that your deluded thoughts and conflicting emotions are without any intrinsic nature, but you cannot apply that understanding to your sensory impressions, you will still be vulnerable to the influence of hope and fear and cling to the notion of emptiness. Dexterity in this practice has therefore not been harnessed properly.

- Have deluded thoughts been revealed as meditation or not?

When you see the empty nature of the thoughts and emotions that arise in your mind and recognise that whatever you see, hear, smell, taste, and touch is also empty by nature, you will be able to use deluded thoughts as part of your meditation. When you can experience all mental processes and sensory impressions in the same meditative way during post-meditation, your deluded thoughts will have been successfully converted into meditation. On the other hand, if you cannot deal with your mental processes and sensory impressions during meditation or post-meditation, you will have failed to convert deluded thoughts into meditation.

- Have the necessary qualities been developed or not?

When you can make use of existing causes and conditions to bring out your innate spiritual powers, you have developed the necessary spiritual qualities. On the other hand, if you are unable to make use of the existing causes and conditions for this purpose, you will have failed to give rise to those qualities, even if you have experienced some intimation of the nature of mind.

- Has full comprehension of empirical reality been attained or not?

If you have insight into the unconditioned aspect of the mind and so can maintain that realisation without disregarding the empirical world, you have full comprehension of empirical reality and can maintain your perspective on the relationship between conditioned and unconditioned reality.[32] On the other hand, if your realisation of the unconditioned aspect of mind leads you to denigrate the conditioned aspect of reality, so that you fail to heed the laws of karma, you will have failed to gain full comprehension of the workings of empirical reality.

- Have the seeds for actualising the rupakaya been sown or not?

If you realise mind is imbued with the two qualities of reality (conditioned and unconditioned) and can generate compassion toward the conditioned aspect of reality so that you continue to interact with the world, without losing sight of the non-conceptual state, you have sown the seeds for actualising the enlightened physical body. On the other hand, if you cannot realise the inseparability of the conditioned and unconditioned states, it may be very difficult to be compassionate toward others. You may become very cavalier toward the conventional world, which operates on the principles of interdependent origination, even if you have some realisation of emptiness. This indicates that you have therefore failed to sow the seeds for the actualisation of the rupakaya.

(ii) The Dawning of Inner Experience

At the initial stage of this yoga, you gain insight into the authentic condition of all things as not subject to change or alteration, because the concepts of coming into being, persisting, and going out of being do not apply. You will retain some fixation on the concept of emptiness at this stage, and continue to react in a conventional manner during post-meditation, such as having extreme attachment to people who are close and enmity to people who are distant, because you still cling to interactions between self and others. Most of your dream experiences are still due to deluded thoughts and conflicting emotions. You will also fluctuate quite radically in your meditation practice and your attitude will generally swing from one extreme to the other. For example, most of the time, you feel good about the instructions that you receive and the teacher that you receive them from, your relationship with your teacher will be close, you will be friendly with your fellow practitioners, and you will maintain a sense of conviction in the validity and efficacy of the practice. This positivity can be upset by intermittent experiences of doubt and uncertainty.

At the intermediate stage, your fixation on the concept of emptiness will weaken and the deluded thoughts that arise during meditation will dissipate as they arise, because you have learnt to let things go. Your mind will still cling to sensory impressions through force of habit and you will still be subject to hope and fear. You will feel quite positive at some times and quite low and uncertain at others in post-meditation. Sometimes your dreams will be coloured by deluded thoughts and conflicting emotions and sometimes you will have non-deluded dreams. Your general attitude to your teacher, fellow practitioners, and the practice itself can also become quite ambiguous, because your confidence is sometimes strong and other times dogged by doubts and uncertainty. Superfluous thoughts may also occasionally intrude on your mind so that you might think, 'There is no such thing as enlightenment, no such thing as plunging into lower forms of existence,' and so on.

At the final stage, you will gain full certainty about the root of the two domains of existence (samsaric bondage and nirvanic freedom) and fully comprehend the reality of both internal and external phenomena. You will no longer be haunted by the afflictions of hope and fear and your mind will cease to be clouded by thoughts of emptiness, non-emptiness, peaceful mental states, or agitated mental states. Your mind will become very buoyant, open, and flexible as these fluctuations subside. As soon as you perceive anything through your sensory impressions, those perceptions will be accompanied by the realisation that things are empty by nature.

You may not maintain a clear and spacious mental state during post-meditation, when conflicting emotions and deluded thoughts return, but you can abide in a meditative state. That state is defined as 'the inseparability of self-existing awareness and emptiness' and 'the inseparability of phenomenal appearance and emptiness.' This meditative experience will be continuous but you will still be unable to maintain your mindfulness in post-meditation without effort. You must therefore still make use of mindfulness. You may also still have deluded dreams and latch onto them as if they were real.

You have now attained an advanced level of realisation and a certain amount of arrogance may set in at this state. You could easily imagine that you understand your true condition and might say there is no such thing as nirvana or samsara.

The power of your realisation will mean that very profound, deep, and hard to comprehend things start to make sense to you. You may also realise that your real teacher is within and that this teacher is the nature of mind. Whatever happens in the external world can now be used in a positive way. Nothing will have an adverse effect on you. Hardly a trace of clinging, grasping, and fixation remain and you will no longer be caught up in the affairs of the eight worldly dharmas. There is still the danger of becoming quite arrogant at this level of attainment and you might imagine that you have no further need for instruction or external teachers.

(iii) Maintaining this yoga

You must cut your attachment to three things, even at the level of non-conceptuality: indulging in rich food, collecting clothing, and gossip. It is also advisable to spend time in solitude and practise silence. Only engage in a minimalist approach to ritual practices and offerings; elaborate rituals and offerings are discouraged. Focus on the practices of mindfulness and awareness in non-conceptual meditation and rely less on auxiliary practices such as deity yoga, offerings, and ganachakra pujas, and so on. It will then be easier to abide in a mental state without distraction or fixation. It is advisable occasionally to do some offerings, exercise generosity toward people in need and accumulate merit by engaging in conditioned reality. The cultivation of humility and the generation of compassion will help you stay anchored in the world of interdependent origination.

You should also imitate the qualities and realisations of great meditation masters and fellow practitioners as a way of sustaining your enthusiasm and interest. Become acquainted with the dohas of the Practice Lineage and learn to sing them. If you lack joy, feel uncomfortable, restless, and agitated, or dream of delicious food, use methods within the various Buddhist traditions to counteract these things, such as practising mystic heat yoga, prayer, or physical exercise.[33] Relying on these methods will help to shake any feelings of stagnation. If you realise the final stage of non-conceptual yoga, but feel you cannot move any further forward, go back to the auxiliary practices of Tantra and contemplate the three types of non-attachment. You can also receive further empowerments, confess your defects and mistakes, and engage in prayers. This will all help your realisation become deeper and more profound.

You can also visualise yourself as a Tantric deity, contemplate the sufferings endured by beings in the lower realms, recognise the origin of all this suffering to be mind, and then rest in the natural state so that mind can reveal itself as non-conceptuality. You can also contemplate the pleasures experienced by beings in higher realms or contemplate the nature of the samsaric condition and convert those contemplations into non-conceptuality. You could also contemplate the nature of nirvana. Climb to the top of a mountain and meditate there, using that experience to free mind into the state of non-conceptuality. Go into the market place and release your mind into non-conceptuality. Hold your breath with your eyes wide open and free your mind in non-conceptuality. These are all auxiliary methods for bringing yourself out of an impasse. Gampopa says:

> When meditators reach the stage of non-conceptual yoga,
> The mind should not be left in a neutral state during meditation.
> There should be a definite and distinct sense of fiery awareness.

Tsangpa Gyare says:

> All dualistic conceptions should be consumed by awareness in the yoga of non-conceptuality. Mingle fiery awareness with your various sensory impressions. This is how non-conceptual yoga is used in meditation.

Je Yanggonpa says:

> When mindfulness arises,
> Do not fall into a deliberate meditation.
> Meditate without contrivances
> And a very unique type of awareness will arise.
> This cannot be conceptualised or articulated.
> When this state of awareness is undisturbed
> By investigation and examination,
> Mother and son luminosity will meet
> In the state of non-conceptuality.

When mindfulness arises and you can use that mindfulness to remain in non-conceptuality without distraction, you should leave that authentic state alone without trying to contrive or condition it in any way. Do not meditate on anything else; just remain in that state. Awareness will arise, but this is not an awareness that can be described or conceptualised, so do not try to examine it or investigate it. If you approach the yoga of non-conceptuality in this way, your mind will become totally free of all the conceptual categories belonging to the dual domains of samsara and nirvana. You do not even need to entertain thoughts of conceptuality or non-conceptuality, emptiness or substance, because you no longer need to accept or reject anything.[34] Whatever arises in that mental state will arise vividly, in its full splendour. Everything will reveal itself as the one-flavouredness of mahamudrahood.

This leads to the third yoga of Mahamudra, which is known as the yoga of one-flavouredness.

3. The yoga of one-flavouredness

(i) Differentiating the three stages

The yoga of one-flavouredness is so-called because everything that exists in samsara and nirvana, confusion and enlightenment, is imbued with the same reality; the reality of emptiness. Saraha says:

> The authentic teacher is one who realises
> That everything in existence
> Is flavoured with one meaning:
> The meaning of emptiness.

Shavaripa says:

> There are many rivers in India
> Such as the Ganges and so on
> But they all merge into one ocean that is salty to taste.
> Similarly, when we examine the mind
> We find a mind and mental events
> But in their true authentic condition,
> They all have the same flavour.

In brief, the term 'one-flavouredness' means that no matter what phenomenal appearance or lack of phenomenal appearance, all forms of dualism have one taste. Phagmo Drupa says:

> Phenomenal appearance or non-appearance,
> Mind and emptiness, emptiness and non-emptiness;
> All dualistic concepts are undifferentiated in their true condition.
> The temporal concepts of simultaneity and
> subsequentness do not apply.
> Understanding and non-understanding,
> Meditation and non-meditation,
> Conceptual proliferation and non-conceptuality
> Are also purified in the state of one-flavouredness.

Je Zhang says something similar. Some clarification about the meaning of 'one-flavouredness' might be helpful at this point in case any misunderstandings have been generated inadvertently. Some people dispute the Mahamudra presentation by saying, 'Understanding emptiness and knowing that it pervades everything is the same as realising one-flavouredness.' They assert that the experience of emptiness is all-pervasive and intrinsic to everything and therefore synonymous with the realisation of one-flavouredness. If this were true, even the initial and intermediary stages of non-conceptuality would be equivalent to a realisation of one-flavouredness. That view is unacceptable.

While meditators can realise ultimate reality on the yoga of non-conceptuality they incline toward emptiness, which creates an uneasy relationship with phenomenal experiences. Only on the yoga of one-flavouredness can you realise the integration of emptiness and appearances, which will reveal a genuine sense of unity in diversity. Despite the variety of your phenomenal experiences you now no longer suppress anything. Appearances continue to manifest in their entirety as a unitary perceptual experience, which reveals the indivisible nature of emptiness and phenomena. All dualistic concepts are then subsumed within the experience of one-flavouredness, without losing their individuality. It is therefore said, 'the diversity of phenomena is united in the experience of one-flavouredness.'

The initial stage of one-flavouredness is attained when you realise everything that can be experienced within the domains of samsara and nirvana is flavoured with the nature of Mahamudra. If you can maintain that realisation you will have attained the initial stage of the yoga of one-flavouredness even if there still is a trace of clinging to that experience. The intermediary stage is attained when you understand that the diversity of phenomena is united in the single taste of the authentic condition. Phenomenal appearances and mind reveal themselves to be co-present and indivisible.

You attain the final stage when you realise that the diversity of phenomena all dissolves into the unity of one-flavouredness and evolves from the unity of one-flavouredness. There is this process of devolution and evolution. You will now be able to experience unity from within diversity, and to express diversity by not wavering from the unity of one-flavouredness. This is a sign of having perfected equanimity in the experience of complete peace. No further conflicts arise from dualistic notions in this authentic state of equanimity; you experience the peace of equanimity, where there is no conflict.[35]

The six pairs of criteria that were used to assess the first two yogas are also used here to determine our progress with the third yoga.

- Has ultimate reality been perceived or not?

You have perceived the nature of one-flavouredness if you can deal with whatever arises in the mind by remaining in a state of equanimity without entertaining thoughts of acceptance or rejection. You simply remain in a state of natural clarity without focusing your mind on anything in particular. On the other hand, if you think you can mingle the diversity of experiences with equanimity and cling to distinct experiences, you may have experienced one-flavouredness, but you have not recognised its nature.

- Has dexterity in the practice been developed or not?

You have developed dexterity in this practice if you can make skilful use of the thoughts and emotions that are present in your mind the moment they arise. On the other hand, if you retain any subtle thought of antidotes, you do not have the requisite skill to use the whole gamut of your experience in meditation. Instead of using your mental states as soon as they arise, you become subtly disturbed by thoughts of acceptance and rejection and therefore lack the requisite skill to engage in the yoga of one-flavouredness.

- Have deluded thoughts been revealed as meditation or not?

If you can deal with the sensory impressions that arise from the interactions of mind and its objects, without interference and without indulging in thoughts of bondage or liberation, whatever arises will reveal itself to be meditation. Whatever presents itself to the mind will occur naturally. On the other hand, if you think sensory impressions cause distractions and only add to your delusions so that you must turn away from them to achieve inner freedom; your deluded thoughts have not revealed themselves as meditation. If you deliberately focus on your sensory impressions to make yourself more comfortable with some impressions and to dissociate from others, that is a sure sign your deluded thoughts and emotions have not revealed themselves as meditation.

- Have the necessary qualities been developed or not?

The necessary spiritual qualities have become manifest when you can mix your body, sensory impressions, and mind to display extraordinary feats. On the other hand, if you are unable to mix your body and mental faculties in this way, you have failed to actualise the necessary qualities, even if you have a certain level of realisation of one-flavouredness. You have failed to develop the necessary qualities because of unfamiliarity with the relevant instructions.

- Has full comprehension of empirical reality been attained or not?

You have a full comprehension of the way empirical reality works when you can engage in both samsaric and nirvanic activities with bare awareness based on the realisation that everything is a product of causes and conditions. On the other hand, if you become fixated on the concept of emptiness and denigrate the causal workings of phenomena, you have failed to comprehend empirical reality.

- Have the seeds for actualising the rupakaya been sown or not?

When you realise that the real expression of emptiness is compassion that wells up automatically in every direction, you will unlock the treasure chest of the enlightened body and be able to benefit others. You will then have sown the seed for actualising the enlightened expression of the physical body. On the other hand, if you have been unable to give rise to unhindered compassion, you will not be able to work for the benefit of others and will have failed to sow the seeds for the actualisation of the enlightened body.[36]

(ii) Dawning of inner experience

At the initial stage of the yoga of one-flavouredness, you recognise ultimate reality but an element of clinging to experience remains. There will still be times during post-meditation when you find it difficult to use sensory impressions as part of your practice and you will still occasionally perceive things to have some inherent reality. The faint remnants of your karmic dispositions might occasionally give rise to deluded or confused dreams. At other times, you will have very good meditative experiences, thinking that there is total equanimity between body, sensory impressions, and mind. At this point, it is also possible for you to go through a period where your devotion weakens and compassion diminishes.

At the intermediate stage, you free yourself from thoughts of experiencer and experience and gain a unitary experience of phenomenal appearance and mind. There will be a dramatic drop in the frequency of your deluded dreams and you will be less likely to revert to perceiving things as intrinsically real. Your interpersonal relationships will also undergo changes because your actions will have more potential to impact on others for either good or ill.[37]

At the final stage, various experiences and sensory impressions continue to arise within your state of equanimity, but no matter what these are, you will no longer fixate on them. Having completely separated yourself from the belief in things having inherent existence, your understanding of non-duality will persist, even during sleep. Understanding will be present day and night, without any disruptions between the meditative and post-meditative states. You will find that there is no transitional point between one state and the other, because meditation will flow naturally into post-meditation. It is called a 'meditative continuum' for this reason. Your meditation is just like a river, where each section of the river is the same as every other section.

There will still be times when you do not have complete certainty and you experience things without fully comprehending them, but you will have no real fixation on your sensory impressions in post-meditation, so all of your experiences of the phenomenal world will have a sense of mental clarity and spaciousness.[38] However, a subtle form of dualistic thinking may still be present. You will continue to have dreams, but they will have become very light because you no longer cling to them. You may also have no dreams at all for significant periods of time. It is said that psychic powers can also develop at this point. You might also have visions where you communicate with male and female deities and the emotional affliction of jealousy will no longer arise.[39]

(iii) Maintaining this yoga

The yoga of one-flavouredness is maintained by relying on solitude the majority of the time. However, you should also be members of a community.[40] The way to maintain this yoga is generally not different from the previous one. You might start to think there is no difference between meditation and non-meditation, mindfulness and non-mindfulness, but these thoughts should be discouraged. Continue to rely on the use of mindfulness and do not become distracted.

At the initial and intermediate stages of one-flavouredness, you sometimes need to resort to auxiliary practices to increase your merit, generate humility, encourage pure perception, and foster compassionate attitudes and you may have come to rely on these skilful methods a great deal. If that is the case, you should now cut down on these auxiliary practices. Continue to work with situations that are workable and beneficial, without allowing yourself to get side-tracked by unhealthy situations. Never minimise the importance of engaging in wholesome and beneficial activities. Je Gomtsul says:

> When you realise non-duality
> You should not abandon wholesome deeds.
> Even if you realise non-meditation
> Do not cut off the feet of skilful deeds.
> When you realise actions require no acceptance or rejection
> Continue to bear responsibility for your actions.
> From fear, your actions may cause others to act unskilfully.
> If you realise there is no need for hope and fear
> It is still very important not to let conflicting emotions run wild.

Maintain a balance between the perspectives of the ultimate and relative truths in this way. It may happen that you are able to realise the final stage of one-flavouredness without experiencing any changes in your dealings with other people. You may still be ineffectual in that and experience none of the extraordinary or unusual psychic powers or visions that are regarded as signs of spiritual unfoldment. This can be caused by breaking your samaya vows or various contaminations from others. In such a situation, engage in the practice of confession and purification. There are many other helpful practices, such as making *tsa tsas* (small clay stupas), placing a flower in front of each one and saying this prayer, 'May I (so and so) be free of contaminations.' Other formulas can be recited in this context as well. You can also recite mantras that are designed to remove contaminations.

Having engaged in some of these curative practices, you might experience some evidence of their success. Do not indulge in elation when your practices succeed or fall into depression when they do not. Instead of attributing the cause of these failures or fluctuations to some kind of evil spirit, understand that they are nothing but constructions of your mind. Regenerate the conviction that all experiences are a creation of mind and that the nature of mind is spacious and open, just like the sky without centre or periphery. You will realise the yoga of one-flavouredness by maintaining this attitude.

If you have this attitude, you will have no fear of the unknown and no exaggerated forms of excitement; just a steady improvement and progress in your practice. If you practise in this way, you can never be corrupted. On the other hand, if you suddenly give rise to a proliferation of jealousy or some other conflicting emotions and experience mood swings during the yoga of one-flavouredness, you should not blame that on external situations or on the environment. Instead, think that a demon has taken hold of your mind.[41] Remind yourself of this, instead of allowing yourself to be carried away by extreme mental states. To relate to and cope with these mental states, make use of the auxiliary methods for creating merit. Everything that upsets your equilibrium should be treated as a demonic manifestation. Gampopa says:

> During the yoga of one-flavouredness, which is about seeing unity in multiplicity, do not spend too much time contemplating general meanings; contemplate your inner experiences.[42]

Tsangpa Gyare says:

> If you attain the initial stage of one-flavouredness,
> You should pray again and again,
> 'I wish to benefit others to alleviate their suffering.'
> It is important to have these aspirations,
> And to create favourable causes and conditions
> For accomplishing this task.[43]

Je Yanggonpa says:

The sensory impressions should be left alone;
Even though they are unceasing,
They will reveal themselves
As manifestations of ultimate reality.
If there is no fixation on the concept
Of things coming into or not coming into being;
The nature of reality will be revealed.
Without preventing phenomenal appearance
From coming into contact with mind,
But simply letting things be
Is how we rest in a meditative state.
Not indulging in conceptualisation;
Deluded thoughts and conflicting emotions,
Become self-liberated on the path.

You realise the yoga of one-flavouredness by ceasing to view phenomenal appearance as bad and by relinquishing your fixation on it. Your sensory impressions, phenomenal appearances, deluded thoughts, and emotional conflicts are not to be avoided; you simply relinquish fixation and clinging. This is what has to be understood. If you practise in this way, the pollution of meditative experiences will be cleared and the realisations you have accumulated will merge with the natural condition of your own being.

4. The yoga of non-meditation

(i) Differentiating the three stages

This yoga is called 'non-meditation' because there is no object of meditation in a very fundamental sense. There is no specific object of meditation because you have realised the authentic condition, you have apprehended ultimate reality. The *Kalachakra Tantra* says:

Because there is no specific object of meditation,
No meditation or meditator,
And no entity to be apprehended;
Meditation is devoid of images.

'Non-meditation' emphasises an approach without a meditator and with nothing to meditate on. It cuts through these dualistic concepts. Saraha says:

Our own natural condition has no origin

So how can we say there is anything to meditate upon?
Don't entertain thoughts of meditation
Or something to meditate upon.
These dualistic ways of thinking
Make you lose the enlightened mind.

Some people say, 'Simply overcoming certain dualistic ways of thinking will lead to the realisation of non-meditation.' If that were the case, we would realise non-meditation at the stage of the yoga of non-conceptuality, but that does not happen. The yoga of one-flavouredness could also be equated with the realisation of non-meditation by this logic. However, that is impossible. 'Non-meditation' means that even extremely subtle forms of dualism about meditation and meditator, which may have persisted throughout the path, have now vanished. No distinction whatsoever remains between meditation and post-meditation. Mindfulness or lack of mindfulness has also ceased to be an issue, because there is only realisation. All other concerns have dropped away. The essence of non-meditation is meditation without effort. The yoga of non-meditation is therefore effortless meditation. Savaripa says:

Anyone who attains realisation
No longer needs to be concerned
With meditation or meditator.
Just as we cannot imagine the sky to exist,
Emptiness cannot be an object of meditation.
Anyone who attains realisation
Experiences unceasing bliss,
All dualistic notions have blended into one
Like water mixed with milk.

Je Zhang says:

When we attain the yoga of non-meditation,
Awareness no longer has any support.
A real yogi has nothing to meditate on
So there is no meditator either.

The yoga of non-meditation is also divided into an initial, intermediate, and final stage. The initial stage is revealed when all sensory experiences become meditation, without your using mindfulness or cultivating a meditative state. You will have no notion of meditation or of being a meditator; you will just experience everything as illusion-like. There is a very subtle form of clinging to this experience at the initial stage.[44] However, at the intermediate stage, even that clinging has disappeared. The experience of meditation becomes a total one, whether asleep or awake, during the day or at night, you are established in real spontaneity. Whatever arises in the mind during post-meditation reveals itself to be self-transparent and luminous. The recognition that deluded thoughts and conflicting emotions are self-transparent and luminous is the attainment of the intermediate stage of non-meditation. When the faintest tiny stains of delusion and conflicting emotion automatically reveal themselves as wisdom, the merging of the mother and son luminosity takes place and you realise the final stage of non-meditation. Again, the six pairs of criteria can be used to determine your success with this yoga.

- Has ultimate reality been perceived or not?

You have perceived the true nature of non-meditation when you cease to need mindfulness or deliberately train in meditation and your experiences become purified by themselves. On the other hand, if you still think there is something to practise or train in or that the mind can be made more vivid and clear, you have failed to perceive the ultimate nature of this yoga.

- Has dexterity in the practice been developed or not?

Dexterity in the yoga of non-meditation is attained when you cease to be disturbed by even the most subtle dualistic thoughts and have no trace of uncertainty about your understanding of the nature of mind. You are no longer separate from wisdom and have complete dexterity in the practice of non-meditation. On the other hand, if you are still disturbed by subtle dualistic thoughts and retain some uncertainty about whether you have recognised the nature of mind, you have not developed dexterity in this practice.

- Have deluded thoughts been revealed as meditation or not?

When the storehouse consciousness reveals itself as fundamental wisdom, without your needing to reject anything, deluded thoughts have become meditation. On the other hand, when you apprehend your body, phenomenal appearances, and mind separately and retain some hidden and unresolved defilements and subtle fixation upon experience, you have failed to realise deluded thoughts as meditation.

- Have the necessary qualities been developed or not?

You have developed the necessary qualities of non-meditation when you see your physical body as a rainbow body and your mind as the luminous expression of the dharmakaya. Various multi-dimensional spiritual realms will be revealed to you through this realisation. On the other hand, if you are unable to see body and mind in this way and remain confined to your conventional view of the world as a container and beings as the contained, you are still constrained by a very subtle form of impure perception. If you have not managed to break out of this confinement, the necessary qualities of the yoga of non-meditation have not become manifest.

- Has full comprehension of empirical reality been attained or not?

You have a full comprehension of empirical reality if you can use various spiritual abilities, such as power, fearlessness, and so on to operate as an enlightened being in the world. On the other hand, if you are still subject to the idea that your body is a product of your karma, your experiences are a product of your karmic traces and dispositions, and your mind is a product of delusions, these defilements will obstruct your enlightened qualities. When you cannot make use of these qualities, you have failed to comprehend the workings of empirical reality.

- Have the seeds for actualising the rupakaya been sown or not?

When you realise that the sphere of reality and wisdom are inseparable and reveal themselves as a unity in the form of the dharmakaya, and when you can work for the benefit of others through your body, speech, and intention, you have actualised the enlightened expression of the physical body. On the other hand, if you still need to contemplate pure perception, without being able to see this very body and this very world in a different light, the actualisation of the enlightened expression of the physical body has not yet been achieved.

Meditators realise non-meditation in this way. To arrive at the final stage of the yoga of non-meditation is to attain full and complete enlightenment.[45] We can achieve this in our lifetime, although it is said we do not quite achieve complete enlightenment in this lifetime. But Tsangpa Gyare says:

> While non-meditation is the seat of dharmakaya, the non-meditation that in most cases is attained is not a complete state of realisation.

Je Gomtsul says:

> The yoga of one-pointedness is where we understand the mind. The yoga of non-conceptuality is where we understand the reality of

> emptiness. The yoga of one-flavouredness is where we understand the nature of phenomenal appearance. The yoga of non-meditation... that I do not understand!

Thus, he does not comment on non-meditation. Many of Je Phagmo Drupa's disciples claimed to have experienced the yoga of one-flavouredness. Gotsangpa, Tukju, and Orgyenpa also spoke about the intricacies and complexities of the yoga of one-flavouredness but they do not elaborate as much on the yoga of non-meditation. The reader should be warned that it is not easy to attain the fourth yoga. These days, when meditators claim to have realised one-flavouredness or non-meditation, many fail to appreciate the differences between these Four Yogas and lack sufficient understanding of them. They may claim to have achieved this or that yoga out of pride but you should not give too much credence to what they say.

(ii) Dawning of inner experience

At the initial stage of non-meditation, most of your dualistic thoughts have subsided and you have no need to deliberately employ mindfulness or make an effort to stay in meditation. Whatever phenomenal appearances you meet are revealed as meditation. Everything you experience will generally be an extension of the meditative state; you will not waver from that. In post-meditation, the mind might retain a certain element of uncertainty and suffer from a lack of mental clarity, which originates in the storehouse consciousness. Even though no new deluded thoughts are being generated in the storehouse consciousness because we now perceive it as neutral, our lack of clarity about phenomenal appearances is a subtle form of defilement that has not yet been uprooted from the storehouse consciousness. In post-meditation the nature of mind cannot possibly lead to the creation of fresh karma; however, whatever arises in the mind does not yet manifest as wisdom, so a very subtle residue of clinging may remain. It is also possible to cling to dream experiences as real because you have failed to recognise your dreams to be dreams.

At the intermediate stage, even the most subtle dualistic thoughts have been purified. You are now in a continual state of meditation day and night. Your meditation is total. In post-meditation, very subtle forms of uncertainty remain. Whatever arises in the mind will be vivid and clear, but there will still be a subtle form of defilement when you are awake and asleep.

At the onset of the final stage, you only experience certainty about everything. Even the most subtle defilements have either vanished or become wisdom and are revealed as inseparable from self-existing luminosity. Two different manifestations of luminosity now merge: self-existing luminosity and realisation luminosity. These are no different from the realisation of dharmakaya. The dharmakaya finds its expression in and through the nirmanakaya. This physical body manifests for the benefit of sentient beings, due to their karmic conditions, for as long as there is a need. As long as there is suffering, there will be the continuous manifestation of nirmanakayas as the physical expression of dharmakaya. This working for the benefit of others is accomplished spontaneously rather than deliberately.

(iii) Maintaining this yoga

The three stages of non-meditation are traditionally presented this way. We might ask, 'What kind of non-meditation can we realistically expect to attain in this life?' The answer would be realisation with the following characteristics: the conviction that your mind is the mind of enlightenment, with fundamentally nothing to reject as intrinsically bad and nothing to cultivate as intrinsically good. You no longer need to purify anything because defilement has no intrinsic existence and no method can purify something that has no reality. You will have no obsessive thoughts about death, mortality, or life because your meditation has become continuous and there is no longer any separation between meditation and post-meditation. Gampopa says:

> Don't pursue meditative experiences during non-meditation and do not hanker after them.

Even at this stage, it is important to remain unconcerned about meditative experiences and refrain from evaluating them. You should not think, 'this experience is good' and 'that experience is bad.' Most defilements feed off a mind that is devoid of attention and there is no better way to become more attentive than by employing mindfulness. You learn to remain focused by resting in a mindfulness that is not manufactured. Your task is to realise ordinary mind. There is hardly any difference in the way you maintain the yoga of one-flavouredness and the way that you maintain the yoga of non-meditation. Tsangpa Gyare says:

> The initial stage of non-meditation
> Is like the yoga of one-flavouredness;
> The way to maintain them is very similar.
> The best form of non-meditation
> Is the same as the enlightened state;
> Where there is no need for deliberation.

Je Yanggonpa says:

> Look closely and try to see
> The meditator and the object of meditation.
> Look closely at your awareness
> There is no duality there!
> If you relax in that state
> There will be bare awareness
> Without manufactured mindfulness.
> When that awareness is maintained
> You will meditate day and night.

To stay in non-meditation is to let go of thoughts about the object of meditation and meditator. Non-meditation is letting go of dualistic thoughts while maintaining awareness without support. This awareness is not attached to anything other than itself. You do not cultivate a manufactured mindfulness. Just allow bare awareness to be, without fixation. The way not to rely on manufactured mindfulness was described in detail in an earlier section of the text. The feeling of being in meditation day and night, which is associated with non-meditation, can also arise in the previous yogas; even at the level of one-pointedness. You might also have a sense of being without a meditator or meditation object on the yoga of non-conceptuality. Then at the level of one-flavouredness, whatever you meet may be revealed as meditation thereby eradicating any distinction between meditation and post-meditation. Nonetheless, the distinctive feature of the yoga of non-meditation is genuine realisation. All these experiences are only proximate experiences on the other yogas because they are tinged with meditative experiences and do not result in realisation. The genuine realisation of non-meditation has not occurred. It is very important to understand this and not assume that the realisation of non-meditation is present in the previous three yogas.

In conclusion, a full explanation of the Four Yogas should really be done from the standpoint of personal experience. However, that is not so easily done, especially for the later yogas. Since I have no personal experience of my own in these yogas, my task is made even more difficult. I have therefore relied on the experiences of previous lineage masters and stayed very close to the original writings of Gampopa, his major and minor disciples, and the writings of other mahasiddhas, all of whom are undisputed experts in the field of meditation. I have in fact devoted considerable space to a discussion of the yogas, more than is usual for meditation manuals. This was made possible by gathering the essential points from the existing meditation literature.

5. Their vital significance

The fundamental problem that we experience on the spiritual path is clinging to the notion of an independent, self-sufficient, and inherently existing self. As the *Ratnavali* says:

> As long as there is clinging to the notion of the self in relation to the psychophysical constituents...

The *Pramanavarttika* says:

> Whenever there is the belief in an immutable, unchanging 'self'
> There is the perception of an 'other.'

The *Bodhicharyavatara* says:

> All the harm and anguish of this world
> Is caused by clinging to an unchanging self.
> Our afflictions, fears and miseries
> Are all caused by this great devil.

The root of cyclic existence—the root of our state of confusion—lies in the dualistic notion of self and other. Until you can fully free yourself from this fixation on dualism all kinds of confusions will continue to arise in your mind and you will wander about endlessly in the samsaric condition. You might search for spiritual freedom, but if you fail to understand the cause of your negative patterns, conflicting emotions, and delusions, you will never be able to identify the real culprit for your lack of freedom, and despite your best intentions you will not deal with your delusions in a skilful way. For instance, you may try to engage in wholesome actions, resist engaging in harmful ones, familiarise yourself with the teachings, and contemplate spiritual matters, but you will incur no real profit from this. While it is obviously quite beneficial to engage in these things and it may go some way toward ameliorating your fixation on a self, these things will not be sufficient to help you to deal with habitual fixations.

You might think that since the notion of an unchanging, permanent self is the cause of your perilous state, it would be best to meditate on selflessness. You could then cultivate a frame of mind that is obsessed with preventing fixation on the self until you convince yourself that there is no self. However, instead of providing you with a proper insight into your real predicament, this approach will only lead to another form of fixation. This fixation on self-extinction is the other extreme to selfishness; it is the extreme of nihilism as opposed to eternalism. You must be very clear about what you are practising.

If you meditate without really understanding properly what the self is, you will only get lost in meditative experiences and deviate from the path. Many deviations are possible. Four types of errors and three types of deviations were discussed in a previous chapter. Failing to develop a proper understanding of the self and becoming fixated on your meditative experiences will only provide the grounds for the creation of fresh karma during post-meditation situations because you will not have overcome your clinging. You will thereby only perpetuate the samsaric condition. The real key to successful meditation is therefore to relinquish fixation. Saraha says:

> If we become attached to meditative experiences,
> Cherish them, and hold them close to our hearts;
> It will cause further disturbances,
> Even if that attachment is very small.

He also says:

> People who hold onto the notion that self has an enduring essence
> Are as deluded as cattle.
> People who hold onto the notion of there being no self at all
> Are more deluded still.

Again, he says:

> Whatever you are fixated on; let that go.

You should think constantly about relinquishing any forms of grasping, clinging, craving, and fixation to meditative experiences. You can expect to have all kinds of experiences in meditation for two reasons. Firstly, there are many different meditations that we can do, such as meditations with sign which involve visualisations, and meditations without sign where there is nothing to visualise, and different meditative experiences are associated with each technique. Secondly, each person has his or her own karmic history and all kinds of experiences are possible based upon that history. Whatever the case, the important thing is to learn to let go. That is the best method of all that we can use on the path. Gampopa says:

> All kinds of experiences arise on the path of meditation, but there is no better method for making progress on that path than not latching onto anything.

The ability to let go is what will enable our karmic traces and dispositions to resolve themselves. Whatever we experience due to our karmic inheritance will be purified and our deluded thoughts and conflicting emotions will be liberated as soon as they arise. There will be no time for them to corrupt our minds. The simultaneous self-liberation of deluded thoughts and conflicting emotions can occur precisely because nothing that arises in mind can create a disturbance or sow karmic seeds if we do not latch onto it. All of our sensory impressions, physical experiences, and conceptual phenomena will then be revealed as an expression of our own authentic state. Gampopa says:

> Most of what you experience
> Comes from your karmic inheritance.
> When you become acquainted with letting go,
> There is no need to deliberately abandon or renounce anything.
> Holding onto things only strengthens fixation.
> If you can let things go,
> It does not matter what arises in your mind;
> It will be liberated at that instant.

He also says:

> When we cease to hold onto things,
> Anything and everything can arise in the mind,
> Without having a defiling impact on our mental continuum.

Again, he says:

> When mind is free of dualistic thoughts,
> Anything and everything can arise in it.
> Instead of creating delusions,
> It is revealed as an expression of our authentic state.

Furthermore, he says:

> If you do not hang onto anything
> Deluded thoughts are self-liberated at their inception.
> Without craving or clinging
> Everything remains in a state of equanimity.
> When this is understood
> Meditation will be continuous.
> This is the best form of phowa[46]
> Because birth and death are not experienced
> In our authentic state.
> When we have no fixation on anything,

> There is only the continuous manifestation of luminosity.

The explanation for achieving self-liberation by renouncing our mental fixation is as follows. Abandon dualistic fixation on an unchanging, permanent, and immutable self and on an unchanging, permanent, and immutable other. This will dismantle your mistaken belief in the psychophysical constituents being the locus of the self. When you realise that the psychophysical constituents have no essence, your conflicting emotions will cease to operate. When the conflicting emotions cease to operate, liberation is achieved. The *Mulamadhyamikakarika* says:

> When we relinquish thoughts of self and other,
> We cease to cling to the skandhas
> As the locus of the self,
> And all conflicting emotions
> And delusory thoughts subside.

This is why our meditation texts place such an emphasis on non-fixation, non-clinging, non-grasping, objectlessness, signlessness, directionlessness, non-rejection, non-cultivation, non-abandonment, and freedom from hope and fear. These concepts all make the same point. You must become acquainted with methods for achieving non-fixation and so on. The Four Yogas should also be cultivated with that understanding. Whatever level of yoga you are practising, try to stay with it without wavering and without becoming too fixated on experiences that are associated with it. An attitude of non-clinging, non-grasping, and non-fixation should be maintained at all times.

THE FOUR YOGAS AND THE MAHAYANA PATHS AND STAGES

If we compare the Four Yogas of Mahamudra to the general Mahayana approach, we might ask, 'Is there a match between the Paths and Stages of Sutra and the Four Yogas of Mahamudra?' There are no extant writings of Gampopa and his disciples that explicitly explain this point but later masters, such as Tuchen Shang, have said the Four Yogas can be matched up with the Paths and Stages of Sutra.[47] Tuchen Shang says:

> The Mahamudra journey is an instantaneous one
> So we cannot really speak about its paths and stages.
> However, people of limited understanding
> Like to think of everything in these terms.

To satisfy the hearts of the confused
The Sutric Paths and Stages
Can be matched with the Four Yogas.

Tuchen Shang calls Mahamudra an instantaneous path because there is no separating it from our authentic state. Our authentic state is Mahamudra. We cannot divide this authentic state into levels or stages because it is a state of complete totality. The authentic state is therefore indivisible from its own side, so it cannot be understood in terms of paths and stages from the perspective of ultimate reality. A commentary on the *Madhyamakavatara* says:

> From its own side, as it exists within itself, so ultimate reality is indivisible and devoid of empirical characteristics.

It also says:

> Since ultimate reality is devoid of empirical characteristics, it cannot be seen. It is not something we can speak about. This is not just true for ordinary beings; even enlightened beings cannot describe it. There is nothing to be described.

The *Sphutartha* says:

> In the Sutric teachings, there is no such thing as seeing or meditating upon the 'path of seeing' when emptiness is realised. No separation can be made between the path of seeing, the path of meditation, and so on.

Why so? Ultimate reality is not something that can be divided from its own side. We can however speak about paths and stages in relation to our individual experiences and levels of comprehension. The descriptions of the Paths and Stages can be enlightening for anyone who is confused about how to approach practice. The Sutric Paths and Stages and the Four Yogas of Mahamudra should be seen as complementary in this way. The *Sphutartha* says:

> The realisation of ultimate reality that takes place on the yoga of non-conceptuality corresponds to the Sutric path of seeing, and the first bodhisattva *bhumi* called 'stage of joy.' The yoga of one-flavouredness corresponds to the path of meditation and the yoga of non-meditation corresponds to the path of no more learning, which is the same as buddhahood.

The non-dual perception of ultimate reality is equivalent to attaining the first bodhisattva bhumi on the path of seeing.[48] As we become more familiar with that non-dual perception, we will embark on the path of meditation, which encompasses the second to tenth bodhisattva bhumis. The path of non-meditation equates with buddhahood and the eleventh bodhisattva bhumi. The yoga of non-conceptuality, the path of seeing, and the first bodhisattva bhumi are the same. By implication, the yoga of one-pointedness equates with the Sutric path of application, even though it is not explicitly stated here. Tsangpa Gyare says:

> We should not be too concerned about the Paths and Stages,
> But if we wish to think about our meditation practice
> In relation to conventional Mahayana teachings;
> The ngondro practices of mandala offerings and so on
> Correspond to the path of accumulation.
> The arising of meditative experiences
> Corresponds to the path of application.
> The yoga of non-conceptuality
> Corresponds to the path of seeing.
> The occurrence of realisation
> Corresponds to the path of meditation.
> The experience of one-flavouredness
> Corresponds to the eighth bodhisattva bhumi.
> The yoga of non-meditation
> Corresponds to the eleventh bodhisattva bhumi,
> Which is the path of no more learning.[49]

Tsangpa Gyare even includes the ngondro practice in this verse, saying ngondro and other practices that accumulate merit and reduce defilements are to be equated with the path of accumulation. He also equates the advanced stages of the yoga of one-pointedness with the path of application, the yoga of non-conceptuality with the path of seeing, the realisation of non-duality up to the third stage of yoga of one-flavouredness with the path of meditation, and the initial and intermediate stage of non-meditation with the ninth and tenth bodhisattva bhumis. The final stage of non-meditation is equated with the eleventh bodhisattva bhumi, or buddhahood. This corresponds to the final Sutric path of no more learning. Je Gotsangpa says:

> The path of accumulation is the preparatory stage. The yoga of one-pointedness is therefore equated with the path of accumulation and the path of application. The yoga of non-conceptuality is equated with the path of seeing and the first bodhisattva bhumi.

> The yoga of one-flavouredness is equated with the second to seventh bodhisattva bhumis on the path of meditation. The first two stages of the yoga of non-meditation are equated with the remaining three bodhisattva bhumis on the path of meditation. The final stage of non-meditation is equated with the path of no more learning, which is the eleventh bhumi of buddhahood.

I personally feel there is a slight difference between the Sutric approach and the Four Yogas of Mahamudra. The primary characteristic of the Sutric method is the notion of paths and stages while the Mahamudra tradition is known as the authentic or uncontrived path and its defining characteristic is the emphasis on meditation. From the ultimate point of view, there is no difference between the Sutric Paths and Stages and the Four Yogas of Mahamudra because their final goal is the same. However, from the point of view of practice, there is a difference. One of the most fundamental differences is their respective time frames. The Sutric teachings encourage practitioners to delay their enlightenment so they can work for the benefit of others. The Mahayana attitude is that we resist the urge to attain enlightenment quickly. It is said we should spend up to three countless aeons before we attain the eleventh bhumi of buddhahood. The Mahamudra attitude is rather different. We do not try to delay enlightenment. We have to think we can attain enlightenment at any time if the circumstances are favourable. It does not have to take us such a long time to achieve that goal. This is also true of ordinary paths and roads where we have both main thoroughfares and side streets.

If we match the Four Yogas with the Sutric Paths and Stages with this understanding in mind, we could say the three stages of the yoga of one-pointedness correspond to the path of accumulation. The three stages of the yoga of non-conceptuality correspond to the path of application. The three stages of the yoga of one-flavouredness and the first two stages of the yoga of non-meditation correspond to the path of seeing and the path of meditation. This covers all ten bodhisattva bhumis. The final stage of non-meditation corresponds to the path of no more learning, which is the bhumi of buddhahood.

This seems the best approach to matching the Four Yogas with the Sutric Paths and Stages. It was mentioned earlier that the transition from the final stage of the yoga of one-flavouredness to the initial stage of yoga of non-meditation is not clear-cut. One stage flows into the other without a clear demarcation line. It is also difficult to draw a line between the final stage of the yoga of non-conceptuality and the initial stage of one-flavouredness. This has to be acknowledged.

Nonetheless, if we take into account the differences between the twelve stages of the Four Yogas and rely on the available meditation instructions, we could safely say there is no unitive experience of one-flavouredness during the initial stage of the yoga of non-conceptuality. Therefore, someone on the initial stage of non-conceptuality would not have a full understanding of ultimate reality so we cannot comfortably equate the yoga of non-conceptuality with the path of seeing and the attainment of the first bodhisattva bhumi. Further study is needed to clarify these differences and meditation experts should pay some attention to this area. That is just my personal feeling.

Other people may object, on the grounds that this statement is contrary to what past masters such as Tsangpa Gyare, Gotsangpa, and so on have said. This difference of opinion poses no real problem because the past masters were referring to a completed form of the yoga of non-conceptuality in their comparisons. For example, complete one-flavouredness is realised when we have no fixation on the meditative experiences associated with it. Some people have objected to the correlation of our lineage, saying it is very difficult to assess experiences on the yoga of non-conceptuality when we are trying to equate all three of its stages with the path of seeing. These critics say:

> One-pointedness, non-conceptuality,
> One-flavouredness, and non-meditation are the Four Yogas.
> The yoga of one-pointedness
> Should be equated with the path of seeing.
> The yoga of non-conceptuality
> Should be equated with the first to seventh bhumis.
> The yoga of one-flavouredness
> Should be equated with the three highest bhumis.
> While the yoga of non-meditation
> Is the ground of buddhahood.

I have seen no writings by past masters to support this claim. Maybe there are such texts. Even if there are, they would not contradict the way we have related the Four Yogas to the Sutric teachings here. No text in existence could contradict the way the Four Yogas have been correlated to the Sutric Paths and Stages by past masters of the Practice Lineage because no sutras or tantras invalidate that comparison. The way this critic marries the Sutric Paths and Stages with the Four Yogas does not gel, because there is no textual support for such a claim. Other people have stated:

> While we can embark on the path of seeing in this life,
> The qualities of that path will only be realised in the hereafter.

This assertion is also quite unfounded and is made by people who do not fully understand the teachings. These people are effectively arguing that we may embark on the path of seeing but we will fail to realise the qualities of that path. There is no textual support for the claim we should automatically realise the qualities of the path of seeing as soon as we embark on that path. If that were the case, a woman who realises the path of seeing would automatically assume the body of a 'universal king' or *chakravartin*. If we were expected to attain all the qualities of the path of seeing as soon as we embarked on that path, we would have to say many Indian and Tibetan masters and even the Buddha's own immediate disciples, did not embark on the path of seeing because they did not display all of the qualities of the path of seeing. The *Dasabhumika Sutra* says:

> A bodhisattva is likely to be reborn as a chakravartin once he or she attains the first bhumi. If he then goes through the process of renouncing home, entering the wilderness, and meditating, he is likely to finally attain buddhahood.

Other people say that the enlightened mind is like the egg of a garuda, which has the infant garuda trapped inside it. We may realise the nature of mind to be the same as our authentic state but not have the capacity to manifest our great buddha qualities in this life because we have not achieved release from bondage to our body and karmic inheritance. Nevertheless, we will become completely freed of such restrictions at the time of death, at which time the luminous nature of mind will be fully experienced and we will assume the illusory body of a sambhogakaya manifestation. Thus it has been said.

There are also people who object to this assertion and who compare it to saying 'the sun shone today but will not illuminate anything until tomorrow.' This objection is obviously wrong, precisely because most Tantric teachings say that we realise our authentic state as dharmakaya at the time of death and assume the body of nirmanakaya in the bardo. The *Caturdeviparipeccha* says:

> When this physical karmic body disintegrates,
> Our spiritual power will reconstitute
> That body in its nirmanakaya form.
> It will then permeate stillness as well as movement
> The way space encompasses everything.
> Understand that it remains that way.

The *Samputa Tantra* says:

> When the physical body in its conventional form is overcome

That very body becomes the body of a god or goddess.

Opponents who objected to the previous example would fall foul of these Tantric teachings. Je Zhang says:

Even when you recognise the non-dual nature of ultimate reality
Don't expect all suffering and misery to immediately disappear
Or to develop all the qualities of an enlightened being.
Even if you attain the path of seeing
You may not be able to display all the qualities of that path;
Yet who could deny you have attained it?
When the early morning sun shines
But fails to melt the ice or warm the earth
No one denies the sun exists.

The immediate realisation of the path of seeing does not automatically mean all the qualities of the first bhumi will become manifest in full force. For example, the moon that is barely visible is still the moon, a child that is very small is still a human being and a lion cub is still a lion. Just because all the qualities of realisation are not on full display does not mean we have not had that realisation. Tsangpa Gyare says:

Even amongst the shravakas there are two kinds of beings:
Some are flamboyant and some are simple.
Even amongst the bodhisattvas there are two kinds of beings:
Some are famous and some are anonymous.
Even amongst the tantrikas there are two kinds of beings:
Some practise in secret and some in public.
Even in terms of realisation there are two kinds of insight:
One that is expressible and one that is demonstrable.
The paths, stages, and their qualities
Are contingent upon the meditators;
On their level of training and the power of that training.
This will determine whether a meditator
Is able to perform extraordinary feats
And work for the benefit of others or not.
Some bodhisattvas fulfil the needs of sentient beings
And others fail to fulfil them.
This is due to the quality of their practice.

In brief, the Sutric teachings have Paths and Stages but there will always be differences in the attainments of individuals. There are flamboyant shravakas and simple shravakas, famous bodhisattvas and anonymous bodhisattvas. From the perspective of the Four Yogas, your progress and accomplishments will mostly depend upon the type of person you are, your level of training, the power of that training, and your ability to effect the things in this life. If you wish to achieve the sublime power of transformation, you must work hard on both the worldly path and the sublime path of Tantra.

This completes my explanation of the Mahamudra meditation of ultimate certainty, the differentiations between each of the Four Yogas, and the methods for crossing the Paths and Stages of buddhahood.

Footnotes

Introduction

1 This is not a philosophical debate about whether there is a material world out there or not. If we reflect on this, we will see that what we thought to be completely objective and independent of the mind is inextricably bound up with our attitudes, concepts, and ways of perceiving things. Unless the mind has become completely purified of defilements, we cannot have an objective view of the world.

2 The world exists as a network of relationships, where everything is dependent upon everything else; nothing can exist by itself. Buddhism makes a distinction between 'things as they appear' (*snang lugs*) to the mind and 'things as they are' (*gnas lugs*) in reality. We instinctively think objects in the external world are independent of mind and are solid and self-existing entities but that is not how things are in reality. Things exist in a state of interrelationship to everything including mind. Mind and the external world have the same nature.

3 Karmic traces and dispositions (*vasanas, bag chags*) are the habitual tendencies that are stored in our unconscious minds.

4 Three states of enlightenment: shravakas, bodhisattvas, and buddhas.

BOOK ONE

2 Common Tranquillity and Insight

1 Tashi Namgyal is referring to meditation in retreat situation here, where we are discouraged from worrying too much about ultimate or relative truth. Thinking about the two levels of truth and inter-relatedness during meditation can lead to distraction. It is the same with practising medicine and astrology or associating with monks and lay people. These activities may lead to distraction and result in a loss of concentration. Tashi Namgyal is obviously not saying meditators should not do these things at all, but if you engage in them during serious practice situations, they might disturb your tranquillity.

2 Teachings that expound the reality of things are called definitive teachings

(*nitartha, nges don*) because they have direct meaning and should be taken literally. Teachings that expound conventional meanings are called interpretive teachings (*neyartha, drang don*) because they require interpretation and cannot be taken literally. For example, some sutras say that you can attain enlightenment by reciting mantras for a period of time. If such statements could be taken literally, attaining enlightenment would be easy. Sutras only say these things because some people do not have the time or capacity to devote to study and meditation. Conventional teachings are sometimes called *thar bstan* in Tibetan, where *thar* means 'to liberate' and *bstan* meaning 'teachings given with that intention.' These teachings do not contain the ultimate truth. The *Jataka Tales* are *thar bstan*. For example, they contain a story about the Buddha in a previous lifetime, when he manifested as a tigress who sacrificed herself for the sake of her cubs. This story has to be interpreted as a metaphor for the importance of compassion, which can instil spiritual aspirations in those who hear it. They are wonderful stories, but they do not represent the way things actually are. People have different needs, but if you are serious about spiritual matters, you should pay attention to definitive teachings.

3 Dullness comes about from getting caught up in mental proliferation and losing your concentration, not from the moral issues behind your judging mind. It is important to put your judgemental mind to rest when you meditate. You should not analyse whether something is wholesome or unwholesome, worthy or unworthy because that will only generate more confusion and you will lose your mental clarity.

4 The Four Noble Truths (*chatur-arya-satya, bden pa rnam bzhi*) are the truth of suffering (*duhkha-satya, sdug bsngal gyi bden pa*), the truth of the origin of suffering (*samudaya-satya, kun 'byung gi bden pa*), the truth of its cessation (*nirodha-satya, 'gog pa'i bden pa*) and the truth of the path (*marga-satya, lam-gyi bden pa*). The basic orientation of any Buddhist practice has to be grounded in the context of these Four Noble Truths. What is a satisfying life? What gives meaning to life? You have to answer, 'A satisfying life is a happy life' and then ask yourself what kind of happiness you should be looking for. Overcoming defilements and obscurations is all about finding happiness. It allows us to understand that when we think we are seeking happiness, we are actually bringing harm to ourselves most of the time. The conventional self is not something to be disregarded. The Four Noble Truths are based on the assumption that our experiences are important and show us the way toward happiness and away from suffering. How else could we conceive of going through the process of recognising suffering, finding where that suffering originates, looking at the possibilities of its cessation, and finally embarking on the noble eightfold path

that leads to nirvana? All this is possible because the relative existence of a self is never denied in Buddhism. What is denied are the various misconceptions that we hold about a hypothetical or metaphysical self. These are notions that no two people from different intellectual backgrounds can ever agree upon.

5 The attitude of the shravakas is selfish because they are only interested in improving their own existential condition. If a bodhisattva becomes self-centred and inward looking, he has fallen from his original aim and become distracted. A bodhisattva's attitude degenerates from a concern with the benefit of others to a concern with one's own benefit.

6 Dullness (*styana, rmugs pa*) and mental agitation (*auddhatya, rgod pa*) constantly recreate each other because we are always swinging from one extreme to the other. These obstacles are returned to in Book Two.

7 There is no reason to stop meditating just because you are tired. However, if mental dullness or stupor keep on repeating themselves, no matter how hard you try to concentrate during meditation, you should discontinue the session. Forcing yourself to meditate will only lead to further obstacles. You have to cultivate a concentrated mind with a firm but gentle discipline, without trying too hard or allowing the mind to become too loose. You should make a disciplined effort to meditate regularly and consistently without pushing too hard. You can try different things to alleviate the obstacles. If you feel drowsy, you can correct your posture and make sure you are eating the right amount of food. If you feel agitated, you should concentrate more on your buttocks and hips to help yourself feel more grounded. You can also narrow your eyes a little. If you feel drowsy, you should concentrate more on your shoulders and head and straighten your spine, expand your chest and open your eyes wide. The lighting can also make a difference, if the light is too bright in the room it can generate agitation and if it is too dim, it can lead to stupor and dullness. Too much cold may make you prone to agitation and too much warmth may make you prone to dullness. What we really need is a perfect world.

8 This is the title for a collection of four texts by Asanga, including the *Bodhisattvabhumi*.

9 Pliancy of body and mind (*prasrabdhi, shin sbyangs*) is also translated as 'perfect ease.'

10 The six transcendental actions (*paramitas, pha rol tu phyin pa drug*) are generosity (*dana, sbyin pa*), moral discipline (*sila, tshul khrims*), patience (*ksanti, bzod pa*), vigour (*virya, brston 'grus*), concentration (*dhyana, bsam gtan*), and discriminative awareness (*prajna, shes rab*).

11 The nine stages of tranquillity meditation, which consist of deepening stages of meditative equipoise, are discussed at length in chapter three.

12 The primary afflictions are the five poisons of pride, jealousy, desire, anger, and ignorance. The secondary afflictions are all the other mental conflicts that arise from those basic poisons, such as spite, resentment, covetousness, and so on. All mental afflictions are related to pride, jealousy, anger, and desire. Ignorance is not really an emotional affliction; it is the precondition for the emotional afflictions.

13 Our temporal goal is improving ourselves as human beings and our ultimate goal is enlightenment.

3 Common Tranquillity Meditation

1 Analytical meditation (*vicara-bhavana, dpyad bsgom*) is a form of insight meditation (*vipashyana, lhag mthong*) and is conceptual by nature.

2 The text lists hair and hole separately, but if you put them together, that is what you get.

3 The five psychophysical constituents (*panca-skandha, phung po lnga*) are consciousness (*vijnana-skandha, rnam shes kyi phung po*), feeling (*vedana-skandha, tshor ba'i phung po*), habitual dispositions (*samskara-skandha, 'du byed kyi phung po*), perceptual experience (*samjna-skandha, 'du shes kyi phung po*), and the physical body (*rupa-skandha, gzugs kyi phung po*).

4 The eighteen spheres (*dhatu, kham*) include six sense organs (eye, ear, nose, tongue, body, and mind), six sense consciousnesses (eye-consciousness, ear-consciousness, nose-consciousness, tongue-consciousness, tactile-consciousness, and mental-consciousness) and six objects of consciousness (form, sound, smell, taste, touch, and phenomena of composite and non-composite things).

5 The twelve interdependent links (*dvadasa-pratityasamutpada, rten 'brel bcu gnyis*): 1) ignorance, 2) karmic formations, 3) consciousness, 4) mind-body complex, 5) six sense fields, 6) contact, 7) sensory impressions, 8) craving, 9) clinging, 10) becoming, 11) rebirth, 12) decay, old age, and death.

6 We begin with the deliberate and focused practice of mindfulness until we start automatically to catch ourselves becoming distracted or drowsy through repeated practice. This is the process of awareness. Awareness is like an alarm system that immediately alerts you to whatever is happening. It has none of the deliberate effort of going back to the object of meditation or of trying to stay focused. You just relax and allow whatever comes up to arise, but as soon as distraction sets in, you automatically become aware of it. Awareness increases through the practise of mindfulness. The basic idea is not to get caught up in thoughts.

7 Meditative concentration (*samadhi, ting nge 'dzin*) is a state of undistracted concentration or undivided meditative equipoise. However, even when we are absorbed in meditative concentration, the mental flow of consciousness has not totally ceased. Subtle forms of mental activity are still taking place allowing us to

be aware of objects and making the mind vulnerable to the occasional disturbance. However, the mind will largely remain in a state of mental equilibrium.

8 It is not essential to attain all nine stages of tranquillity to attain enlightenment. Even if you do attain the ninth stage of tranquillity, you may still be a scoundrel. If you do not practise shamatha in conjunction with vipashyana, you will not develop the qualities necessary for enlightenment. You may even lose interest in meditation altogether, because you have become so absorbed in concentration. The power of concentration will help enormously when you engage in insight meditation however, because it is easy to get distracted when using concepts in your meditation, if you do not have a stable mental state. This is why shamatha is so important, not because shamatha by itself will lead to any great spiritual realisation.

4 Common Insight Meditation

1 The third type of insight is the proper one because it arises from understanding the true nature of things.

2 We have to rely on tranquillity meditation when we engage in insight meditation, because we are trying to use concepts to break everything down. We normally just solidify things even more when we use concepts. When we use concept to break down the rigidity of our conceptual worldview, we are using them in a meditative way and we need a basis in shamatha meditation to do that. It is not true that concepts and meditation do not go together; it is just that we normally have no control over our thoughts, concepts, and ideas. It is imperative that we gain this control.

3 The nature of mind (*sems nyid*) is to be distinguished from the deluded consciousness (*sems*), which gives rise to the mental events (*sems byung*) that seize on specific objects of experience. The nature of mind is a key Mahamudra concept, which will become apparent throughout the remainder of the text.

4 Buddhism does not say we must get rid of ego, it says we should overcome our mistaken notions of ego. We mistakenly think something exists over and above our psychophysical constituents. That idea of ego is a myth; it does not exist. If we think of ourselves as composite phenomena, we still have an identity. It is just not an abiding and permanent one. That is one reason why it is possible for all of us to become enlightened. We may currently experience enormous difficulties, be afflicted by anxiety, depression, and fear, and fail to display any qualities of enlightenment whatsoever, but we can aspire to that state because we do not have any fixed psychic principle. If our true nature were fixed, it would be impossible to attain buddhahood. Buddhism has an elastic view of the ego, which makes our whole existence very flexible.

5 The 'selflessness of persons' (*pudgala-atman, gang zag gi bdag pa*) is distinguished from the 'selflessness of phenomena' (*dharma-atman, chos kyi bdag pa*). While the shravakas of early Buddhism realised the former, it is said that they did not realise the latter, or at least not to the same extent as a bodhisattva does. The Mahayana path emphasises the emptiness of both self and phenomena, while the so-called Hinayana only emphasised the selflessness of persons.

6 Without the methods of insight meditation, it will be extremely difficult to appreciate the insubstantiality of self or ego, because our instinctual belief in that self is so strong. We cannot say, 'If I meditate for long enough, I will just realise the insubstantiality of ego.' It does not work that way. We have to make a deliberate and consistent effort to see through this illusion. What does it mean to say, 'The self is a composite thing?' or 'There is no unified thing called self?' If you use concepts to dismantle those ideas, what have you done? You have gradually liberated yourself from the tyranny of this notion of a self. You have demolished the concept of self and ego through analysis, by working out the relationship between self and your own experiences and you will gradually gain a conceptual understanding of the self as a composite phenomenon.

7 The fourfold reasoning (*catuskoti, mtha' bzhi*) comes from Nagarjuna's *Mulamadhyamikakarika*, which says, 'A thing does not arise from itself, from other, from both itself and other or from neither self nor other.' If a rice seed could produce itself without dependence upon other external causes or conditions, it should be able to give rise to itself at all times and in any circumstances. If rice were produced from something other than a rice seed, anything could give rise to anything else. A rock could give rise to rice or darkness could come from light. There must be a homogeneous relationship between cause and effect. If rice could come from both itself and other, we would have the same problems and if rice could arise from no cause at all, it would mysteriously come into existence from nowhere. Some people say the soul has no cause and has simply come into being of its own accord. How is that possible? Anything that has come into existence must at one time have not existed. It must also go out of existence again at some point. It is therefore impossible by definition for something eternal to have been created at some point in time. This fourfold reasoning is meant to establish the notion of emptiness; that things can only arise from many inter-related and inter-linked causes and conditions. Everything arises because of dependent origination (*pratityasamutpada, rten 'drel*). Some people argue that the world has come into being because a divine being produced it. If you apply this logic, you have to ask, 'If God is the cause and the world is the effect, how come this creation is not continuous? Why did an act of creation come about and then stop?'

8 We are attempting to overcome conceptual proliferations (*vikalpa, rnam rtog*),

not concepts themselves. When we think about something, it only gives rise to more thoughts about that thing, which gives rise to even more thoughts. We just cannot stop; our thoughts breed like rabbits. One concept begets five concepts and those five concepts beget ten more and so on. This only generates confusion, which is what we need to overcome. The way these concepts and thoughts manifest is the obstacle because they are polluted or defiled by our desires, anxiety, anger, resentment, and so on. If we were free from these afflicted emotions, we would have no trouble with our thoughts and concepts. It is only when we consolidate and solidify concepts, such as the notion of pure ego, that we encounter problems. These ideas are constructed out of fear and anxiety; the fear of losing our identity or of becoming non-existent.

9 Letting the mind rest in its own natural state (*sems nyid ngal so*) is a key term in Mahamudra meditation and will be returned to in book two.

10 Phenomenal appearances are said to be illusion-like (*sgyu ma lta bu'i*) because of their insubstantial nature. They are not however said to be actual illusions, only to have the appearance of an illusion.

11 We may have some experience when we are engaged in purely intellectual activity, but that has nothing to do with meditative experience. The intellectual way of thinking is a discursive and extremely crystallised one, which separates subject from object, knower from known. A meditative way of thinking breaks down or overcomes the separation between subject and object. You are not necessarily aiming for objective knowledge, such as you would be within the scientific sphere; you are trying to find meaning in life. This thinking is not undertaken for excitement or mental stimulation, but it is absolutely essential for understanding what it means to be a human being.

5 Misconceptions About Common Meditation

1 The Mahamudra view is that while we must use analysis to establish a proper view, it is not necessary to employ in-depth analysis. While that is for scholars, and there is no need for meditators to be scholars, meditation is as necessary for scholars as analysis is for meditators. Meditators who do not use any analysis fall into subjectivism because they only have their own experience to rely on and that could very well be deluded. There is no way of verifying or validating our own subjective position. If we practise analysis in conjunction with meditation, we can validate our experiences and make sure that we have proper understanding. Having proper understanding is therefore just as important as having direct experience.

2 Analysis (*vicara, dpyod pa*) helps us to experience certain things. While that experience is direct and non-conceptual, it would not have manifested if you had

not analysed things beforehand. Without analysis, all you have are experiences that you cannot validate. You do not know whether they are delusory experiences or not. Some people think that they are experiencing emptiness when nothing is happening in the mind but that is incorrect. If you do not read and think about meditative experiences, you will not necessarily know if your experiences are deluded. You might very well think you had a direct experience of selflessness or emptiness just because your mind was devoid of mental processes. Only analysing and having a conceptual knowledge of these things will enable you to know what the experience of emptiness means.

3 The integration of tranquillity and insight meditation is extraordinarily important in the Mahamudra tradition. You can use a certain amount of analysis in tranquillity meditation but not the kind of analysis you would employ in Madhyamaka exercises.

4 Direct perception (*pratyaksa, mngon sum*) is a form of inference (*anumana, rjes dpag*), according to Buddhist logic (*pramana, tshad ma*). While we do come to understand the nature of emptiness through reasoning in this way, reasoning can only provide us with a conceptual understanding of emptiness because it is only based upon inference. There are therefore two extreme approaches we can take: the path of quietude, which claims the cessation of thought leads to realisation, and the path of logic, which claims that reasoning leads to an understanding of reality. Atisha and Gampopa are saying that reasoning alone will not lead to an understanding of emptiness and nor will Hwashang's quietest approach.

5 These versions of reality are known as a 'non-affirming negation' (*prasajya-pratisedha, med dgag*) and an 'affirming negation' (*paryudasa-pratisedha, ma yin dgag*).

6 Tashi Namgyal is making a distinction between conditioned experiences and unconditioned realisations. However, unconditioned is not a good description in this context. Realisations are irreversible but experiences are not. Experiences can be positive or negative, but realisations are always wholesome. Experiences are determinate in that you have an experience 'of something.' Realisations are indeterminate; they are not realisations of any particular thing so much as an encompassing state. We are also conditioned by our experiences, dispositions, and idiosyncrasies, but realisation is universal. The understanding of emptiness or ultimate reality is universal, while experiences are articulated or alluded to by specific individuals. Our meditative experiences will therefore be unique even though we may be doing the same practices as everybody else.

7 Many people say meditation should lead to a state of absorption. The Buddhist tradition also lists different levels of absorption but these absorptions have no real spiritual values. Many Tibetans criticised the early form of Zen Buddhism,

represented by the Chinese master Hwashang Mahayana, because they thought he was merely practicing these absorptions and cultivating a mind that is devoid of mental activity as the state of enlightenment. However, history has shown that this was not actually Hwashang's position. His critics simply imposed a certain view on him and then criticised that view. Tashi Namgyal does not feel there are any grounds for their criticism because Hwashang never subscribed to that view. Nonetheless, certain Zen masters in the West seem to emphasise an absence of thought in meditation so the basis for this criticism is and must have been a reality amongst some meditators.

8 This refers to the Gelugpa meditation system established by Tsongkhapa (1357–1419).

9 To fixate on emptiness is to adopt the nihilistic view. If we operate in the world with this nihilistic view, we may develop a complete disregard for morality, because if nothing ultimately has enduring essence, anything is permissible. The middle view is to understand that while the nature of everything lacks inherent existence, this does not mean nothing exists. All religious and metaphysical systems posit views of the world that are meant to comfort us. The world may be impermanent, illusory or even non-existent, but they say there is some greater reality hidden behind it all, which is unchanging, perfect, and enduring. The Madhyamaka view is the complete opposite of that. To realise emptiness is not to realise some occult reality hidden behind our everyday experiences of the world. To realise the nature of the world in which we live is to realise emptiness. Religion and philosophy have this preoccupation with looking for an ideal world, but this is a complete contradiction to the world we know. This may be called God or the absolute, but it is always presented as a mechanism of comfort for life's transiency. They all share the notion that whatever is eternal and unchanging is good and whatever is impermanent and transient is bad. The Buddhist view is that we should embrace the idea of impermanence and insubstantiality rather than seek for some overriding occult reality.

10 Shamatha meditation is non-conceptual. We just pay attention to the object of meditation. All things that exist are knowable and we utilise what is knowable as objects of concentration in shamatha. In insight meditation, we are trying to comprehend the relationship between things that exist and their nature, which is emptiness. How does emptiness relate to everything that is knowable? We also try to distinguish between two types of wisdom: wisdom that comprehends the extent of things and wisdom that comprehends the nature of things. Both wisdoms are related to the insight we gain through vipashyana meditation. However, we should not think of shamatha and vipashyana as two separate techniques or that we cannot realise insight without doing shamatha meditation. There are no

absolutes when it comes to these two practices; there is no clear-cut distinction. It is advisable to practise shamatha until you develop a certain proficiency in it and then engage in vipashyana. Shamatha meditation is the same in Hinayana, Mahayana, and Vajrayana. Insight meditation is what distinguishes each yana because insight deals directly with the proper world view and that world view will change from one yana to the next. The Hinayana world view is about dependent origination, which is understood only in relation to the human condition. The Mahayana world view applies the notion of causality to the world at large. We really have to embrace analysis in Mahayana vipashyana meditation, but that is not so important in Mahamudra meditation. The standard Mahayana approach to vipashyana is to engage with the external world while Mahamudra practice uses the mind as the object of analysis. Mahamudra says that if we can realise that the nature of mind is empty, we will automatically be able to apply that insight to everything else that exists.

11 Two-fold essencelessness (*atma-dvaya, bdag gnyis*) is essenceless of the perceiver (*pudgala-atma, gang zag gi bdag nyid*) and the essenceless of the objects of perception (*dharma-atma, chos kyi bdag nyid*).

12 Concepts are used in vipashyana meditation to lead to a non-conceptual understanding of reality. The traditional example of rubbing two sticks together so they will catch fire and burn each other up, symbolises the way we use concepts to break down our rigid ideas. This automatically leads to a non-conceptual understanding of things. If we do not use concepts to break down our rigid conceptual notions, we will not attain non-conceptuality. We have very little chance of realising anything if we have no conceptual understanding of it. It is very difficult to experience anything that is completely free from concepts and we are not trying to reject our concepts in Mahamudra meditation. We just let our concepts be so that they cease to have any hold over us. Recognising your concepts, ideas, thoughts, and emotions to be insubstantial is the realisation of vipashyana meditation.

BOOK TWO

1 An Explanation to Arouse Confidence

1 Dharmakaya and Mahamudra refer to the same reality, but tend to be used in different contexts. When we want to emphasise the more subjective aspect, we use the term dharmakaya and when we want to emphasise the objective aspect, we use the term dharmadhatu. Dharmadhatu means emptiness generally, dharmakaya means emptiness in relation to consciousness and Mahamudra encompasses

both the subjective and objective aspects. The dharmakaya also encompasses the subjective and objective dimensions, but we need to understand the subjective differently in the context of dharmakaya, where it means that the emptiness of mind and the emptiness of the external world are identical.

2 Mahamudra would not be all-encompassing if it could be located somewhere. It is pointless to try to locate space when space itself is the precondition for any kind of locality. Trying to locate Mahamudra would also be a mistake, because Mahamudra encompasses samsara and nirvana, physical and mental, and everything else that exists or does not exist.

3 Mahamudra can only be divided into ground Mahamudra (*gzhi phyag chen*), path Mahamudra (*lam phyag chen)*, and fruition Mahamudra (*'bras bu phyag chen*) in relation to individuals. From the point of view of ultimate reality; no such division is possible.

4 Some people have greater understanding than others, which is why we have three types of people: ordinary beings have no understanding of their true nature, bodhisattvas have a better understanding of it, and buddhas have complete understanding. This relates to the notion of two-fold purity (*dag pa gnyis*): primordial purity (*rang bzhin dag pa*) and temporal purity (*glo bur dag pa*). Primordial purity is our buddha nature, which has been pure and uncorrupted from the beginning. Temporal purity comes about through eradicating our obscurations and defilements. Primordial purity is the same in everyone while temporal purity will vary. In other words, there is no difference between ordinary beings and buddhas from the view of primordial purity, but there are enormous differences in terms of their temporal purity. Buddha nature is intrinsically pure but we do not recognise it because of ignorance. We have to remove our ignorance to increase our temporal purity. The approaches of Sutra, Tantra, and Mahamudra employ different methods to achieve this.

5 All of these mudras have the experience of unity in common, which is emphasised in the experience of bliss associated with each mudra. Karmamudra involves unity with another person, jnanamudra involves unity with a deity, dharmamudra involves unity with the phenomenal world, and the Mahamudra is all-encompassing unity. Each mudra has an accompanying experience of bliss. Mahamudra is the final experience of 'great bliss' or *mahasukha*.

6 The five wisdoms (*pancajnana, ye shes lnga*) are the wisdom of the authentic state (*dharmadhatu-jnana, mnyams pa nyid kyi ye shes*), mirror-like wisdom (*adarsa-jnana, me lung lta ba'i ye shes*), the wisdom of discrimination (*pratya-vekasana-jnana, sor rtog ye shes*), the wisdom of equanimity (*samata-jnana, mnyams nyid ye shes*), and the wisdom of accomplishment (*krtyanusthana-jnana, bya ba grub pa'i ye shes*).

7 The three aspects of a buddha's being (*kaya, sku*) are the authentic aspect (*dharmakaya, chos kyi sku*), the communicative aspect (*sambhogakaya, longs sku*), and the manifest aspect (*nirmanakaya, sprul pa'i sku*).

8 The word mudra has many additional meanings, such as seal, mark, signifier, gesture, and symbol. Mudra can stand for all kinds of things in the context of both Sutra and Tantra and it means something different again in Mahamudra. We need to understand that words have no intrinsic meaning; they just assume the meanings we ascribe to them.

9 Buddha nature (*tathagatagarbha, de bzhin snying po*) can be found in the sutras belonging to the third turning of the wheel of Dharma, specifically the sutras associated with the Yogacara school. In the early sutras, buddha nature was presented as an embryonic thing, but by the late Mahayana sutras, such as the *Uttaratantrashastra*, and the Vajrayana tantras, it was understood as the principle of innate enlightenment. The Kagyu and Nyingma schools both understand buddha nature in the latter sense; our inherently enlightened nature, which needs nothing added to it and nothing taken away.

10 The aspects of buddha's being are usually enumerated as three or four. The fourth kaya is the essential aspect of buddha's being (*svabhavivakaya, ngo bo nyid sku*), which is the unity of the other three kayas. While the three kayas can be separated conceptually, there is no separation between them in reality.

11 The karmamudra, dharmamudra, jnanamudra, samayamudra, and mahamudra are translated as action seal (*las kyi phyag rgya*), reality seal (*chos kyi phyag rgya*), wisdom seal (*ye shes kyi phyag rgya*), commitment seal (*tshig gi phyag rgya*) and great seal (*phyag rgya chen po*) respectively. In Tantric literature, the action seal usually involves sexual union with a consort, the reality seal involves imagining oneself in sexual union, the wisdom seal involves the external representation of the deity, the commitment seal involves the relationship between teacher and student, and the great seal is the union of great bliss and emptiness.

12 This teacher refers to Sakya Pandita (1181–1251), the renowned scholar and hierarch of the Sakya School of Tibetan Buddhism and a vocal opponent of the Mahamudra and Dzogchen traditions.

13 The dohas came directly from the mahasiddha's own experiences. In the Kagyu tradition, from Marpa until Gampopa's time, the sole practice of the mahasiddhas was Mahamudra. Gampopa introduced the monastic system of the Kadampa to the Kagyu tradition and it is said that he 'formed one stream,' meaning the Mahamudra stream of transmission and the monastic stream became one in the Kagyu school.

14 What distinguishes Tantric practice from Mahamudra is that the bliss we experience in Tantric practices is convertible, whereas the bliss we experience

in Mahamudra is inconvertible. The Tantric experience of bliss is embellished because it is tinged with things such as sexual desire or grasping. For example, tummo practice is done to sublimate our libido. Instead of avoiding pleasure, we use pleasure to experience transcendence. Therefore, a convertible or embellished bliss is associated with our physical and mental sensations. The pure experience of bliss in Mahamudra is not contingent on the various stages of bliss associated with physical sensation. Tantric practice utilises four centres in the body through specific methods meant to bring about the experience of bliss. Mahamudra experience is quite distinct from this manipulation of the bodily centres, although related to it. The Mahamudra experience of bliss should not be confused with the bliss of these other Tantric practices.

15 The *Vajramala* is saying that there is no need to engage in excessive analytical meditation of the five psychological constituents, six sense fields, and eighteen elements and so on. From the Mahamudra point of view, it is not necessary to engage in this analysis too much. Nor should we get caught up in the Tantric creative-imagination and fulfilment stages, the recitation of mantras, visualisations of deities and so on. This does not mean that we should avoid them completely, but we need to understand that they are only techniques. We should focus on what these techniques are meant to help us realise, instead of getting fixated on the techniques themselves.

16 The *brahma-loka* is the name for the highest of the celestial worlds in Buddhist cosmology. The 'abode of the gods,' it consists of twenty successive heavens that are located above our human plane of existence.

17 This critic is Sakya Pandita again.

18 Tantric empowerments (*dbang, abisheka*) are given to ripen the practitioners and initiate them into particular Tantric practices. The Anuttarayoga tantras typically consist of four empowerments: the common 'vase empowerment' (*caturabisheka, bum dbang*) and three uncommon empowerments called the 'secret empowerment' (*guhyabisheka, gsang dbang*), 'wisdom empowerment' (*prajnajnanabisheka, shes rab ye shes kyi dbang*), and the 'fourth empowerment' (*caturtha, dbang bzhi pa*). The wisdom empowerment is associated with the practice of sexual yoga where the sexual energy is sublimated to give rise to the experience of bliss and the fourth empowerment, which is associated with the equanimity of all things.

19 While the critic mentioned here is saying that emptiness is realised through analysis, Tashi Namgyal says the emptiness we realise in Mahamudra is not the same as the emptiness we experience through analysis.

20 Relative wisdom is associated with taking empowerments, engaging in sexual yoga, and so on, while ultimate wisdom comes from overcoming all concepts and ideas in the realisation of inconvertible bliss. You can only experience temporal bliss in

the Tantric practices, because they are conditional. For example, the practice of tummo is conditional because you rely on physical images to produce physical and mental bliss. You will experience unconditional and inconvertible bliss in Mahamudra without doing anything. Tantric bliss can be the cause for a realisation of mahamudra bliss, because they are related rather than independent experiences. The former come from practices associated with the third empowerment and the latter from practices associated with the fourth empowerment, but you cannot say they arise independently of each other.

21 Mahamudra deals directly with the nature of mind so there is no real need for empowerments. You need only receive the transmission and explanation of the lineage. Mahamudra is the nature of mind itself; it is not something an empowerment can bring so you cannot receive an empowerment that will add anything new to it.

22 We enter into the natural state (*gnas lugs*) of our own being by simply being aware of what arises in the mind with simple naked awareness. This is still a contrived form of awareness, but it will lead to intrinsic awareness because it is natural for our mind to be aware. The natural state is not some kind of abiding or substantial entity; it is luminous yet empty, it is beyond existence or non-existence and so unable to be found.

23 Ordinary mind (*tha mal gyi shes pa*) is a Mahamudra term, which means that the nature of mind is identical with the mind we already have. The nature of mind is not lurking somewhere beneath our normal deluded consciousness; it can be realised by understanding the mind in its ordinary manifestations. Understanding the nature of ordinary mind is to understand the nature of mind. This is slightly different to the Dzogchen view, where we make a distinction between the nature of mind and the empirical mind, because the empirical mind is regarded as completely deluded. The nature of mind, which they call 'mind itself', is quite different in character. In Mahamudra, temporality and atemporality, differentiation and non-differentiation, appearance and reality coexist; they are not separable. The nature of mind cannot be perceived as separate from our thoughts, concepts, and ideas.

24 We don't need to cultivate these attitudes because the realisation of the nature of mind includes the paramitas. Non-duality is synonymous with generosity, non-exclusion is synonymous with morality, and non-discrimination is synonymous with patience. Non-exclusion, non-discrimination, non-acceptance, non-abandonment, non-attachment and non-conception are the same, because they all involve non-conceptuality, which is wisdom. If you have wisdom, or the understanding of emptiness, everything else will follow from that.

25 Deity yoga is divided into the creative-imagination (*utpattikrama, bskyed rim*) and fulfilment stage (*sampannakrama, rdzogs rim*). The creative-imagination

stage is comparable to our experiences of birth and the fulfilment stage is comparable to the process of death. We have birth, rebirth, and the process of dying. In the first stage, we construct increasingly more elaborate visualisations and in the second, we dissolve everything to the point where the mind is brought down to the simplest focal point, which is luminosity or the clear light of bliss. The first stage involves the integration of the deity into ourselves as a way of understanding the inseparability of emptiness and appearance, and the second involves suspending our gross and subtle mental functions in a state of deep meditative bliss where we have the experience of luminosity.

5 The Stages of Identification

1 These are nature (*vastu, ngo bo*), essence (*prakriti, rang bzhin*), and characteristic (*rnam pa*).

2 The Mahamudra presentation of the nature, essence, and characteristic of mind is the same as dharmakaya, sambhogakaya, and nirmanakaya. The nature of mind is dharmakaya, the essence of mind is sambhogakaya, and the characteristic of mind is nirmanakaya. Only in relation to the nature and essence of mind can we talk about mind as unoriginated, unceasing, and unconditioned. We can conceptualise the characteristic of mind as temporal and unceasing because of its interactions with the temporal world. We see a relationship between mind and the nature of mind in this respect.

3 We could not operate without the characteristic of mind. We are therefore not trying to stop all mental processes; we are simply trying to bring about a change in the patterns of mind and the way it operates.

4 *Tathagatagarbha* is the same as buddha nature and has to be understood in relation to the nature and essence of mind; the emptiness and luminosity aspects. The characteristic of mind has some determinate form, because even an enlightened being needs to have a mind that functions. The Mahamudra teachings do not often use the term buddha nature but it is the same as the nature of mind.

5 Luminosity (*prabhasvara, 'od gsal*) is the innate non-conceptual clarity aspect of intrinsic awareness inseparable from emptiness.

6 Self-awareness (*svasamvitti, rang rig*) is the mind's ability to be aware of itself. It is the nature of consciousness to be self-aware because consciousness is naturally self-illuminating.

7 The cause of enlightenment is luminosity and the attainment of buddhahood is to realise that luminosity. Cause and the effect are the same, because nothing new has come into being. It is a process of unveiling rather than a process of replacement where something called 'deluded consciousness' is replaced by something called 'wisdom consciousness.' The early Buddhist view was that ordinary consciousness

is deluded and buddhahood is attained when we acquire wisdom consciousness. However, that is quite a discontinuous view of our basic nature. The Mahamudra view is that there is no such discontinuity.

8 Our reactions to things become habituated until they become the dispositional tendencies that form our character. These tendencies are gathered in our storehouse consciousness as karmic traces and dispositions (*vasana, bag chags*) where they continue to influence our mental states, reactions, biases, and preferences. The karmic imprints determine the way our minds perceive the phenomenal world. The mind cannot perceive the world independently of them, because all of our perceptions are informed by them.

9 Coemergence (*sahaja, lhan cig skyes pa*) means arising and existing together. The nature of mind and the empirical mind, the nature of mind and the nature of phenomena, reality and phenomenal appearances are all coemergent. They are two aspect of the same thing; not something separate where one thing precedes the other.

10 This Tantric understanding of bodhichitta is different to the understanding found in the Mahayana context. In the Mahayana, bodhichitta means 'enlightened mind' or buddha nature, while in the Tantric system, bodhichitta refers to sexual energy. 'The melting of bodhichitta' means the melting of sexual energy, which is a complex yogic exercise that involves transmuting the libido into the experience of great bliss.

11 Ignorance and wisdom are coemergent in ordinary sentient beings. When we say that the nature and essence of mind are coemergent with the characteristic of mind, this implies that ignorance and wisdom are coemergent. We cannot talk about them in terms of any temporal or causal priority. The term 'coemergent' is supposed to make the point that no priority is involved. You cannot say the nature of the mind gives rise to all these mental processes, thoughts, concepts and emotions. There is no temporal priority because one thing does not come before the other.

12 Coemergence emphasises the fact that we do not devalue the characteristic of mind by saying, 'All these thoughts, concepts, and mental processes are bad; I have to realise the nature and the essence of mind.' We have to understand their codependency. As samsaric beings, we do not have a proper understanding of the essence and nature of mind but we should not go to the other extreme and reject the empirical determinations of mind. Realising the nature and essence of mind does not mean going beyond the characteristic of mind; the mind that we know, the ordinary mind. The characteristic of mind is ordinary mind. It cannot be rejected because nature, essence, and characteristic are inseparable. We can talk about emergence and dissipation in relation to the characteristic aspect.

The understanding that arises through our practice is also associated with the characteristic of mind. Whether we understand more or understand less is also determined by the characteristic of mind. How much insight we have, how well we do, how well we advance, all of this is determined by the characteristic of mind.

13 The nature of mind does not undergo change, but the thoughts, concepts, and ideas that arise in mind do change. They are not separable however, because the nature of thoughts and the nature of mind are the same. 'The nature of thoughts is dharmakaya,' as the Kagyu Mahamudra prayer says. The nature and essence of mind do not change, the characteristic of mind does change, but all three nonetheless coexist, because the nature and essence of mind are present within the characteristic of mind. We should not think of the characteristic as something separate from these other two aspects.

14 This is the view of Tsongkhapa.

15 This critic is Sakya Pandita.

16 The problem is not conceptuality; the problem is conceptual proliferation (*vikalpa, rnam rtog*). This refers to our tendency to elaborate, to interpret, and to become excessively caught up in concepts.

17 It may appear paradoxical, but the Mahamudra perspective is that any state of mind is to be regarded as ordinary mind, whether it is peaceful or agitated. Ordinary people and meditators all have concepts, thoughts, and emotions. What differentiates meditators from ordinary people is that meditators have cultivated awareness and developed discriminating wisdom, while ordinary people have not. Many people think that meditators have no concepts and enlightenment means the cessation of all mental activity. That is not the case. What differentiates an enlightened being from an ordinary person are the changes to their understanding and reactions. An enlightened person still has to use thoughts and concepts but his or her mind is no longer governed or limited by them. Ordinary people have no ability to control their thoughts and thus they become the victims of their own belief systems.

18 From a Mahamudra point of view, the mind is purified when defilements become self-liberated. We do not have to get rid of them. If we allow these to manifest and let them go, they will become liberated by themselves. All Buddhist practices are geared towards purification of the mind. But Mahamudra has a special technique, which does not literally involve purifying the mind in the traditional sense. It achieves the same goal nonetheless. The practice of Mahamudra is not supposed to make you happy with your aggression and negativities so that you do nothing about them. The whole point of Mahamudra is that by refusing to dwell on our mental processes, they become self-liberated. The mind becomes purified

of these things and you become free of them. Most approaches employ antidotes or technique to purify our defilements. The Mahamudra understanding is that our tendency to dwell on things is what solidifies our problem with negative emotions and mental states. If we can learn to let go of these things in the moment they occur, they will not have any negative effect.

6 Integrating Meditation and Post-meditation

1 *Vikalpa* is a very difficult term to translate. I have translated it here as 'discursive thoughts' but in other places as 'conceptual proliferation.' The Tibetan word *rnam rtog* does not mean 'thoughts,' which is where the problem arises, because that has led to mistranslations of non-conceptuality as overcoming thoughts so that many people think we are trying to achieve a thoughtless state when we eliminate vikalpa. We are trying to overcome the endless proliferation of concepts, not to overcome thoughts.

2 *Shravakas* or 'hearers' are people who may listen to the teachings but do not practise them. *Pratyekabuddhas* or 'solitary realisers' are people who have embarked on a spiritual path independently of any tradition and without a teacher. They may have realised certain things on their own but are unable to appreciate the depth and extent of the reality of things so they are said not to attain a state of complete enlightenment, even though their attainment is an enlightened state. An appreciation of the reality of things can only arise from the practice of mindfulness that is done by bodhisattvas. Pratyekabuddhas fall short of the final goal, not from lack of wisdom as much as from a lack of compassion. They need inspiration from another realised being such as a Buddha to inspire their compassionate aspect. It is said that pratyekabuddhas may go to a graveyard, find a bone and ask, 'Where does this bone come from?' They instantly realise that the bone comes from birth. Then they ask, 'Where does birth come from?' and realise that birth comes from craving and grasping. They continue in this way until they gain insight into the twelve links of dependent origination spontaneously, realising a certain level of spiritual insight quite independently of any teachings or system.

3 The four negative forces are: 1) delusion, 2) the five psychophysical constituents, 3) death, and 4) the internal and external forces that seduce us into harmful actions.

4 There is a degree of effort involved in mindfulness, but as your mindfulness gradually becomes more subtle and can arise spontaneously, it becomes awareness. Awareness is an unconditional state; it is the luminosity of mind. There is no conscious effort applied in being aware. The gaps between thoughts are a glimpse of ordinary mind; we also need to realise that thoughts themselves are an expression of ordinary mind. They are the creative activities of ordinary mind. The gaps themselves are an unconditioned state of awareness.

[5] These twelve types of mindfulness within the context of the Four Yogas of Mahamudra are examined in the final chapter.

[6] We can have certain meditative experiences (*vetana, nyams*) in association with meditation. These experiences are different to realisation (*adhigama, rtogs pa*), because they are transient and fluctuating while realisations are permanent. Once we have realised something, we cannot lose it. We may have certain experiences that are associated with luminosity or emptiness, but that is different from realising the nature of mind, because these experiences reveal something, while a realisation of the nature of mind has no empirical content. You can no longer talk about somebody realising, perceiving, or knowing something. Meditative experiences and realisation are discussed at length in the following chapters.

[7] The meditative experiences of bliss, clarity, and non-conceptuality have a mundane and a transcendent aspect. Anyone who has meditated for some time can have these experiences to some extent. A general sense of physical and mental well-being is the experience of bliss. Being focused with a sense of sharpness is the experience of clarity. When thoughts and concepts subside and we experience a spaciousness that is free from mental agitation, we are experiencing non-conceptuality. That basic level of experience can happen to anyone from time to time and those experiences get refined through repeated practice. To experience them properly, you need to relate them to realisation, rather than remaining on the level of experience without realisation. Realisation is always accompanied by experiences, but experiences are not always associated with realisation. We have to understand that distinction. You will also become caught in your meditative experiences if you become attached or fixated on them. Some experiences can be quite strong and have powerful emotional overtones, which may be mistaken for realisation and instead of something associated with your meditation practice. You might think that you have realised something, which can become an obstacle to your progress.

[8] When we have direct experience of the nature of mind, it will not be comparable to a direct experience of anything else because other direct experiences have definable characteristics. That is why Sharipa says, 'Look! Look! But do not look at anything.' In this context, 'look' means that there is nothing to look at. It is the same with space. People say they have seen space, but if you question them further, they will say, 'Space is just space, you can't define it.' You cannot define the direct experience of the nature of mind either. A direct experience of the nature of mind is not even comparable to meditative experiences, because meditative experiences have the definable qualities of bliss, clarity, and non-conceptuality. We cannot say the nature of mind is good, bad, pleasant, or unpleasant, because it is not an entity. It is not anything. As soon as you start to think otherwise, you

have reduced the nature of mind to a thing. The line, 'Look! Look! But do not look at anything,' is not a zen riddle designed to stop your thinking and give you a glimpse of non-conceptuality. This statement does not violate conventional logic. It is simply saying that if the nature of mind has no definable characteristics, you cannot perceive it to be anything whatsoever.

9 It is difficult to maintain mindfulness in everyday life, but once awareness arises naturally, it becomes easier to integrate mindfulness and worldly activities. However, as we may still fail to do that, Tashi Namgyal advises us to integrate our daily life with meditation because it can be helpful to integrate mindfulness with certain daily activities. You go back to the object of attention, such as gardening, making a pot of tea, and so on. Our mind is not normally engaged with the things we do. Mindfulness is about trying to be present with whatever we are doing. It is practically impossible to be mindful all the time, because mindfulness requires effort, but we can be aware all the time. That is like having a continuous state of meditation.

10 Each of the Four Yogas is divided into three stages: an initial, intermediate, and final stage. These divisions are explained at length in the final chapter.

7 Eliminating Meditative Deviations

1 People sometimes think that the practices of generosity, patience, effort, and vigour are related to relative reality and have no ultimate reality. Other people think they can reduce everything to emptiness by uttering the mantra of emptiness. These are all incorrect ways of understanding the inseparability of relative and ultimate reality. The whole point of these four aberrations is to emphasise this point. We should not separate ultimate reality from the phenomenal world or think that emptiness is something abstracted and disconnected from everyday experiences.

2 Meditative experiences can be very exciting or uplifting, while realisation may not produce any dramatic feelings and you may fail to appreciate its significance. This is reflective of how we live our daily lives. Many people are addicted to emotional dramas because they think it is better to be stirred up than to have no emotional experiences at all and the same is true for meditation. We can have very good meditation experiences or very difficult and upsetting ones but realisation may not produce anything like that. Something just clicks in your head and you say 'ah ha.' Nothing dramatic takes place. You might therefore fail to appreciate it.

3 The critic is saying that unless you understand Mahamudra, there is no such thing as Mahamudra and if you do understand Mahamudra, there is no possibility of being sidetracked or lost. In other words, you either understand Mahamudra or you do not. The critic's other point was that you cannot use concepts to understand Mahamudra because using concepts is not part of Mahamudra.

However, according to the Kagyupa system of Mahamudra, concepts are not to be denigrated or rejected. The problem is not that we have concepts and thoughts; the problem is that we do not understand the nature of those concepts and thoughts. To understand the nature of thoughts and concepts is liberating. That is no different to Mahamudra. Furthermore, Mahamudra is all-encompassing so it must by definition encompass thoughts, concepts, emotions, and everything else besides.

4 Shantideva is saying that we meditate on emptiness by using concepts in analytical meditation.

5 It is very common for different Buddhist schools to criticise one another and that is healthy. Otherwise, you might end up with people being burned at the stake as heretics. As Mahayana Buddhism continually emphasises, different teachings are necessary because people have different predilections, personalities, and characteristics and require different methods to attain the same goal. There is really no conflict from that perspective. However, on a more individual level, you either approach something in one way or the other. You have to be very clear about following your chosen path and not mixing things up. That sometimes may involve criticising others, which is what is happening here. It is a friendly sort of criticism. They are not saying, 'If you don't believe what we believe, something drastic will happen.'

6 This is still a product of our karmic traces and dispositions (*vasanas, bag chags*). When the mind becomes more settled, what remains dormant or unconscious can rise up and manifest as different experiences. The *bag chags* rise to the fore and we have the opportunity to work through our karmic imprints until they no longer influence our perceptions or behaviour. If you read Milarepa's life story, his exchanges with Gampopa are very much like that. Gampopa goes home after receiving some instructions, has all these amazing dreams and then goes running back to Milarepa saying, 'What does it all mean?' Milarepa might say, 'Such-and-such karmic imprint gave rise to that dream but don't it take too seriously; just go back and keep practising.' He says that again and again. The same kind of exchange took place between Milarepa and his teacher Marpa. People who have great skill in harmonising the psychic energies are more vulnerable to this, while people whose meditation is less continuous, who go back and forth between ordinary things and meditation, may not experience these things with the same level of intensity.

7 The five signs are mirage, smoke, fireflies, flames, and a clear sky. The eight beneficial qualities are realised either by perfecting the psychophysical yoga practices of the Anuttarayoga tantras or by mastering Mahamudra meditation. They are attaining the body, speech, and mind of an enlightened being and realising the five wisdoms.

8 In the Mahamudra context, attachment refers to the emotional side and fixation refers to the cognitive side. Fixation is *'dzin pa*, which is cognitive fixation on an object. Attachment is *chags pa*, which is the emotional element involved in fixation. Even fixation on the dualistic concept of subject and object is *'dzin pa*. All the emotional conflicts of anger, jealousy, pride, attachment, and so on arise from that fixation. Fixation is what hinders our understanding of emptiness. If there were no fixation, there would be no attachment. Fixation is the fundamental barrier that we need to overcome if we are to attain enlightenment. Lhalungpa uses the word 'grasping' for *'dzin pa* and 'craving' for *chags pa*.

9 These realms are discussed at length in chapter six. According to Buddhist cosmology, the sensual realm is our realm of existence. It also includes the lower levels of gods. The realm of form is above the sensual realm and is where the more superior gods reside. Above that is the formless realm, where disembodied and passive forms of consciousnesses are said to dwell. The Buddhist texts also present these realms as different levels of consciousness that can be attained and they are listed in detail in the meditation manuals of both the Theravada and Mahayana. We can traverse these levels of meditative concentration and meditative absorption by means of tranquillity meditation. These attainments relate only to tranquillity meditation. Buddhist cosmology also says people literally rise upward or fall downward in terms of rebirth; we go up and down within these realms. Our sensual realm is grosser than the other two realms. Buddhist cosmology also states that time is relative, so we cannot say how long beings live in the higher realms, because our measurement of time is not relevant to them. Meditators who become attached to these meditative absorptions will not disappear into formlessness. This admonishment is more a warning than a description of actual events. It is a skilful use of the teachings because sometimes you need to frighten people a little to make them do things. We need to be careful about our meditative experiences or we might very well lose the opportunity to become enlightened. This does not mean a little attachment is a major problem, but if you fail to deal with your attachment as it arises, it will consolidate until you do have a real problem.

10 We fall from higher to lower states of rebirth because mind is totally inactive in the high realms. We simply live off our positive karmic stock until it is consumed and then get thrown back to lower states of existence because of the karma we created previously. Some karmic traces and dispositions come to fruition and others remain dormant, depending on our circumstances and situation. If the appropriate causes and conditions are present for a particular karma, it will come to fruition. Otherwise, it will remain dormant.

11 Lhalungpa translates this as 'absorption,' but absorption is a better translation for *snyoms 'jug* and 'cessation' is better for *gog pa*, which is the word used here

by Tashi Namgyal. *Gog pa* refers to the cessation of all thoughts and mental activities, it is about entering into deeper and deeper states of consciousness and trying to block out all sensations, feelings, and sensory impressions. Cessation experiences are associated with the formless realm and are called *jhanas* in the Theravada tradition.

12 Cessation with discrimination relates to not having a full understanding of emptiness. Nonetheless, the shravaka experience of cessation is different from other types of cessation. Some commentators have failed to make or do not wish to make that distinction. They want to present the shravaka understanding as a lack of achievement. Mahayana literature sometimes presents arhats as people who need to do more work before they achieve enlightenment. Tashi Namgyal is saying we should have a more balanced outlook. Even according to the literature itself, it is clear the shravaka type of cessation is different from the cessation of the absorptions and trance states. Shravaka practitioners, such as the non-returners and arhats, have gone beyond samsara; they will not return to the samsaric condition. Even people who have achieved the highest level of absorption have not gone beyond the peak of worldly existence, and sooner or later, will regress. There is a fundamental difference between the shravaka understanding and the absorption states. The shravakas have realised selflessness, while someone who has become fixated on different absorptive and trance states has had no such realisation. However, arhats need to deepen their understanding of emptiness. They have a proper understanding of the selflessness of persons but not of the selflessness of ultimate reality. We do not need to associate these levels of understanding with Theravada and Mahayana adherents. A mahayanist could turn out to be an arhat and a Theravadin could be a bodhisattva or Buddha. It is more about a person's realisation than about the doctrine they are following.

13 As we whittle away our karmic traces and dispositions, we have meditative experiences that are more positive. If we do not handle them properly, these experiences will increase instead of being overcome. When we handle our emotions properly, we can transform desire into bliss, aggression into clarity, and dualistic conceptions into wisdom. That is why they make a distinction between *sags rje* and *sems nyid*. The meditative experience of bliss, clarity, and non-conceptuality takes place on the level of *sags rje*, which means 'still tarnished by the karmic traces and dispositions.' When you attain realisation, those same experiences are called *sems nyid,* which means 'transcendental and untarnished by pollutants.' That is the difference. If you become attached to these experiences, you are actually increasing the elements of *sags rje* and they will become more and more of an obstacle. We need to be aware of this rather than getting paranoid about it. The more we crave these experiences, the more elusive they become. If we

do not crave them, they will arise naturally and can lead to realisation.

14 Allowing ourselves to be overwhelmed by meditative experiences is what Trungpa Rinpoche called 'spiritual materialism.' One of the major players in this whole thing is ego. These meditative experiences may make you think you are really getting somewhere, that you are superior to other people or even that you are enlightened. All kinds of things can happen because the ego is so influential. It is so easy to deceive ourselves. Self-deception plays such a major part in our lives precisely because of ego.

15 Shravakas are said to fall short of buddhahood because they lack sufficient insight into ultimate reality and they lack compassion. The dualistic notion of self and other arises from a strong notion of self. If you begin to realise that there is no immutable self within, you will gradually come to understand that the other has no enduring essence. When you realise the interdependence of subject and object, it obviously becomes easier to feel compassion. You are no longer constantly thinking of everything 'other' to your ego as something to be enjoyed, used, consumed, or attacked, destroyed, and pushed away. A whole new way of relating to things will open up. Shravakas still have a subtle sense of other and lack the ability to overcome all of their emotional conflicts. They have overcome the usual suffering experienced by ordinary people because they have relinquished egocentricity and belief in a permanent self.

16 We deal with these deviations by knowing that they are a problem. We have to be aware that these types of problems are possible. If you are aware of them, you will be able to deal with them. If you get too excited about these experiences, you will lose your awareness and get carried away by the deceptive allurement of these meditative experiences. Meditative experiences are meaningful, of course, but they should not be taken too seriously. As human beings, we are addicted to experiences. We are always chasing after new or novel experiences. Meditative experiences may be viewed in this experimental way with negative or drastic consequences. The fundamental points are not to get too attached to them and not to mistake them for realisations. Everything else is auxiliary.

17 We let things be by just noticing what arises in the mind without creating a commentary about it. Just notice it and let it go. We try to be more accommodating and maintain our awareness without being completely overwhelmed. We need to observe what is going on without thinking, 'I should not be doing this' or 'this is the same thing that always comes up.' It is important not to approach meditation like this. If it becomes hard to stick with whatever arises in your mind, just go back to watching the breath until you feel ready to return to vipashyana exercises again.

18 We realise the nature of mind by switching back and forth between shamatha and vipashyana meditation. If you are unfamiliar with meditation, you concentrate

on the shamatha aspect and only do a little vipashyana, until your ability to concentrate increases. Even when you are comfortable with vipashyana, observing your thoughts may still sometimes become too much at times so you can just go back to shamatha for a while. You do not have to perfect shamatha before you can introduce vipashyana. You can still do a little vipashyana when you are still new to shamatha and you do not leave shamatha behind once you have become proficient in vipashyana. Combining the practices in this way is called *zhi lhag zung 'jug*. *Zhi* is short for *zhi gnas* or 'tranquillity meditation,' *lhag* is short for *lhag mthong* or 'insight meditation' and *zung 'jug* means 'unity.' We traverse the Mahamudra path by practising 'the unity of shamatha and vipashyana.'

19 There are four stages of attainment on the shravaka path: the stream-enterer (*sotapanna*), once-returner (*sakadagami*), non-returner (*anagami*), and foe-destroyer (*arhat*).

20 The eight worldly concerns are loss and gain, praise and blame, pleasure and pain, and disgrace and fame.

21 The centres or chakras of the body are part of Tantric physiology and can be found at the crown, forehead, throat, heart, and below the navel.

8 Determining the Originless Nature of Mind

1 There is no direct translation for *lada*; it is a technical term for the conviction that develops through meditative experiences. It is the basis for determining the nature of mind or ultimate reality, the emphasis being on ultimate rather than relative reality. We understand the nature of mind without getting too caught up in the meditative experiences of bliss, mental clarity, and non-conceptuality. Without lada, it is quite possible to get overwhelmed by these experiences and fail to progress. Lada is also about realising that we do not need to rid ourselves of thoughts and concepts because they have no enduring essence of their own. We simply need to understand their nature.

2 While time has no intrinsic reality, that does not mean the three times do not exist at all, it just means time is relative. To realise that is to realise the insubstantiality of time. You may transcend thoughts of the three times during the unitive experience of meditation, but you will have a concept of time during post-meditation. We need to make that distinction. We have to think in terms of the inseparability of relative and ultimate truth. That is the non-dualistic way of looking at the whole thing.

3 Unless we have some feeling of humility (*mos gus*) toward the masters of the lineage, we cannot make any progress. *Mos gus* is actually two words, *mos* means 'longing' or 'inclination' and *gus* is 'humility.' The Tibetan tradition sometimes uses the analogy of a hook and ring. Humility is a ring and the blessing of the

lineage is a hook. If your ring of longing connects to the hook of the lineage's blessing, you will make progress more rapidly. We can learn only when we are open. If our mind is already full due to our preoccupation or pride, it will be very difficult to learn anything. The traditional teachings say you should not be like a pot turned upside down or a pot with a hole in it or nothing that enters you will be retained. If you are open and receptive to the blessings of the lineage, you will progress much more quickly. If you become familiar with the kindness of Marpa, Milarepa, Tilopa, Savaripa, and the other mahasiddhas quoted in this text, their blessings will seep through and you may make more progress.

4 Thoughts and the nature of mind are not the same, but the nature of thoughts and the nature of mind are the same. Both are both empty and therefore free of the defiling tendencies. You have to appreciate this distinction. Our thoughts are the product of delusions and defilements unless we are enlightened. That is why the Lineage Prayer says the nature of the thoughts is dharmakaya. It does not say thoughts are dharmakaya.

5 Emptiness does not mean that nothing exists; it is the experience of unity in diversity. The diversity of phenomenal experiences does not cease; you just realise that all experience has the same nature. Some religious and philosophical traditions say multiplicity is unreal and we have to realise one reality. From the Mahamudra view, to see unity in multiplicity is one error and to see unity at the expense of multiplicity is another. We have to see unity and multiplicity as non-dual. All physical entities are part of an interconnected network of events and processes rather than singular entities. The belief in things and entities is a conceptual imputation, but that does not discredit the reality of the things we perceive entirely. The Mahayana teachings sometimes use the example of Indra's net to illustrate this point. If you undo one knot in the net, all the others knots are affected. The reality of this physical world functions in a similar way.

6 'Indestructible mind' is *vajrachitta* where *vajra* means 'indestructible' or 'diamond-like' and *chitta* is 'mind.'

7 Bliss is a temporal experience, but the nature of bliss is no different from the nature of mind. The nature of bliss is unchanging and permanent because the nature of mind is unchanging and permanent.

8 Tashi Namgyal is challenging more conventional Tantric practices here, where dream yoga is emphasised as the process of becoming aware of luminosity while dreaming. The Mahamudra view is that experiencing luminosity during our dreams is not the issue; the real issue is our attitude when we wake up. Are we still fixated or attached to that dream experience or are we able to determine its nature to be emptiness and therefore no different to the nature of mind? That is the essential point.

9 Confidence (*dad-pa, sraddha*) is often translated as 'faith' but many people do not like the theistic connotations of that word. The Buddhist teachings say confidence is developed in three stages: confidence with a sincere heart (*dang ba'i dad pa*), confidence with conviction (*yid ches kyi dad pa*) and inconvertible confidence (*'dod pa'i dad pa*). Confidence with sincere heart is where you have genuine sincerity and interest but no real experience or practice. You start out on the journey with that kind of confidence and that develops into some kind of conviction about how it actually might work. As that conviction is further strengthened, it matures into the inconvertible confidence that comes from direct experience. It is not a question of either 'having' or 'not having' confidence. We can have more or less of it. Confidence will grow and mature if we handle it properly. We are not required to take a leap of faith in Buddhism. All that is required is a willingness to work with the practice and confidence will come. If you practise long enough, confidence will come. There will be fluctuations, because as human beings, we go up and down, but a genuine sense of progress will take place if we stick with the practice.

10 All of these practices are to be undertaken in a retreat environment so post-meditation is also being discussed within that context. You do these practices for five days, ten days, and so on, but you should not take a break from awareness when you break from your formal practice. You have to maintain your awareness throughout the three fundamental actions of eating, walking, and sleeping.

9. Transforming Adversity on the Path

1 The point of this section is not that we should use methods, but that we employ them in a different way. Instead of thinking that techniques will be a solution to our problems, we apply a technique that allows our problems to resolve themselves. Instead of thinking that we have a solution for a specific problem—as if the problem and solution were completely independent of one another—we resolve the problem by understanding it. This is a different kind of understanding to mere knowledge; it is an understanding that comes from practice. The whole idea of transforming adverse circumstances and situations is very suggestive. We do not need to battle with and overcome adversity, we can make it part of our growth. We do not eliminate it from our self-perception; we incorporate it into our identity through a certain form of understanding. That type of understanding is wisdom. Things are only a problem when we fail to understand them or when we rigidly compartmentalise them and see them partially or in fragments. The aspects of ourselves that we find unacceptable or undesirable can aid our progress if we understand them properly.

2 Tashi Namgyal is saying the appropriate time to use this method is after we have

gained some insight into the nature of reality. The Mahayana Paths and Stages identify a meditative experience of spiritual heat (*usmagata, drod*) that occurs at an advanced stage of the path of application.

3 The creative-imagination stage (*utpattikrama, bskyed rim*) and the fulfilment stage (*sampannakrama, rdzogs rim*) are the two aspects of Tantric practice, the former involving the visualisation of deities and the latter involving dissolving those deities into emptiness. The creative-imagination stage corresponds to conventional shamatha and the fulfilment stage to conventional vipashyana. Tantra has some very elaborate visualisations of deities and their mandalas, which are equivalent to trying to visualise an epic play, where you have to remember all the characters, how they stand in relation to one another, what their roles are, and so on. There are also simple mandalas, where you only need to visualise a central deity such as Chenresig. Then there are ever simpler visualisations, which relate to the fulfilment stage, that deal with the psychophysical energy pathways and give rise to the experience of non-duality or emptiness. The fulfilment stage is about realising emptiness. Deities are symbolic representations of our wisdom potential. Imagination plays an important role in our lives and when we can imagine something and give it shape and form, we can relate to it. Having power over wisdom means to visualise these deities and incorporate them into ourselves so that we no longer perceive them as something that possesses power while we do not. The human mind constantly conceptualises and imagines things so the Tantric system makes use of that tendency instead of trying to reject it. Instead of discarding our mental activities, we make use of them to discover what is simple. As the Tantric teachings say, 'We arrive at the simplicity of mind through elaborate mental activity.'

Some people think that they don't have to do shamatha because they are practising deity yoga but visualisation is just another form of tranquillity meditation. If you think you have gone beyond shamatha practice or feel superior to someone doing shamatha, you have made a mistake. Tantric practices are just another way of doing shamatha. Visualising deities is tranquillity meditation and dissolving the visualisation into emptiness is insight meditation. Tranquillity meditation is nothing other than concentrating the mind. Whether you are concentrating your mind on an external object or on the specific details of the deities, you are still concentrating. If your practice is devoted to insight into reality, it is insight meditation. To realise that the nature of the deities is mental, and therefore insubstantial, is what constitutes insight meditation. Tantric practice is not about imagining deities as beings hovering in space, you are to see them as projections of your own mind. That is part of the realisation of insight. We use visualisations to enhance our concentration because some people find it easier to concentrate if they visualise something and others find it easier to concentrate on the breath or an external object. Standard shamatha does not deal directly with your conflicting emotions, while visualising a deity deals with them directly because the deities are symbols of those emotions. All the emotional disturbances originate from four basic emotions and all the deities are symbolic manifestations of one of those emotions. Shamatha enhances our visualisation practice, because without grounding in shamatha, visualisation can become a source of distraction or entertainment. Shamatha practice can be boring, but the visualisations can become a form of mental gymnastics because there are so many things you can think about. You can be constantly preoccupied. Visualisation should not be approached that way, because even that will become boring if you do it for long enough.

4 Even though this is a Mahamudra text, we can still use Tantric methods whenever appropriate. Tantrism is about self-transformation and Mahamudra is about self-liberation. However, self-liberation may not always work and when it is not working, we can use the methods of transformation. We may have mindfulness, awareness and so forth, but still experience problems that obstruct our progress. There is a need to deal with them, which is why we introduce the methods of transformation. We can choose to use or not to use Tantric techniques when we are practising Mahamudra. Mahamudra is a state of being that we attain; it has nothing to do with technique. Tantra is all about techniques that work with our body and mind.

5 We are advised to retreat into the wilderness, not because the wilderness has some intrinsic value attached to it, but because it is upsetting. We should be moving toward what we find difficult, not running away from it. We grow as people when we deal with difficulties and are unable to stretch our resources or potential when we are afraid to face things. We may never discover what we are capable of, if we back off when things become difficult. Instead of seeing difficulty as something to be avoided, we should see it as an opportunity for growth. If we cannot change our perspective and face our difficulties, we will always be tiptoeing around situations without really confronting anything. Those same fears will haunt us; they will not disappear and may even become stronger and more powerful over time.

6 Even though we hear the Mahamudra instructions on not grasping, not judging, and treating our experiences with equanimity and acceptance, it is very difficult to get used to that feeling. If our mind is calm during meditation, we are happy, and if our mind is agitated, we become despondent about having such a terrible meditation session. We automatically think this way. Tashi Namgyal is saying we do not need to think like this. The very fact that we are sitting in meditation means we are dealing with our minds differently to our everyday life approach. You might think there is a difference between an agitated and calm state of mind

but that's only because you don't really understanding what meditation involves. Even when the mind wanders off in meditation, it will still be working if you have this attitude. Meditation works when the mind is calm and it works when the mind has completely lost it.

7 Tashi Namgyal is not saying we should become a mad person, he is saying we should behave like a mad person in the sense of not being bound by ordinary conventions, value judgements, and so forth. Meditators should learn to let go and stop being so rigid and fixated on things. We always want security, we always want everything to be fixed and predictable; but life is not predictable. If you keep on accumulating fixed value systems and attitudes and insist on believing that this is how the world is, you will become very deluded. That is not how the world is. 'To be just like a mad person' means to let go of those fixations and false certainties.

8 It is best not to think there is a particular way to experience these things. It is very difficult for Western people to accept that; we want everything to be so clear. However, nothing is made clearer by forming rigid ideas about the way we should experience things. That will always depend on the individual. Tashi Namgyal is just providing a general guideline for these experiences here.

9 There are diversions in terms of mindfulness and there are diversions in terms of how we conceptualise our experiences. We may be mindful and attentive during meditation but we may still be misled in our conceptualisations during post-meditation. We will then have less chance of deepening our insight because we are too eager to make sense out of the whole thing conceptually instead of just persisting with the practice. It is important to be informed about what we are doing but we should not over-indulge in making sense of it. Persisting with the practice is its own reward. You just have to learn to be present. If you are constantly trying to work out where you are at, you will not be present.

10 Some people may be able to rely solely on the Mahamudra method of self-liberation, but most of us will experience disturbing thoughts and emotions that create obstacles to that practice. Subtle thoughts and emotions are much easier to deal with, but when more violent and vivid ones arise, it can throw us off our practice. Tashi Namgyal is saying that we have to learn not to worry about them. Worrying and perceiving these disruptions as bad automatically creates more problems. We introduce the method of transformation at this point, but unlike the Mahayana approach where some kind of antidote is necessary, we transform our problems by learning to regard them as positive phenomena. We transform thoughts and emotions by learning to accommodate and accept them. Just accommodate them; don't think that you need to gain some insight into them. You cannot have insight into your disturbing thoughts unless you learn to accommodate them, just as you

cannot get to know another person unless you accommodate them and show your acceptance and understanding. Accommodation is the important thing; insight comes from that.

11 Rechungpa and Gampopa were the two main students of Milarepa.

12 As we progress with our practice, we cease to think of the goal as something to achieve at a later date. The goal is already here. We are not concerned about it, hoping to get somewhere and fearing we may not. We drop those ideas and just try to remain in a natural state, making no separation between the nature of mind and practice. Many Westerners tend to think there has to be a fixed method, but even in secular life there is no 'one' way that works in every situation. The methods we used when we were naive are different to the ones we use when we are more experienced. We cannot use the same attitude and method throughout the spiritual journey. The practices and teachings are based on skillful means and correspond to our predilections, capacities, and experience.

13 Gampopa is saying we should not think of discarding our thoughts and concepts. 'Do not abandon the disturbing concepts of inner mind' (*nang sems gyi rnam togs mi pong ba*); 'view these disturbing thoughts as very beneficial' (*rnam togs gyur din gyi lta ba*); 'see them as indispensable' (*mi dam rol ma lta ba*). Instead of thinking of defilements, delusions and disturbing thoughts as inessential and to be eradicated, view them as something we cannot do without. We need them to make progress on the spiritual path. Gampopa then says, 'We should learn to love them' (*snying du sdug bsngal lta*). When someone is very beautiful, we say *lta snying sdug bsngal*, which literally means 'suffering engendered by looking.' People say beauty fills you with joy, but that happens only if you are lucky! However, *snying du sdug bsngal lta* does not mean that we suffer in this context; it means we should see the disturbing concepts and thoughts as lovable, from the heart. We have to realise that they are no different to their nature. Thoughts and concepts are something we have to understand and overcome, but we don't do that by getting rid of them. We have to see disturbing thoughts as our friends because, 'Disturbing thoughts and concepts are our companion' (*rnam rtog trogs yen*). 'Disturbing thoughts and concepts are part of our path' (*rnam rtog lam yen*); no other path exists apart from the one that deals with disturbing thoughts. 'Disturbing thoughts are fuel for the fire of wisdom' (*rnam rtog shes rab push bying*), because they are necessary if we wish to give rise to wisdom. It is important to know we can make use of and transform disturbing thoughts and concepts by learning to admire, incorporate, and love them, rather than discard or transcend them.

14 The difference between transformation and vipashyana is that we actually think about our thoughts and emotions in the technique of transformation while we

are simply being aware of them in vipashyana meditation. Instead of simply being aware of your anger, you think about it and try to develop friendliness toward it; you try to love and embrace your anger. Instead of feeling frustrated or thinking that your meditation has been disturbed by thoughts and emotions, you regard them as no problem. The vipashyana method is about understanding the nature of mind, while the method of transformation is about understanding the nature of mind through your disturbing thoughts and emotions. This is not strictly speaking a part of Mahamudra meditation, as Tashi Namgyal makes clear, but we can utilise Tantric methods in this context.

15 When we visualise deities in the Tantric system, the visualisation is not about the deities, the deities are about us. We begin by visualising deities we can handle and gradually move to disturbing manifestations we may not necessarily be able to handle. They might be stark naked, in sexual embrace, drinking blood out of a skull cup, wearing garlands of skulls around their necks, and looking so ferocious and disturbing they are almost demonic. We can transform our negative emotions by identifying with their enlightened aspect in this way, utilising our thoughts and imagination as part of meditation to gradually transmute the emotional poisons into ambrosia.

16 It is a myth to think we are either confident or insecure. Real confidence can only be built on a lack of confidence. We develop confidence by trying to work with and understand our insecurity. Only superficial types of confidence exist independent of insecurity, such as excessive pride, arrogance, and so on. Real confidence comes when we accept our limitations and know the full range of our capabilities, shortcomings, weaknesses, and strengths. Someone who does not know their own strengths and weaknesses cannot have real confidence

17 The five elements are earth, water, fire, wind, and space.

18 If we cease to view health and illness as separate and opposed, that insight will naturally give rise to spiritual growth. If we do not have that insight, we will be unable to incorporate these experiences into our meditation practice. We can talk about health and illness on the relative level, but health and illness have no intrinsic essence to fixate on or cling to. We see all kinds of people on television who are suffering from eating disorders. They are not seeking ill health, but that is exactly what they get because of their obsession with health. Obviously, this is an exaggerated approach, but this attitude exists within all of us. Health is something we want and ill health is the most evil thing we can experience short of death itself. Tashi Namgyal is saying that health and ill health are not just something that happens to our body, they also have a lot to do with our mental attitude.

19 We are advised to relate to physical pain in the same way we would relate to illness. If you can gain some familiarity with this in relation to your minor aches and

pains, you might be able to transfer that same attitude to major physical afflictions when they occur. You don't need a detailed knowledge of the physical elements to work with them. We should just stay with whatever occurs in our mind and deal with our mental reactions to those experiences. We identify ourselves with the pain, instead of thinking, 'I have pain in my knee, I have pain in my shoulder.' Try to see yourself and your pain as the same. We are always thinking, 'This is happening to me, I don't want it, I should not have it, I should get rid of it.' But here we are simply trying to be aware of the pain and identify with it. If the pain becomes unbearable, we should stop. We have to be skilful here and not take it too far. On the other hand, if we shift our position or change our posture as soon as we experience any discomfort, we will derive no benefit from the experience. Sometimes the pain will subside automatically, just from identifying with it in this way. Pain does not just occur on a physical level, it is a mental thing. Mental pain comes from our mental attitude and our mental attitude is not different from the nature of mind. It is possible to realise the nature of mind even within pain. That pain will then become transformed.

20 Tibetans have a saying, 'the essence of meditation is not concentration but familiarity.' This is actually a Tibetan pun. *Gom* is 'meditation' and *kom* is 'familiarity.' *sGom pa ma yin kom ba yin* is the Tibetan expression, which means that when you become familiar with practice, it actually becomes meditation because you can do it effortlessly. It can be very taxing and painful when you have to exert yourself constantly. Takpo Tashi Namgyal is saying that we start by practising slowly, then as we get used to it, our capacity gradually develops to a point where we have the ability to cure ourselves of illness. We are aiming toward that ideal; we do not start from that ideal. We start from where we are, which is to be always struggling with health and illness. As we deal with that struggle, and learn to practise properly, we may develop the ability to transform our illness as part of our spiritual practice, just as the Kagyu masters of the past were able to do. Familiarity is a very important concept. From this perspective, real well-being is about not struggling with health or illness.

21 Mother luminosity (*'od gsal ma*) is the same as our buddha nature; our potential or capacity to become enlightened. We cannot realise our buddha nature simply by knowing about it. We need to engage in practice and develop different insights. These insights are known as son luminosity (*'od gsal pu*), because just as a son is born from a mother, insight is born from our buddha nature. Son luminosity goes through many levels of change but mother luminosity does not change. They are nonetheless the same. For example, the sun is always bright but there will be more or less illumination, depending on the cloud cover. We could say that son luminosity is the expression of mother luminosity. We also realise mother

luminosity through son luminosity. The luminosity we experience through practice is no different from mother luminosity; however the latter is not something that we can currently access because it is obscured by the clouds of delusions. Sometimes they are referred to as the rays of the sun and the sun itself. The rays of the sun are not different from the sun. *O' zer* is 'rays' and *nyi ma* is 'sun,' so *o' zer* and *nyi ma* are not different.

22 The Mahamudra and Tantric teachings talk about mother and son luminosity and the importance of reuniting them. Mother luminosity is the same as our intrinsic awareness, which is called *rig pa*, which has been present right from the beginning. Son luminosity is the awareness we develop through meditation. When we attain realisation, a reunion between the mother and son luminosity takes place so that they become one. This is called *'od gsal ma pu sde* or the 'fusion of the mother and son luminosity.'

23 Everything we think about and everything we experience is dependent on our concepts so both life and death are conditioned by mind. For that reason, it is said that 'death results from conceptual proliferation.' The kind of world we live in is always conditioned by the kind of mind we have. We may think things are actually independent of mind but the things that happen to us and the way we experience events is dependent on our mind because mind conditions everything we experience. That is not to say that mind literally creates something out of nothing, just that nothing can occur without mind. For this reason, even birth and death are created by mind. Life and death are relative concepts because they are tied up with the kind of beings we are. If we lived for only a week, we would think about life and death in a very different way. Death does not exist as some kind of objective reality, which is why death results from conceptual proliferation. We do not die because of our concepts, but the way we think about these things and the way we are is dependent on our karmic inheritance. We should not only look for scientific explanation about our body and mind; we should also think of it in relation to karma. All of these factors are relevant to our experience of death. Death is therefore conditional; it only has meaning to living beings.

24 Buddhism does not formulate an eternal life from which we fell and became mortal because somebody sinned. We are mortals because that is the kind of being we are. We cannot be otherwise. However, from the perspective of ultimate reality, there is no death. As Gampopa says, 'How can we think of death in relation to that?' When the nature of dharmakaya is pure and uncorrupted, how can we find death there? There are these two perspectives; the relative view where death is related to the kind of beings we are and the ultimate view where life and death are meaningless. Ultimate reality has nothing to do with coming into being and going out of existence so life and death have no relevance. Those two levels coexist. It is

not like deathlessness is found from having eternal life. Deathlessness is found in the momentariness of our lives as we live them. We just have no intimation of that higher state of being.

10 Four Yogas of Mahamudra

1 Whether you are an instantaneous-type (*chig char ba*), an intermediate-type (*thod gyal*), or a gradual-type (*ring gyis pa*), it does not qualify or preclude you from practising Mahamudra.

2 Intellectual understanding (*jna, go*), meditative experience (*vetana, nyams*), and realisation (*adhigama, rtogs pa*) are all necessary components for attainment in the Four Yogas of Mahamudra. Intellectual understanding is having a general idea about what the nature of mind, ultimate reality, and emptiness mean. This is followed by the fluctuating meditative experiences of bliss, clarity and non-conceptuality during practice. That is followed by realisation, where your comprehension and insight into reality and the nature of mind becomes more stable. An immediate cognition of ultimate reality in the Four Yogas can only occur with the comprehension that comes about through all three factors. Some Westerners do not seem to acknowledge the difference between understanding and experience, while others think intellectual understanding and meditation are incompatible. However, we need to have all three. Intellectual understanding alone or experience alone is insufficient; they must both be brought to bear on our practice so that genuine realisation can develop.

3 Someone can only have an instantaneous-type of understanding because they already possess the qualities of humility and courage. The teachings present instantaneous realisation more as a possibility than as something we can actually do. Some people may have that capacity, but they are very rare. Most of us have to slog away and do the hard work, attaining intellectual understanding, meditative experiences, and then realisation. Anyone who is capable of an instantaneous understanding would have developed those qualities in past lives. We do not get anything without meriting it.

4 Rare individuals may attain realisation without first gaining intellectual understanding, just as a musical prodigy knows how to play music without having to study it in detail, but most of us need intellectual understanding. We just need to see it as a means to an end and not as the end in itself. The goal is not to have a better intellectual understanding; the goal is to have an immediate meditative realisation of what we are trying to understand. Intellectual understanding will definitely help to steer us in the right direction. Many people have all kinds of misconceptions about practice and its aim, so we need to have a clear conceptual framework around what we are doing. That understanding is an indispensable

tool, but it is only a tool.

5 It is very important to distinguish between meditative experience and realisation in the Mahamudra tradition, which is why the mahasiddhas are always saying, 'Don't mistake experience for realisation.' Experiences will fluctuate. You may think everything is going wonderfully well and then you may think you are going backwards and nothing is working, but you should be able to deal with both scenarios because they are really the same experience. It is all meditative experience. We should not just regard good things as meditative experience. The *Ocean of Certainty*, *Moonbeams of Mahamudra*, and other Mahamudra texts all say we will experience all kinds of urges and mental images while meditating, but we should regard everything as meditative experiences that are not fundamentally good or bad. They are something we need to work with rather than some kind of deviation. According to Mahamudra, all meditative experiences can be turned into good experiences if we deal with them properly. The goal of practice is to learn to come to terms with bad experiences and see them as an indispensable part of meditation through the techniques of vipashyana or transformation. Bliss, luminosity, and non-conceptuality are also to be found in bad experiences. To see that bliss is also present when there is a lot of discomfort is the dawning of realisation. When we can handle our experiences that way, we will start to have realisations.

6 The Sanskrit terms *adhigama* and *jna* were translated by the Tibetans as *rtogs pa* and *go*, *rtogs pa* meaning a 'direct, intuitive, unmediated recognition or true perception of ultimate reality' and *go* meaning 'theoretical knowledge consisting of an intellectual grasp of a concept or idea.'

7 Phagmo Drupa was one of the famous 'three men of Kham,' along with Dusum Khyenpa and Saltong Shogam, who were amongst Gampopa's five most pre-eminent disciples. These three siddhas were staying at Gampopa's monastery and drinking, dancing, and singing dohas every evening. The monastic disciplinarian could not control them and he became so desperate, he went to Gampopa and said, 'Either these three go or I'll have to stop being the disciplinarian.' Gampopa had no choice but to say, 'Maybe they should go.' The three men of Kham were asked to leave the monastery. However, as they were leaving, they danced around and left many footprints in the rocks. The disciplinarian realised they were not ordinary people and called them back, saying he would make an exception for them and let them stay at the monastery.

8 While maintaining our awareness during meditation is quite difficult, if we can do so, we will occasionally have glimpses of mental clarity and realise that mental clarity is always there. It becomes more continuous with persistent practice until it is self-present rather than something we have to make present. The clarity of

the mind is like the sun. There is never a day without the sun, but some days are cloudier than others. Meditation is about realising this lucidity of mind, rather than trying to bring it about anew. If you can have that understanding, you will learn to maintain that mental clarity more continuously. That is more natural than not having clarity, because clarity is part of the nature of mind.

9 Because we can now perceive unity in diversity, without needing to obliterate the various sensory impressions and multiplicities of the phenomenal world, the interactions between the external world and the internal workings of our minds have been brought into unison.

10 Fundamentally, there is no difference between deluded consciousness (*sems*) and intrinsic awareness (*rig pa*), in terms of their nature. The difference lies only within our own experience. *Rigpa* gives us the opportunity to realise ultimate reality and *sem* separates us from that reality, but the nature of *sem* and the nature of *rigpa* are the same, because they are both grounded in the same reality.

11 One-flavouredness means that we should not become too fixated on our dualistic ways of thinking or on anything. Most religions encourage people to become fixated. You might become fixated on the duality of pure and impure, for example. 'Buddha is pure and I am impure.' The duality of samsara and nirvana is mentioned. Nirvana is liberation and samsara is bondage. However, you should not become too fixated on that, thinking that samsara is inherently evil and nirvana is inherently pure. We need to realise that these polar realities have the same nature. The nature of samsara is no different from the nature of nirvana, which is why Nagarjuna says, 'Samsara and nirvana are identical.' You should not be misled into thinking samsara is the same as nirvana, because samsara and nirvana have the same nature.

12 Things are said to be 'like an illusion' (*sgyu ma lta bu'i*) in Buddhism but they are never said to be actual illusions. We are meant to see the insubstantial and interdependent nature of the phenomenal world, not to dismiss the world as unreal. That would be to fall into the extreme of nihilism. Regarding things as completely real and substantial is to fall into the extreme of eternalism.

13 Trying to develop confidence by hanging onto your experiences instead of being with whatever you are experiencing will only create further confusion. Hanging onto a positive experience may give you comfort and you can base your confidence on that. But you are only basing you confidence on an attempt to concretise that experience to make it more real. You are trying to solidify the whole thing (*ngo 'dzin*). If you do that, you cannot have any fresh experiences because you are still involved with the idea of solidifying experiences you've already had and are unable to let go of that. Your confidence will be built on that solidification and will therefore be false. You should be basing your confidence on the fact that you are

meditating and have the capacity to accommodate all of your experiences, the bad as well as the good.

14 Integration (*yugananda, zung 'jug*) is based on disentangling ourselves from our conceptual proliferations so that we can see that mind and reality cannot be separated. The Mahamudra teachings are not saying that mind and reality are the same however. The mind is not the same as reality; mind is inseparable from reality. The mind and the world arise together.

15 We cannot understand the totality of this experience on the yoga of one-flavouredness because our notion of emptiness is still only a partial one. We are less fixated on our experiences, thoughts, perceptions, sensations, and feelings, but we have become fixated on emptiness. We see emptiness as a separate reality rather than something that cannot be found outside those very experiences. It is so easy to side with one thing or the other and much easier to think of emptiness in relation to things that are pleasant than in association with things that are uncomfortable or painful. Nonetheless, they are the same reality from the ultimate point of view. We only attain this yoga when we understand that the experience of *ro chig* occurs from both sides. Our attitudes and perceptions can be warped in a certain direction and fall into a state of partiality where there can be no understanding of *ro chig*. We have to understand emptiness in relation to all the terrible things as well as the good ones if we hope to experience the single flavour of everything.

16 The storehouse consciousness is a neutral state that does not respond to things from its own side. We can therefore rest in that level of consciousness and experience very peaceful states of meditation. Some people mistake this experience for the attainment of non-meditation, but the fourth yoga is not about having nothing to meditate on. Resting in the storehouse consciousness is more like being in a state of unconsciousness than being fully present. Non-meditation has nothing to do with being unconscious; it means you no longer need to make an effort to be aware. You can experience the yoga of non-meditation even when the mind is very busy. You are always in a state of meditation.

17 Even trying to be mindful can become a habit and we need to go beyond that. This is a very systematic text. Tashi Namgyal explains how we develop and practise mindfulness, by paying attention to a physical object, the breath, and so on, and then by focusing our attention on the thoughts and emotions that arise in the mind, because unless we can gain some understanding of the nature of our thoughts and emotions, we will not give rise to insight. We have to begin by making an effort but we also need to learn how to go beyond habit because a habit can become an addiction. Meditation is more about gaining insight into our thoughts and emotions than about developing a concentrative state. We can

develop a very concentrated mind, but that's just one aspect of meditation and a very early stage of meditation at that. A concentrated mind is necessary, but not a sufficient condition for developing spiritual understanding.

18 We first learn to be mindful and then we learn to transfer that mindfulness into awareness. When we gain insight into the workings of mind through awareness, we can carry that insight into post-meditation, whatever we are doing. The real point is to see how meditation spills over into everyday life. Tashi Namgyal may be exaggerating slightly, but if you have real presence of mind it will make no difference what you are doing, even jumping up and down or running around. Even on the yoga of one-pointedness it is very important not to think that thoughts and emotions are the cause of your distraction. The cause of distraction is being alarmed by your thoughts and emotions. This is what you have to understand on the yoga of one-pointedness. You cannot say, 'I'm a bad meditator because my mind is busy all the time.' You are not a bad meditator because your mind is busy; you are a bad meditator for allowing yourself to get overwhelmed by that busy mind. The key issue is to maintain your awareness in relation to whatever is arising. We all begin with the yoga of one-pointedness, so instead of thinking of the Four Yogas as unusual or beyond your reach, you have to understand that you have already begun. It is just a matter of going from there.

19 The path of no more learning (*mi slob pa'i*) is the fifth bodhisattva path and equates with the attainment of perfect buddhahood.

20 The world has two aspects, a transcendental and an empirical one, which cannot be separated. Due to the delusions and obscurations of mind, we only perceive the world as it is presented through our senses, but that is just one aspect of things. The other aspect is the transcendental dimension, which we begin to understand through meditation. The inseparability of these two aspects is called the 'union of the two truths.' Relative truth is what we perceive normally through our senses and our concepts and ultimate truth is the transcendental aspect of emptiness. However, ultimate truth is the nature of relative truth. We have to understand that the transcendental—or suprasensory—reality is present within the sensory world. It has no form or shape so can only find expression through the phenomenal world. We cannot therefore conceptualise it or comprehend it. We are completely immersed in the world around us through our habits, conflicting emotions, and conceptual confusions, but as we go from the first to the second yoga, we begin to change and see something more than our familiar world. On the yoga of one-flavouredness, we start to realise that the transcendental is actually part of our everyday experiences; we just did not know it. One-flavouredness means merging the transcendental with the empirical. We cease to see them as two separate domains of existence, the state of enlightenment and the state of confusion.

21 It is only when we reach the yoga of non-conceptuality that we gain our first glimpse of ultimate reality. We do not just perceive ultimate reality; we see that it is inseparable from empirical reality. We cannot glimpse ultimate reality on the yoga of one-pointedness. This is merely the development of the ability to stabilise the mind so that we can sit without too much disturbance and is therefore called a 'worldly meditative state.' The yoga of one-flavouredness is where we have a real unitive experience. Unitive experience does not mean everything becomes blurry or amorphous. For example, if you experience a state of rapture when engrossed in some music you enjoy, it is as if the music and you have become the same but that does not mean you have become the sound. That is a unitive experience.

22 Consciousness is severed because it has become transformed. Ordinary consciousness is no longer operating and the storehouse consciousness has been pacified. Ordinarily, when we see something or hear something, we perceive it through our sense organs, recognise it through our sense consciousnesses, label it as pleasant or unpleasant, and give rise to an emotional reaction based on that judgement through our afflicted consciousness. That reaction leaves an impression in the storehouse consciousness and these impressions accumulate until they constitute our habits, predilections, personality, and so on. These impressions are stored in an unconscious way and remain dormant until we come across situations that trigger us, when we will respond from these karmic traces and dispositions stored there. Consciousness is severed when the storehouse consciousness has been completely purified and this cycle of action and reaction no longer operates.

23 This is the point at which we see meditative experiences are feeling-based and contingent on physical and mental factors, while realisation is independent of these factors and therefore lasting.

24 We have the illusory-like experience of karma because even our karmic experiences have no intrinsic reality. Karmic cause has no intrinsic reality of its own, karmic effect has no intrinsic reality of its own, and the agent who is subject to that karmic cause and effect has no intrinsic reality.

25 We also have to distinguish between causality and karmic cause and effect because not everything is karma. When we talk about karma, we are talking about cause and effect in relation to the mind. Karmic cause and effect ceases to have any relevance to someone who has attained full realisation. Karma only has relevance to someone who is subject to karmic law because of their own karmic tendencies.

26 The Four Yogas are not discrete stages; it is more about deepening our experience or understanding. The Four Yogas are really about dealing with our experiences in a way that develops more certitude and confidence rather than about constantly leaving experiences behind because they have been superseded. It is not as if your previous understanding was a distorted product of your delusions and you have

now arrived at something more valuable.

[27] At the level of one-pointedness, we start to develop insight into ultimate reality when we experience bliss, clarity, and non-conceptuality because those experiences lead to realisation.

[28] We have to learn not to overly rely on meditative experiences if we wish to progress with our practice. Each of the yogas is accompanied by relevant experiences, which become more and more subtle as the yogas progress. At the beginning, we have to rely on our understanding and experiences, but we gradually rely less on these things as realisation gradually becomes the dominating influence. These six criteria are about not relying too much on our experiences. Over-reliance on experiences is just another way of perpetuating our conventional mode of relating. Tashi Namgyal is constantly reminding us to be more open and non-judgemental, to work with hope and fear, and to resist becoming too bogged down in acceptance and rejection.

[29] Pure vision (*visuddha-bhasa, dag snang*) means that we see everything as an expression of ultimate reality. We cultivate pure vision by trying to see things as they are, rather than from an egocentric point of view. We just see, just hear, just taste, just smell, and just touch in a depersonalised way.

[30] We can make offerings to the lineage masters and Tantric deities, perform special ganachakra offerings, and receive transmissions that empower us to do certain practices within the Tantric context. Buddhism talks about two accumulations: of merit and wisdom. We accumulate wisdom by meditating and developing some insight into emptiness. We accumulate merit by making offerings, performing pujas, engaging in compassionate activities, or working for a centre or monastery. A deficiency in our stock of merit may hold us back from accumulating wisdom so merit is extremely important. From the perspectives of the two truths, merit works on the relative level and wisdom works on the ultimate level. We need to work on both levels. We may be meditating diligently, but if we have no generosity in our hearts, we restrict our development on the relative level, which makes it much more difficult to progress. We encounter various internal or external disruptions to our practice, which are called 'spiritual obstacles' or 'disruptions to the practice' (*pa chi*). We need to practise generosity by making offerings to counteract these obstacles. We practise generosity in two ways: upward generosity and downward generosity. Upward generosity (*chir pa*) is making offerings to sublime and sacred objects and downward generosity (*sbyin pa*) is directed towards ordinary sentient beings. This is how we replenish our stock of merit.

[31] If we become attached to the experiences of bliss, clarity, and non-conceptuality, we will not appreciate deluded thoughts. The aim of meditation is to allow deluded thoughts to arise and disperse into those experiences so that they assume

the qualities of bliss, clarity, and non-conceptuality. We have to make sure that our mind does not automatically latch onto these positive experiences and constantly try to recapture or recreate them. Each experience is unique. Experiences can be similar but no two experiences are ever the same. Learning these teachings is extremely important but they are only general guidelines. Our individual experiences will be quite unique.

32 When we no longer see the things of the world as having enduring essence, we will see that it operates because everything is interdependent. This is not just a conceptual thing. We realise it and perceive it that way. It is only because we do not see things this way that our minds are so full of delusions. We have so much anger, craving, grasping, and fixation because we are trying to freeze the world. If we can see everything as dependent origination, we will see everything as a process. Nothing is fixed, except for our concepts and ideas.

33 Any situation can be used as part of non-conceptual yoga to bring us out of that state of inertia. We can use pujas, rituals, yogic exercise, or physical exercise to stimulate ourselves. At the beginning, we try to minimise these practices, but if you get to a point where you think you are stuck, you can start doing these auxiliary practices to bring yourself out of that stuckness. You do them in such a way that they are not seen as something different. They are an extension of non-conceptual yoga practice. Buddhism has many objects of prayer. We have the Buddha and the Indian and Tibetan teachers and mahasiddhas, and we have all the symbolic representations of enlightened qualities in Tantric Buddhism. You can pray to Tara, Chenresig, or Vajrapani, the list is endless. We generally address our prayers to the lineage masters. Buddhist prayer works in a different way, because we are not necessarily based on the assumption that there is somebody out there to help us. You are invoking the object of your prayer and seeking inspiration, but you do this to gather all the positive and wholesome qualities you have, bundle them up and project them into the future. Prayers come to fruition when two conditions are met; your own stock of merit and the inspiration of the object of your prayer. The coming together of those two is what matures the prayer. Prayer is a form of wish or aspiration. It is called *mon lam* in Tibetan, which means literally 'path of aspiration.'

34 When we realise that the nature of everything is emptiness, we no longer have to think in terms of emptiness or non-emptiness. Conceptual categories just drop away. We are in the state of being with whatever is, without distinguishing between meditation or non-meditation, emptiness or non-emptiness, samsara or nirvana, freedom or bondage. That is from the point of view of ultimate truth. We still have to make distinctions on the level of relative truth, but we are no longer bogged down by these conceptual categories.

[35] Progress through the last three yogas is a deepening of realisation rather the experience of different realisations. We can experience various things but we can only realise one thing: our own authentic state. That realisation of ultimate reality can only be deepened. We can glimpse reality or we can have a more intimate knowledge of it.

[36] Compassion will arise if we have a real understanding of emptiness. Tashi Namgyal says, 'emptiness is the essence of non-directional compassion' (*stong nyid snying rje snying bo can*). This kind of compassion emanates everywhere. There is no independent self-existing subject here and no independently existing object there. If the self existed as a self-sufficient entity, there would be no need for compassion and it would be very difficult to give rise to compassion. Compassion is not something we have a choice about; we have to give rise to compassion if we want to make spiritual progress. We have to work on the relative as well as absolute level. Compassion includes feeling, emotion, and cognition; we must bring all that to bear on the practice of compassion. An enlightened being's physical body (*rupakaya*) is the product of compassion and mental body (*dharmakaya*) is the product of realising the nature of mind. Even an enlightened being needs a body to interact with others. Our own bodies are the product of our karma, but an enlightened being's body is the product of compassionate activities. Compassion has many different levels, but we usually speak about two kinds: 'compassion with object' (*migs dzi ma snying rje*) and 'compassion without object' (*migs ma snying rje*). As you advance on the path, there will only be compassion without object. That is what brings about the physical manifestation of enlightenment. With the realisation of the nature of mind comes the manifestation of enlightened mind.

[37] Harm, in this context, means 'unintentional harm.' We have to be very careful not to do any unintentional harm because our actions have more impact at this level. Even though our capacity to impact on others is very limited, we can still hurt people in the process of trying to do something good. Not all the harm that people suffer is caused by a deliberate intention to hurt them so we have to take responsibility for how we behave.

[38] The terms here are *rjes snang*, which means 'phenomenal appearance in the post-meditative state' and *rjes shes*, which means 'the experience of the mind in the post-meditative state.'

[39] The notion of competitiveness is now gone, because if there is no jealousy, there is no reason to be competitive. Whatever you want to do, you will do because it is worthwhile or necessary, not because you want to compete with someone else. The emotional affliction of jealousy is more easily overcome than some others because it is only a secondary emotion; a combination of several other basic emotions.

40 The practices that you do in solitude should work in your favour when you participate in the community. The reason you practise on your own in the first place is because you lack the confidence to practise when everything is busy. It is easy to get distracted, easy to have no time, easy to get caught up in things. As you gain confidence and proficiency in the practice, you need to learn to be in a community. Our goal is not to live in solitude; it is to live with others. We have to go full circle to do that properly. Tashi Namgyal mentions solitary individual practice in relation to the first stage of each of the yogas. Retreat practices are very important at the initial stages of each, but your view becomes more expansive as you move onto the second stage. Your views of solitude and community should be dismantled so that you do not value one over the other.

41 The 'demon' here is just the experiences themselves; there is no other demon. The demon is the mind that goes from one extreme to the other.

42 This means not relying too much on understanding and relying more on inner experiences. This emphasises the realisation of the yoga of one-flavouredness.

43 We need to keep our aspirations and goals in mind when we are doing Mahamudra practice. Creating favourable conditions includes not forgetting other sentient beings and not focusing on ourselves to the point that we sever our ties with everyone and everything. We need to have contact with others so that we have the ability to benefit others on a grander scale in the future. That should be our aspiration.

44 Subtle clinging is an unconscious or instinctive type of clinging; it is not a conscious thing. These are subtle forms of fixation. The defilements may diminish, but even if we are very advanced in the practice, we still have to work with our karmic traces and dispositions. *Tu ma* means 'defilement.' It is a very exact word. Very subtle forms of defilement from the past are still there, even if no new defilements are being created. We still need to work with these last remaining traces of defilements on the yoga of non-meditation as they gradually come into consciousness. We will then become more certain and begin to see everything more clearly, because the defilements are still what you might call 'blind spots.'

45 Perfect and complete enlightenment (*samyaksambuddha*) is the term for the final endpoint of the bodhisattva's journey. As the bodhisattva Paths and Stages demonstrate, there are degrees of enlightenment and bodhisattvas who are coursing through the bhumis are all enlightened to varying degrees. The final attainment is perfect and complete buddhahood.

46 The transference of consciousness (*phowa*) is the practice of imagining that your consciousness is a ball of light and trying to eject it through the crown of your head into one of the buddha-fields. This is a preparatory practice for the time of death, when you would try to effect this transference realistically.

[47] The Sutric path of the bodhisattva is divided into five paths (*panca-marga, lam lnga*) and ten stages (*dasa bhumi, sa bcu*), which are progressively traversed by the bodhisattva, from the stage of an ignorant sentient being to the stage of a fully awakened Buddha. The path of accumulation (*sambhara-marga, tshogs lam*) and the path of application (*prayoga-marga, sbyor lam*) lead directly into the path of seeing (*darsana-marga, mthong lam*). This is followed by the path of meditation (*bhavana-marga, sgom lam*), which contains the ten bodhisattva stages and culminates in the path of no more learning (*ashaiksha-marga, mi slob lam*), which is regarded as the eleventh stage of perfect and complete enlightenment (*samyaksambuddha*).

[48] The first bodhisattva stage (*bhumi, sa*) is actually attained on the path of seeing and the other nine bhumis consist of the path of meditation. These first six bhumis are called joy (*pramudita, rab tu dga' ba*), stainless (*vimala, dri ma med pa*), illuminating (*prabhakari, 'od byed pa*), brilliant (*arcismati, 'od 'phro ba*), difficult to conquer (*sudurjaya, shin tu sbyang dka' ba*), and directly facing (*abhimukhi, mngon du gyur ba*). The seventh to tenth are called far advanced (*durangama, ring du song ba*), immovable (*acala, mi gyro ba*), unerring intellect (*sadhumati, legs pa'i blo gros*), and cloud of Dharma (*dharmamegha, chos kyi sprin*).

[49] The path of no more learning is also known as the path of completion.

Quoted People

Aryadeva (third century): a scholar of the Madhyamaka system in southern India, best known for his *Catusataka* (*Four Hundred Verses*).

Asvaghosa (80–150): A Kashmiri Vedantist famous for his debating skills, he converted to Buddhism after being defeated in debate by Aryadeva and subsequently attained realisation. His most famous work is the *Buddhacarita* (*Acts of the Buddha*).

Asanga (300–370): Exponent of the Yogacara school and half-brother of Vasubandhu, reputedly received teachings from Maitreya in Tusita heaven.

Atisha (982–1054): Atisha Dipankara Shrijnana, forefather of the Kadampa school of Tibetan Buddhism, he was a major figure in the revival of Buddhism in Tibet. His most famous work is the *Bodhipathapradipa* (*Lamp for the Path to Enlightenment*).

Baram Darma Wangchuk (twelfth century): disciple of Gampopa and founder of the Baram Kagyu.

Barawa (1321–1403): Barawa Gyaltsen Pelzang, disciple of Rangjung Dorje, the third Karmapa, fled to Bhutan after civil disorder in his native Gtsang led to religious persecutions.

Bodhibhadra (eleventh century): A teacher of Atisha and great scholar, who resided at Nalanda University.

Chandragomin (seventh century): a famous lay Indian master and scholar who dressed in white robes. Renowned for his ability to understand texts by reading through them once. He famously challenged Chandrakirti to a debate that lasted many years because he was able to consult with a vision of Chenresig each evening. Writings include *Twenty Verses on the Bodhisattva Vow* and *Letter to a Disciple*.

Chandrakirti (600–650): Abbot of Nalanda University and the disciple of Nagarjuna, best known for the *Madhyamakavatara* (*Introduction to the Middle Way*), a commentary on Nagarjuna's major work. The founder of the prasangika division of Madhyamaka philosophy.

Darika (tenth century): one of the eighty-four Indian mahasiddhas, known as the 'slave-king of the temple whore.' An Indian king from Saliputra who, along with his minister Tengipa, grew disgusted with worldly life before meeting their guru Luyipa in a cemetery. They received Cakrasamvara initiation after offering themselves as the initiation fee. Luyipa sold him to a prostitute in Orissa, where he worked for twelve years before attaining Mahamudra.

Dharmakirti (seventh century): reinterpreted the work of Dignaga. Renowned as the founder of Buddhist logic. His theories became normative in Tibet and his seven treatises of valid cognition are still part of the monastic curriculum.

Dignaga (480–540): pioneer of Buddhist logic and indirect student of Vasubandhu. Combined aspects of Yogacara and Sautrantika with his innovative logical methodology. Wrote important works on abhidharma and pramana, including the *Pramanasamuccaya* (*The Treatise on Systems of Cognition*).

Dombipa (eleventh century): one of the 84 Indian mahasiddhas, known as the 'tiger rider,' he was a king from Magadha who abdicated his throne after being caught consorting with a low-caste woman. A student of Virupa, he meditated in the forest for twelve years before attaining Mahamudra.

Drikhungpa (1143–1217): Je Drikhungpa Kyobpa Jigten Sumgon, one of the foremost disciples of Phagmo Trupa and founder of the Drikhung Kagyu.

Dusum Khyenpa (1110–1193), the first Karmapa, met Gampopa at the age of thirty and studied with him for three years. Also received teachings from Rechungpa and other disciples of Milarepa. Studied and practised meditation for twelve years and developed miraculous powers. Received extensive instructions from many dakinis in Uddiyana. Founder of the Karma Kagyu.

Gambhiravajra: Kashmiri Pandita, famous for conjuring up Vajrasurya in a cemetery, receiving secret teachings in visions and attaining siddhis.

Gampopa (1079–1153): Gampopa Sonam Rinchen, took ordination as a novice monk in the Kadampa tradition when twenty-six, heard of Milarepa three years later and immediately experienced intense devotion. Found Milarepa after many hardships and received the complete Kagyu teachings from him. Established the monastic lineage of the Kagyu tradition and 'mixed the two streams' of Tilopa's Mahamudra and Atisha's Kadampa teachings.

Gomchung (1120–1178): Gomchung Sherab Jangchub, nephew of Lord Gampopa and youngest son of Gampopa's elder brother, he held the chair of Gampo monastery for a brief time after Gomtsul.

Gomtshul (1116–1169): Gompa Tsultrim Nyingpo, nephew of Lord Gampopa. He was the Abbot of Gampo monastery after Gampopa died, Gampopa's institutional heir and the principal teacher of Lama Zhang.

Gotsangpa (1180–1258): Gotsangpa Gonpo Dorje, the founder of the upper Drukpa Kagyu. Recognised as the reincarnation of Milarepa, a wandering yogi who left many footprints in the Himalayas. He never stayed in the same place twice and is connected to the practice of Chakrasamvara.

Hwashang Mahayana (eighth century): the Chinese monk who participated in the Samye debate of the eighth century and established the approach of Sutric Mahayana in Tibet. His doctrine is characterised as a form of quietude, where thoughts are suppressed and karmic cause and effect is discredited.

Indrabodhi (eighth century): the legendary king who received the root text of the *Guhyagarbha Tantra* from Vajrapani when it fell from the sky. Studied with the mahasiddha Kukuraja, who practised in a cave in the company of a dog. Indrabodhi attained enlightenment and then passed on his realisation to Kukuraja.

Jnanagarbha (eight century): intellectual heir to Bhavaveka, the founder of the svatantrika-Madhyamaka tradition, he was an influential thinker and the teacher of Shantarakshita.

Kamalashila (740–795): Abbot of Nalanda University before he was invited to Tibet to carry on the work of his teacher Shantarakshita. Defeated Hwashang Mahayana in the Samye debate. A Yogacara-Madhyamakan, he wrote the three-part *Bhavanakrama* at the request of King Trisong Detsen.

Kotali (ninth century): one of 84 Indian mahasiddhas, a peasant who hoed mountain fields for his subsistence, he met the scholar-monk Santipa who gave him instructions to apply to his ploughing.

Krsnacarya (tenth century): a nath siddha who authored the caryapada songs, but failed to attain complete awakening. Conceited and hasty, he refused to listen to his dakini advisor, disobeyed his guru Tantipa and came to a nasty end. Tantipa attributed his failings to incomplete meditation and failing to unite insight and skilful means.

Lavapa (ninth century): disciple of Indabuti and a teacher of Kukkuripa and Tilopa, he passed the Dream Yoga practice and the six yogas of Niguma to Tilopa. Dissolved into light at his death, leaving ony a palm-sized portion of his crown behind.

Lingrepa (1128–1188): Lingchen Repa Pema Dorje, Tibetan mahasiddha, the only yogi disciple of Phagmo Drupa, he founded the Drukpa Kagyu and passed those teachings along to Tsangpa Gare, the guru of Gotsangpa.

Longchenpa (1308–1364): a major teacher in the Nyingma school. Along with Sakya Pandita and Je Tsongkhapa, he is commonly recognised as one of the three main manifestations of Manjushri. Best known for his works on Dzogchen, especially the *Seven Treasures* (*Choying Dzod*). He collected the heart-essence teachings of Guru Rinpoche, Vimalamitra, and Yeshe Tsogyal. Abbot of Samye, he spent most of his life travelling or in retreat. He had many disciples but remained a simple hermit, often dwelling in caves.

Lorepa (1187–1250): an accomplished yogin who spent years meditating in isolated retreat. A seminal figure in the early history of the Drukpa Kagyu and a student of Tsangpa Gyare.
Maitripa (eleventh century): he was expelled from Vikramasila University for practising with alcohol and a consort in the monastery. Demonstrated his realisation by crossing the Ganges on a mat and then lived as a mahasiddha, and meditated in the forest for twelve years. He became a leading exponent of Mahamudra, had many disciples, and was one of the main gurus of Marpa.
Marpa (1012–1097): embraced Buddhism at an early age, first as a Sakya, then sold all his possessions and set out for India to become a disciple of Naropa. Also studied with Jnanagarbha, Kukuripa, and Maitripa. Spent many years translating Buddhist texts into Tibetan. Marpa made two more trips to India to collect further teachings. Marpa's four great disciples were Milarepa, Meton Tshonpo, Tshurton Wangpo, and Ngogton Chokyu Dorje.
Milarepa (1040–1123): most famous yogi of Tibet, his early life was full of misery and hardship. He learned magic to avenge his family and killed many people. Overcome with regret, he sought a master who could help him and eventually found Marpa, who put him through years of ordeals and hardship before imparting the teachings he had received from Naropa. Milarepa practised for years in isolated mountain caves and attained enlightenment. He is famous for his spiritual song and had many disciples, including Gampopa and Rechungpa.
Nagarjuna (150–250): founder of the Madhyamaka school of philosophy, which systematised the emptiness teachings in Prajnaparamita. One of the most influential thinkers of Buddhism and famous for *Madhyamakakarika* (*Fundamental Verses of the Middle Way*).
Naropa (1016–1100): born to a royal family in Bengal and destined to be a king, he married early but left the marriage after eight years to become ordained. He becoming an abbot at Nalanda University until one day a dakini appeared and challenged his understanding, suggesting he seek out the mahasiddha Tilopa for instructions. After enduring many trials, Naropa found and trained with Tilopa, who subjected him to further severe trials before he attained mastery of the teachings.
Pawo (1440–1503): born in Yarlung in Central Tibet, he was given the title pawo or 'hero' as a result of the supernatural powers he displayed at a young age. Initially a Nyingma master, he became a student of the seventh Karmapa and was one of his spiritual heirs. The Karmapa establishing him as the head of Sekhar Guthog, the place where Marpa and Milarepa had lived.
Phagmo Drupa (1110–1170): disciple of Gampopa and founder of the Phag-

mo Kagyu. One of the famous Three Men of Kham, along with Dusum Khyenpa and Saltong Shogam, he received Gampopa's complete transmission of Vajrayana and Mahamudra teachings.

Rangjungpa (1284–1339): the third Karmapa, he sat up straight at the age of three and proclaimed himself Karmapa. Born to a Nyingma family, he received the full transmission of the Nyingma tradition in addition to the Karma Kagyu, wrote many volumes on Dzogchen and founded the Karma Nyingtik lineage. He unified the Kagyu Mahamudra and Nyingma Dzogchen, introduced a revised system of astrology, after having a vision of the entire universe contained within his body. His most famous text is the *Profound Inner Meaning* (*Zab mo nang don*).

Rechungpa (1088–1158): one of the most important students of Milarepa, he founded the Rechung Kagyu lineage and was important in the transmission of the Cakrasamvara cycle as the *Demchog Nyengyü*. He met Milarepa at the age of eleven and spent many years studying and practising with him. He travelled to India three times and obtained the teachings and transmissions that Marpa missed, such as the entire 'nine-fold cycle of the formless Dakinis.' He compiled the Six Equal Tastes and hid it as terma, where it was recovered by the terton Tsangpa Gyare, founder of the Drukpa lKagyu.

Sakya Pandita (1182–1251): notable for his exceptional scholarship, regarded as an emanation of Manjushri, and as the fourth Forefather and sixth Sakya Trizin. He composed many important and influential texts on Sutra and Tantra, including *Clarifying the Thought of the Sage* and *Discriminating the Three Vows*.

Santipa (ninth century): a famous scholar-monk of the brahmin caste at Vikramasila. He recognised that Kotali, one of his students who had been meditating on Mahamudra for the past twelve years, had attained realisation. He himself had been too busy teaching to attain much, so he asked Kotali to be his guru, and attained highest realisation.

Saraha (eighth century): a Buddhist monk and noted scholar, he was expelled from his monastery for drinking and became a wandering tantrika until he met a young woman of the arrowsmith caste. The name Saraha can be translated as 'one who aims through the heart of duality.' Denounced by the royal court he recited spontaneous songs known as *Dohakosa* (*Three Cycles of Doha*), which are famous throughout Bengal.

Savaripa (tenth century): from the untouchable caste, he initially made his living hunting animals, until Avalokiteshvara manifested and taught him the Dharma, after which he meditated on compassion and attained Mahamudra after twelve years. He is also known as Sri Savari, 'the peacock-wing wearer'

and the 'mountain-hermit.' He was the guru of Maitripa.
Shantideva (695–743): A scholar at Nalanda University and an adherent of the Madhyamaka school, famous for his *Bodhicharyavatara* (*Guide to the Bodhisattva's Way of Life*).
Sthirmati (sixth century): Indian Buddhist scholar-monk, renowned for his numerous and detailed commentaries on Yogacara and Abhidharma works of Vasubandhu and for a commentary on the *Kasyapa-parivarta*.
Subhagini (tenth century): the dakini from whom Tilopa recieved the mystic heat (*candali*, *tummo*) transmission.
Tashi Namgyal (1511–1587): a lineage holder of the Dagpo Kagyu, he also trained in the Sakya lineage. A scholar and yogi, his famous works *Moonbeams of Mahamudra* and *Clarifying the Natural State* are classic texts still widely studied to this day.
Tengipa (tenth century): the Brahmin minister to king Indrapala (see Darika above); he also became a disciple of the mahasiddha Luyipa. Sold to a wine seller woman in Jintapura because of his great pride, he spent twelve years working as a rice-husker before attaining Mahamudra.
Tilopa: (988–1069), the founder of the Kagyu lineage, Tilopa practised the *Chakrasamvara Tantra* teachings for twelve years at Somapuri. Expelled from the monastic community for taking a consort, he travelled throughout India, meeting many teachers and receiving instructions. He pounded out the oil of sesame seeds (*tila*) for a living and frequented desolate places. He received direct Mahamudra transmission from Vajradhara.
Tsangpa Gyare (1161–1211): a disciple of Lorepa, he founded the Drukpa Kagyu school and was the guru of Lorepa and Gotsangpa. He was the first Gyalwang Drukchen Rinpoche.
Vasubandhu (330–400): The younger half-brother of Asanga, he composed the *Abhidharmakosa,* the famous Sarvastivada treatise on abhidharma. He later converted to Mahayana Buddhism under the influence of Asanga.
Virupa (837–909): a monk at Somapuri for twenty-four years before being ejected for eating the monastery's pigeons. Famed for consuming miraculous amounts of alcohol, he wandered around performing miracles. He inspired the Tibetan Sakya lineage.
Yanggonpa (1213–1258): Yanggonpa Gyaltsen Pel, a disciple of Gotsangpa and child prodigy who was able to spontaneously utter religious invocations and predict future events. He was a master of the upper Drukpa Kagyu lineage.
Zhang (1123–1194): Lama Zhang was a disciple of Gomtsul and the founder of the Tsalpa Kagyu.

Quoted Texts

Sutra

Acintyaguyha Sutra (The Inconceivable Secrets Sutra), *gsang ba bsam gyi mi khyab pa'i mdo*

Aksayamatinirdesa Sutra (The Sutra Taught by Inexhaustible Intellect), *blo gros mi zad pas bstan pa*

Aksayamatipariprccha Sutra (Sutra Requested by Unending Intelligence), *blo gros mi zad pas zhus pa'i mdo*

Astasahasrika-prajnaparamita Sutra (Perfection of Wisdom in 8,000 Stanzas), *shes rab kyi pha rol tu phyin pa khri brgyad stong pa*

Atyayajnana Sutra (Sutra on the Wisdom of the Verge of Passing), *'da' ka ye shes*

Arya-buddhasamgiti Sutra (Recitation of the Names of Noble Buddha Sutra), *sangs rgyas 'phyag pa sdud pa'i mdo*

Avatamsaka Sutra (The Sutra of Buddha Avatamsaka), *sangs rgyas phal po che mdo*

Badrakalpika Sutra (Sutra of the Auspicious Aeon), *skal bzang mdo*

Bhadrapalapariprccha Sutra (Badrapala's Request Sutra), *bzang skyong gi zhus pa'i mdo*

Bodhisattvapitaka (Bodhisattva Basket), *byang chub sems pa'i sa gang sa*

Candrapradipa Sutra (Moon Lamp Sutra), *zla ba sgron ma'i mdo*

Caturdharmanirdesa Sutra (Showing the Four Dharmas Sutra), *chos bzhi bstan pa'i mdo*

Dasabhumika Sutra (The Ten Bhumi Sutra), *sa bcu pa'i mdo*

Dasacakra-ksitigarbha Sutra (The Bodhisattva Ksitigarbha Vow Sutra) *sai snying po 'khor lo bcu pa'i*

Dasadharmaka Sutra (Ten Dharma Sutra), *phyogs bcu pa'i mdo*

Dharmaraja Sutra (The Dharma King Sutra), *chos kyi rgyal po'i mdo*

Dharmasamgiti Sutra (Recitation of Names for the Dharma Sutra), *chos yang dag par sdud pa'i mdo*

Dharmadhatu-prakrtyasambhedanirdesa Sutra (Demonstrating the Indivisible Nature of Dharmadhatu), *chos kyi dbyings kyi rang bzhin dbyer med par bstan pa'i mdo*

Dharmatacala Sutra (The Sutra of Non-wavering Dharmata), *chos nyid mi g.yo ba'i mdo*

Dharmatasvabhavasunyatacalapratitsarvaloka (Sutra Unwavering Dharmata Sutra), *chos nyid mi g.yo bar mdo*

Gaganaganjapariprccha Sutra (Requests of Gaganaganja Sutra), *nam mkha' mdzod kyis zhus pa'i mdo*

Gandavyuha Sutra (The Flower Ornament Sutra), *sdong po bkod pa*

Hrdaya Sutra (The Heart Sutra), *snying mdo*

Jnanalokalamkara Sutra (The Ornament of the Realm of Wisdom Sutra), *ye shes snang ba rgyan*

Jnanamudra Sutra (The Seal of Wisdom Sutra), *ye shes phyag rgya'i mdo*

Kasyapapariprccha Sutra (Questions of Kasyapa Sutra), *'od srungs gi l'eu mdo*

Kasyapapanvarta Sutra (Kasyapa Requested Sutra), *'od srungs kyis zhus pa'i mdo*

Lalitavistara Sutra (Noble Profound Representation Sutra), *rgyas cher rol pa'i mdo*

Lankavatara Sutra (The Sutra of the Arrival of Lanka), *lang kar gshegs pa'i mdo*

Mahakarunanirdesa Sutra (The Teaching on Great Compassion Sutra), *snying rje chen po bstan pa'i mdo*

Mahakarunapundarika Sutra (The White Lotus Sutra), *snying rje pad ma dkar po'i mdo*

Maharatnakuta Sutra (Great Jewel Heap Sutra), *dkon mchog brtsags pa'i mdo*

Mahayanaprasadaprabhavana Sutra (Faith and Meditation in the Great Vehicle Sutra), *theg chen la dad pa sgom pa'i mdo*

Mahosnisa Sutra (Great Ushnisha Sutra), *gtsug tor chen po'i mdo*

Maitreyapariprccha Sutra (Questions of Maitreya Sutra), *byams pa'i gi l'eu mdo*

Maitreyapradasthana Sutra (Liberation of Maitreya Sutra) *byams pa'i rnam par thar pa*

Manjushrivikridita Sutra (Representation of the Manifestation of Manjushri Sutra) *'jam dpal rnam par rol pa'i mdo*

Prajnaparamita Sutra (The Great Perfection Sutra) *pha rol tu phyin mdo*

Prajnaparamita-ratnagunasamcayagatha (Perfection of Wisdom in 8,000 Lines and its Verse Summary) *mdo bsdus pa*

Prajnaparamitasamcayagatha (Condensed Perfection of Wisdom Sutra), *phags pa mdo sdud pa*

Pratimoksha Sutra (Sutra of Individual Liberation), *so thar mdo*

Ratnakuta Sutra (The Jewel Mound), *dkon mchog brtsags pa'i mdo*

Ratnamegha Sutra (Clouds of Noble Jewels Sutra), *dkon mchogs sprin mdo*

Saddharmaparigraha Sutra (The Sutra that Fully Embraces the Sacred Dharma), *dam pa'i chos yongs su 'dzin pa'i*

Saddharmapundarika Sutra (The Sutra of the White Lotus of Genuine Dharma), *dam chos pad ma dkar po'i mdo*

Sagaramatipariprccha Sutra (Sagaramati Requested Sutra), *blo gros rgya mtsho zhus pa'i mdo*

Samadhinirmocana Sutra (Clarification of Thought Sutra), *dgongs pa nges par 'grel pa'i mdo*

Samadhiraja Sutra (The King of Meditative Absorption Sutra), *ting nge 'dzin gyi rgyal po'i mdo*

Saptasatika-prajnaparamita Sutra (The Perfection of Wisdom in 700 Lines Sutra), *sher phyin bdun brgya pa*

Savadharmapravrttinirdesa Sutra (The Sutra Demonstrating the Non-origination of all Things), *chos thams cad 'byung ba med par bstan pa'i mdo*

Silasamyukta Sutra (Possessing Moral Ethics Sutra), *tshul khrims dang ldan pa'i mdo*

Tathagatacintyaguhyanirdesa Sutra (Teachings on the Secrets of the Tathagata Sutra), *de bzhin gshegs pa'i gsang ba'i mdo*

Tattvaprakasa Sutra (Teaching Suchness Sutra), *de kho na nyid bstan pa'i mdo*

Upalipariprccha Sutra (Requests of Upali Sutra), *nye bar 'khor gyis zhus pa*

Varmavyuhanirdesa Sutra (The Teaching on the Armour of Vyuha Sutra), *go cha bkod par bstan pa mdo*

Vajrasamadhi Sutra (Vajra-like Meditative Absorption Sutra), *rdo rje ting nge 'dzin gyi mdo*

Viradattagrhapatipariprccha Sutra (The Sutra Requested by Viradatta), *dpa' sbyin gyi zhus pa'i mdo*

Visesacintapariprccha Sutra (The Request of Visesacinta Sutra), *khye par sems kyi zhus pa'i mdo*

Shastra

Abhidharmakosha (The Treasury of Abhidharma by Vasubandhu), *mngon pa mdzod*

Abhidharmakosha-bhasya (Auto commentary on the Treasury of Abhidharma by Vasubandhu), *mngon pa mdzod rang 'grel*

Abhidharmasamuccaya (The Compendium of Abhidharma by Asanga), *mngon pa kun btus*

Abhisamayalamkara (The Ornament of Clear Realisation by Maitreya), *mngon rtogs rgyan*

Ahapramanasamyak (The Perfect Measure of Buddha's Words by Trisong Deutsen), *bka' yang dag tshad ma*

Avikalpapravesadharani-tika (Commentary on the Dharani of Entering Non-conceptuality by Kamalashila), *rnam par mi rtog par la 'jug pa'i gzungs kyi rgya cher 'grel pa*

Bhavanakrama (The Stages of Meditation by Kamalashila), *sgom pa'i rim pa*

Bodhisattvacharyavatara (The Entrance to the Bodhisattva's Way of Life by Shantideva), *byang chub sems dpa'i spyod pa la 'jug pa*

Bodhichittavivarana (The Commentary on the Mind of Enlightenment by Nagarjuna), *byang chub sems kyi 'grel ba*

Bodhipathapradipa (The Lamp for the Path to Enlightenment by Atisha), *byang chub lam gyi sgron ma*

Bodhisattvabhumi (Bodhisattva Stages by Asanga), *byang sa*

Bodhisattvabhumi-vrtti (Commentary on the Bodhisattva Stages by Gunaprabha), *byang sa bstan*

Caryasamgraha-pradipa (Summary of Conduct by Atisha), *spyod bsdus*

Catuhsataka (Four Hundred Verses by Aryadeva), *bzhin brgya pa*

Dasatattva (Tenth Bhumi of Suchness by Vimalakirti), *de khon na nyid bcu pa*

Desanastava (Hymn to the Teachings by Candragomin), *bshags bstod*

Dharmadhatustava (In Praise of Dharmadhatu by Nagarjuna), *chos dbyings bstod pa*

Drstisamksepta (The Condensed View by Naropa), *lta ba mdor bsdus*

Madhyamakahrdaya-karika (Essence of the Middle Way by Bhavaviveka), *dbu ma snying po*

Madhyamakavatara (Entrance to the Middle Way by Chandrakirti), *dbu ma la 'jug pa*

Madhyamakopadesa (Concise Pith Instructions by Atisha), *dbu ma'i man ngag*

Madhyantavibhaga (Distinguishing the Middle from Extremes by Maitreya), *dbus dang mtha' rnam par 'byed pa*

Mahayanasutralamkara (The Ornament of Sutras by Maitreya), *theg pa chen po'i mdo sde rgyan*

Mulamadhyamakavrttiprasannapada (Lucid Words by Chandrakirti), *dbu ma'i rtsa ba'i 'grel pa tshig gsal ba*

Mulamadhyamika-karika (The Fundamental Verses on the Middle Way by Nagarjuna), *dbu ma rtsa bai tshig le'ur byas pa sehes rab ces bya ba*

Nirvikalpaprakarana (Proof of Non-conceptuality by Shantarakshita), *tshogs chos bkra shis phun tshogs*

Prajnaparamitopadesa (The Prajnaparamita Pith Instructions by Ratnakarasanti), *shes rab kyi pha rol tu phyin pa'i man ngag*

Pramanavarttika (Commentary on Valid Cognition by Dharmakirti), *tshad ma rnam 'grel*

Pramanasamuccaya (The Compendium of Valid Cognition by Dignaga), *tshad ma kun las btus*

Ratnavali (Precious Jewel Garland by Nagarjuna), *rin chen 'phreng ba*

Satyadvayavibhanga-vrtti (Commentary on the Two Truths by Jnanagarbha), *bden gnyis 'grel pa*

Satyadvayavatara (The Entrance into the Two Realities by Atisha), *bden pa gnyis la 'jug pa*

Siksamuccaya (Collection of Transcendental Instructions by Shantideva), *pyod pa rol bsdus pa*

Sphutartha (Radiant Commentary: the Abhisamayalamkara by Haribhadra), *'grel pa don gsal*

Sravakabhumi (The Stages of the Hearers by Asanga), *nyan thos pa'i sa*

Suhrllekha (Letter to a Friend by Nagarjuna), *bshes pa'i springs yig*

Trayastrimsat-parivarta (Chapter on the Gods in the Abode of the Thirty-three), *sum cu rtsa gsum pa'i le'u'i mdo*

Udanavarga (A Collection of Verses from the Buddhist Canon compiled by Dharmatrata), *ched du brjod pa'i tshoms*

Uttaratantra (Unsurpassed Tantra by Maitreya), *rgyud bla ma*

Yogacarabhumi (Treatise on Bhumis by Asanga), *rnal 'byor spyod pa'i sa*

Tantra

Abhidhana Tantra (Master of Articulation Tantra), *mngon par brjod pa'i rgyud bla ma*

Amanasi (Twenty-six Teachings of No Mental Activity), *a ma ni si skor nyer drug*

Bharvanarthasiddhi (Accomplishing the Meaning of Meditation Tantra), *sgom pa don grub*

Buddhasamayoga (Equalising Buddhahood), *sangs rgyas mnyam sbyor*

Buddhakapala Tantra (Skullcup of Enlightenment Tantra), *sangs rgyas thod pa*

Candraguhyatilaka (Tantra Secret Moon Essence), *zla gsang thig le*

Caturaksa Mahamudra (Four Syllables of Mahamudra), *phyag rgya chen po yi ge bzhi pa*

Guhyacintya Tantra (Tantra of the Inconceivable Secret), *gsang ba bsam gyis mi khyab pa'i rgyud*

Guhyasamaja Tantra (Secret Assembly Tantra), *gsang ba 'dus pa*

Guhyatattva (Secret Fundamental Nature), *gsang ba'i de kho na nyid*

Hevajra Tantra (The Heart of Non-dual Realisation Tantra), *rgyud brtags gnyis*

Jnanagarbha Tantra (The Essence of Wisdom Consciousness Tantra), *ye shes snying po rgyud*

Jnanasiddhi Sadhana (Sadhana for Accomplishing Wisdom Consciousness), *ye shes grub pa'i sgrub thabs*

Kalachakra Tantra (Wheel of Time Tantra), *dus 'khor*

Kalachakra-mulatantra (The Kalachakra Root Tantra), *dus 'khor rtsa rgyud*

Mahamudra-tilaka (The Sphere of Mahamudra Tantra), *phyag chen thig le*

Manjushri-mulatantra (The Manjushri Root Tantra), *'jam dpal rtsa rgyud*

Manjushrinama-samgiti (A Praise to Manjushri by Eight Maidens), *'jam dpal mtshan brjod*

Samcaya Tantra (Condensed Tantra), *bsdus rgyud*

Samdhivyakarana Tantra (Tantra That Prophesies Realisation), *dgongs pa lung bstan gyi mdo*

Samputa Tantra (Tantra of Perfect Union), *yang dag par sbyor ba*

Samvarodaya Tantra (The Manifestation of Samvara), *bde mchog 'byung ba*

Sarvabuddhasamayoga (Equalising Buddhahood), *sangs rgyas mnyam sbyor*

Subahupariprccha Tantra (Tantra of the Questions of Subahu), *dpung bzang gi zhus pa'i rgyud*

Sri-Anavila Tantra (The Glorious Tantra of the Stainless King), *rgyud kyi rgyal po dpal rnyogs pa med pa*

Suryacandra sadhana (The Accomplishment of the Sun and Moon), *nyi zla grub pa*

Yogasapta (The Sevenfold Yoga), *sbyor ba bdun pa*

Vairocanabhisambodhi (The Tantra of the Enlightenment of Vairocana), *rnam snang mngon byang*

Vajradakini Tantra (The Indestructible Dakini Tantra), *rdo rje mkha' 'gro rgyud*

Vajramala (Indestructible Thread), *rdor 'phreng*

Vajramala-akhyata (The Explanatory Tantra of the Vajramala), *bshad rgyud rdor 'phreng*

Vajrapanjara Tantra (Vajra Dome Instruction Tantra), *rdo rje gur*

Tantric Commentaries

Caturmudraniscaya (The Definitive Explanation of the Four Mudras by Nagarjuna), *phyag rgya bzhi gtan la dbab pa*

Dohakosa (Collection of Spontaneous Vajra Songs by Saraha), *do ha mzod*

Dvikramatattvabhavana-nama-mukhagama (The Oral Instructions of Manjushri by Buddhajnana), *'jam dpal zhal lung*

Guhyasiddhi (Accomplishment of Secrets by Mahasukha), *gsang ba grub pa*

Hevajra-pindartha (Commentary on the Heart of Non-dual Realisation Tantra by Vajragarbha), *rdo rje snying 'grel*

Jnana-tilaka (The Sphere of Primordial Wisdom by Gambhiravajra), *ye shes thig le*

Padmini (The Lotus Endowed, a Commentary on the Kalachakra), *pad ma can*

Pancakrama ('Five Stages' of the Guhyasamaja Completion Stage by Nagarjuna), *rim lnga*

Pradipoddyotana ('An Illuminating Lamp' for the Guyhayasamaja Root Tantra by Chandrakirti), *'grel pa sgron gsal*

Sekanirdesa (Empowerment of the True Teachings by Maitripa), *dbang skur nges bstan*

Vimalaprabha Stainless Light (Commentary on Kalachakra), *'dri med 'od*

Tibetan Texts

brda rtsa (Energy and Symbol by Maitripa)

bsngags 'os bsngags bstod (Hymns of Praise)

bu mo rin chen gyis zhus pa'i mdo (The Sutra Requested by the Girl Ratna)

byang chub lam rim chen mo (The Great Treatise of the Stages to Enlightenment by Tsongkhapa)

de kho na nyid rab tu mi nges pa'i rgyud (Gaining Certainty in Absolute Suchness Tantra)

do chung mdzod brgyad (The Treasury of Eight Lesser Pairs)

do ha skor gsum (Three Cycles of Spontaneous Vajra Songs by Saraha)

dus bzhi mnyam sbyor kyi ye shes (The Wisdom of the Equality of the Four Times)

gab pa mngon phyung gi skor (Cycle of the Disclosure of the Hidden by Savari)

grub pa sde bdun (The Seven Texts of the Mahasiddhas)

grub snying ('Heart of Accomplishment' Dohas of the Indian Mahasiddhas)

gsang sbyor (Guhyasamaja Yogas)

gsang spyod (Secret Union Yoga)

lta ba'i 'dod pa mdor bstan pa (Concise Explanation of Philosophical View)

lhan cig skyes sbyor (The Means of Realising Coemergence by Gampopa)

lhan cig skyes sbyor bsam gyis mi khyab pa'i rgyud (The Tantra of Inconceivable Coemergence)

lhan skye sam gyi mi yab pa'i gyud (Tantra Unleashing Coemergence)

mdo sil bu (Sutra Pieces)

nam mkha'i lta bu'i ting nge 'dzin gyi mdo (Space-like Samadhi Sutra)

phyag chen tshig bsdus (Essential Mahamudra Instruction by Maitripa)

phyag rgya chen po rab tu mi gnas pa'i rgyud (Complete Non-dwelling Mahamudra Tantra)

phyag rgya chen po tshig bsdus pa (The Summary of Mahamudra by Naropa)

rtogs pa rgyas pai mdo (Sutra of Expanding Realisation)

sa'i snying po khor lo bcu pa'i mdo (Sutra of the Ten Wheels of Ksitigarbha)

sa yi dngos gzhi (Four Pillars of Merit)

sems nyi ngal so (Resting in the Natural State by Longchenpa)

snying po skor drug (Heart Teachings Cycle)

theg sgron (The Lamp of Mahayana by Serdingpa)

ting 'dzin dam pa'i mdo (The Most Excellent Meditative Concentration Sutra)

thub pa dgongs gsal (The Illuminated Thought of the Buddha) *tshogs cho bkra shis phun tshogs* (Auspicious Prosperity and Happiness of the Common Dharma by Gampopa)

tshogs chos chen mo (The Great Accumulation of Dharma by Gampopa)

ye shes gsal byed (Illuminating Primordial Wisdom)

zhu lan (Answers to Questions by Gampopa)

Topics Outline

BOOK TWO: AN EXTENSIVE DESCRIPTION OF THE UNCOMMON SYSTEM OF MAHAMUDRA MEDITATION

PART I: THE PRELIMINARIES

PART II: MAHAMUDRA MEDITATION

~ The Stages of Virtuous Practice ~

~ Consolidating our Meditative Experiences ~

Index